Anecdota Oxoniensia

TEXTS, DOCUMENTS, AND EXTRACTS

CHIEFLY FROM

MANUSCRIPTS IN THE BODLEIAN

AND OTHER

OXFORD LIBRARIES

SEMITIC SERIES—PART XII

THEOLOGICAL TEXTS FROM COPTIC PAPYRI

EDITED

*WITH AN APPENDIX UPON THE ARABIC AND COPTIC VERSIONS
OF THE LIFE OF PACHOMIUS*

BY

W. E. CRUM, M.A.

HON. PH.D. BERLIN

OXFORD

AT THE CLARENDON PRESS

1913

Price Twenty-five Shillings net

The *Anecdota Oxoniensia* comprise materials, chiefly inedited, taken direct from MSS., particularly those preserved in the Bodleian and other Oxford Libraries. These materials fall into five classes: (1) unpublished texts and documents, or extracts therefrom, with or without translations; (2) texts which, although not unpublished, are unknown in the form in which they are to be printed in the *Anecdota*; (3) texts which, in their published form, are difficult of access through the exceeding rarity of the printed copies; (4) collations of valuable MSS.; (5) notices and descriptions of certain MSS., or dissertations on the history, nature and value thereof. They are issued in four Series:—

I. *Classical.* II. *Semitic.* III. *Aryan.* IV. *Mediaeval and Modern.*

Anecdota Oxoniensia

THEOLOGICAL TEXTS FROM
COPTIC PAPYRI

EDITED WITH AN APPENDIX UPON THE ARABIC AND COPTIC
VERSIONS OF THE LIFE OF PACHOMIUS

BY

W. E. CRUM, M.A.

HON. PH.D. BERLIN

Oxford
AT THE CLARENDON PRESS

1913

OXFORD UNIVERSITY PRESS
LONDON   EDINBURGH   GLASGOW   NEW YORK
TORONTO   MELBOURNE   BOMBAY
HUMPHREY MILFORD M.A.
PUBLISHER TO THE UNIVERSITY

RESPECTFULLY DEDICATED

TO THE

PHILOSOPHICAL FACULTY OF

THE UNIVERSITY OF BERLIN

PREFACE

THE papyrus fragments here published were acquired in the winter of 1905–6 by the late Lord Amherst of Hackney, who kindly entrusted me with their publication. During the course of printing they became the property of Mr. J. Pierpont Morgan. Professor Sayce, who had already seen them at the dealer's in Luxor,[1] was told that they had been brought from Hou, some 30 miles below Denderah. There is no internal evidence as to their *provenance*. Probably they had been part of the library of one of the monasteries once numerous in that district.[2] It is melancholy to reflect that these poor remnants of some thirty volumes—assuming each script to indicate a distinct volume—are all that have survived.

The language in which the texts are written is a pure Saʿidic, such as one might expect in the district whence they came. Peculiar however is, in several cases,[3] the superlineation, which I have tried to reproduce in print as nearly as may be.[4] This matter of superlineation is one to which various scholars have given attention—notably M. Amélineau[5]—but as yet no systematic, statistical investigation has shown how it may be used as a means towards determining the dates of manuscripts.

Neither, in the present case, can any very definite indication of age be had from palaeographical features, the script of most of our papyri, including both the finest (No. 13) and the roughest (Nos. 8, 16) types, being of the class which it is still necessary vaguely to assign to about the 7th century.[6] For No. 7 a *terminus ante quem* is indeed given, since its author was

---

[1] That Prof. Sayce saw these identical fragments is proved by his having then and there copied part of one, that printed here as No. 25, fol. 14.

[2] The presence here of two Lives of Pachomius might suggest one of the Pachomian foundations, seven at least of which lay close around Hou. It may be observed that the position of Tabennêse, as being 10 m. from Shenesêt (Bo. 25), is confirmed by Av. 12 b ll. al ẕ ... (cf. Amélineau *Géogr.* 469 n.). There is still obscurity as to some of these names (cf. Ladeuze

173 ff.). For شلست (Am. 569) = ⲦⲤⲎ, I would suggest شلست ⲬⲈⲦⲤⲎⲦⲈ.

[3] Particularly Nos. 1, 4 (fol. 3), 7, 9, 11, 12, 15, 16, 18, 23. Examples of similar abnormal usage can be seen in Br. Mus. Cat., Pl. 10, nos. 278, 967.

[4] The frequent comma in the text of No. 25 is, as elsewhere, merely a word-divider; the + above ⲏ the breathing.

[5] In the Introduction to his *Œuvres de Schenoudi*, Paris 1907.

[6] Most of the Turin papyri should belong to this period. *V.* also Brit. Mus. Cat., Pll. 8–10.

patriarch from 578 to 605; and this, considering the paucity of datable
uncial hands, is not without importance. It may perhaps be assumed that
the rest of the collection also is of about that age.

Though so fragmentary, these papyri include remnants of more than one
interesting work: foremost probably, as also most extensive, the new Lives
of Pachomius (Nos. 24, 25); then the Sermon attributed to Gregory
Nazianzen (No. 9) and that above referred to, bearing the name of
Damianus (No. 7). A certain historical value attaches to the evidence, in
No. 13, for a Coptic version of the anecdotes embodied by John of Maiuma
in his *Testimonies*; nor is a fresh addition to Enoch literature (No. 3),
even when manifestly of late origin, without its interest. Indeed there
are few of the remaining pieces but contribute something, either in the
persons whom they mention or the relations which they show to other
works, to enlarge our knowledge of Coptic literature.

Little need be said regarding the manner of publication. Though all
revised once, several (*e.g.* No. 25) more often, my copies cannot claim
finality. The dark colour of the papyrus in some cases, in others faded
ink or a damaged surface, made certainty well nigh unattainable. I have
preferred to abstain from many a seemingly obvious completion of *lacunae*,
where reflection showed that such was not the sole restitution possible
and the several alternatives would have overloaded the page unduly. The
translations aim at literalness, so long as that remained intelligible.

In an Appendix I have taken the opportunity to attempt a preliminary
estimate of two hitherto unstudied Arabic versions of the history of
Pachomius and to give summary accounts of the various Sa'idic recensions,
a critical edition whereof is promised by Professor Théodore Lefort.

A list of the principal abbreviations used will be found at the head of the
Appendix.

My grateful thanks are due to Lady Amherst for her kindness in leaving
the papyri at my disposal and to the Delegates of the Press for generously
undertaking their publication; to Prof. Nau for lending me his copy of the
Metaphrastic text of the Pachomian biography (*Paris* 881), to Prof. Pietschmann for facilitating my use of an important Arabic MS. (*v.* p. 176), and
to Marcus bey Simaika for a valuable communication (*v.* p. 175); also to
Sir Herbert Thompson and Mr. H. I. Bell for help in verifying occasional
references otherwise beyond my reach.

CONTENTS

No.   PAGE

1. Ruth iv. 5–10 1
2. Lectionary 2
3. Enoch, Legend relating to 3
4. The Virgin, Life of 11
5. The Virgin, Death of 17
6. Sermon 18
7. Sermon by Damianus of Alexandria 21
8. Sermon 33
9. Sermon by Gregory Nazianzen 36
10. Sermon 53
11. Sermon 57
12. Dialogue (ἐρωταπόκρισις) 58
13. Anecdotes (*cf.* Πληροφορίαι of John of Maiuma) . . . 62
14. Apocryphal Acts of an Apostle 64
15. Mark the Evangelist, Martyrdom of 65
16. Philotheus of Antioch, Martyrdom of 68
17. From another MS. of the same 70
18. Psate of Psoi, Martyrdom of 73
19. Apa Moui, Martyrdom of 75
20. An unidentified Martyrdom 80
21.   „   „ 82
22.   „   „ 83
23.   „   „ (?) 85
24. Pachomius, Life (?) of 86
25. Pachomius, Life of 94
26. Apollo and Ammonius, Anecdote of 162
27. Hôr, Narrative relating to 164
29. Monkish Narrative 167

PAGE

APPENDIX 171
    On Paris, *MS. arabe* No. 261 . . . 172
    On the Cairo edition 174
    On Amélineau's text 176
    On *Cod. Vatic. Arab.* No. 172 . . . 177
    On the Sa'idic Recensions 183
    Table of Correspondence 189
    Table of Sequence 191

ADDITIONS AND CORRECTIONS 194

INDEX 195
    Persons 195
    Places 196
    Coptic 197
    Greek 200
    Arabic 204
    Subjects 204

FACSIMILES OF THE MANUSCRIPTS

No. 1.

Ruth iv. 5–10, with *lacunae*. This is clearly by the scribe of no. 9, and lay together with those fragments. But I have assumed that it has merely a fortuitous connexion with them, for it is improbable that the long biblical passage would be cited by the preacher of a sermon. Nor can I recall a Coptic MS. which contained both a biblical and a non-biblical text.[1] Sir H. Thompson's text (*A Coptic Palimpsest*) is unfortunately deficient here.

→ *Recto.*

ⲙⲟⲩ [ⲉⳍⲛ-]
ⲧⲉϥⲕⲗⲏⲣⲟ·
ⲛⲟⲙⲓⲁ ·　ⲧ[
✝ⲁⲩⲱ ⲡⲉⲧ-　ⲛ[
(*lacuna*)　✝ (*lacuna*)
　　　　ⲛ̄ⲧⲉⲧⲟⲛ[ⲛ
[ⲛ]ⲟⲙⲓⲁ' · ⲛ̄　ⲉⲣⲟϥ' · ⲁⲩ[ⲱ]
ⲧⲟⲕ' ⲇⲉ' ⲭ̄ⲓ　ⲡⲁⲓⲡⲉ ⲡⲙ[ⲁⲣ-]
ⲙ̄ⲙⲟⲥ' ⲛⲁⲕ'　ⲧⲩⲣⲓⲟⲛ' ⲉ[ⲧ-]
ⲉⲡⲁⲙⲁ'　ⳍ̄ⲙ̄ⲡⲉⲥⲣⲁ[ⲏⲗ'] *sic*
ϫⲉⲁⲛⲟⲕ'　✝ⲡⲉⲧⲭ̄ⲓ ⲇⲉ
ⲛ̄ϯⲛⲁϣϫⲓⲧⲥ'　ⲉⳍⲟⲩⲛ' ⲉⲡⲡ[ᵃ

margin

↑ *Verso.*

[ⲡⲉϫⲁ]ϥ ⲛ̄-
[ⲛⲉⲡⲣⲉ]ⲥⲃⲩ-
[ⲧⲉⲣⲟⲥ ⲙ̄]ⲛ-
(*lacuna*)
ⲉⲗⲓ-]
ⲙⲉⲗ[ⲉⲭ ⲧⲏ-]
ⲣⲟⲩ' · ⲁⲩⲱ
ⲛⲉⲧϣⲟⲟⲡ'
ⲧⲏⲣⲟⲩ' ⲛ̄ϫⲉ-
ⲗⲁ̄ⲓⲱⲛ ⲙ̄ⲛ
ⲙⲁⲗⲗⲱⲛ'
ⲛ̄ⲧⲟⲟⲧⲥ' ⲛ̄-
ⲛⲱⲉⲙⲙ' · ⲁⲩⲱ *sic*

[ⲙ̄ⲡⲉⲛ]ⲧⲁϥ-
[ⲙ]ⲟⲩ ⲉⳍⲛ-
ⲧⲉϥⲕⲗⲏⲣⲟ-
ⲛⲟⲙⲓⲁ ⲛϥ-
ⲧⲙ̄ϭⲱⲧⲉ ᵇ
(*lacuna*)

ⲫⲩⲗⲏ [ⲙ̄-]
ⲡⲉϥⲗⲁ[ⲟⲥ .]
✝ⲛ̄ⲧⲱⲧⲛ̄'
ⲧⲉⲧⲛⲟ̄
ⲙ̄ⲙⲛⲧⲣⲉ
ⲙ̄ⲡⲟⲟⲩ' ·

margin

ᵃ Should be ⲉⲃⲟ[ⲉⲥ.　ᵇ Here Thompson's text (p. 267), which fills the gap thus: ⲉⲃⲟⲗ ⲛ̄ϭⲓ ⲡⲣⲁⲛ ⲙ̄ⲡⲉⲛⲧⲁϥⲙⲟⲩ ⲉⲃⲟⲗ ⳍⲙ̄ⲡⲉϥⲥⲡⲏⲩ ⲁⲩⲱ ⲉⲃⲟⲗ ⳍⲛⲧⲉ- (*i.e.* probably six lines of our MS.).

1 Unless it be a volume with 'Exodus and the Canons of Apa Athanasius' in the catalogue

No. 2.

Fragments of a Lectionary. Text in one column. The sequence of foll. 1 and 2 is obvious; that of fol. 3 uncertain.

I have to thank Dr. Anton Baumstark for the following valuable observations:—'The Bohairic directories indicate Ps. xcvii. 1 ff. and Eph. iv. 20–v. 14 as lections for Low Sunday (*Dom. in Albis*); *v.* Lagarde's *Orientalia* 8; likewise Ps. xxviii. 3 ff. and Titus ii. 11–iii. 7 for Epiphany; *l.c.* 10. With the Blessing of the Water at Epiphany Ps. l. 7 might well be connected; note that it was read in Egypt at a similar rite (Foot Washing) on Holy Thursday. The divergences in detail of the lections, here and in the far younger Bohairic uses, are of small moment compared with the remarkable agreement, maintained over so long a period, to which these important fragments testify.'

The only other Lectionary on papyrus known to me is a small fragment (no. 12) in the Strassburg University Library, which shows a lection ending 1 John iii. 11 (or 2 John v.?) followed by Acts ix. 36 ff. and, on its other side, an unidentified passage from St. John's Gospel.

Fol. 1. ↑ *Recto* (?).

]o̅ȳc̅ (*red*) [a]
]тоти . (*black*)
]ϩ' ап .
ш]пйшоп
]аγ єт

→ *Verso.* Ps. xcvii. 1, 2.

(*red*) пепро[кеілленон]
со со[
(*red*) χω [епxоеіс ноγxω ивирре]
(*black*) xеап[xоеіс еіре нϭепшпнре]
ϩст[оγxо нач нϭі течоγналл]
аγω [печϭвоі етоγаав .]
апx[оеіс оγωнϩ евоλ лепечоγxаі]

[a] From a Pauline Epistle.

Fol. 2. → *Recto.* Ps. xcvii. 2–5.

сγнн лепе[лт]о евоλ н[нϩе-]
оноc тн[р]оγ . [a]
ачрплеєγє лепечна н[іакωв]

↑ *Verso.* Eph. v. 17–20.

[λ]а єіле xео[γпе] поγωш й-
[пx]оеіc . аγω [л]пртϩе ϩноγн-
[рп] паі етеоγн оγлйтшна'

[a] тнроγ not elsewhere. *Cf.?* Ps. lxvi. 2.

ⲁⲩⲱ ⲧⲉϥⲙⲉ ⲙⲡⲏⲓ ⲙⲡ[ⲓⲏⲗ]
ⲁⲡⲉⲣⲱⲟⲩ ⲧⲏⲣⲟⲩ ⲙⲡ[ⲕⲁϩ ⲛⲁⲩ]
ⲉⲡⲟⲩϫⲁⲓ ⲙⲡⲉⲛⲛⲟⲩ[ⲧⲉ]
ⲡⲕⲁϩ ⲧⲏⲣϥ ϯ ⲗⲟⲅⲗⲁⲓ ⲙ[ⲡ-]
ⲛⲟⲩⲧⲉ
ϫⲱ ⲛⲧⲉⲛⲧⲉⲗⲏⲗ ⲛⲧⲉⲛ-
ⲯⲁⲗⲗⲉⲓ ⲉⲣⲟϥ
[ⲯⲁⲗⲗⲉⲓ ⲉⲣⲟϥ ϩⲛⲟⲩ]ⲕⲓⲑⲁⲣⲁ

[ϣⲱ]ⲟⲡ ⲛϧⲏⲧϥ ⲁⲗⲗⲁ ⲛ̄ⲧⲉⲧⲛ-
[ϫⲱ]ⲕ ⲉⲃⲟⲗ ϩⲙⲡⲉⲡⲛⲁ · ⲉⲧⲉⲧⲛ-
[ϣⲁ]ϫⲉ ⲙⲡⲛⲉⲧⲡⲉⲣⲏⲩ ϩⲛϩⲉⲛ-
[ⲯⲁⲗ]ⲙⲟⲥ ⲙ̄ⲛϩⲉⲛⲥⲙⲟⲩ ⲙ̄ⲛϩⲉⲛ-
ϣⲇⲏ ⲙ̄ⲡⲛⲁⲕⲟⲛ ⲉⲧⲉⲧⲛϫⲱ'
ⲁⲩⲱ ⲉⲧⲉⲧⲛⲯⲁⲗⲗⲉⲓ ϩⲙⲡⲉⲧ-
ⲛϩⲏⲧ' ⲉⲡϫⲟⲉⲓⲥ · ⲉⲧⲉⲧⲛϣⲡ

ⲟⲗ. 3. ↑ *Recto* (?).   Ps. l. 7–9.

margin

) ⟌ ⟍ ⟎ ⲯⲁⲗⲧⲏⲣ[ⲓⲟⲛ

ⲕ) ⲕⲛⲁⲥⲉϣϭⲱⲟϣⲧ [ⲛⲟⲩϭⲩⲥⲥⲱⲡⲟⲥ]
ⲉⲃⲟⲗ' ϩⲙⲡⲉⲥⲛⲟϥ' ⲛ̄[ⲡϣⲉ ⲧⲁⲧⲃⲃⲟ]
ⲕⲛⲁϫⲟⲕⲙⲉⲧ ⲉⲃ[ⲟⲗ ⲛϧⲏⲧϥ ⲁⲩⲱ]
ᵃⁱᶜ ⲧⲁⲟⲩⲃⲁϣ'ᵃ ⲛ̄ϩ[ⲟⲩⲉⲟⲩⲭⲓⲱⲛ]
[ⲉ]ⲕⲛⲁⲧⲣⲁⲥⲱⲧ[ⲙ ⲉⲩⲧⲉⲗⲏⲗ ⲙⲛⲟⲩ-
          [ⲟⲩⲛⲟϥ ᵇ
[ⲥ]ⲉⲛⲁⲧⲉⲗⲏⲗ' ⲛ̄[ϭⲓ ⲛⲕⲉⲉⲥ ⲉⲧⲑⲃⲃⲓⲏⲩ]
[ⲕⲧⲉ] ⲡⲉⲕϩⲟ ⲛ̄ⲥ[ⲁⲃⲟⲗ ⲛⲛⲁⲛⲟⲃⲉ]
[ⲁⲩⲱ] ⲛⲁⲁⲛⲟ[ⲙⲓⲁ ⲧⲏⲣⲟⲩ ϥⲟⲧⲟⲩ ⲉⲃⲟⲗ]

→ *Verso* (?).   Ps. xxviii. 8 and Titus
ii. 11 (?).

margin

[ⲧⲉⲥⲙⲏ ⲙⲡϫⲟ]ⲉⲓⲥ · ϥⲕⲓⲙ' ⲉⲧⲉⲣⲏⲙⲟⲥ
[ⲡϫⲟⲉⲓⲥ ⲛⲁⲕⲓⲙ] ⲉⲧⲉⲣⲏⲙⲟⲥ' ⲛ̄ⲕⲁⲇⲏⲥ·
]———...
ⲡⲣ]ⲟⲥ ⲧⲓⲧⲟⲥ — (*red*)
]———...
[ⲁⲡⲉϩⲙⲟⲧ ⲅⲁⲣ ⲙⲡ]ⲛⲟⲩⲧⲉ ⲡⲉⲛ- (*black*)
[ⲥⲱⲧⲏⲣ ⲟⲩⲱⲛϩ ⲉⲃ]ⲟⲗ' ⲛⲣⲱⲙⲉ' ⲛ[ⲓⲙ
]ⲁϥ' ⲉ .. ⲕ[
]ⲧⲉ ... [

ᵃ Elsewhere ϯⲛⲁⲟⲩⲃⲁϣ.
ᵇ The end of this must have been inserted above or below the line.

No. 3.

These remnants of a new text connected with the once extensive Enoch
literature are, owing to my failure to discover elsewhere any guiding version
of the story[1], printed in a merely tentative sequence. An alternative order
might, for instance, begin with foll. 2, 6, 8. All is so ill preserved that
scarcely a phrase can be translated without hesitation. Pronouns, of
decisive importance for the intelligence of the narrative, are too often
missing or, owing to imperfect context, ambiguous. Needless to say, the

[1] The recently published Ethiopic 'Clement' (Grébaut, *ROC.* xvi. 230) is of no help.

Both Enoch's mother and sister—assuming 'my son' and 'my brother' to have their literal meaning—have parts in this legend.[1] That the latter is the speaker in foll. 7, 9, is an assumption based simply upon the traditional relationship of the Sibyl to Enoch[2] and the probability that prophetic information would be ascribed to her wisdom. A gnostic element in the work might perhaps be recognized in fol. 2, but the references to the persons of the Trinity would suffice to separate this text from the more venerable literature relating to Enoch.

Fol. 1. ↑*Recto.* margin   → *Verso.*

	]к[	[.]е[	ꝏр[
	[ϥ · є	[. .]пє[	єϥ[
	ϯ[єпаі]пє пр[аи]	[.]є стω[т є]ϥ-	[.]оүк єϥ[
	ūпϣнрє [n̄-]	ϣаннаү єро-	поү . аи[
]є ūпар-	пиоүтє єϥ-	оү ꝍпиєгūнт-	тє · ϥпа[
[хат]гєλос аϥ-	ꝍꙏ оос n̄са-	ϣаϥтє тн-	хєпо[
[к]ꙏаϥª єхn̄n̄ꙏ ꙏꙏ а-	оүиаꙏꙏ ūпϥ̄-	роү єϣагааү	n̄ꙏоис .[
[аϣ]є n̄таїкаі-	єïωт · аϥ-	ϥпассꙏаïсоү	тєϥꙏоꙏ · [
[ос]гүн аϥєï-	паꙏтϥ̄ єхn̄-	n̄тєгпоү n̄-	ꙏ[. .]ϣєꙏ
[пє] n̄кєаꙏꙏє-	ūп[ат]ᵇ ūпєϥ-	тєтєн[ꙍ]їкω̄	ꙍꙏпко[
[λо]ϥ n̄хωωрє	єï[ωт] єϥхω	тнр̄с β[ω]к єп-	є[.]ꙏ ꙏꙏа[
[. . . . .] о [n̄]ϣаꙍ	ꙏꙏ[ос] хєꙍ̄	тако · [аλ]λа	[. .]гєп[
	па[єіω]т ū-	ϣïn[є .]тꙏ .	
	пр[. . .]ūпϥ̄	n̄са[. . . .]ꙏꙏᶜ	

ª Or таαϥ.   ᵇ Altered.   ᶜ n̄]тоϥ пса[оүрω]ꙏ[є?

Fol. 1. *Recto.* . . . the archangel (ἀρχ.) and he placed him (it?) at (upon?) the ba[lan]ces of righteousness (δικαιοσύνη), and broug[ht] other mighty angels (ἄγγ.), . . . being flame (?) . . . . .

[1] In an Ethiopic legend his mother's name is Bareka (*Livre des Mystères*, p. 138, ed. Grébaut, *Patr. Or.* vi).

[2] *V.* my note *ZNTW.* 1911, 352. I may here add that the sibylline quotation in the Turin papyrus is to be referred to the Tiburtian Sibyl; *cf.* Sackur, *Sib. Texte u. Forsch.* 181; further, as to the invocations of Enoch on grave stones, *v.* H. Thompson in Quibell's *Saqqara*, 1912, p. 48.

Prof. Pietschmann has referred me to certain versions of the History of Alexander, wherein the Sibyl appears as Solomon's sister (A. N. Vesslovsky's work on the *History of the Novel*, vol. i, 1886, and his article in *Vizant. Vrem.* 1897). On Tabitha associated with Enoch and Elias, *v.* also Steindorff's *Apok. des Elias* 92.

. . . which is (?) the name (?) of the son of God, sitting on His father's right.   He cast himself at His father's feet, saying, ' O (?) my father, do not . . . . .

Verso. . . . 'tremble (?) if he behold them in all their wickedness which they do, he shall straightway write them down and all thy image[1] (εἰκών) shall go to destruction.   But (ἀλλά) rather (?) seek for ' . . . . .[2]

. . . *nothing intelligible in col. 2.*

Fol. 2.   → *Recto.*   ↑ *Verso.*

	[.]ⲛⲟⲩ[. .]ⲟⲛ .	[. . ⲁⲛⲁ]ⲗⲁ[ⲙ-]
	ⲣⲱⲙⲉ ⲛ[ⲁⲓ-]	[ⲃ]ⲁⲛⲉ ⲙⲙⲟϥ ⲉ-
	ⲕⲁⲓⲟⲥ ⲉⲧ[ⲉⲡⲁⲓ-]	[ⲧ]ⲡⲉ · ⲁϥⲛⲟⲓ ⲛ̄ⲛ̄-
	ⲡⲉ ϊⲁⲣ[ⲉⲁ ⲁϥⲣ̄-]	[ⲙⲩⲥⲧⲏ]ⲣⲓⲟⲛ
]ⲛ	ϩⲟⲧⲉ ϩⲏⲧϥ [ⲙ-]	[ⲉ]ⲑⲏ[ⲡ] ϩⲛⲛⲁⲓ- ⲉ[
]ⲉ	ⲡⲛⲟⲩⲧ[ⲉ ⲁⲩⲱ]	ⲱⲛ ⲙⲡϫⲓⲥⲉ ⲛ[
]ⲁⲡⲟϥ[a]	ⲡⲛⲟⲩⲧⲉ ⲟ[ⲛ]	[ⲁⲩ]ⲱ ⲛⲛⲟⲩⲥ ϫ[
]ϩⲁ-	ⲉⲣⲉⲛⲉϥ[ⲁⲙⲙⲉ-]	ⲧⲏⲣⲟⲩ ⲉⲑⲏⲡ ⲉⲛ[
]ⲡⲉ	ⲗⲟⲥ ⲙⲉ ⲙⲙ[ⲟϥ]	[ϩ]ⲛⲛⲁⲓⲱⲛ ⲙ- ⲣⲉ[
]ϫⲓ	[ⲉ]ⲧⲃⲉⲡ . . [	[ⲡ]ⲟⲩⲟⲉⲓⲛ · ⲁⲩⲱ ⲁϥ[
]ⲡⲉ		[. . .]ⲓⲁ ⲛⲛ[ⲛ̄[
]ⲛ̄		

* Or ϫⲡⲟϥ.

Fol. 2. *Recto.*   . . .[3]righteous (δίκαιος) man, namely Iar[ed, and he] feared God.   [And] the [an]gels (ἄγγ.) of God al[so] loved him[4] by reason of . . . . .

Verso.   . . . took him up (? ἀναλαμβάνειν) to heaven and he knew (νοεῖν) the [mys]teries (μυστ.) that are hidden in the *aeons* (αἰών) of the height, and all the minds (νοῦς) that are hidden in the *aeons* (αἰ.) of light, and . . . of the (*pl.*) . . . . .

---

[1] The human race.

[2] Perhaps : seek out a man to mitigate the

[3] Presumably ' son of a], or something similar.

[4] *Lit.* (if my suggestion be accepted) ' And God also, His angels loved him '.   But this con-

Fol. 3. ↑ *Recto.* ? margin   → *Verso.* margin

Recto:

```
              ⲙⲡ[. . .]ⲉ[
              ϩⲟ[.]ⲩ [ⲉ]ϥⲁϩⲉⲣ[ⲁ-]
              ⲧϥ ϩⲓϫⲙⲡⲧⲟ-
              ⲟⲩ· ⲉⲓᵒⁱᶜ ⲟⲩⲁ[ⲅ]ⲅⲉ-
              ⲗⲟⲥ ⲛ̄[ⲧⲉ ⲡⲛⲟⲩ-]
]ⲧ           ⲧⲉ ⲁϥⲟⲩⲱⲛ[ϩ]
]ⲅⲙⲛ-        ⲛⲁϥ ⲉⲃⲟ[ⲗ ⲉϥ-]
]ϣⲁϫⲉ        ⲙⲏⲣ ⲉϫⲛⲧ[ⲉϥ-]
]· ⲁ-        ϯⲡⲉ ⲛⲟⲩⲙ[ⲟ-]
]ϥⲧⲙ-        ⲭ̄ϩ ⲛ̄ⲛⲟⲩⲃ [ⲉ-]
]ϫⲓ          ⲣⲉⲟⲩⲕⲗⲟⲙ [ⲛⲁ-]
]ⲟ̈ⲥ         ⲧⲁⲙⲁⲛⲧ[ⲓⲛⲟⲛ
              ?
```

Verso:

```
                    ]ⲛⲁ
        ⲥⲁ. ⲉⲛⲱⲭ ⲡ-
        ϣⲏⲣⲉ [ⲛⲓ]ⲁⲣⲉⲗ                    ϩ̣[
        [ϫⲓ ⲙⲡⲉ]ⲓϫⲱ-                      ⲟⲉ[ⲓ
        ⲱⲙⲉ ϩⲛⲧⲁϭⲓϫ                       ⲡⲁⲙ[
        [ⲛⲅ]ⲟϣ ⲛ̄ϩⲏ-                       ⲛⲁ[
        [ⲧ]ϥ ⲛⲧⲟⲩⲱⲛϩ                      ⲙ̄ⲡⲉ[
        [ⲉ]ⲃⲟⲗ ⲙ̄ⲡⲣⲁⲛᵒⁱᶜ                   ⲙⲉϩ[
        [ⲡⲉ]ϫⲉ ⲉⲛⲱⲭ                        ⲡ̄ⲥ[
        [ⲛ]ⲁϥ ᵃ ϫⲉⲛⲓⲙ                       ⲧ̄ϥ[
                   ?
```

ᵃ Not ⲡⲁⲥ.

Fol. 3. *Recto.* . . . while he stood upon the mount, lo, an angel (ἄγγ.) of God appeared unto him, girt about his loins with a golden girdle, a crown of adamant (ἀδαμάντινος) being [upon his head . . . . .

Verso. . . . 'Enoch, son of Iared, [take] this book of my hand and read therein and reveal the(?)[1] name.' Enoch said unto him, 'Who [art thou?' . . . . .

Fol. 4. → *Recto.*   ↑ *Verso.*

Recto:

```
        ]ⲉⲧ[       ⲡⲁ[
        ]ⲛⲧ[       ⲱⲙ[. . . ⲡⲛⲟⲩ-]
        ]ⲧ[        ⲧⲉ ⲛ[ⲁⲭⲁⲣⲓⲍⲉ]
]ⲁⲛⲟⲩϣ            ⲛⲁⲕ [ⲛ]ⲟⲩⲣ[ⲁⲛ]
]ⲁϣⲱⲡⲉ            ⲛⲥⲟⲉⲓⲧ ⲉ[ϩⲟⲩ-]
]ⲟⲩ ⲉⲓⲧⲉ          ⲉⲣⲱⲙⲉ ⲛⲓⲙ
]ⲉⲥⲟⲗ-            ⳗⲥⲉⲛⲁϫⲓⲧⲕ ⲉⲧ-
]ⲥϩⲁⲓⲥⲟⲩ          ⲡⲉ ϩ̄ⲙⲡⲉⲕ-
```

Verso:

```
        ]ⲧⲉ.           ⲱⲙ[
        ]ⲛ[            ϩ̈ⲓϫ[
        ]ⲣⲡ.           [.]ⲧ̄ⲛ[
[. . . .]ⲕⲟⲥ ⲛ̄ϥ-      ⲫⲁⲥ[ⲓⲟⲥ ⲙ̄ⲡϫⲟ-]
ϫⲓ ⲛⲧⲁⲡⲁⲥ-            ⲉⲓⲥ ⲧ̄ⲅ . [
[ⲅⲉ]ⲗⲟⲥ ⲧⲁⲙⲟϥ         ⲡⲁⲣⲑⲉ[ⲛⲟⲥ
ⲉⲣⲟⲟⲩ ϩ̈ⲓϫⲙ-          ϫⲉⲥ . [
ⲡⲧⲟⲟⲩ· ⲁϥ-            ⲛⲁⲉⲓⲣⲉ[
```

[1] Perhaps 'my', ⲡⲁ-.

]ϫⲓⲛⲧⲉϥ-	ⲥ[ⲱ]ⲙⲁ ⲛ̄ⲥⲉⲕⲁ-	ϭⲛ ϣⲟⲙ[ⲧ]ⲉ	ϣⲟ ⲛ̄[ⲣⲟⲙⲡⲉ] [a]
]ⲉ ⲙⲡⲁ-	ⲁⲕ ⲟⲛ̄ⲧⲙⲛ̄ⲧⲉ	ⲛ̄ⲥⲫⲣⲁⲅⲓ[ⲥ]	ϭⲓϫⲙ[ⲡⲕⲁϩ
]ⲁⲁϥ ⲉⲧ-	[ⲛⲟ]ⲩⲡⲟⲑⲩⲕⲏ	ⲁⲩⲱ ⲡⲉ[..	ϣⲁⲧⲛ̄[
]ⲛ̄ⲛ̄ⲧϥ̄-	[..]ⲧⲉ ⲟⲩⲥⲓⲉ	[.]ⲩ . ⲛⲉϩⲁⲓ .	ⲛⲟⲩ .. [
?	]ⲡ[	]ⲧ	
	traces of two lines.	]ⲙⲉ	

[a] Stroke over ⲛ̄ not certain.

Fol. 4. Recto. . . . 'God [shall grant ($\chi\alpha\rho\iota\zeta\epsilon\sigma\theta\alpha\iota$)] thee a name (?) famous [above] all men. Thou shalt be taken to heaven in thy body ($\sigma\hat{\omega}\mu\alpha$) and shalt be set in the midst of the store-house (? $\dot{\alpha}\pi\circ\theta\dot{\eta}\kappa\eta$ [1])' . . . . .

Verso. . . . whereof the angel ($\ddot{\alpha}\gamma\gamma$.) had told him upon the mount. He found three seals ($\sigma\phi\rho\alpha\gamma\iota\varsigma$) and the . . . writings . . . . .

. . . the ho[ly one ($\ddot{\alpha}\gamma\iota\circ\varsigma$) of the Lo]rd . . . .[2] vir[gin ($\pi\alpha\rho\theta$.)], that . . . should spend . . . hundred [years] upon [the earth,] all but . . . . .

Fol. 5. ↑ *Recto* (?).   → *Verso* (?).

	]ⲛ̄[	ⲙⲏ[	ⲙⲉ[
	]ⲟⲩ-	?	
ϣⲟϫ[ⲛⲉ] ⲛⲟⲩ-	ⲣ . [	]. ⲡ .	ⲁϥϭⲛ̄[ⲧϥ ϫⲉⲡ-]
ⲱⲧ ⲡ[ⲉ]ⲧⲛ̄ϩⲟⲛ-	ⲉϫ[	]ⲉ ϭⲛ-	ⲣⲁⲛ [ⲙ]ⲡⲉⲡⲛ-
[ⲧ]ⲟⲩ ⲛ[ⲧ]ⲟⲟⲩ ⲥⲉ-	ⲧⲏ[	?	ⲛⲁ ⲉⲧ[ⲟⲩⲁⲁⲃ]
ⲉⲣⲟⲙⲙⲉ ⲛ̄ⲧ-	ⲙⲉ[	]ⲉ	✓ Ⲡⲉϫⲉ ⲉⲛⲱⲭ
[ⲡ]ⲉ ⲙ̄ⲡ̄ⲡⲕⲁϩ	ⲱ[	]ⲟⲕ	ⲛⲁϥ ϫⲉⲡⲁ-
Ⲡⲣⲁⲛ ⲙⲡⲉⲓⲱⲧ	ⲥⲏ[	]ⲕ	ϫⲟⲉⲓⲥ ⲉⲓ[ⲥ ϣⲟ-]
[.]ⲱϩ ⲛⲡⲙⲉϩ-	ⲛ[	] ⲉⲃⲟⲗ	ⲙⲛ̄ⲧ ⲛⲣⲁⲛ
ϣⲟⲙⲛ̄ⲧ ⲛ̄ .	ⲧ[	]ⲉⲧ-	ⲛⲁϩⲟⲣⲁⲧⲟⲛ
[.]ⲛ ⲉⲧⲟⲓ̈ϫⲛ̄-	ⲡ[	]ⲛ	ⲁⲓ̈ϭⲛ̄ⲧⲟⲩ ⲉ[ⲩ-]
		?	[ⲥ]ⲛϩ ϭⲛ̄ⲛϫⲱ-
		?	ⲱⲙⲉ[

[1] In the Book of Enoch 'store-houses' are mentioned, but the Greek words are *typical* θησαυρός (ch. xi, xviii).

[2] ⲧⲛ[ⲛⲟⲟⲩ ⲧ-] 'send the', might be read;

Fol. 5. Recto (?). . . . 'a single purpose is in them.[1] They it is do guide heaven and earth. The name of the Father is written (?) [2] on the third . . . that is upon ' . . . . .

Verso (?). . . . and he found [it to be the] name [of] the [Holy] Ghost (? πνεῦμα). Enoch said unto him, 'My lord, lo, three invisible (ἀόρατος) names have I found written in the book (?) . . . . .

Fol. 6. → *Recto.*   ↑ *Verso.*

]ϣ[	]ⲁϭ	[. . . .]ⲛϭ	
]ⲡ	ⲓⲉϱ[. . . . .]ⲡ	ⲍ̄ⲡ̄[. . .]ⲁⲡⲉ	ⲟⲛ[
ϣ ⲛ̄-	ⲃⲟⲗ . . . . .ⲟ	ⲕ . . . ⲛⲧⲉⲩ-	ϯⲁⲡ . . ⲁⲡ[
ⲡϣⲁϫⲉ ⲛ-	ⲙ̄ⲡⲕⲟⲓⲧⲱ̄	ⲡ[ⲟⲩ ⲛⲧ]ⲁⲥⲥⲱ-	ϯϫ[ⲓ] ⲉⲕⲓ̈ⲃ[ⲉ ⲛ̄-]
[ⲛ̄ϩⲉ]ⲗⲗⲏⲛ ⲙ̄-	ⲛⲧⲡⲁⲣⲑⲉ-	ⲧⲁ ⲉ[ⲧ]ⲉϥⲱ-	ⲧ̄ⲡ̄ⲧⲁⲙⲁ[ⲁⲩ]
]ⲥⲱⲧⲙ	ⲛⲟⲥ ⲉⲥⲛⲕⲟ-	ⲛⲏ ⲛⲉⲛⲱⲭ	ⲙⲛ̄ϣϭ[ⲟⲙ
] . ϫ	ⲧ̄ⲕ ⲛ̄ϧⲏⲧϥ	ⲡⲉⲥⲥⲟⲛ ⲡⲉ-	ⲉⲧⲣⲁϣ[
]ⲓ̈ⲛⲉ	⳨ⲡⲉϫⲁⲥ ⲛⲁϥ ϫ[ⲉ-]	[⳨]ⲁϭ ⲛⲁϥ ϫⲉ-	ⲛ̄ⲕⲉⲓ[
]ⲧⲁ-	ⲉⲛⲱⲭ ⲡⲁ-	ⲉⲛⲱⲭ ⲡⲁⲥⲟ̄	ϯϫ[
ϩⲣⲁ̈ⲓ	ϣⲏⲣⲉ ⲙⲁⲣ[ⲟⲛ]	[ϩ]ⲱⲛ ⲉϧⲟⲩⲛ	ⲛ̄[
]ⲁ	ⲉϧⲟⲩⲛ ⲉⲡⲕ[ⲟⲓ-]	ⲉⲣⲟⲓ̈ ⲛ̄ϭⲟ[ϣⲧ]	ⲛ̄[
]ⲉ	[ⲧ]ⲱⲛ ⲛⲧⲏ[	[ⲉ]ⲃⲟⲗ ⲙ̄ⲡⲣ[	[

Fol. 6. Recto. . . . the words of the Greeks (? ἕλλην) . . . hear . . . . outside . . . . . the bed-chamber (κοιτών) of the virgin (παρ.), wherein she slept. She said unto him, 'Enoch, my son, let us go into the bed-chamber (? κοι.) and let us (?)' . . . . .

Verso. . . . at the moment when she heard the voice (φωνή) of Enoch, her brother, she said unto him, 'Enoch, my brother, come in unto me and look forth. Be not . . . . when] I took suck of my mother. It is impossible that I should [be?] again (*or* other)' . . . . .

---

[1] ? the Trinity.

[2] Reading ⲥⲏϱ, though as following prep. ϧⲛ would be preferable.

Fol. 7.　↑ *Recto.*　　　　　　→ *Verso.*　margin

p. ⲓⲁ (or ⲣⲁ)

margin

ⲉⲕⲟ[ⲉ	[		[. . ⲛ]ⲛⲟⲃⲉ
[. . . . .]ϥⲣ̄ ⲛ[ⲟ-]	. ⲡⲉ[	?	[ⲛ]ϥϥⲓ [ⲛⲛⲁ]ⲧⲁ-
ⲃⲉ ⲟⲛⲟⲩⲙⲛⲧ-	[　　ⲉⲕ-]	[ⲛ]ϣⲟⲣ[ⲡ	ⲑⲟⲛ ⲛ[ϥⲧ]ⲁ-
ⲕⲟⲩ[ⲓ] ⲛϩⲏⲧ·	ⲉϥ[ⲟ]ⲧϥ ⲉⲃⲟⲗ	[ⲥ]ⲟⲁⲓ ⲛⲛ̄ⲛ[ⲟ]ⲃⲉ	ⲗⲟⲟⲩ ⲉ[ⲕ]ⲉⲥⲁ
ⲙ̄ⲡⲟⲩⲙⲛⲧ-	ⲛ̄ⲕⲉⲥⲟⲡ·	ⲙ̄ⲡⲛⲁⲅⲁⲑⲟⲛ	ⲉϥϣⲁⲛⲛⲁⲩ
ϣⲁϥⲧⲉ· ⲛ̄　 /Ⲡⲉϫⲉ ⲉⲛⲱⲭ	ⲙ̄ⲡϣⲏⲣⲉ ⲛ̄-	ⲉⲛⲛⲟⲃⲉ ⲉⲩ-	
ⲡⲉⲕⲥⲉⲟ ⲡⲉⲩ-	ⲛⲁⲥ ϫⲉⲟⲩⲕ-	ⲡⲣⲱⲙⲉ· ⲥⲉ-	ⲥⲱⲕ ⲡⲁⲣⲁ
ⲛⲟⲃⲉ ⲛ̄ⲥⲱⲟⲩ	*sic* ⲕⲟⲩⲛ [. ⲙ]ⲡⲉⲡ-	ⲛⲁⲭ[ⲁⲣ]ⲓ̈ⲍⲉ	ⲛⲁⲅⲁⲑⲟⲛ
ⲧⲁⲭⲏ· ⲁⲗⲗ[ⲁ]	ⲛⲟⲩⲧⲉ [†] ⲛⲟⲩ-	ⲛⲁ[ⲕ] ⲙⲡⲁⲥ-	ϣⲁϥϥⲓ ⲙⲡⲉϥ-
ⲉⲕⲉⲕⲱ ⲙ̄[ⲡ-]	ⲁⲅⲅⲉ[ⲗⲟ]ⲥ ⲟⲛ̄-	[ⲧ]ⲉⲗⲟ[ⲥ ⲛⲧ]ⲙⲛⲧ-	ⲟ[ⲣ]ⲁⲃⲇⲟⲥ ⲉⲧ-
ⲕⲁϣ ⲟⲓ̈ϫ[ⲙ-]	ⲧⲡ[ⲉ] ⲛϥ̄ⲕⲁ-	ⲁϣⲁⲛⲉⲟⲧⲏϥ	[ⲟⲛ]ⲧⲉϥϭⲓ̈ϫ
ⲡⲕⲁⲗⲁⲙ[ⲁⲣⲓ-]	[ⲁϥ	ϭ[. . . .]ⲉⲧ[. .]	[ⲛⲟ]ⲩⲛⲁⲙ ⲛ̄ϥ-
ⲟⲛ ϭ[			ⲧ[ⲁⲗⲟ]ϥ ⲉϫⲛ-

Fol. 7 (1st fol. of quire 14).[1] *Recto.* . . . 'if] thou fi[nd (?) . . . . . he sinned through cowardice and error, thou shalt not write their sins against them hastily (ταχύ), but (ἀλλά) thou shalt put the reed into the reed-case (καλαμάριον) . . . . .

. . . delete[2] it again.' Enoch said unto her, 'Doth not God then (οὔκουν) [appoint?[3]] an angel (ἄγγ.) from heaven and (doth) he (not) [set? him' . . .

Verso. . . . 'first (*or* before [thou]) write the sins and the good-deeds (ἀγαθός) of the sons of men, thou shalt be granted (χαρίζειν) the angel (ἄγγ.) of mercy' . . . . .

. . . 'sins and he taketh the good-deeds (ἀγ.) and placeth them on another side. If he see the sins drawing (down the balance) beyond (παρά) the good-deeds (ἀγ.), he taketh his staff (ῥάβδος), that is in his right hand, and layeth it upon' . . . . .

---

[1] So if this is *recto*; if *verso*, it indicates p. 14, or (reading ⲟ̄ⲅ̄) p. 104.

[2] Perhaps ⲉⲕⲉϥⲟⲧϥ 'thou shalt delete'. Enoch deletes sins, *CSCO.*, vol. 42, 236.

[3] *Lit.* 'give'. ϯ, as part of a 2-rad. verb, is more difficult, though as accus., superlined before ⲟⲩ, it is also unlikely. The passage is to me quite obscure.

Fol. 8. → *Recto.*   ↑ *Verso.*

]п[			
]ⲙⲉ			. ⲉ[
ⲉⲣⲉ[. . . .] ⲙⲙⲉ	ⲡⲟ[		ⲙⲉ[
ⲟⲛⲧⲉ ⲙ[ⲡ]ⲟⲩⲉ̈ⲓ	ⲉⲛⲱ[ⲭ	]ⲙⲟ	ⲟ̅ⲡ̅[. . . .]ⲟ̣ⲓ
ⲙⲉ ⲉⲣⲟⲥ ⲙⲡⲟⲩ-	?	]ⲙⲏ	п̅ⲧ[ⲉⲧ]ⲙⲙⲁⲩ
ⲉϣⲟⲩⲟⲛϩ̅ⲥ̅ ⲉⲃⲟⲗ	ⲉⲛⲱⲭ ⲡ[ⲁ-]	]	ⲉ̈ⲓⲥ ⲧⲁ[. .]ⲉⲧ ϣ[ⲱ-]
ⲉ̈ⲓⲉⲙⲛⲧⲉ̈ⲓ	ϣⲏⲣⲉ [	]ⲟ̅ⲡ̅-	ⲡⲉ ⲛⲟⲩ п̅ⲧⲁⲕ-
[ⲛ]ⲅ̅ⲃⲱⲕ ⲡ̅ⲅ̅-	ⲙ[	]	ⲭⲡⲟⲥ ⲛ̅ϧⲏ[ⲧⲥ]
ⲟⲩⲟⲛϩ̅ⲥ̅ ⲉⲃⲟⲗ	ⲉⲡⲉ[	ⲉⲛ]ⲱⲭ	ⲉ̈ⲓⲥ ϣⲟⲙⲛⲧ ⲛ̅-
[ⲟ̣]п̅ⲧⲙⲏⲧⲉ	ⲛⲁⲩ[	]ⲧⲁϩⲟ-	ⲥⲟⲡ ⲁⲥϣⲁⲭ[ⲉ][a]
[ⲙ̣]ⲡⲉⲕⲉ̈ⲓⲱ-	п̅ⲁ[	]ⲣⲁⲛ	ⲟ̅ⲡ̅ϩⲉⲛⲛⲟ[ϭ
[ⲧ] ⲙⲛ̅ⲧⲉⲕ ⲙ[ⲁⲁⲩ]	ⲧⲁ[	]ⲉ	ⲛϣⲁⲭⲉ ⲕⲟ̣. [
[. . .]ⲭ[	ⲭ[	]ⲉ	[.]ⲏⲛ . . ⲱ[

[a]   ⲁϥϣⲁⲭⲉ cannot be read.

Fol. 8. *Recto.* . . . 'they[1] have not known her, they have not been able to make her (? it) known, except (εἰμήτι) thou (first) go and make her (? it) known before (*lit.* in midst of) thy father and thy mo[ther' . . . . .

. . . 'Enoch [my ?] son' . . . . .

Verso. . . . En]och . . . . .

. . . 'of her. Lo, my . . . (*fem.*),[2] what shall (she ?) become (?), (she) whom thou didst beget from (her) ? Lo, three times hath she spoken great (?) words' . . . . .

Fol. 9. → *Recto.*   ↑ *Verso.*

margin		margin	
ⲡⲛⲟⲩⲧⲉ ϭⲱ-	ⲭⲉⲟⲩⲕⲟⲩⲛ	[. .]ⲛⲁϫ̈ⲓ п̅[ⲥ-]	ⲉ̈ⲓⲉⲙⲛⲧⲉ ⲛ-
ϣⲧ ⲉ̣ϩⲣⲁⲓ ⲉϫⲱⲕ ·	ⲡⲟ . . . ⲁⲛ[ⲁ-]	[ⲛⲁ]ⲩ ⲉϩⲣⲁ̈ⲓ ⲉⲧ-	ⲡⲗⲁⲥⲥⲉ ⲛⲕ[ⲉ-]
ⲁϥⲛⲁⲩ ⲉⲣⲟⲕ	ⲗⲁⲙⲃⲁⲛⲉ [	[ⲡⲉ] ⲟ̅ⲡ̅ⲡⲉⲩⲥⲱ-	ⲣⲱⲙⲉ ⲛⲟⲉ

[1] Read? ⲟⲩⲧⲉ 'neither'.

[2]]ⲉⲧ might be completed as ⲕⲉⲧ or ⲉⲉⲧ, were they not so difficult to adapt to the context.

ⲝⲉⲛ̄ⲧⲕⲟⲩⲥⲱ-   ⲡⲣⲱⲙⲉ [ⲉⲧ-] | [ⲙ̅ⲁ] ⲟⲩⲁ ⲭⲉ-   ⲙ̄ⲡⲉⲛⲉⲓ̈ⲱ[ⲧ]
ⲧⲡ ⲁⲩⲱ ⲉⲕⲥⲁ-   ⲡⲉ ⲟⲙⲡⲉϥ[ⲥⲱ-] | [ⲟ]ⲏⲗⲓ̅ⲁⲥ ⲙ̄ⲛ-   ⲁⲁⲙ ⲡϥ̄ⲥⲱ̅-
ⲟⲏⲩ ⲉⲃⲟⲗ ⲉⲡⲉ-   ⲙⲁ ⲉⲓⲙⲏⲧ[ⲉⲓ] | [ⲕ]ⲉⲟⲩⲉⲓ ⲭⲉⲧⲁ-   ⲣ̄ⲅ̄ ⲉⲡⲕⲁⲟ
ⲑⲟⲟⲩ ⲛ̄[ⲓ]ⲙ· ⲡⲉ-   〜ⲁ[ⲛⲟ]ⲕ· ⲡⲉⲭ[ⲁⲥ] | [ⲃⲓ]ⲑⲁ ⲛ̄[. .]ⲕⲁ   ⲡⲉⲭ[ⲁ]ⲥ ⲛⲁϥ
ⲭⲁϥ ⲭⲉ[. . .]ⲉⲓⲁⲩ ᵃ   ⲛ̄ⲁ[ϥ] ⲭⲉ[|]ⲙ̄ⲡⲙⲁ ⲉ-   ⲭⲉ[ⲡ]ⲁⲥⲟⲛ ⲁ
ⲁⲛⲟ[. . . .]ⲛⲉⲣ .ᵇ   [ⲭ]ⲟⲉⲓ̈ⲥ . .[|]ⲉ ⲛ̄ⲟⲏ[ⲧ]ϥ̄   ⲗⲁ[. ⲡ]ⲕⲁⲣⲡⲟⲥ
? |]ⲧⲉⲧ[ⲉⲧⲛ̄[ⲁⲉⲓ ⲉ]ⲃⲟⲗ
                                                 | ⲛ̄ⲟ[ⲏⲧⲕ

ᵃ Possibly ⲁⲅⲓ.   ᵇ Possibly ⲛⲉⲛ.

Fol. 9. *Recto.* . . . 'God (did) look down upon thee and saw thee, how that thou wast a chosen one and removed from all evil.' He said, ...

. . . said,] '[Shall] not then (οὔκουν) [the Lord?] take up (ἀναλαμβάνειν) [any?] man to heaven in his body (? σῶμα), except (εἰμήτι) me?' She (?) said unto [him,] '. . . Lord (?) . . . . .

Verso. . . . shall take two up to [heaven] in their body (σῶμα): one Elias, another Tabitha . . . . . the place where . . . is . . . . .

. . . except (? εἰμήτι) by forming [1] (πλάσσειν) another man, in the fashion of our father Adam, and that he people the earth.' She said unto him, 'Mathusala (?)[2] [is the] fruit (καρ.) that [shall go] forth from [thee'. . . . .

No. 4.

From a version of the Life (?) of the Virgin, identical, in part at least, with Zoega no. cxvii, Clar. Press no. 14 (v. Forbes Robinson, *Apocr. Gosp.*, pp. 10, 14) and Br. Mus. no. 303.[3] In the latter of those fragments there is likewise reference to the Meletians.[4] Our fourth fragment here is perhaps wrongly associated with the other three; it may be from a different MS. and text. So too the third, which has marked differences from the others (v. note on text).

[1] For εἰμήτι (cf. the readings here *ro.* and frag. 8), perhaps ⲉⲓⲉ ⲙⲏ ⲧⲉⲛ-. But 1st pl. 'we form' seems incongruous here.

[2] Reading instead [ⲙ]ⲁⲑⲟⲩⲥⲁⲗⲁ[ⲡⲉ.

[4] F. R., p. 2, ll. 14, 15, 'Say not as the heretics that the Virgin was a " power " (δύναμις, cf. ib. 108, 10); nor say as the Meletians, that she was taken up to heaven in her body.' Mr. Winstedt has kindly collated the text.

Fol. 1. ↑ *Recto.*   → *Verso.*

Recto	margin	margin	Verso
[п겐]а ппероо- оу птакевві- он ꙅппре- паꙅнт ппаꙅ акꙗаст пое ноупетра ак- ꙗі пбоеїт ꙅнт акепт евол еуоуастп ак- тало проепрꙍ- пе ехппеп- [а]пеуе · акепт	margin	margin	еіпе ппеут[а-] еїо пïꙍаке[пп] аꙋр сашꙅ п- ꙅооу еуоу- ꙍп еусꙍ [еу-] еуꙅрапе е- ꙗппа п- таппоуте ꙗокꙅ [евол] ппïꙍак[еіп] ппап[на

Fol. 1. *Recto.* . . . 'in[1] place of the days in which Thou didst humble us, when my heart was sad. Thou didst raise me up like a rock (πέτρα) and didst guide me and bring me forth unto a broad-place.[2] Thou didst cause men to ride over our heads and didst bring [us' . . . . .

Verso. . . . brought their gifts-of-honour unto Joakim and they spent seven days eating and drinking and rejoicing (εὐφραίνειν) over the mercy that God had fulfilled with Joakim and Anna . . . . .

Fol. 2. ↑ *Recto.*   → *Verso.*

Recto	margin	margin	Verso
[пп]оуте ааꙅ [пп]пша е- [т]реꙅꙅïте [П]лнп ппе- [т]парꙝепос шпе пса- песеіоте	margin	margin	а[у]ꙍ[a] нет[вꙍк] пппау еп[еу-] па пшïпе [ет-] ꙅооꙅ ете[пеу-] па пшꙍп[е-] пе · оуꙗе [оу-] оп пïп етпіꙅ-

[a] Or ꙗаі]ппꙍп ет-.

[1] This ode is made up of various Psalm verses (*v.* F. Robinson, p. 11).

[2] F. R. поуꙍшꙅ евол.

ⲁⲗⲗⲁ ⲛⲉⲥⲟ ⲛⲑⲉ	margin	ⲧⲉⲩⲉ ⲛⲙⲙⲁⲩ
ⲛⲛⲉⲓ̈ⲥⲣⲟⲟⲩ-		ⲉⲧⲉⲩϩⲁⲓ̈ⲣⲉ-
ⲡⲉ ⲉⲧⲙⲟⲟⲛⲉ		ⲥⲓⲥ ⲉⲧⲥⲟⲟⲩ
ⲛⲛⲁⲩ ⲛⲓ̈ⲙ		ⲛⲁⲓ̈ [ⲉⲧ]ϭϩⲁ[ⲓ]ᵃ
ϩⲙⲡⲣⲡⲉ ϣⲁ-		ⲛⲟϭ ⲛⲧⲱⲗⲙ
ⲡⲉϩⲟⲟⲩ ⲛⲧⲁⲥ-		ⲉⲧⲙⲛⲧⲛⲟⲩ-
ⲙⲡϣⲁ ⲙⲡⲉⲓ̈-		ⲧⲉ ⲛⲉⲙⲙⲁⲛⲟⲩ-
ⲛⲟϭ ⲛⲧⲁⲉⲓⲟ		ⲏ̅ⲗ ⲉ . . . . ⲉ
ⲛϩⲏⲧϥ ⲉⲧⲣⲉⲥ-		ⲧⲉⲧⲣⲓⲁⲥ ⲉⲧⲟⲩ-
ϫⲡⲟ ⲙⲡⲉⲭ̅ⲥ̅		ⲁⲁⲃ ⲡ̅ⲓ̈ⲱⲧ
Ⲡⲁⲣⲟⲩⲭⲓ̈ ϣⲓ̈-		ⲙⲡϣⲏⲣⲉ
ⲡⲉ ⲧⲉⲛⲟⲩ ⲛ-		ⲙⲡⲉⲡⲛ̅ⲁ̅
ϭⲓ ⲙⲙⲉⲓ̈ⲗⲓⲧⲓ-		ⲉⲧⲟⲩⲁⲁⲃ ⲉⲩ-
ˢⁱᶜ ⲡ̅ⲁⲛⲟⲥ ⲛⲁⲓ̈		ϭⲓ̈ ⲙⲙⲁⲩ ⲙ-
ⲉⲧⲩⲡⲟⲧⲉⲩⲉ		ⲡⲉⲙⲙⲏ ⲙᵇ
ⲉ̣ · [		ⲧⲉⲛⲛⲛ ⲉⲣⲉ-

ᵃ Or (if space would allow) [ⲉⲧϫ]ⲉ ϩⲉ[ⲛ-. ᵇ ⲙⲛ- (? ⲙ̅⁻) is required; then prob. ⲡⲉⲡⲛ̅ⲏ.

Fol. 2. *Recto.* . . . God made him (?) worthy to take her (? it).   Howbeit (πλήν) the Virgin (παρ.) visited not her parents, but (ἀλλά) was like to those doves that dwelt always in the temple, until the day whereon she was worthy of this great honour, that she should bear Christ.   Let the Meletians[1] be now ashamed, that cast suspicion (? ὑποπτεύειν) . . . . .

Verso. . . . and (?) they that [go] with them unto [their] filthy oracles, that is, their dwelling-places ; neither (οὐδέ) any one that believeth (πιστεύειν)

[1] There is little to add to Riedel's account of the Meletians (*Can. Athanas.* xv ff.   My reference there to Renaudot may now be replaced by Evetts, *Patrol. Or.*, v. 200 ff., where their magical practices are specially referred to).   Their heretical tenets are condemned in the other copy of the present text (*v.* note above), their usages attacked Sanê, *ed.* Guidi), and their survival of Siût (Br. Mus. no. 358, if by Bp. Constantine, then also of early seventh century, *v.* Br. Mus. no. 865 n.), and at Achmîm (*Mission* iv. 740; *cf.* Wüstenfeld's *Synax.*, 9th Kihak) are recorded.   Athanasius, in a Festal Letter (Zoega no. cclxxvii, f. 2 = text of Paris 129¹⁴, ff. 87–90, which is same MS. as Br. Mus. no. 173), refers to their traffick-

with them in their filthy heresy (αἵρ.), who ascribe[1] great impurities unto the divinity of Emmanuel, they . . . -ing the holy Trinity (τριάς), the Father, the Son and the Holy Ghost (πν.), taking away the *mê* (μῦ) and the *nê* (νῦ)[2] . . . . .

Fol. 3.   ↑ *Recto.*[a]

margin

ⲁⲩⲥⲫⲣⲁⲅⲓⲍⲉ ⲙ-	[. .]ⲧⲛⲟⲩ
ⲙⲟϥ ϩⲛ̄ⲟⲩⲥⲫⲣⲁ-	[. . .] ⲉⲧⲉⲡ-
ⲅⲓ̈ⲥ · ⲁⲩⲱ ⲙⲙⲛ-	[ⲥⲁ]ⲃⲃⲁⲧⲟⲛⲡⲉ
Ⲥⲁⲛⲁⲓ̈ ⲟⲛ ⲙⲡⲉ-	ⲉⲥϫⲱ ⲙⲙⲟⲥ
ⲥⲟⲗⲥⲗ ⲛϩⲏⲧ ⲉⲥ-	ϫ[ⲉ]ⲙⲁⲣⲏⲧⲱ-
ϫⲱ̄ ⲙⲙⲟⲥ ϫⲉ-	[ⲟ]ⲩⲛ ⲛⲧⲉⲩϣⲏ
ⲉⲓ̈ⲧⲁ̄ⲃⲱⲕ ⲧⲁ-	ⲛⲧⲛⲃⲱⲕ ⲉⲃⲟⲗ
ⲛⲁⲩ ⲉⲡⲧⲁⲫⲟ̄ⲥ	ⲛⲙⲙⲁⲥ ⲛⲧⲛ-
ⲛ̄ⲑⲉ ⲛⲧⲁⲩⲕⲁ-	ϫⲓ̈ⲧⲉ ⲉⲃⲟⲗ ⲛⲥ-
ⲁϥ ⲙⲙⲟ̄ⲥ ⲛ̄ϯ-	ⲛⲁⲩ ⲉⲡⲉϥⲥⲱ-
ⲛⲁϩⲙⲟ̄ⲥ ⲁⲛ	ⲙⲁ ϫⲉⲛⲛⲉⲥⲙⲟ̄ⲩ
Ⲉⲣⲉⲛⲁⲓ̈ ⲇⲉ ϣⲟ̄-	ⲛⲧⲉϥⲁⲫⲟⲣⲙⲏ
ⲟⲡ ⲛⲧⲉⲓ̈ϩⲉ ⲙⲁⲗ-	ⲁⲩⲧⲱⲟⲩⲛ ⲁⲩ-
ⲗⲟⲛ ⲇⲉ ⲛⲉ[ⲣ]ⲉ-	[ⲥ]ⲟⲃⲧⲉ ⲛ̄ⲣϩⲉⲛ-
ⲟⲩⲛⲟϭ ⲛ[. .]ⲣⲃ̄	[ϩ]ⲛ̄ⲏ̄ⲡⲉ ⲉⲛⲁϣⲱ-
[.]ϩ̣[	[ⲟⲩ] ⲙⲙϩⲉⲛ-
	[. . .]ϣⲏⲣⲓ̣[b] . .
	?

---

[a] The superlineation here is so peculiar and different from that on foll. 1, 2, 4, that one may doubt this leaf being from the same MS.   [b] [ⲟⲩⲙⲓ]ⲁⲧⲏⲣⲓ[ⲟⲛ is improbable.

---

[1] *Lit.* 'write'. Or 'speak' (grammatically preferable).

[2] I can suggest no other translation, and even for this the reading requires manipulation. I suppose the consonants of 'Emmanuel' to be intended and some magical or gnostic use of the name ⲉⲗⲟⲩⲏⲗ referred to. *Cf.* wholly vocalic forms like ⲁⲉⲏⲉⲓⲟⲩⲱⲏⲗ (*Rain. Mitth.*, v. 120). That the letters ⲙ, ⲛ were thus pronounced is seen from Hebbelynck, *Mystères*, 34, 117, Paris 131[8], f. 77 (on significance of the letters in name ⲙⲁⲣⲓⲁ).

→ *Verso.*

margin	ⲡⲉⲭ̅ⲥ̅ (in margin) [a]
ⲡⲉ ⲉⲧⲣ[ⲉⲩⲙⲟ-]	ⲉⲧϥϫⲱ ⲙⲙⲟ-
ⲟⲩϣⲉ ⲉⲃ[ⲟⲗ ⲉ]ⲩ-	ⲟⲩ ⲛⲁϥ ϫⲓⲡⲉϥ-
ⲣϩⲟⲧⲉⲡⲉ ⲁ[ⲩ]ⲱ	ϣⲟⲟⲡ ⲛⲙⲙⲁⲩ-
ⲉⲩϣⲧⲣⲧⲱⲣ	ⲡⲉ ⲭⲉϩⲁⲡ̅ⲥ̅
⳥ Ⲉⲛⲉⲣⲉⲛ̈ⲓⲟⲩ-	ⲉⲧⲣⲁ̅ϣ̅ⲡ̅ ⲛⲉ̈
ϩⲁⲓ ⲅⲁⲣ ⲥⲟⲣⲥ	ϩⲓⲥⲉ ⲁⲩⲱ̅ ⲛⲧⲁ-
ⲉⲡⲉⲧⲛⲁⲃⲱⲕ	ⲧⲱⲟⲩⲛ ⲛⲉⲣⲉ-
ⲉⲃⲟⲗ ⲉⲡⲙⲟⲁ-	ᵍⁱᶜ ᵏᵃ ⲟⲩⲕ̅ⲉ ⲛⲃⲟⲗ ⲙⲛ-
ⲁⲩ ⲛⲥⲉⲉ̈ⲣⲉ ⲛⲁⲩ̅	ⲟⲩϣⲧⲟⲣⲧⲣ
ⲛⲟⲉⲛⲡⲉⲑⲟ-	ⲁⲩⲱ ⲁⲩ̅ⲕⲱ̅ ⲛ-
ⲟⲩ· ⲛⲉⲛⲡⲣⲉϥ-	ⲥⲱⲟⲩ̅ ⲛⲛⲁⲓ̈
ⲣⲟⲉ̈ⲥ ⲣⲟⲉ̈ⲥ ⲉ-	ⲧⲏⲣⲟⲩ̅ ⲁⲩⲙⲟ̄-
ⲣⲟϥ̅ⲡⲉ ϫⲉⲛ-	ⲟϣⲉ ⲛ̅ⲙⲙⲁⲥ
ⲛⲉⲩϥ̈ ⲙⲡⲉϥ-	[ⲉ]ⲧⲃⲉⲧⲉ̈ⲥ̅ ⲙⲛ̄-
ⲥⲱⲙⲁ ⲛϫ[ⲓⲟ]ⲩⲉ	ⲁⲛⲁⲅⲕⲏ ⲙ̅ⲛ̅-
ⲛⲉⲣⲉⲟⲩϣⲧ[ⲟⲣ-]	[ⲡⲉϣⲧⲟ]ⲣⲧⲣ
ⲧⲣ ϣⲟⲟⲡ [ⲉⲧ-]	
[ⲃ]ⲛⲛⲧϥ̅ ϫ[ⲉ	

[a] This being the *verso*, the formula [ⲓ̅ⲥ̅ ⲡ]ⲉⲭ̅ⲥ̅ would indicate the last fol. of a quire. (More usually ⲓ̅ⲥ̅ on the last, ⲡⲉⲭ̅ⲥ̅ on first of following quire.)

Fol. 3. *Recto.* . . . they sealed (σφραγίζειν) it with a seal (σφραγίς). And after this also she was not comforted at heart, saying, 'If I go not and see the tomb (τάφος), how they have laid Him, I will not sit down.' But (δέ) these things being so, and moreover (μᾶλλον δέ) as there was a great . . . . which as the Sabbath, she saying, 'Let us arise at night and go forth with her and take her out and she see His body (σῶ.), lest she die on His account (ἀφορμή).' They arose and prepared much spices and . . . (*plur.*) . .

. . . . that they should go forward being afraid and trembling

For (γάρ) the Jews were lying in wait for whoso should go forth to the grave, that they might do them evil; and the watchers were watching it, lest His body (σῶ.) should be taken by stealth; and there was a disturbance on His (?) account, because that . . . . .

. . . words] that He spake unto them, while He was with them, ' Needs must that I should suffer these things and should arise, there being (still) darkness and disturbance.'[1] .And they left all these things behind them and went with her, by reason of her need (ἀνάγκη) and her trouble . . . . .

Fol. 4. → *Recto.*   ↑ *Verso.*

<table>
<tr><td>margin.</td><td>

 na[
ɯa[
ενεϩ ϊ[ετ-]
ϭϊϫππκαϩ κ[
ερεπεγϩητ[a] ϭ[. .]
 νθε ντνει[. .]
εγϲοφοϲπ[ε] ε-
_{sic} ν
περογο ενταγ-
ɯωπε τηρογ
ϭϊππκαϩ
καν εαϥϫι πνο-
[πο]ϲ νθε πππω-
[γϲηϲ] καν εαϥ-
]ππ-

</td><td>

]ω
πε]ϥογο-
[ειν] ανϲιογ
αναχωρει
ναγ ατκακε
ɯωπε ντπα-
ɯε ππεϩοογ
ανετποογτ
τωογν αγει ε-
βολ ϩππεπ-
ϩααγ
Ӆπκατ[απεταϲππα][b]
ππρ[πε
?

</td><td>margin</td></tr>
</table>

[a] πεϥϩητ more probable.   [b] Inevitable, if not too long. Last letters perhaps above the line.

Fol. 4. *Recto.* . . . ever . . . on the earth . . ., his (?) heart being . . . like . . . . . , he being wise (σοφός) beyond all them that had been upon earth, whether (κἄν) when he received[2] the law (νόμ.) like Moses, or (κἄν) when he . . . . .

Verso. . . . his (?) light; the stars departed (ἀναχωρεῖν); darkness was at midday; the dead arose and came forth from the graves. The veil (? καταπέτασμα[3]) of the temple (?) . . . . .

[1] *Cf.* Lemm, *Misc.* lix.   [2] ' accepted ', if this refers to Christ.   [3] *V.* note [b].

No. 5.

Presumably from a Sermon (or Encomium), with reference, on *verso*, to the death of the Virgin. *Cf.* the passages in Forbes Robinson's *Apocr. Gospels*, pp. 65, 83, and in *PSBA*. xxix. 304. The narrative would appear not to be related here by an apostle.

→ *Recto.*

       margin

ⲁϥϯ ⲛⲁϥ ⲛ[ϩⲉⲛ-]
ⲧⲁⲉⲓⲟ ϩⲱⲱ̅[ϥ]
ⲙ̅ⲛ̅ϩⲉⲛⲇⲱ[ⲣⲟⲛ]
ⲉⲛⲁϣⲱⲟⲩ —   ϣ[
ⲁ̅ϥϫⲟⲟⲥ ⲛ̅ⲓ̅ⲱ̅   ⲅⲉⲓ[
ⲥⲛ̅ϥ ϫⲉⲉ̈ⲥ ⲡⲁ-   ⲱⲡ[
ⲕⲁϩ ⲧⲏⲣ̅ϥ̅ ⲙ̅ⲡⲉ̅-   ⲥⲛⲁⲩ ⲁ̣[
ⲧⲟ ⲉⲃⲟⲗ ⲙ̅ⲡⲉⲕ-   ⲁⲩⲙ̅ⲡ[
ⲉⲓⲱⲧ ⲙ̅ⲛ̅ⲛⲉ[ⲕ-]   ⲁϥⲧⲛ̅[
ⲥⲛⲏⲩ ⲙⲁⲣⲟⲩ-
ⲟⲩⲱϩ ϩⲙ̅ⲡⲕⲁϩ
ⲉⲧⲛ̅ⲁⲛⲟⲩϥ
ⲛⲥⲉϫⲓ ⲛ̅ⲥⲉϯ
ⲛ̅ⲥⲉϣⲱⲡⲉ
ϩⲙ̅ⲡⲉⲟⲟⲩ ⲛ̅-
ⲧⲁⲙⲛ̅ⲧⲉⲣ[ⲟ]
ⲙ̅ⲛ̅ⲛⲁⲅⲁ[ⲑⲟⲛ]
ⲙ̅ⲡⲕⲁϩ·
ⲉϣϫⲉ ⲁⲛ[

↑ *Verso.*

       margin

      [ⲡ]ⲏⲩⲉ ⲉⲣⲉⲛⲃⲁ[ⲗ]
      [ⲛ]ⲛ̅ⲁⲡⲟⲥⲧⲟⲗ-ᵃ
      [ⲗ]ⲟⲥ ϭⲱϣⲧ̅ ⲛ̅-
]ⲃⲱⲕ   ⲥⲱϩ ⲉⲩⲑⲉⲱⲣⲉⲓ
ⲙ]ⲡⲏⲩⲉ   ⲙ̅ⲙⲟⲥ ⲙ̅ⲡⲉⲥ-
]ⲧⲏⲟⲩ   ⲉⲟⲟⲩ ⲛⲁⲧϣⲁ-
]ⲛⲟⲥ   ϫⲉ ⲉⲣⲟϥ· ⲁⲩⲱ
]ⲁⲥⲱϣ   ⲛ̅ⲧⲉⲣⲟⲩⲡⲱϩ
]ϫⲁⲉⲙ   ⲛⲙ̅ⲙⲁⲥ ⲉⲙⲡⲩ-
]ⲥϩ   ⲗⲏ ⲛ̅ⲙ̅ⲡⲏⲩⲉ
      ⲁⲛⲉⲑ̅ⲩ̅ⲣⲟⲩⲣⲟⲥ̅
      ⲛ̅ⲙ̅ⲡⲏⲩⲉ ⲣⲁ-
      ϣⲉ ⲁⲩⲱϣ̅ ⲉ-
      ⲃⲟⲗ ⲉⲩϫⲱ ⲙ̅-
      ⲙⲟⲥ ϩⲓⲧⲛ̅ⲧⲉ-
      [ⲥ]ⲙⲏ ⲛ̅ⲧⲁⲥϣⲟ-
      [ⲡⲉ] ⲙ̅ⲙⲟⲥ̅ ⲙ̅-
      [ⲡⲛ]ⲁⲩ ⲛ̅ⲧⲁⲡⲉⲥ̅-
      [ϣⲏ]ⲣⲉ ⲃⲱⲕ ⲉ-
      [ϩⲣⲁⲓ] ⲉⲙ̅ⲡⲏⲩⲉ
      [. . . .]ⲱⲛ[

ᵃ Perhaps nothing instead of ⲗ.

Recto. ... he gave unto him also (?) honours and many gifts (δῶρον).

¹ *V.* Gen. xlvii. 6.

brethren. Let them dwell in the good land and buy and sell and share (*lit.* be) in the honour of my kingdom and the good-things (ἀγαθός) of the land.'[1] If we (?) . . . . .

Verso. . . . to] heaven, the eyes of the apostles (ἀπ.) looking after her, beholding her and her unspeakable glory. And when they[2] had attained with her unto the gates (πύλη) of heaven, the door-keepers (θυρωρός) of heaven rejoiced and cried out, saying, with the voice that had reached her[3] at the time when her Son had gone up to heaven . . . . .

No. 6.

We have here the last words of one Sermon, followed by the title and opening of another; also (fol. 2) a passage, relating to Acts i. 3 ff., which may belong to either or to neither of the preceding. That with its title preserved was pronounced at Christmas, and might be attributed to Basil of Caesarea, if that town's name could be read in the second lacuna. The text, however, does not resemble that of any published sermon by Basil.

Fol. 1. ↑ *Recto.*   → *Verso.*

margin   margin

ϫοειϲ ναϊ ε-	ωτ ⲙ̄ⲡⲡ[επⲡⲁ]	[. . .]ϲ ⲛ̄ϲερω-	λοολε᾿ εϲωⲗ̄ⲡ
ⲃολ ϩιτοοτϥ̄	ετογⲁⲁⲃ [ϣⲁεⲛεϩ]	[ⲃⲥ]ᵃ ⲙ̄ⲡⲁⲏⲣ εγ-	ⲙ̄ⲡϣⲏⲣ ετε-
ⲡεοογ ⲙ̄ⲡει-	ⲛ̄ⲡεⲛεϩ ϩ[ⲁⲙⲏⲛ ·]	]ⲝⲓⲓ ϩⲛ̄-	ⲡϥ̄ⲛⲁϯ ⲕⲁⲣⲡⲟⲥ
		]ⲧⲡε	ⲁⲛ · ⲡϥ̄ⲧⲃ̄ⲃⲟ
		]ⲓⲓⲓⲁ ⲛⲏγ	ⲙ̄ⲡετⲛⲁϯ ⲕⲁⲣ-
		] ?	ⲡⲟⲥ ϩ̄ⲛ̄ⲟγⲟγ-
		] εⲃⲟⲗ	ⲣⲟⲧ · τοτε
		]ⲕⲁⲗⲏ	ϣⲁⲣεⲡογοειε
		]ογ	ϫⲱⲣ ⲙ̄ⲡεϥⲟϩ̄
7 ·̇ ογεϩⲏⲥⲏⲥιϲ ⲛ̄τε [		]ϩⲟγ	εⲱϩ̄ ⲛ̄ⲡεⲛ-
·̣ ⲡεⲡιϲⲕⲟⲡⲟϲ ⲛ̄τⲡ[		]ⲛⲟϥ	τⲁγϫⲁⲁτε ϩⲛ̄-
⸻ ⲛ̄ⲧϣⲟⲣⲡ̄ ⲛ̄ⲕⲁⲛⲡⲁ[ⲇⲟⲕιⲁ		]ⲛϲε	ογτεⲗ[ⲏⲗ] το-
εϥϣⲁϫε ετⲃεⲛ[ϩⲟγⲙιϲε ⲙ̄ⲡεⲛ-]		] ?	τε ϣⲁ[

ᵃ ϩⲱⲗ ϩⲙ- less probable because of the division ϩⲱ-ⲗ.

[1] Perhaps the supposed quotation does not end here.   [2] *Sc.* the angels.   [3] *Lit.* 'been for her'.

[cωτ]ηρ ⲓ̅ⲥ̅ ⲡⲉⲭ̅ⲥ̅ [ⲛⲥⲟⲩⲭⲟⲩⲧⲯⲓⲥ ⲙ-]
[ⲡⲉⲃⲟⲧ ⲭⲟ]ⲓⲁⲭ̅ⲕ̅ : [ⲟⲛⲟⲩⲉⲓⲣⲏⲛⲏ ?

⊦— — — —

[Ⲉ]ⲣϣⲁⲛⲡⲉⲭⲓ-   ⲟ̅ⲣⲁⲓ̈ ⲛⲟ[ⲩϣ-]
ⲙⲱⲛ ⲟⲩⲉⲓⲡⲉ·   ⲛⲏ ⲛ̅ⲭⲟⲣ[ⲧⲟⲥ]
ⲛ̅ⲧⲉⲡⲣⲟⲩⲙ-   ϣⲁⲣⲉⲛ̅ϣ[ⲏⲛ]
ⲡⲉ ⲁⲛⲁⲭⲱⲣⲉⲓ·   ⲟⲓ ⲣⲁϣⲉ ⲉⲃⲟⲗ ⲙ̅-
ⲕⲁⲧⲁ ⲡϣⲁⲭⲉ   ⲡⲧⲱ'·ᵃ ϣⲁ[ⲣⲉ-]
ⲙ̅ⲡⲥⲟⲫⲟⲥ ⲥⲟ-   ⲡⲣⲏ' ⲃⲟⲩⲃ̅[ⲟⲩ]
ⲗⲟⲙⲱⲛ ⲛ̅ⲧⲉ   ⲟ̅ⲛ̅ ᵇ[
ⲡⲁⲏⲣ ⲛⲟⲩⲧϥ̅·   ⲛ̅[
ⲛ̅ⲧⲉⲡⲣⲏ ϣⲁ·   ⲛⲓ[. ⲁⲩ]ⲱ ⲟⲛ
ⲧⲟⲧⲉ ϣⲁⲣⲉ-   ϣⲁⲣⲉⲛϩⲁⲗ[ⲁⲧⲉ]
ⲡⲕⲁϩ ⲧⲁⲅⲟ ⲉ-   ⲉⲓ' ⲉⲃⲟⲗ ⲟ̅ⲛ̅[.]

margin

]ⲟⲉ   ⲁⲁ[·
]ϣⲃⲛⲟ- ᶜ   ⲡⲉⲥ[
]ⲣⲁϣⲉ   ϩⲣⲏⲣⲉ [?ⲧⲟⲩ-]
]ⲟⲩⲉⲗⲟⲟⲩ   ⲣⲏⲥ ⲙ̅ⲡⲉⲧⲛⲓ-
ⲟ'ⲩⲏⲣ ⲛ̅ⲥⲁ-   ⲭⲉ ⲉϩⲟⲩⲛ' ⲟ̅ⲛ̅
]ⲉϣ̅ⲡ̅ⲧⲁⲥ̅-   ⲡⲕⲩⲡⲟⲥ ⲛ̅ⲧ-
[ⲥⲉ] ⲟⲛⲟⲩⲟⲩ-   ⲡⲅⲁⲙⲫⲏ ϣⲁⲛ-
[ⲣⲟ]ⲧ ⲉⲩⲥⲕⲓⲣ-   ⲧⲉⲡⲉϥϣⲏⲛ
[ⲧⲁ] ⲟ̅ⲛ̅ⲙⲙⲁ ⲙ̅-   ⲧ̅ ⲛ̅ⲡⲉⲩⲥ̅ⲧ̅-
[ⲙⲟ]ⲟⲛⲉ' ⲉⲧⲉ-   ⲛⲟⲩϭⲉ· ⲁⲩⲱ
]ⲩ ⲧⲟⲧⲉ   ⲛ̅ⲟⲩⲱϩⲉ ϣⲁⲩ-
ⲥⲏⲥϥⲉ ᵈ ..ϥⲙⲟ-   ⲧ̅ ⲛ̅ⲡⲉⲩϣⲏⲩⲩ
ⲟϣⲉ ⲉⲃⲟⲗ ⲉ-   ᵉᵗᶜ ⲉⲑⲁⲗⲁⲥⲁ ⲛ̅-
ⲧⲉϥⲃⲱ ⲡⲉ-   ⲥⲉⲉⲓⲣⲉ ⲛ̅ⲧⲉⲩ-
                    ⲉⲣⲅⲁⲥⲓⲁ' ⲟ̅ⲛ̅

margin

ᵃ Read ⲧⲟⲩⲱ.   ᵇ ? ⲟⲛ[ⲡⲉϥⲁⲕⲧⲓⲛ].   ᶜ ?ⲧⲉⲛ̅ⲡⲟⲟⲩⲉ.   ᵈ Must be ⲧⲥⲏϥⲉ.

Fol. 1. *Recto.* . . . our] Lord, He through whom (be) glory to the Father and the Holy [Ghost (πν.)] [for ever] and ever. A[men.]

A Sermon (ἐξήγησις) of . . ., the bishop (ἐπ.) of . . ., of Cappa[docia] Prima, discoursing upon the [Birthday of our Sav]iour (σω.) Jesus Christ, [on the 29th day of the month Cho]iahk. [? In peace (εἰρ.). Amen?]

When[1] the winter (χιών) is gone by and the rain hath past (ἀναχωρεῖν), according to (κατά) the words of the wise (σοφός) Solomon, and the air (ἀήρ) is pleasant, and the sun doth shine ; then (τότε) doth the earth put forth a garden of herbs (χόρτος), the trees burst forth in gladness[2] at budding, the sun is fervid in . . . . And the birds likewise (?) go forth from . . .

(*Verso*)   and cover (?) the air while they . . . . . the sky . . . . following . . . footsteps gladly, skipping (σκιρτᾶν) in the . . . pastures. Then

[1] *Cf.* Cant. ii. 11.   [2] *Lit.* 'throw out gladness'.

branch that shall not bear fruit (καρ.) and to dress (*lit.* cleanse) that which is about to bear fruit in gladness. Then (τότε) doth the husband-man sharpen his sickle to reap those that have made progress joyfully. Then (τότε) doth (?) . . . . . . flower . . . southwind of that (?) which[1] bloweth upon the orchard (κῆπος) of the bride[2] (νύμφη), that its trees may give their perfume. And the fishermen put their nets into the sea (θάλ.) and do their business (ἐργασία) in . . . . .

Fol. 2. → *Recto* (?).　　　　　　　　　↑ *Verso* (?).

　　　　　2 illegible lines.　　　　　　　margin

	] ? ⲉⲩ-	ⲧⲉ ⲛⲧ[ⲙⲛⲧ-]	
[ⲟⲩⲱⲛⲅ] ⲉⲃⲟⲗ	ⲭⲛⲟⲩⲥⲉ ⲙ̄ⲙⲟϥ	ⲉⲣⲟ ⲙ̄[ⲧ]ⲉ-	[
[ⲛⲟⲙⲉ] ⲛ̄ϩⲟⲟⲩ	ⲛ̄ϭⲓ ⲡⲉⲛⲧⲁⲩ-	ⲍⲟⲩⲥⲓⲁ ⲛ̄ⲧⲙⲛⲧ-	ⲉⲣⲱ[
[ⲉϥⲉⲓ]ⲣⲉ ⲛ̄ϩⲉⲛ-	ⲥⲱⲧⲙ̄ ⲉⲩ-	ⲛⲟⲩⲧⲉ · ⲟⲩ-	ⲧⲙ ⲡⲉ[
]ϭ ᵃ ⲁⲩⲱ	ⲭⲱ ⲙ̄ⲙⲟⲥ	ⲥⲉ ⲡⲉⲛⲧⲁϥ-	ⲁⲩⲱ ⲟ[
[ⲉϥϣ]ⲁⲝⲉ ⲛⲙ̄-	ⲭⲉⲡϫⲟⲉⲓⲥ	ⲟⲩⲱϣⲃ̄ ⲛⲁ̄ϥ	ⲧⲉⲡϣ[ⲏⲣⲉ ⲧⲉ-]
[ⲙⲁⲩ ⲉⲧⲃ̄]ⲉⲧⲙ̄ⲛ̄ⲧ-	ⲙⲛ ϩⲣⲁⲓ̈ ϩ[ⲛ̄ⲡⲓ-]	ⲛ̄ϩⲏⲧϥ̄ ⲛ̄ϭⲓ	ⲍⲟⲩⲥⲓ[ⲁ
[ⲉⲣⲟ ⲙ̄]ⲡⲛⲟⲩ-	ⲟⲩⲟ[? ⲧⲙⲛ̄]ⲧⲉ-ᶜ	ⲡϫⲟⲉⲓⲥ ⲡⲉ-	ⲛ̄ϫⲱⲕ[? ⲉ-]
[ⲧⲉ] ⲁⲩⲱ ⲉϥ-	[ⲣ]ⲟ ⲙ̄ⲡⲓⲏⲗ	[ⲭ̅ⲥ̅ ·] ⲛ̄ⲧⲱⲧⲛ	ⲃⲟⲗ ⲉ[ϥϫⲱ ⲙ̄-]
[ⲟⲩⲱⲙ] ⲛ̄ⲙ̄ⲙⲁⲩ	ⲡⲁϣ ⲇⲉ ⲛ̄ϩⲉ	ⲙ̄[? ⲟⲩⲟⲉⲓϣ ᵈ]	ⲙⲟⲥ ϫ[ⲉⲟⲩⲛ̄-]
[ⲁⲩⲱ] ⲛⲉϥⲡⲁ-	ϥⲛⲁϯ ⲛ̄ⲧⲙⲛ̄ⲧ-	ⲙ̄ⲡⲛⲉⲭⲣⲟ[ⲛⲟⲥ]	ⲧⲁⲓ̈ [ⲧⲉⲍⲟⲩⲥⲓⲁ
ⲣⲁⲅⲅⲉⲓⲗⲉ ⲛⲁⲩ	ⲉⲣⲟ ⲛ̄ϭⲓ ⲡⲉ-	ϫⲉⲕⲁⲥ ⲛ̄ⲛⲉϥ-	ⲉⲕⲱ ⲛ̄ⲧⲁϥ[ⲅ-]
ⲉⲧⲙ̄ⲉⲓ ⲉⲃⲟⲗ	ⲧⲉⲙⲛ̄ⲧⲁϥ ⲙ̄-	ⲧⲱϣⲉ ⲛ̄ⲟⲩ-	ⲭⲏ · ⲁⲩⲱ ⲟⲩⲛ̄-
ⲟ̅ⲛ̅ⲑⲓⲗⲙ ⲁⲗⲗ=ᵇ	ⲙⲁⲩ ⲛ̄ⲧⲁⲅⲟⲑⲉ̄-	ⲙ̄ⲡⲁⲧⲥⲟⲟⲩ	ⲧⲁⲓ̈ ⲧⲉⲍⲟⲩⲥ[ⲓⲁ
ⲉϩⲱ ⲉⲡⲉⲣⲏⲧ	ⲧⲓⲁ ⲙ̄ⲡⲧⲟⲗ ·	ⲉⲡϣⲏⲣⲉ ·	ⲉⲭⲓⲧⲉ · ⲁⲩⲱ
ⲙ̄ⲡⲉⲓⲱⲧ	ⲡϫⲟⲉⲓⲥ ⲉⲛⲉ	ⲙ̄ⲡⲱⲧⲛ̄ ⲁⲛⲡⲉ	ⲙ̄ⲡⲣ̄ϣ̄ⲡⲏⲣ[ⲉ]
ⲡⲁⲓ̈ ⲛ̄ⲧⲁⲧⲉ-	ϩⲣⲁⲓ̈ ϩⲙ̄ⲡⲉⲩ-	ⲥⲟⲩⲛ̄ ⲛⲉⲟⲩⲟ-	ⲱ̄ ⲡⲁⲙⲉⲣⲓⲧ
ⲧⲏⲥⲟⲧⲙⲉϥ	ⲟⲉⲓϣ ⲕⲛ[ⲁϯ]	ⲉⲓϣ ⲙ̄ⲡⲛⲉ-	ϫ[ⲉ]ⲁϥⲕⲱ ⲙ̄-
ⲛ̄ⲧⲟⲟⲧ ⲡⲉ-	ⲛ̄ⲧⲙⲛ̄ⲧⲉ[ⲣⲟ]	ⲭⲣⲟⲛⲟⲥ ⲛⲁⲓ̈	ⲡⲥⲟⲟⲩⲛ ⲛ̄ⲛⲉ-
ϫⲁϥ ϫⲉⲓ̈ⲱ-	ⲙ̄ⲡⲓⲏⲗ ⲉϥϫ[ⲱ]	ⲛ̄ⲧⲁⲡⲉⲓⲱⲧ	ⲭⲣⲟⲛⲟⲥ [ϩⲁ]ⲧⲉ-

ᵃ One expects ⲙⲁⲉⲓ]ⲛ.　　ᵇ *Sic.* A strange abbreviation; recurs in col. 2, penult.　　ᶜ This line may begin ⲥⲭ . [Either MS. or copy is faulty. The proper text of v. 6 follows below.　ᵈ Here again more space seems indispensable to the sense. In preceding line ? ⲡⲉϫⲁϥ.

[1] ⲙ is difficult: possibly ' of Him that '.　　　　　　[2] *Cf.* Cant. iv. 16.

ϩⲁⲛⲛⲏⲥ ⲙⲉ̄	ⲙ̄ⲙⲟⲥ [ⲛⲁⲩ ϫⲉ-]	ⲕⲁⲁⲩ ϩⲁⲧⲉϥⲉ-	ⲍⲟⲩⲥⲓⲁ ⲙ̄ⲡϣⲏ-
ⲁϥⲃⲁⲡⲧⲓⲍⲉ	ⲡⲉⲓⲱⲧ ⲛⲁ-	ⲍⲟⲩⲥⲓ̈ⲁ ⲙⲁⲩ[ⲁ-]	ⲣⲉ ⲉϣϫⲉⲛ̄-
]	ϯ ⲛⲧⲙ̄ⲛ̄ⲧⲉ-	ⲁϥ· ⲁⲛⲟⲕ ⲉ[ⲓ-]	ⲕⲁ ⲛⲓⲙ ⲉⲧⲥ-
	[ⲣ]ⲟ· ⲁⲗⲗ= ⲉⲩ-	ⲑⲉⲱⲣⲉⲓ ⲛ̄[	ⲉϫⲛ̄ . . [
	[ϣⲁ]ϫⲉ ⲉⲡⲉ-	ϣⲏⲣⲉ [	

Fol. 2. *Recto.* . . . appearing[1] during forty days, doing signs (?) and speaking with them concerning the kingdom of God ; and, eating with them, He charged (παράγγ.) them not to go forth from Jerusalem, but (ἀλλά) to wait for the promise of the Father, 'the which ye have heard from me.' He said, 'John indeed (μέν) did baptize (βαπτ.) . . . . .

they then, that had heard him asking Him, saying,[2] 'Lord, dost Thou (μή) at this time (?) . . . . . the kingdom to Israel?' But (δέ) in what manner shall he that hath not the authority (αὐθεντία) and the power give the kingdom? 'Lord, wilt thou, at this time, give the kingdom to Israel?' When He said unto them, 'The Father shall give the kingdom,' they rather (ἀλλά) spake of the . . . . .

Verso. . . . the kingdom and the power (ἐξουσία) of divinity. What, then, was it that the Lord [Christ?] answered them? 'Ye[3] . . . . . times] and the seasons (χρόνος),' that He might not impute ignorance unto the Son. 'It is not yours to know the times and the seasons (χρ.) which the Father hath set within His own power (ἐξ.).' I behold (θεωρεῖν) . . . Son . . . . .

. . . the Son . . . power (ἐξ.), . . . to fulfil . . ., saying,[4] 'I have power (ἐξ.) to lay down my life (ψυ.) and I have power (ἐξ.) to take it up.' And be not astonished, O beloved, that He placed the knowledge of the seasons (χρ.) within the power (ἐξ.) of the Son, when everything that . . . on . . . . .

No. 7.

This Sermon has an unusual interest from containing the mention—so rare in Coptic literature—of contemporary historical persons and events. Not only was it pronounced at Alexandria in the cathedral church[5] by the patriarch Damianus,[6] its author, but this in presence of the emperor Maurice's

1 Acts i. 3.

2 Text of following clause not in order.

4 John x. 18.

5 καθολικὴ ἐκκλ. *V.* Rossi, *Papiri*, ii. IV. 59 c (*v.* below on these texts). *Cf. PSBA.* xxvii. 171.

Ostr. no. 18, and Krüger in *PRE*[3]. iv. 439.

envoy, Constantine Λάδρυς.[1] With him was Amantius, apparently a prominent eunuch.[2] Constantine's mission to Alexandria is mentioned, though
without year, by John of Nikiou.[3] If it were but possible to identify, among
the various earthquakes of this period, one shortly previous to that mission,
we might arrive at the date of the latter. It was one, at any rate, which
shook Syria (v. below), and, to judge by the title of the present sermon,
presumably Egypt also. Evagrius records an earthquake, affecting Antioch
and its suburbs, in Oct. 589.[4] In the foregoing (or same?) year Agapius
mentions one, likewise at Antioch, and in 591 and 599 others, not localized[5];
while John of Nikiou describes one which devastated Antioch, the east and
'the isles' in this reign.[6] The title of our sermon is but a fragment—that
a considerable part of it is lost may be estimated from a comparison between
the length of gaps in fol. 10 and in the parallel passage in the Turin MS. (v.
below)—so that the effects of the earthquake, to which it no doubt made
reference, are unknown. Nor can it be decided whether the words here used
as to Constantine and the Egyptian magnates are to be connected with
those disturbances to which he, according to John of Nikiou, put an end.[7]

   This text has further value in being the means of ascribing certain of
the Turin fragments to their true author. F. Rossi, *I Papiri*, ii. IV. 56–62
have been assumed[8] to belong to the sermon of Athanasius, *ib.* ii. I. 5 ff.;
but their identity in several passages with our text now shows them to be
due to Damianus. And besides the passages actually identical, there are
among Rossi's fragments others, which (though neither facsimiles nor
descriptions of this group are given) it is tolerably certain must belong to
the same work. One of these[9] has importance in that it names four places
which suffered through the earthquake—doubtless that referred to in the
title of our present text: Berytus and Aradus with [   ]ϥⲉⲛⲏ and
ⲁⲅⲣⲓⲏⲏ. These Lemm seeks[10] (as Στεφάνη and the island Ὀρεινή) in

---

[1] Theoph. Simoc. viii. 9 and 13, *Chron. Pasc.*
an. 602 (*PG.* 92, 972). The latter has variant
Λάρδις. The three titles here given him are a
usual combination in that age, *e. g.* Cairo Pap.
67002 (*ed.* J. Maspero in the *Catal. Gén.*); the
two first in Pap. Oxyrh. 138.

[2] A strange coincidence: Amantius had been
the name of a powerful eunuch executed by
Justin I. When one finds this eunuch (or yet
another namesake?) reappearing as Theodora's
envoy to Egypt (Zoega clxvi), one suspects that
the name had grown legendary.

[3] Pp. 298, 532. What his office in Egypt was
is not clearly stated: three words (*masfen, makua-
nen, šeyûm*) are indiscriminately used by the
translator, sometimes (as on pp. 295, 296) to
designate the same official. De Ricci, *PSBA.*
xxiv. 107, and M. Gelzer, *Leipz. Hist. Abh.* xiii.
33, take him for the prefect.

[4] vi. 8. *Cf. Chron. de Michel* ii. 359, and
others on pp. 351, 352, 373.

[5] *Ed.* A. Vasiliev in *Patr. Or.*, pp. 180, 187.

[6] P. 536.

[7] P. 532. The Coptic verb here, literally 'receive', is not often found as 'take into custody',
which seems to be the present meaning.

[8] By O. von Lemm, *KKS.* 280, 321 ff. That
the Turin collection once included still another
homily on the Nativity, and that by Cyril, is clear
from the fragment Rossi, ii. II. 5 = III. 2. Presumably to this belongs the fragment ii. IV. 77 b,
referring to Nestorius as the speaker's opponent
'in the midst of the σύνοδος'. It may be noted
that Rylands, no. 73, is a text very similar to these.
(In its 2nd line read ⲭⲉⲁⲛⲟⲩⲩⲟⲥ, *cf.* Rossi,
ii. IV. 57 c.)

[9] Rossi, ii. IV. 60 c.

[10] *L. c.* 324.

Paphlagonia and Ethiopia respectively; but one would here rather expect localities not so far distant from the Syrian coast. I would propose either for the first name Sophene, and for the second Auranitis[1] (whether the district south of Damascus or that between Palmyra and the Euphrates); or merely ὀρεινή, 'the highlands,' for the latter, and σεφενη = ? σεφηλά, 'the low country, coast,' for the former.[2]

Fol. 1. ↑ *Recto.*   → *Verso.*

                                        margin

— · · · — · · · — · · · —

ΟΥΛΟΓΟ[C] ΕΑϤΤΑΓΟϤ ЙϬΙ ΠΡΑ-
ΚΙΟC ΑΠΑ ΔΑΜΙΑΝΟC ΠΑΡΧЙ-
ΕΠΙCΚΟΠΟC ЙΡΑΚΟΤΕ· ΕΤΒΕ-
ΠΕΧΠΟ ЙΠΕΝCΩΤΉΡ ΙС ΠΕΧ̅С
ΠΕΝΧΟΕΙC ЙCΟΥΧΟΥΤΨΙC Й-
ΠΕΒΟΤ ΧΟΪΑΚ̅Ϩ· ΑΥΩ ΕΤΒΕΠШΑ-
ΑΗ ЙΠΜΟΥ· ЙΠΚΪΤΟ ЙΤΑϤ-
[. . . . .Н̣Ϩ]ΗΡΙϹ[Τ]ΩС ЙЙΠΟΛΙ-
[ΤΕΥΟΜ]ΕΝΟϹ Ε . [ΑΗ]ΑϹΚΑΖΕ
[. . . . .]ΑΪ ΕΤΩΡ̅Π̅ [Н]ЙΚΑ ЙΠΑ-
Ε]ΜЙΤΟΥ Н[Α]Υ ЙΪΩΤ ЙЙ-
]ΕΤΠ̅ . [

Ⴭ [. .]ШНМ ϦΙ[Κ]ΩС[ΤΑΗ]ΤΙΝΟC ΠΠ[ΑΤ-]
Ⴭ ΡΙΚΙΟC ΠΕΤΕШΑΜΟΥΤΕ ΕΡΟϤ
Ⴭ ΧΕΠΛΑΡΤΗC· ϦΜΠΤΡΕϤΤΙ-
Ⴭ ΜΟΟΥϤ ЙϬΙ ΜΑΥΡΙΚΙΟC Π̅Ρ̅Ρ̅Ο
Ⴭ ΕΡΑΚΟΤΕ ΕΤΡΕϤΧΙ ЙΠΑΡΧ̅Ω̅
Ⴭ ΤΗΡΟΥ ΗΚΗΜΕ· ΑΥΩ ΕϤЙΜΑΥ
Ⴭ ЙϬΙ ΠΠΑΤΡΙΚΙΟC ЙΠϦΥΠΑ-
Ⴭ ΤΟC· [Μ]Π̅ΠΕCΤΡΑΤ[НΛΑ-]
ΤΗC· ΜΝΑΜΑΝΤΪΟ[C . . . . CΙ-]
ΟΥΡ̅ ЙΠΠΑΡΧΩΗ ΤΗΡ[ΟΥ ΗΚΗ-]
ΜΕ ΑΥΩ ΠΑΗΜΟC ΤΗ[ΡϤ]
[.]Μ ΗΤΠΟΛΙC ΤΗΡϹ [
[.]ΓΑ ——————⟨Ο[

Fol. 1. *Recto.* A discourse (λόγος) which the holy (ἅγιος) Apa Damianus, the archbishop (ἀρχιεπ.) of Alexandria, pronounced concerning the Birth of Our Saviour (σωτ.) Jesus Christ, Our Lord, upon the 29th day of Choiahk; and concerning the terror (?) of death[3] and the earthquake, that did . . . the most exalted (?? ὕψιστος) of the citizens (? πολιτευόμενος[4]), compelling (? ἀναγκάζειν) . . . . . to seize the goods of . . . . . that had not any (?) . . . . .

[1] It will be objected that ϹΟΦΕΝΗ (even with possibly preceding article Τ-) is a word too short to fill the line, and that the other is an unauthenticated equivalent . . . .

[2] Or again ΔΑ]ΦΕΝΗ for Δάφνη (of Antioch) might be geographically possible, though ortho-

graphically improbable, besides being too short for the gap.

[3] Reading ШΛΑϦ, though hitherto not found in Sahidic.

[4] Πόλις would, in the context, seem more likely. The sense is utterly obscure.

Verso. . . . the Younger (?)[1] and Constantine the patrician (πατρ.), who was called Lartês[2]; when Maurice the king sent him unto Alexandria, to take (into custody?) all the magnates (ἄρχων) of Egypt. And the patrician (πατρ.) and consul (ὕπατος) and general[3] (στρατηλάτης) was present, and Amantius the . . . eunuch[4] and all the magnates (ἀρχ.) of Egypt and all the populace (δῆμος) . . . . . of the whole city (πόλις) . . . . .

Fol. 2. ↑ *Recto* (?). | → *Verso* (?).

margin | margin

ϩⲟⲛ ᵃ ⲧⲏⲣⲟⲩ	ⲡⲉⲩⲁⲅⲅⲉⲗⲓⲥ-
ⲙ̄ⲡ̄ⲛⲉⲕ̄ⲧⲁⲓⲟ	ⲧⲏⲥ ·
Ϥ Ϣ̄ ⲓ̅ⲥ̅ ⲡⲉⲧⲉⲡⲱϥ̄-	ⲁⲩⲱ ⲡⲙⲁⲣⲧⲩ-
ⲡⲉ ⲧⲁⲓⲟ ⲛⲓⲙ	ⲣⲟⲥ ·
ϩⲓⲥⲙⲟⲩ̄ ⲛⲓⲙ	ⲙ̄ⲡ̄ⲡⲁⲛⲭ̄ⲱ̅ⲍ
ⲉ̈ⲓⲛⲁⲣ̄ⲑⲉ ⲛ̄ⲟⲩⲁ̄	ⲡⲉⲧⲣⲟⲥ ·
]	ᵃⁱᶜ ⲁⲩⲱ ⲡⲙⲁⲧⲩ
	ⲣⲟⲥ ·
	[. . .]ⲉ̈ϫⲁⲛ ᵇ

ⲧⲏⲣⲟⲩ ⲛ̄ⲧⲉⲕ-	ⲃⲉ ⲙ̄ⲡⲙⲉⲕⲉ-
ⲕⲗⲏⲥⲓ̈ⲁ ϣⲁ-	ⲟⲟⲥ ⲛ̄ⲧⲉⲕ-
ϩⲣⲁⲓ̈ ⲉⲧⲉⲛ-	ⲙ̄ⲛ̄ⲧⲛⲟⲩⲧⲉ
ⲙ̄ⲛ̄ⲧⲣⲉϥⲣ̄-	ⲛⲓⲙ ⲡⲉⲧⲛⲁⲣ̄-
ⲛⲟⲃⲉ · ⲁⲩⲱ	ᵃⁱᶜ Ϥ ⲡⲉϥⲛⲟⲩⲥ
ⲙ̄ⲡⲟⲩϭ[ⲛ ⲑⲉ ⲛ̄-]	ⲛ̄ⲣⲙ̄ⲙ̄ⲡⲉ
ϫⲱⲕ ⲙ̄[ⲡⲉⲕ-]	?
ⲧⲁⲓⲟ ⲙⲙ̄ ·	

ᵃ ⲁⲟϩⲟⲛ.   ᵇ ? ⲁⲩⲱ ⲡ]ⲉⲩⲁⲅ[ⲅⲉⲗⲓⲥⲧⲏⲥ.

Fol. 2. *Recto* (?). . . . all [Thy] glory (? δόξον[5]) and Thy honours. O Jesus, whose is all honour and all blessing, I shall be like unto one . . . . the evangelist (εὐαγ.), and the martyr (μάρτυρος) and head, Peter, and the martyr (μάρ.) . . . . .

Verso (?). . . . all [the . . .] of the church (ἐκ.), down to our sinfulness.[6] And they did not find [means to] complete the . . . honour of . . . . of the greatness (μέγεθος) of Thy divinity? Who shall make his understanding (νοῦς) celestial . . . . .

[1] I do not know whether ϣⲏⲙ (like ϩ̄ⲣⲣⲉ), with a name preceding it, can = *junior*. Whether in Lepsius, *Denkm.* vi. 102, nos. 9, 10, 19 &c., Murray, *Osireion*, pll. 26, 31, it has this meaning or is mere humility, may be doubted. Perhaps read ⲟⲩϣⲏⲙ, the town of Ausîm.

[2] *Lit.* ' the Lartês '.

[3] These complimentary titles designate merely Constantine.

[4] Space would allow ⲡⲛⲟϭ ⲛ- or ⲡⲁⲣⲭⲓ- ' the chief eunuch '.

[5] I cannot find this form in literary use, though it had acquired a legal meaning. *V.* Rylands Catal., no. 139.

[6] *I.e.* ' to me, Damianus '.

Fol. 3. → *Recto* (?).   ↑ *Verso* (?).

margin   margin

ⲛⲁϣⲧⲉⲭⲛⲉ-	ⲡⲉⲧⲛⲁϣ[ⲟⲓⲥ-]	[ⲧ]ⲙⲛⲧⲛⲟⲩ-	ⲁϣ ⲛϣⲟⲅⲱ-
ⲁⲗⲟⲕⲉⲓ ⲛⲧ-	ⲧⲟⲣⲓⲍⲉ ·	[ⲧ]ⲉ · ⲡⲕⲟⲩⲓ̈	ⲃⲉ ⲧⲉⲧⲛⲁϣ-
ⲉⲕϭⲓⲛⲉⲓ ϣⲁ-	ⲏ̅ ⲛϥ̅ϫⲗⲟⲛⲟ[ⲅ-]	[ϩ]ⲛⲟⲩⲗⲏⲧⲓ̈ⲁ	ⲱϣ ⲉⲃⲟⲗ ⲛ̅-
ⲣⲟⲛ ·	ⲣⲁⲫⲟⲩ ·	[ⲁ]ⲩⲱ ⲡⲛⲟϭ	ⲑⲉ ⲛⲟⲩⲥⲁⲗ-
ⲅϣ ⲙ̅ⲙⲁⲛⲟⲩⲏⲗ	ⲏ̅ ⲡⲉϥⲥⲉⲛⲉⲁ-	ϩⲛⲡⲉϥϩⲟⲟⲩ ·	ⲡⲓⲅ̅ ⲛ̅ⲥⲉⲉⲧ-
ⲡϣⲏⲣⲉ ⲙ̅-	ⲗⲟϭⲉⲓ ⲛⲧⲉⲕ-	[ⲁ]ϣ ⲛ̅ⲥⲡⲟⲧⲟⲩ	ⲕⲱⲙⲓⲁⲍⲉ
ⲡⲛⲟⲩⲧⲉ	ϭⲓⲛϫⲡⲟ ⲱ̅	[. . .]ⲡⲕⲁⲣⲱϥ	ⲛ̅ⲧⲉⲕⲉⲡⲓⲧⲏ-
ⲕⲁⲧⲁ ⲧⲉϥ-	ⲙ̅ⲙⲁ[ⲛⲟⲩⲏⲗ]	[ⲛⲉⲧⲛ]ⲁϣϣⲁ-	ⲙⲓ̈ⲁ ϣⲁⲣⲟⲛ̅
ⲙⲛ̅ⲧⲛⲟⲩⲧⲉ	ⲡⲛⲟ[ⲩⲧⲉ ⲙ̅-]	[ϫⲉ . . .]ⲅⲥ	ⲅ̅Ⲡϣⲱⲥ ⲙ̅ⲙⲉ
ⲅⲅ̅Ⲉⲙⲉϥϣⲓ̈ⲃⲉ	ⲙⲉ [	]ⲏ	ⲛⲧⲁϥⲕⲱ ⲛ̅-
ⲉⲙⲉϥⲡⲱ-	ⲡⲣⲱ[ⲙⲉ	?	ⲧⲉϥⲯⲩⲭⲏ
ⲱⲛⲉ · . .	ⲗⲱⲧ[		[ϩ]ⲁⲛⲉϥ[ⲉⲥⲟⲟⲩ]

       ]ⲉⲕⲱ

Fol. 3. Recto (?). . . . shall be able fitly to account for (τεχνεαλογίζειν [1]) Thy coming unto us, O Emmanuel, Son of God according to His divinity ? It (?) altereth not, it is not transformed . . . . .

. . . Who] shall be able to narrate (ἱστορίζειν) or (ἤ) who shall record (χρονογράφειν) or (ἤ) who shall trace (γενεαλογεῖν) Thy birth, O Emmanuel, true (?) God . . . man . . . . .

Verso (?). . . . divinity ; the young in age (ἡλικία) and the old (*lit.* great [2]) in His days? What lips . . . silence . . . . shall be able to speak . . . . . ? What throat shall be able to cry out like a trumpet (σάλ.) and belaud (ἐγκωμιάζειν) Thy sojourn (ἐπιδημία) with us, true shepherd, that did lay down His life (ψυ.) for His [sheep . . . . .

Fol. 4. ↑ *Recto.*   → *Verso.*

    margin   margin

ⲉⲓⲙⲉ ϩⲓⲧⲛ̅-	ⲧ[	]ⲓ̈	ⲅ̅ϩⲟⲙⲟⲗⲟϭⲉⲓ
ⲛⲓⲙ ⲙ̅ⲡ̅ⲛ̅ϣϭⲙ	ⲙ[	]ⲧⲉ	ⲛⲁⲛ ⲙ̅ⲡⲉⲛ-

same.   ² Not the phrase of Dan. vii. 9.

ⲛ̄ⲗⲁⲥ ⲛ̄ⲥⲁⲣⲝ̄	ⲡ[	]ⲟⲛ	ⲧⲁϥ ϣⲱ-
ⲉⲩⲉⲛⲉⲁⲗⲟ-	ⳟⲡⲉ[	]ⲱ	ⲡⲉ ·
ⲅⲉⲓ ⲙ̄ⲡⲉⲭⲡⲟ̄	ⲁⲗ[ⲏⲑⲱⲥ	]ⲱⲣ	ⳟ ⲧ̄ⲛⲁⲕⲁⲁⲕ
ⲙ̄ⲡⲉⲛⲥⲱ-	ⲡⲉ[	?	ⲉⲃⲟⲗ ⲁⲛ ⲱ̄
ⲧⲏⲣ̄ ·	ⲉ[	?	ⲅⲁⲃⲣⲓⲏⲗ
ⲁⲗⲏⲑⲱⲥ ⲡⲁ-	ⲡ[		ⲟⲩⲇⲉ ⲛ̄ⲧ̄-
]ⲣⲁⲥ			ⲛ̄[ⲛⲁ

Fol. 4. *Recto.* ... learn (it?) through whom? Fleshly (-σάρξ) tongue hath not power to trace (γενεαλογεῖν) the birth of our Saviour (σωτήρ). Verily (ἀληθῶς) my ..... grow old .....

Verso. ... confess (ὁμολογεῖν) unto us what befell. I will not release thee, O Gabriel, neither (οὐδέ) will we .....

Fol. 5.   → *Recto.*   ↑ *Verso.*

	[ⲡⲭⲟ]ⲉⲓⲥ ⲛ̄ⲙ̄-	ⲭⲁⲓⲣⲉ [ⲙⲁⲣⲓⲁ]	
	ⲙⲉ ·	ⲧⲥⲱϣⲉ ⲉⲧ-	
	Ⲭⲁⲓⲣⲉ ⲙⲁⲣⲓⲁ	ⲧⲃ̄ⲃⲏⲩ ⲉⲧⲉ-	
	ⲧⲉⲕⲗⲟⲟⲗⲉ	ⲣⲉⲡⲙⲁ[ⲣ]ⲕⲁ-	[
]ⲉ	ⲉⲧⲁⲥⲱⲟⲩ	ⲣⲓⲧⲓⲥ ⲛ̄ϩⲏ-	ⲙ[
[Ⲭⲁⲓⲣⲉ ⲙⲁ]ⲣⲓⲁ	ⲉⲧⲣ̄ⲟⲩⲟⲉⲓⲛ̄	ⲧⲥ ⲉⲧⲉⲡⲁⲓ-	ⳟ ⲭⲁⲓⲣⲉ
]ⲁ	ⲉⲛⲉⲧϩⲙⲟ-	ⲡⲉ ⲡⲉⲛⲭⲟ-	? [
] ⲉⲧⲧⲟ	ⲟⲥ ϩⲙ̄ⲡⲕⲁ-	ⲉⲓⲥ ⲓ̄ⲥ̄ ⲡⲉⲭ̄ⲥ̄	ⲛ̣ⲟⲩⲃ[
[ϩⲓⲱ] ⲉⲧⲉⲡⲉⲩ-	ⲕⲉ ⲙ̄ⲡⲑⲁⲓ̈-	?	?
]ⲟⲩⲱⲛⲉ [a]	ⲃⲉⲥ ⲙ̄ⲡⲙⲟⲩ		
]ⲡⲉⲧⲩ̇-	ⲭⲁⲓⲣⲉ ⲧⲉⲛ-		
]ⲉ ⲛ̄ⲓⲁ-	ⲧⲁⲥϭⲛ [ϩⲙⲟⲧ]		
[ⲕⲱⲃ	ⲡⲭ[ⲟⲉⲓⲥ ⲛ̄ⲙ̄-]		
	[ⲙⲉ		

^a Or]ⲟⲩⲱ ⲡⲉ (*fem.*).

Fol. 5. (*Possibly not a part of this MS.*) *Recto.* .. Hail (χαῖρε)]

Mary .... [garment (?)] that is [on thee ?], which is their ... stone [1]
... which they ... Ja[cob [2] .....

 ..., the Lord is with thee. Hail (χ.) Mary, light (*levis*) cloud [3] which illumineth them that sit in darkness and the shadow of death. Hail (χ.) thou that hast found [grace], the Lord [is with thee .....

 Verso. ... Hail (χ.) (Mary), pure meadow, wherein is the pearl (μαργ.) [4] which is our Lord Jesus Christ .....

 ... Hail (χ.) ..... gold (?) .....

Fol. 6. ↑ *Recto* (?).   → *Verso* (?).

	[ⲧⲉⲧ]ⲉⲙ[ⲉⲥ]ⲉ-	ⲧⲏ [ⲧⲡ]ⲁ[ⲣⲑⲉ-]	ⲧ[ⲡ]ⲁⲣⲑⲉⲛⲟ[ⲥ]
ⲡⲉⲛⲧⲁⲥⲭⲡⲟ[ϥ]	ⲡⲉⲓⲟⲩ[ⲙ]ⲉⲓ ⲉ-	ⲛⲟ[ⲥ ⲉ]ⲧⲟⲩⲁ[ⲁⲃ]	[ⲭⲉⲉ]ⲣⲃⲏⲕ ⲉ-
ⲡⲁⲣⲁ ⲡ[ⲉⲭⲣⲟ-]	ⲛⲉⲟ ⲉⲡⲥⲟⲗⲥⲗ	ⲙⲁⲣⲓⲁ ⲉⲥⲕⲟⲥ-	ⲧⲱⲛ ⲙⲡⲉⲓ-
ⲛⲟⲥ ⲛ̄ⲧⲙⲛⲧ-	ⲛ̄ⲛⲁⲧⲟⲣⲁ ⲙⲡ̄-	ⲙⲉⲓ ϭ̄ⲛⲉⲡⲓⲥ-	ⲛⲟϭ ⲛⲟⲩⲉ ⲉ-
ⲣⲉϥⲙⲓⲥⲉ·	ⲛ̄ⲭⲟⲗⲙⲉⲥ ⲛ̄ⲙ̄-	ⲧⲙⲙⲉ ⲛⲓⲙ· *sic*	ⲧⲟⲣⲓⲡⲏ ⲉⲧⲥⲉ-
⳩ⲗⲁⲓⲥ ⲉⲣⲟⲓ ⲱ̄ ⲧ-	ⲙⲁ ⲛ̄ⲥⲱ· ⲙ̄ⲡ̄-	ⲉⲥϭⲟⲗϭ ϩ̄ⲙ̄ⲡ-	ⲡⲏ ⲉⲃⲱⲕ
ⲡⲁⲣⲑⲉⲛⲟⲥ ⲉ-	ⲛⲥⲩⲛⲧⲉⲭⲓⲁ	ⲉⲥⲗⲁⲥ ⲉⲥⲧⲟⲩ-	ⲡⲉⲭⲁⲥ ⲉⲛⲁⲩ
ⲧⲟⲩⲁⲁⲃ ⲭⲉⲉⲣ-	ⲛ̄ϫⲓ ⲟⲣⲁϥ· ⲧⲉ-	ⲭⲏⲩ [a] ϩ̄ⲛⲉⲥⲃⲁⲗ	ⲉⲧⲉϣⲡⲓⲣⲉ
ⲃⲏⲕ ⲉⲧⲟⲛ	⳩ⲧⲉⲙⲉⲥⲃⲱⲕ ⲉ-	ⲃⲁⲗ ⲉⲧⲥⲓⲛⲥⲱ-	ⲛ̄ⲧⲁⲥϣⲟⲡ-
ⲙ̄ⲡⲉⲓⲛⲟϭ ⲛ̄-	ϩⲟⲩⲛ ⲁⲩⲛⲓ ⲉⲡ- *sic*	ϣⲧ ⲉⲧϣⲟⲩ-	ⲡⲉ [
[ⲁⲡ]ⲁ[ⲛⲧ]ⲛⲙⲁ	ⲧⲏⲣϥ ⲉϥϩ̄ⲛ	ⲉⲓⲧ· ⲁ[ⲩⲱ]	?
[.....]ⲉⲓⲛⲟϭ	ⲉϩⲟⲩⲛ ⲉⲡⲣ̄ⲡ[ⲉ]	ⲙⲉⲥⲣⲱⲃ ϩ̄ⲛ-	
	⳩ⲧⲉⲧⲉⲙⲉⲥ[	ⲛⲉⲥϭⲓϫ ⲛ̄ϭⲓ	
	[..]ⲛ ⲉⲩϣ[	[ⲧⲡⲁⲣ]ⲑⲉ[ⲛ]ⲟⲥ	

[a] Here Rossi, 62 c.

---

[1] Or '... to thee' (*fem.*), ⲟⲩⲱ being a verb.
[2] Or 'jasper stone' ⲱⲛ]ⲉ ⲛⲓⲁ[ⲥⲡⲓⲥ.
[3] *Cf.* Cairo, *Theotokia* 195 (= Tuki 100) and Isa. xix. 1, which verse is similarly used in χαιρετισμοί, though differently interpreted, by Joh. Damas. (*PG.* 96, 693) and Theod. Stud. (*ib.* 99, 725). It is remarkable that the Ethiopic (Fries, *Weddâsê Mâryâm*, 38), renders ‏خفيف‎ by *za-ba-'aman* 'true', taking it for ‏ﺧﻔﻲ‎: a contribution towards proof of translation from the Arabic. Nothing can of course be deduced from these coincidences as to the early existence of a Saïdic *Theotokia*; the specimens in Samannûdî's *Scala*

(Paris MS. 44, f. 21) show indeed true Sa. forms, but may point (in the 13th century) to a version from Bo. But if Simeon Ḳuḳaya (*ca.* 520) be, as Euringer (*Or. Christ.* 1911, 215 ff.) plausibly suggests, author of the *Theotokia*, the present passages, in a work dating only some 80 years later, and by a writer of Syrian origin, have an added interest.

[4] *Cf.* Cairo *Theot.*, 178; also, besides Usener's article (in *Theol. Abh. f. Weizsäcker*), Rossi, *l. c.* ⲁⲩⲱ, ⲓ̈ⲁⲥⲡⲓⲥ ⲛ̄ⲟⲩⲱ; Bezold, p. xl and § 68: and Lagarde, *Aeg.* 48, 22 (= F. Robinson, p. 53) where read ⲱⲛⲓ for ⲟⲩⲱⲛⲓ.

Fol. 6. Recto. . . . 'him whom she hath borne, out of (παρά) the time (χρ.) of bearing.' Tell me, O holy Virgin (παρ.), whither thou goest for (?) this great meeting[1] [and] this great . . . . .

. . . She who never desired (ἐπιθυμεῖν) the distractions (*lit.* consolations) of the market-place (ἀγορά) nor the festivities[2] of the drinking-place, nor meetings (συντυχία) for merrymaking. She who never entered a house that was near to the[3] . . . . . She who did not . . . . .

Verso. . . . holy Virgin (? παρ.) Mary, adorned (κοσμεῖν) with all knowledge (ἐπιστήμη), sweet in her tongue, preserving her eyes[4] from vain glances. And the Virgin doth not work with her hands . . . . .

. . . Tell me, O] Virgin, whither goest thou, this great distance, to the hill-country (ὀρεινή)?[5] 'I hasten and go,' saith she, 'to see the marvel that hath happened . . . . .

Fol. 7. → *Recto.*

margin

ⲧⲁⲥ̄ⲣⲏⲏ ⲉⲧⲉⲧ̄	ϥⲱⲱⲣⲉ ⲉⲃⲟⲗ
ⲕⲉⲥⲟⲟⲩ ⲡⲉ-	ϯⲛⲁⲛⲁⲩ ⲭⲉⲛ̄ⲕⲓ̈- (sic)
ⲃⲟⲧⲛⲉ ·	ⲃⲉ ⲛⲧⲁⲩϣⲟⲟⲩⲉ
ϣⲁⲛⲉ · ⲁⲩⲭⲉ	ⲙ̄ⲡ̄ⲛ̄ⲥⲁⲡⲉ-
	ⲭⲣⲟⲛⲟⲥ ⲁⲩⲙ̄[ⲧ̄ⲟ̄]
	ⲛⲉⲣⲱⲧⲉ ·
	Ⲁⲣⲏⲅ[a] ⲣⲱ̄ ⲉⲩⲣ̄-
	ϩⲁⲗ ⲙ̄ⲙⲟⲓ
	[ϩⲙ̄ⲡ]ⲛ̄ⲧⲁ[ⲩ-]

[a] Here Rossi, 62 c.

↑ *Verso.*

margin

ⲙ̄ⲡⲉϥⲭⲟⲉⲓⲥ	⳦ⲛⲁϣ[
ⲉⲥⲛⲏⲩ ⲉⲣⲁⲧϥ[b]	ⲛⲁⲥ . . .
ⲛ̄ⲧⲉϥⲙⲁⲁⲩ	ⲁⲛ ⲉⲓ ⲛⲁ[ⲓ
ⲁϥⲭⲓ ϭⲟ̄ⲥ̄	ⲭⲟⲉⲓⲥ ⲁⲩⲱ
ⲁϥⲥⲕⲓ̈ⲣⲧⲁ	ⲧⲙⲁⲁⲩ ⲙ̄ⲡⲁ-
ⲁϥⲭⲓ ϭⲟ̄ⲥ̄	ⲭⲟ[ⲉⲓⲥ ⲉⲓ]
[ϩⲓⲑ]ⲏ ⲙ̄ⲡ . . .	

[b] Read ⲉⲣⲁⲧⲥ.

---

[1] Ἀπάντημα is rare apparently. Διανόημα would fit, though less appropriate. Or? ⲁⲡⲁⲛ-ⲧⲏ ⲙⲁ-.

[2] *V. Can. Athan.*, p. 66 n. To the instances there add *Triadon*, ed. Lemm, § 368 = تَنْزِه (parallel to εὐφραίνειν), and Paris 131[6], f. 9 (? same MS. as Br. Mus., no. 362): ⲁⲥϣⲱⲡⲉ ⲙ̄ⲙⲟⲓ ⲉⲓⲁⲛⲁⲭⲱⲣⲉⲓ ⲙⲁⲩⲁⲁⲧ ⲁⲓⲭⲱⲗⲙ ⲙ̄ⲡⲟⲩⲥⲟⲡ ⲉϥⲟⲣⲓⲧⲟⲩⲱⲓ ⲁⲩⲱ ⲁⲓⲕⲁⲁⲥ ϩⲙ̄ⲡⲁϩⲏⲧ ⲉⲧⲙ̄ⲧⲣⲁⲃⲱⲗ ⲛⲙ̄ⲙⲁϥ. There-

[3] 'Temple' seems unlikely, though my copy suggests it.

[4] *Lit.* 'preserved in her eyes'. *Cf.* Ps. cxviii. 37.

[5] *Cf.* Luke i. 39.

upon a saint appears, bidding ⲟⲛⲧⲱⲥ ⲕⲛⲁ-ⲙⲟⲩⲣ ⲙ̄ⲡⲛⲉⲧϩⲓⲧⲟⲩⲱⲕ ⲭⲉⲁϥϯ ⲙ̄ⲧⲟⲛ ⲛⲁⲕ, and quoting I Pet. ii. 23. In this latter passage, and in Brit. Mus. Cat., no. 217 n., the meaning can hardly be the same as in the others. In Mingarelli 295 it is equally obscure (*cf.* Stern, *Gram.*, p. 388).

Fol. 7. *Recto.* . . . the barren woman. Yet (ἔτι) other six months is it,[1] until . . . . womb] swollen.[2] I shall see how that the breasts, which were dried up, after the (proper) time (χρ.) have become full of milk.' Perchance[3] indeed they have deceived me [in that] which [they . . . . .

Verso. . . . of (?) his Lord, when she came up to his mother, he leaped[4] and jumped (σκιρτᾶν), he leaped [in the] womb (?), ere (?) . . . . .

. . . 'How (? what) . . . . . come unto me (?) [my ?] Lord and the mother of my Lord '[5] . . . . .

Fol. 8.　→ *Recto.*　　　　　　　↑ *Verso.*

ератϥ ⲙ̄ⲡⲉϥ-	ⲧⲓ̈ⲁ ⲙ̄ⲡⲟⲩ[ⲙⲛⲱ-]	[. .]ⲛ ϣⲁϫⲉ ⲙⲛ̄-	ϣⲱⲡⲉᵃ ⲛⲁⲓ̈ ⲛ̄-
ⲥⲧⲣⲁⲧⲏⲣⲁ-	ⲁⲟⲥ ⲁⲁⲅ[ⲉⲓⲁ]	[ⲡⲉⲩ]ⲉⲣⲏⲩ ⲁⲓ̈-	ⲟⲩⲡⲉⲣⲉⲧ[ⲏⲥ ·]
ⲧⲏⲥ ·	ϫⲉⲁⲡⲡⲁ̄ [ⲙⲛ̄-]	[ⲧ]ⲉⲓ ⲉⲅⲟⲛ̇ⲑⲛ ·	⳦ⲁⲛⲟⲕ ⲁⲓϭⲓ ⲙ̄-
⳦Oⲩⲥⲧⲣⲁⲧⲱⲣ	ⲧⲙⲉ ⲧⲱⲙ[ⲛⲧ]	[Ⲡⲉ]ϫⲁϥ ⲛ̄ϭⲓ ⲡⲣⲓⲉ-	ⲙⲁⲩ ⲛⲧⲁⲙ̄-
ⲉϥⲏⲩ ⲉⲣⲁ-	ⲉⲛⲉⲅⲉⲣⲏ[ⲩ ·]	[ⲣⲟ]ⲯⲁⲗⲧⲏⲥ	ⲧⲁ ϩ ⲣ ⲏ ⲛ ⲡ̄-
ⲧϥ ⲙ̄ⲡⲉϥ†	ⲁⲧⲁ ⲓ ⲕⲁⲓ̈[ⲟⲥⲩ-]	[ⲁⲁⲅ]ⲉⲓⲁ ϫⲉⲡⲛ̇ⲏ	ⲧⲉⲕⲙⲁⲁⲩ
ⲣⲱⲛ ·	ⲛⲏ ⲙⲛ†[ⲣⲏ-]	[ⲛⲁ]ⲟⲩⲱϣϥ ⲟⲩ-	ϫⲉⲉⲥⲛⲁϫ-
Oⲩϣⲟⲥ ⲉϥ	ⲛⲏ †ⲡⲓ̈ ⲉ-	[ⲃⲉ]ⲡⲛⲟⲩⲏ ⲉⲡⲉ-	ⲡⲟⲕ ⲡ̄ⲥⲟⲩ-
ⲛⲏⲩ [ⲉⲣⲁⲧ]ϥ	ⲛⲉⲅⲉⲣ[ⲏⲩ]	[ϩⲣⲟⲟⲩ] ⲡⲛⲉⲕ-	ⲧⲉ ⲛ̄ⲡⲉϩⲓⲟ̄-
[ⲙ̄ⲡ]ⲉϥⲉⲥⲟⲩ	ⲛⲧⲏ[	[ⲕⲁⲧⲁϩⲣⲁ]ⲕⲧⲏⲥ	ⲟⲩⲉ ϩⲓⲟ̄ⲏ ⲙ-
[ⲧ]ⲉⲱⲥ ⲱ̄ ⲛⲁ-	?	] ?	ⲡⲉⲕϫⲟ[ⲉⲓⲥ]
[ⲙ]ⲉⲣⲁⲧⲉ ⲟⲩ-		]ϣⲉ	ⲛ[ⲧⲟⲕⲡⲉ ⲓⲱ-]
[ϣ]ⲡⲏⲣⲉⲧⲉ			ϩⲁⲛⲛⲏⲥ [ⲡⲁ-]
[ⲧⲟ]ⲓ̈ⲕⲟⲛⲟⲙⲓ̈ⲁ			ⲙⲉⲣⲓⲧ

ᵃ Here Rossi, 61 c.

Fol. 8. *Recto.* . . . coming] to his general (στρατηλάτης); a . . . . .[6] (στράτωρ) coming to his recruit (τίρων) ; a shepherd coming to his sheep. Howbeit (τέως),[7] O my beloved, a marvel is the dispensation (οἰκονομία) [of God . . . .] of the singer (ὑμνῳδός) David,[8] 'Mercy and truth are met

---

[1] Luke i. 36.
[2] *Cf.* the phrases in Rossi, ii. 1. 10 b.
[3] Here, I assume, the preacher resumes.
[4] Luke i. 44.
[5] *Ib.* 43.

[6] 'Groom' is the sole meaning offered for this. Probably a mistake for a high military title.
[7] 'Meanwhile' seems unsuitable. Perhaps read ὅμως.
[8] Ps. lxxxiv. 10.

together; righteousness (δικαιοσύνη) and peace (εἰρ.) have kissed one another' [1] .....

Verso. ... talked one with another, whilst yet (ἔτι) they were in the womb. The hieropsalt (ἱεροψ.) David said,[2] 'Deep answereth unto deep at the voice of Thy cataracts (κατ.)' .....

... be unto me servant (ὑπηρέτης). It is I have taken away the barrenness of thy mother; for she shall bear thee and thou shalt prepare the ways before thy Lord ..... John, my beloved .....

Fol. 9. ↑*Recto.*　　　　　　　→ *Verso.*

　　margin　　　　　　　　　　　　margin

Καθαριϩε ⲡⲛⲉ-	ⲱⲧ[	]ⲉⲛ	ⲧⲁϩⲟ [c] · ⲛ̄ⲡⲉ-
ϩⲓⲟⲟⲅⲉ ⲉⲧⲥⲟ-	𝒱Ⲡⲉⲡ[	] ⲙⲁⲣⲛ̄-	ⲧⲁⲕⲟⲛⲓⲁ ⲛ̄ⲛ-
ⲟⲙⲉ ϩⲓⲑⲏ ⲛ̄-	ⲛⲁⲛ[	] ⲙⲡⲉⲡ-	ϣⲁⲙⲥⲉ ⲧⲁϩⲟ
ⲡⲉⲕϫⲟⲉⲓⲥ ·	𝒱Ⲛ̄ⲧⲟⲕ ⲡ[ⲉ	]ⲁⲙⲛⲥⲓ-	ⲱ̄ ⲙⲁⲣⲓⲁ ⲧⲡⲁⲣ-
𝒱Ⲛ̄ⲧⲟⲕⲡⲉ ϯⲛⲁ-	ⲡⲉϥϣⲁ[	ⲥⲏ]ⲙⲁⲛⲉ	ⲑⲉⲛⲟⲥ ·
ⲃⲁⲡⲧⲓϩⲉ [a] ⲉⲃⲟⲗ	ϭⲓⲝ ⲉϥ[	ⲉ]ⲧⲃⲉⲡⲉⲓ-𝒱Ⲁⲣⲙⲥⲉ ⲛ̄ⲧⲟ
ϩⲓⲧⲟⲟⲧⲕ̄ ·	ⲙ̄ⲡⲉϥ[	[ϣⲁⲙ]ⲥⲉ ⲉⲧ-	ⲟⲩⲡⲁⲣⲑⲉⲛⲟⲥ
𝒱Ⲁⲙⲟⲩ ⲧⲉⲛⲟⲩ	𝒱Ⲛ̄ⲧⲟⲕ ⲡ[ⲉ	] ⲉⲃⲟⲗ ⲙ̄-𝒱Ⲁⲣⲙⲉⲥⲓⲱ̄ ⲙ̄ⲙⲟ
ⲡⲃⲁⲓ̈ϣ̄ⲙ̄ⲛⲟⲩ-	ⲁⲥⲡⲉ[	]ⲡⲉⲓ	ⲙⲁⲩⲁⲁⲧⲉ ·
ϭⲉ ⲉⲧⲧⲁⲓ̈ⲏⲩ	ⲛ̄ⲧⲉⲡⲁ[	ⲉⲛⲥⲙⲩ̊	ⲛ̄ⲧⲟ ⲟⲩⲡⲁⲣⲑⲉ-
ⲡ̄ⲕ̄ⲕⲁⲑⲁⲣⲓ̈ϩⲉ	ⲁⲩ[	]ⲛ	ⲛⲟⲥ ?
[ⲡ̄]ⲛⲉϩⲓ̈ⲟⲟⲅⲉ	𝒱		
[ϩⲓ]ⲑⲏ ⲙ̄ⲡ- [b]			

[a] Here Rossi, 61 c.　　　[b] ⲡⲉⲕϫⲟⲉⲓⲥ.　　　[c] Here Rossi, 58 c.

Fol. 9. *Recto.* ... Make clean (καθαρίζειν) the crooked paths before thy Lord.[3] Thou it is by whom I shall be baptized (βαπτ.). Come now, honoured bearer of good-tidings, make clean (καθ.) the paths before the.....

... Thou .... Thou ....

Verso. ... signify (σημαίνειν) [4] ... because of this first-born (?) that ... out from .....

---

[1] Rossi, ii. IV. 94, Fr. vi ⲙ̄ⲟ appears to expatiate on this.
[2] Ps. xli. 8.

[3] The verb used recalls Isa. lvii. 14.
[4] Occurs in Rossi, 62 c, but I cannot identify the two passages.

ⲧ ... reached thee (not).   The pangs (ἀγωνία) of the first-born[1] befell thee not, O Maria the Virgin (παρ.).   Thou didst bring forth, thou a virgin. Thou didst deliver[2] thyself, thou a virgin . . . . .

Fol. 10. → *Recto.*   ↑ *Verso.*

margin   margin

ⲃⲱⲗ[a] ⲉⲃⲟⲗ · ⲧⲉ-	ⲟⲙ̣[	]ⲏ̄	ⲙ̄ⲡ̄ⲥⲉⲣⲁⲫⲓⲛ
ⲅ̄ⲗⲟⲟⲗⲉ ⲙ̄ⲡⲉⲧ-	ⲟⲛ ⲙ̣̄[	]ⲕ̄ⲏ	ⲛ̄ⲁⲅⲛⲁⲙⲓⲥ
ⲙⲟⲟⲛⲉ ⲙ̄ⲡⲥⲱ-	ⲛⲟⲥ[? ϭⲗⲟⲙ-]	] . ⲅ[e]	ⲙ̄ⲡ̄ⲡⲉⲭⲣⲟⲛⲟⲥ
ⲡⲧ ⲧⲏⲣϥ̄ ·	ⲅ̄ⲗ̄ⲙ ⲙ̄ⲙⲟϥ [ⲛϩⲉⲛ-]	[ⲙⲏⲛ]ⲥⲓⲃⲧ	ⲡⲁⲣⲭⲏ ⲙ̄ⲡ-
ⲅ̄ⲡⲉⲧ†ⲫⲣⲉ ⲙ̄-	ⲧⲟⲉⲓⲥ ϥ̄	[ⲙⲛ]ⲡⲣⲏ ·	ⲛⲉⲍⲟⲩⲥⲓⲁ
ⲡⲥⲱⲛⲧ ⲧⲏ-	ϩⲓⲱⲟⲩ ⲛ[	[ⲙⲛ]ⲡⲟⲟⲩ ⲙ̄ⲡ-	ⲙ̄ⲡ̄ⲕⲟⲥⲙⲟⲕ-
ⲣϥ̄ ⲁ†ⲉⲣⲱⲧⲉ	ⲛⲁⲙⲓⲥ[ⲉ	[ⲛ̄ⲥⲓⲟ]ⲩ · ⲙ̄ⲡ-	ⲣⲁⲧⲱⲣ ⲛ̄ⲧⲟⲕ
ⲛⲁϥ ϩⲱⲥ ⲕⲟⲩⲓ̈	ⲅ̄ⲩ̄̄[c] ⲡⲉⲓⲟⲩ[ⲟⲙϥ]	[ⲛϣⲏ]ⲛ ˢⁱᶜ ⲛ̄ ⲧⲥⲱ-	ⲡⲉ ⲡⲉⲅⲁⲙⲓ̈
ϩⲓⲧⲛⲧⲟⲩⲉⲣⲱ-	ⲙ̄ⲙⲁⲕⲁ[ⲣⲓⲟⲥ]	[ϣⲉ] ⲡϣⲱⲙ	ⲅ̄ⲟⲣⲧⲟⲥ ⲧⲏⲣⲟⲩ ·
ⲧⲉ ⲛ̄ⲗⲟⲕⲓⲕⲏ	ⲅ̄ⲩ̄̄ ⲛⲛⲏⲥ[d]	[ⲙ̄ⲛⲡⲉ]ⲁⲣ	ⲅ̄ⲩⲱ ⲡⲉⲭⲁϥ
ⲅ̄ⲡⲉⲧⲙⲉⲣⲉ-		[ⲡⲉⲭⲓⲱ]ⲛ ⲁⲩⲱ	ϫⲉⲙⲙⲁ ϣⲟⲟ-
ⲙⲁ ϣⲟⲡϥ̄[b] ⲁϥⲱ-		[ⲡⲉⲕⲣⲩⲥ]ⲧⲁⲣ°	ⲟⲡ ⲛⲁⲩ ϩⲛ̄-
[ⲣ]ⲃ̣̄ ⲉϩⲟⲩⲛ ϩⲛ̄-			ⲙⲁ [ⲛϭ]ⲟ̣ⲓ̣[ⲗⲉ

ᵃ Here Rossi, 58 c.   ᵇ *Cf.* ⲡⲉⲧⲙⲉⲣⲉⲡⲧⲏⲣϥ ϣⲟⲡϥ ⲟⲩⲇⲉ ⲙⲉⲩⲉϣⲟⲣϥ ⲉϩⲟⲩⲛ ⲉⲩⲙⲁ ⲛⲟⲩⲱⲧ in Damianus' *Synodikon, Miss.* i. 38, line 7. I propose to re-edit this text shortly, having identified it with that in Chabot's *Chron. de Michel* ii. 325 ff. *Cf.* my *Ostraca*, no. 18 n.   ᶜ Here Rossi, 59 a, b.   ᵈ Perhaps with Rossi ⲛⲉⲓⲧⲟ[ⲉⲓⲥ.   ᵉ Here Rossi, 56 a, b.

Fol. 10. *Recto.* . . . dissolved.   Thou (*fem.*) dost nurse[3] Him that shepherdeth all creation.   He that giveth food unto all creation, thou gavedst Him milk when (ὡς) a child, with thy reasonable (λογικός) milk. He whom no place may hold was confined within . . . . .

. . . swathed Him in bandages . . . . O this blessed (μακ.) manger, O these[4] . . . . .

Verso.   . . . the] hills [and] the sun and the moon and the stars and the

[1] So far recorded only as a Bohairic form, though Peyron (280 b) knew the Saʻidic.

[2] *Lit.* (reading ⲁⲣ̄ⲙⲉⲥⲓⲱ) ʻdidst act mid-wife'. *Pap. Bruce*, p. 259, uses the verb as

here.   Perhaps for ⲧⲙⲉⲥⲓⲟ (*cf.* Steindorff, *Gram.*², § 262).

[3] Reading ϩⲗⲟⲟⲗⲉ with Rossi.

[4] ʻIncorruptible bandages' (Rossi).

trees of the field; the summer and the spring (ἔαρ), snow (χιών) and ice (κρύσταλλος) . . . . .

. . . the Cherubim] and the Seraphim, the powers (δύναμις) and the seasons (χρόνος)[1] the principalities (ἀρχή) and the powers (ἐξ.) and the rulers (κοσμοκράτωρ), Thou it is art the Creator (δημιουργός) of them all. And he saith, 'There was not place for them in the lodging' . . . . .

Fol. 11. ↑ *Recto.*   → *Verso.*

margin   margin

┼ᵃ ϩⲓⲱⲟⲩ ⲛϩⲉⲛ-	ⲉⲃⲟⲗ · ⲙ[ⲁⲣⲟⲩ-]	]ⲧⲁⲕⲟ ⲛϭⲓ	ϫⲉ ⲛϭⲓ ⲡⲡⲉⲧⲩ̇-
ϩⲟⲓⲧⲉ ⲉⲛⲁϣⲉ	ϫⲓᵇ ϣⲓⲡⲉ [ⲧⲉⲛⲟⲩ]	[ⲛⲡⲁ]ⲣⲁⲛⲟⲙⲟⲥ	ⲁⲁⲃ ⲡⲉⲅⲁⲅⲅⲉ-
ⲥⲟⲩⲉⲛⲧⲟⲩ ⲉⲅⲟ	ⲛϭⲓ ⲡⲟⲩ[ⲱⲛϣ]	]ⲓⲑⲁⲧⲏⲥ ᵉ	ⲗⲓⲥⲧⲏⲥ ⲉϥ-
ⲙ̅ⲙⲓⲛⲉ ⲙⲓⲛⲉ	ⲉⲑⲟⲟⲩ ⲛ[ϩⲁⲓⲣⲉ-]	[ⲛⲁⲓ] ⲉⲧⲟⲛⲟ-	ϫⲱ ⲙ̅ⲙⲟⲥ ϫⲉ-
ϩⲟⲓⲛⲉ ⲉⲧⲃⲉ-	ⲧⲓⲕⲟⲥ . [ᶜ	]ⲛⲉ ᶠ ⲛϣⲟ̅ⲙ̅	ⲛⲉⲙⲙⲁ ϣⲟⲛ-
ⲡϣⲱⲙ ϩⲉⲛⲕⲟ-	ⲑⲏⲡ ϩⲛ[ⲧⲡⲟ-]	sic	
ⲟⲩⲉ ⲉⲧⲃⲉⲧⲉⲡ-	ⲗⲓⲥᵈ ⲉⲧⲥ[ⲱⲧⲙ ⲉ-]	[ⲛⲧ ⲙⲙ]ⲛⲧⲛⲟⲩ-ᵍ	ⲟⲡ ⲛⲁⲩ ϩⲙⲡ-
ⲣⲱ· ⲡⲛⲟⲩⲧⲉ	ⲣⲟⲛ ⲛ̅ⲡⲟⲟⲩ ·]	[ⲧⲉ ⲉ]ⲩⲡⲱⲣϫ̅	ⲙⲁ ⲛϭⲟⲓⲗⲉ
ϫⲉ ⲡⲁⲛⲙⲓⲟⲣ-	Ⲡⲁⲣⲉϥϫ[ⲓ ϣⲓⲡⲉ]	[ⲙ̅ⲡⲉⲓ]ⲱⲧ ⲉⲃⲟⲗ	ⲁⲅⲱ ϫⲉⲁⲩϫⲙ-
ⲅⲟⲥ ⲥ̅ⲗ̅ⲙⲓⲱⲙ	ⲛϭⲓ [	[ⲙ̅ⲡϣⲏ]ⲣⲉ ⲙⲛ-	ⲗⲱⲙⲉϥ ⲛϩⲉⲛ-
[ⲛ̅]ϩⲉⲛⲧⲟⲉⲓⲥ	ⲡ[	[ⲡⲉⲛⲡ̅ⲁ̅ ⲉ]ⲧⲟⲩ[ⲁ̅-]	ⲧⲟⲉⲓⲥ ⲁⲩϫ[ⲧⲟⲩ]
? ?	?	[ⲁⲃ ⲙⲁ]ⲣⲟⲩ-	ϩⲛⲟⲩⲟⲙⲉϥ [
		ⲛ̅]ϭⲓ	ⲉⲣⲉⲡⲟⲩⲟⲙ[ⲉϥ
			ⲁⲣϫⲓ ⲙ̅ⲡ[
			[. .]ϛ ⲛⲟⲑⲉ ⲛ

ᵃ Here Rossi, 56 c.   ᵇ Probably = Rossi, 57 b.   ᶜ ? ⲛ[ⲁⲓ ⲉ-].   ᵈ 'Hidden for us' (Rossi).   ᵉ First visible letter not very like ⲩ.   ᶠ ? ⲉⲧ[ⲟⲛⲟⲙⲁ]ⲍⲉ.   ᵍ The prolonged stroke over ⲛ demanding ⲙ, one cannot read ϣⲟⲙⲛⲧ ⲛⲟⲩ[ⲥⲓⲁ.

Fol. 11. *Recto.* . . . clothe them[selves?] in garments of great price, of divers sorts, some because of the summer, others because of the winter. But (δέ) God, the Creator (δημιουργός), is swathed in bandages . . . . .

. . . Let [them] be shamed [now], the evil wolves of [here]tics (αἱρετικός)

[1] Read θρόνος with Rossi.

[that are] hidden in the city (? πόλις), that hear us to-day.   Let him be [shamed] . . . . .

Verso. . . . [Let them] perish, the presumptuous (? αὐθάδης) transgressors (παράνομος), [they] that name (? ὀνομάζειν) three divinities, dividing the Father from the Son and [the] Holy [Ghost (πν.).[1]   Let] them . . . . .
. . . the holy evangelist (εὐαγγ.) . . . ,[2] saying,[3] 'There was not place for them in the lodging,' and 'they swathed Him in bandages and laid Him in a manger.' [Him whom] the manger did . . ., thou (*fem.*) didst take . . . . . like . . . . .

No. 8.

From a Sermon, treating here of the Last Judgement.   The inability of the righteous to aid the wicked in that day is similarly alluded to in Homilies by John *Jejunator* and Theophilus.[4]

Fol. 1.   → *Recto.*   ↑ *Verso.*

<table>
<tr><td>ⲙⲙⲛⲧⲉϥⲓⲏⲛ</td><td>ⲓ̈ⲱⲧ ⲛⲁⲛⲟⲩϥ</td></tr>
<tr><td>ⲭⲉⲟⲩⲟⲓ ⲛⲁⲓ̈</td><td>ⲉⲛⲉⲛⲡⲉⲕ-</td></tr>
<tr><td>[ⲡⲁ]ⲓ̈ⲱⲧ ⲉⲕ-</td><td>ⲭⲡⲟⲓ ⲭⲉ[</td></tr>
<tr><td>ⲛ[ⲁ]ⲕⲁⲁⲧ ⲛ-</td><td>ⲉⲛⲁⲩ [ⲉⲣⲟⲕ]</td></tr>
<tr><td>ⲥⲱⲕ ⲛⲧⲉ-</td><td>ϭⲛ̅ⲛⲉⲓ̈ϩⲓⲥⲉ</td></tr>
<tr><td>ⲡⲉϥⲓⲱⲧ ⲟⲩ-</td><td>ⲱ ⲡ[ⲁ]ⲓⲱⲧ ⲙ̅ⲡ-</td></tr>
<tr><td>ⲱϣⲃ ϭⲛ̅ⲟⲩ-</td><td>ϣϭⲟⲙ ⲛ̅ⲙⲟⲓ̈</td></tr>
<tr><td>ⲣ̅ⲓ̈ⲙⲉ ⲙ̅ⲡⲟⲩ-</td><td>ⲉⲃⲟⲏⲑⲉⲓ̈ⲁ</td></tr>
<tr><td>ⲁϣⲁϩⲟⲙ·</td><td>ⲉⲣⲟⲕ ⲙ̅ⲡⲉⲓ̈-</td></tr>
<tr><td>ⲭⲉⲟⲩⲟⲓ ⲛⲁⲓ̈</td><td>ⲙⲁ· ⲉⲃⲟⲗ</td></tr>
<tr><td>ⲡⲁϣⲏⲣⲉ</td><td>ⲭⲉ ⲁⲓϩⲓⲥⲉ</td></tr>
<tr><td>ⲙ̅ⲡ̅ϣϭⲟⲙ ⲙ̅-ᵃ</td><td>ⲉⲓ̈ϯⲥⲃⲱ ⲛⲁⲕ</td></tr>
<tr><td>margin</td><td>margin</td></tr>
</table>

ᵃ ⲙⲙⲟⲓ.

---

[1] What relation this heresy bears towards the distinctive position of Damianus himself (v. Kruger's article, *PRE*.) is not clear.   In Rossi, 57 b c (if parallel here) the sect in question are named Πλατωνίτης.

[2] A Greek verb.

[4] Budge, *Copt. Hom.*, 38 *inf.*, 71 *inf.*

Fol. 1. *Recto.* . . . wretchedness, (saying,) 'Woe is me, my father! Thou wilt leave me behind thee?' And his father shall make answer, with weeping and groaning, 'Woe is me, my son! [I] have not power [to' . . . . .

Verso. . . . 'my] father, it were good if thou hadst not begotten me. For . . . to see [thee?] in these distresses. O my father, I have not power to help ($\beta o\eta\theta\epsilon\hat{\imath}\nu$ [1]) thee here. Because I was at pains and taught thee' . . . . .

Fol. 2. ↑*Recto.*　　　　　　　→ *Verso.*

ⲙⲁ̅ⲣⲟ̅ⲙ ⲡ̅ⲧ̅-
ϧ̣ⲉ ⲉⲩⲙⲁⲁⲩ
[ⲛⲁ̅]ⲓⲕⲁⲓⲟⲥ
ϧ[ⲙⲡ]ⲙⲁ ⲉⲧⲙ̅-
ⲙⲁⲩ ⲉⲥⲁ̅-
ⲙⲁϧⲧⲉ ⲛ̅ⲧ̅-
ϭⲓⲝ ⲛ̅ⲧⲉⲥ-
ϣⲉⲉⲣⲉ ⲛ̅ⲣ̅ϥ̅-
ⲉⲣⲛⲟⲃⲉ ⲛ̅ⲧⲉ-
ⲧⲁⲡⲟⲫⲁⲥ̣ⲓ̇ⲥ
ⲉⲓ̇ ⲉⲃⲟⲗ ϧⲓⲧⲙ̅-
ⲡϫⲟⲉⲓ̇ⲥ ⲓ̅ⲥ̅
margin

ⲛ̅ⲧⲉⲥⲅ[ⲉⲉ-]
ⲣⲉ ϫⲉⲉⲩⲛⲁ-
ⲛⲟϫⲥ ⲉⲛ[ⲕⲟ-]
ⲗⲁⲥ̅ⲧ̅ [. .]ⲉ
ϣⲁⲥⲱϣ ⲉⲃⲟⲗ
ⲛ̅ϭⲓ ⲧⲉⲥⲅⲉ-
ⲉⲣⲉ ϫⲉⲟⲩⲟⲓ̇
ⲛⲁⲓ̈ ⲧⲁⲙⲁⲁⲩ
ⲙ̅ⲛ̅ϣϭⲟⲙ ⲙ̅-
ⲙⲟⲓ̈ ⲉⲃⲟⲏ-
ⲑⲉⲓⲁ ⲉⲣⲟ· ⲉ-
ⲃⲟⲗ ϫⲉⲁⲓϧⲓⲥⲉ
margin

Fol. 2. *Recto.* . . . groaning and thou shalt (?) find a righteous ($\delta i\kappa\alpha\iota\sigma\varsigma$) mother there, clasping the hand of her ill-doing daughter and the judgement ($\dot{\alpha}\pi\dot{\sigma}\phi\alpha\sigma\iota\varsigma$) coming forth from the Lord Jesus . . . . .

Verso. . . . her daughter, because they are about to cast her to the torments ($\kappa\dot{\sigma}\lambda\alpha\sigma\iota\varsigma$) . . .[2] her daughter will cry out, 'Woe is me, my mother! I have not power to help ($\beta o.$) thee. Because I was at pains' . . . . .

---

[1] Nominal for verbal forms are not uncommon; of this same verb, *e.g.* Brit. Mus. no. 370, Ry-　lands no. 340.

[2] ⲧⲟⲧⲉ probably too long for the gap.

Fol. 3.   → *Recto.*

ρι]ϫε ϭιⲁ-
[ϣⲁ]ϩⲟϫ ϫ-
[ⲡⲉ]ⲟⲩⲟⲛ ϣⲱ-
ⲡ[ⲉ ⲛⲧ]ⲉⲥϭⲉ
ⲉⲛⲉϩª ⲡⲧ̄-
ϩⲉ ⲉⲩⲟⲟⲛ ⲛ̄-
ⲁⲓⲕⲁⲓⲟⲥ ⲉϥ-
ⲁϫⲁϩⲧⲉ ⲛ̄ⲧ-
ϭⲓⲝ ⲙ̄ⲡⲉϥ-
ⲥⲟⲛ ⲛ̄ⲣⲉϥⲉⲣ-
ⲛⲟⲃⲉ · ⲛ̄ⲧⲉ-
ⲧⲁⲡⲟⲫⲁⲥⲓⲥ̄
margin

margin (left)

↑ *Verso.*

ⲡⲱ[ϫ-]
ⲡⲉⲟⲩ[ⲟⲛ ϣⲱ-]
ⲡⲉ ⲛ̄ⲧⲉ[ⲥϭⲉ]
ⲉⲛⲉϩ [
} Ⲟⲩⲟⲓ [ⲛⲁⲛ]
ϫⲁⲣⲉⲛⲧⲱ-
ⲟⲩⲛ ⲧⲏⲣ ⲙⲉ
ⲉⲣⲟⲛ ⲙ̄ⲙⲁⲩ-
ⲁⲁⲛ ⲧ̄ⲛⲡⲱϩ
ⲛ̄ⲛⲉⲛϩⲏⲧ
ⲧ̄ⲛϣⲏϣ ⲕ̄ⲛⲣ-
ⲙⲉⲥ ⲉϫⲱⲛ
ⲙ̄ⲡⲁⲧⲉⲡⲉ-
margin

margin (right)

ª *Cf.* Mark xiii. 19.

Fol. 3. *Recto.* . . . weeping and groaning, the like of which never was. And thou shalt find a righteous (δίκαιος) brother clasping the hand of his ill-doing brother and the judgement (ἀπόφ.) . . . . .

Verso. . . . the like of which never was. Woe [unto us]! Let us arise and weep over ourselves and break our hearts and scatter ashes upon us, ere the . . . . .

Fol. 4. ↑ *Recto.*

ϩⲛ[ⲧ]ⲙⲏⲧⲉ
ⲛ̄ⲛⲉⲧⲟⲩⲁⲁⲃ
[ⲙⲛ̄ⲛ]ⲁⲡⲟⲥ-
ⲧⲟⲗⲟⲥ ⲉⲩ-
ϫⲡⲓ̈ⲟ ⲙ̄ⲙⲟⲛ
ⲟⲩⲙⲉⲛⲧⲁⲛ-
ⲁⲁⲩ · ⲙⲏ ⲛ̄-

margin (left)

→ *Verso.*

mostly
illegible

ϫⲉⲧⲉⲛⲉⲣ-

margin (right)

<table>
<tr><td>

ρωη ηατωλλ
αη ⲧⲡⲧⲙ-
ϭη ϣⲁϫⲉ ⲉ-
ϫⲱ · ⲉⲩϫⲡïⲟ
ⲙⲙⲟη ϫⲉⲉⲧ-

</td><td>

ϩⲟⲧⲉ ⲉ̅ϩ̅ⲏ̅- *sic*
ⲧⲟⲩ ⲛ̅ⲡⲣⲱⲙⲉ
ⲡⲁⲣⲁ ⲡⲛⲟⲩ
ⲧⲉ · ⲉⲕ-
ϣⲁⲛϫⲟⲟⲥ
    margin

</td></tr>
</table>

Fol. 4. Recto. . . . in the midst of the saints [and] the apostles (ἀπ.), upbraiding us for the things we have done. Shall not (μή) our mouths be shut and we find not a word to say, whilst they upbraid us for that . . . . .

Verso. . . . because we fear men more than (παρά) God. If thou say . . . .

No. 9.

This Homily does not appear among the works ascribed to Gregory Nazianzen.[1] The connected foll. 5, 6, 7 contain the author's name; they belong therefore to the title-page, fol. 1; while foll. 3, 4, connected by their subject-matter, appear immediately to precede fol. 5. But since the title relates to Rom. iv. 15, therefore foll. 11, 12, 13 must belong to this same text, dealing as they also do with that verse. Again, repentance being the subject of foll. 3, 4, 5, therefore fol. 2 probably comes near these. Finally, I have noted (on my copy) that foll. 8, 10 appear, from their present shape, to lie near to fol. 7; they too, then, should belong to this sermon; while fol. 9, dealing, like the last, with charity,[2] should probably be placed close to them.

Cf. also No. 1.

Fol. 1. → *Recto.*

[ⲟⲩϩⲟ]ⲙⲉⲗⲓⲁ’ [a] ⲛ̅ⲧⲉ ⲡϩⲁⲅⲓⲟⲥ’ ⲅⲣⲏⲕⲱ-
[ⲣⲓⲟⲥ] ⲡⲉⲑⲉⲟ̅ⲗⲟⲅⲟⲥ’ ⲡⲉⲡⲓⲥⲕⲟⲡⲟⲥ’
[ⲛ̅ⲛⲁ]ⲍⲓⲁⲛⲍⲟⲥ’ ⲉⲁϥⲧⲁⲩⲟⲥ’ ⲉⲧⲃⲉ-
] ? ⲉⲧ · ⲩϩ . . [ⲡ]ⲁⲡⲟⲥⲧ[ⲟ-]

↑ *Verso.*

[+]   ]ⲙⲉ ·
ⲉⲧⲃⲉⲟⲩ ϯⲛⲁ-
ϫⲟⲟⲥ’ ϫⲉⲉⲩ-
ϣⲁⲛⲉⲓ ⲉⲃⲟⲗ’

ⲡⲁⲩⲗⲟ[ⲥ ⲉϥ-]
ϫⲱ’ [ⲙⲙⲟⲥ’]
+ϫⲉⲡ[ⲙⲁ’ ⲉⲧⲉ-]
ⲙ̅ⲡ̅ⲛ[ⲟⲙⲟⲥ’]

     [a] Above this line another, or an ornament. The six lines of title are in a sloping script.

---

[1] Nor among those of his namesakes.

[2] On Zoega p. 19 is the title of a homily by Gregory on charity. Its text is unpublished.

[λος] ετογααβ' ϫεπμα' ετεμῆ[ο-]
[μ]ος' ῇϙητϥ' ῑῆπαραβαϲιϲ ᵃ

ηα]ηογϲ'	πεγϙωβ [
]ετρε-	ματε ηϙ[
]τηϣα-	ηεϫ ϭραγϭη
ϫεη]τηϭη-	ῆϲωϲ' · εγ-
μαη]ηει	+ϫω' ῑῑμοϲ
]τϥ	ϫετῆϯ
?	ϙτηη ετ-
	.ω ?

ϙῆτεκκλη-	ῇϙητ[ϥ' ῑῑη-]
ϲια' · αλλα' ϫιη-	παρα[βαϲιϲ'·]
τεϯηογ' εγ-	+εκϫω' [ῑῑμοϲ'
ϙμοοϲ' ϙῆ-	ϫεογ [ω̅ παγ·
τϲ̅γηαϫιϲ' ·	λοϲ' · [
[+ε]γϣαηϲω-	ϙῑῑτλο[
τῑῑ' ετλεϫιϲ'	εροη [
ῆτεκεογει	ϲοη[
εῑ ῑῑῆϲωϲ'	+ειμε[
ϣαγ̅ρπωβ̅ϣ̅'	ῆτῆ[
μπεηταγ-	ϫε[
[ϲ]οτμεϥ' ῆ-	?
[τ]εγηογ ·	?
[. .]ηạϲωτῑῑ'	

ᵃ After this I read ҋ., very doubtfully. It did not seem to be ⲁⲙⲏⲛ.

Fol. 1. *Recto.* A Homily (ὁμιλία) of St. (ἅγιος) *Gregory the Theologian* (θεόλ.), *the bishop* (ἐπ.) *of Nazianzus, which he pronounced concerning* .... *the holy apostle* (ἀπ.), *namely,* ' *The place wherein there is not law* (νό.), *there is not transgression* (παράβασις).' [1]

. . . good (?) . . . that . . . the word (?) whereby (?) we point out (? σημαίνειν) . . . . .

. . . . ., cried (-κραυγή) after her, saying, We give heed unto . . . . .

Verso. . . . Wherefore ? I will tell.   (It is because) whenever they come forth from the church, nay (ἀλλά) from the moment that they are seated at service (σύναξις), if they hear the lesson (λέξις) and there follow another (lesson) after it, straightway they forget what they have heard.   Let them (?) hear . . . . .

. . . Paul, [who] saith, ' the place wherein there is not law, there is not transgression.'   What sayest thou, O Paul ? . . . . .

[1] Rom. iv. 15.

Fol. 2. ↑ *Recto.*   → *Verso.*

Recto		Verso	
ⲙⲱⲩⲥⲏⲥ			ⲡ̄ⲡⲟⲗⲓⲧⲉⲩ[ⲉ]
ⲁϥϯ ⲡⲛⲟⲙⲟⲥ			ⲛ̄ϣⲟⲣⲡ̄'
ⲁϥϫⲟⲟⲩ ⲛ̄-		]ⲡⲁ-	+ⲁⲗⲗⲁ' ⲉϣⲁϥ-
ⲛⲉⲡⲣⲟϥⲏ-		[ⲛⲁ̄ⲃ] ⲅⲁⲣ ϩⲟ-	ϫⲟⲟⲥ' ϫⲉ-
ⲧⲏⲥ' ⲁⲩⲱ'	ⲡⲉ[	[ⲗ̄ⲥ ⲁ]ⲩⲱ ⲥⲁⲥⲱ-	ⲉⲓⲥ ϩⲏⲏⲧⲉ'
ⲙ̄ⲡⲟⲩⲡⲓⲥ-	+ⲉⲓⲥ ϩⲏⲛ[ⲧⲉ]	[ⲟⲩ] ⲛϭⲓ ⲧⲁⲉⲧⲡⲱ	ⲁⲕⲟⲩϫⲁⲓ
ⲧⲉⲩⲉ· ⲙ̄ⲡ-	+ϫⲓ ϣ[ⲓⲡⲉ	]ⲟ ⲟⲩⲛⲁᵇ	ⲙ̄ⲡⲣ̄ⲕⲟⲧⲕ̄'
+ⲛ̄ⲥⲱⲥ' ⲁⲡϣⲏⲛ-	ⲉⲃⲟⲗ [	ⲛ]ϭⲓ ⲧⲉⲧⲡⲱ	ⲉⲣ̄ⲛⲟⲃⲉ'
ⲣⲉ' ⲙ̄ⲡⲛⲟⲩ-	ⲙⲏ[	?	ϫⲉⲉⲛⲉⲡⲉ-
ⲧⲉ' ⲧⲱⲟⲩⲛ̄	ϣⲁⲣ[	[ⲉⲣϣ]ⲁⲛⲟⲩⲅⲁ'	ⲑⲟⲟⲩ' ⲉⲡⲁⲓ
ϩⲓⲟⲩⲛⲁⲙ	ⲟⲛ ⲛⲥ[ⲛ-]	[ϯ]ⲡⲉϥⲟⲩⲟⲓ	ϣⲱⲡⲉ' ⲛ̄-
ⲙ̄ⲡⲉϥⲉⲓⲱⲧ'	ⲧⲁⲩⲣ[	[ⲉⲡⲉ]ⲭ̄ⲥ̄ ⲉⲧⲃⲉ-	ⲙⲟⲕ' · ⲉⲧⲉ-
+ⲁϥⲉⲓ ⲉϥϣⲁ-	ⲁⲛⲟⲕ [	]ⲛⲟⲃⲉ	+ⲡⲁⲓⲡⲉ' ϫⲉ-
ϫⲉ' ⲛ̄ⲙⲙⲁⲛ	ⲧⲉ ⲉⲧ[ⲛ-]	?	ⲧⲉⲕⲡⲟⲗⲓ-
ⲉϥϫⲱ' ⲙⲙⲟⲥ' ·	ⲧⲁϥⲉ[	?	ⲧⲓⲁ' ⲧⲏⲣⲥ̄'
+ϫⲉⲉϣϫⲉⲁⲓ-	ⲛ̄ⲕⲁ ⲛ[ⲓⲙ	] ⲉⲃⲟⲗ	ⲡⲉ ⲧⲙ̄ⲕⲟ-
ϫⲟⲟⲩ ⲛ̄ⲛⲁ-	ⲉⲃⲟⲗ ⲁ[ᵃ	?	ⲧⲕ̄' ⲉⲡⲛⲟⲃ-
ⲡⲣⲟϥⲏⲧⲏⲥ'	ⲥⲉⲡⲏⲧ [ⲉ-]	]ⲩϣⲱⲡⲉ'	ⲃⲉ' ⲛ̄ⲕⲉⲥⲟⲡ·
ⲉⲧⲟⲩⲁⲁⲃ'	ⲃⲟⲗ' ⲙ̄[ⲙⲟⲓ	]ⲟⲩⲱϣ'	+ⲧⲙⲉⲧⲁⲛⲟⲓⲁ'
ⲛⲏⲧⲛ̄' ⲁⲩⲱ'	+ⲛ̄ⲧⲁϥ[ϫⲟⲟⲥ]	[ⲉⲧ]ⲣⲉϥⲧⲁⲗ-	ⲙ̄ⲡⲛⲟⲃⲉ'-
ⲁⲩϣⲁϫⲉ' ⲛ̄ⲡ-	ⲁⲛ' ⲛ̄ϭⲓ [ⲡⲛⲟⲩ-]	[ϭⲟⲟ]ⲩ' · ⲙⲉϥ-	ⲡⲉ ⲧⲙ̄ⲕⲟⲧⲕ̄'
ⲙ̄ⲛⲧⲛ̄' ⲉϫⲙ̄-	ⲧⲉ' ϫ[ⲉⲁⲙⲏ-]	ⲟⲩⲛⲟϥ'	ⲉⲣⲟϥ' · ⲉⲣ-
ⲡⲁⲣⲁⲛ· ⲡⲉ-	ⲉⲓⲧ[ⲛ̄ ϣⲁⲣⲟⲓ]	[ⲛⲉⲧⲡ̄]ⲱ' ⲉϥ-ᶜ	+ϣⲁⲛⲡⲣⲱⲙⲉ'
margin	margin	ⲉ]ϫⲱϥ'	ⲕⲟⲧϥ' ⲉⲡⲛ̄-ᵒ
		margin	ⲧⲏ̄ⲣ̄
			margin

ᵃ ⲁⲩⲱ or ⲁⲗⲗⲁ.   ᵇ ⲛⲁϣⲧ?   ᶜ Not an epithet of ⲉⲧⲡⲱ.

Fol. 2. *Recto.* ... Moses. He gave the law (νόμ.), He sent the prophets (πρ.) and they believed (πίστ.) not. Afterward the Son of God arose upon His Father's right, and came and spake with us, saying, 'If I have sent my holy prophets (πρ.) unto you and they have spoken with you in my name . . . . .

. . . Lo, I am put to shame (?) through . . . . all things . . . . . they flee from [me']. Hath not God said, 'Come unto me[1] . . . . .

Verso. . . . for (γάρ) my [yoke] is easy and my burden is light' . . . . . the burden . . . . [If] one betake him to Christ by reason of . . . sin (?) . . . . disease(d ?) [and ?] desire that He would heal them, He doth not [lay a heavy ? bur]den . . . . .

. . . 'and first thou live strictly (πολιτεύειν).' But (ἀλλά) He saith,[2] 'Behold, thou hast been made whole; turn not again to commit sin, lest a worse thing than this befall thee,' which is (to say,) ' Thy whole way-of-life (πολιτεία) is (that) thou turn not unto sin again.' Repentance (μετ.) of sin is not returning thereto. If a man turn unto God . . . . .

Fol. 3. ↑ *Recto.*   → *Verso.*

τε' εϥογ-			π̅cωϥ' ·
ωϣ' εμετα-			+ϩεπκοογε'
ποει· εϥϫι			αγωω' ϩ̅μ-
+π̅πτγποc'	ρπ̅	]ηα	πιωογ'
πο[γσλο]ο̅σε'	πο[	]τβλ-	εγαϣε' π̅-
ερερατ̅c̅	κο[	]ϣ̅κ̅'	cαπϫοϊ·
ταϫρηγ'	βε' [	] ετϩι-	+ϩεπκοογε'
εϫπ̅πκαϩ'	+Gιω[	]ατε	εγϩμοοc'
ερετεcαπε'	τπ̅[	]ποcε	εβολ' ϩ̅μ-
πηϩ' εϩραϊ	πα[	?	πϫοϊ· ϩεπ-
ετπε ερε-	ϫε[	]cωτπ̅	+κοογε' εγ-
πεcποειϣ'	ϫε[	?	αϩ'ε ρατογ'
ϫοcε' επεγ-	ϩμ[	]ορ εϥ-	ϩιπϫοϊ π̅-
ερηγ'· π̅θε'	τ[	?	πογσπ̅ μα
+π̅πρωμε'	σ[	]εμπ-	π̅ρμοοc'
εϥπαϥ' τεϥ-	πε[	]. εϩε	ϣαπτογ-

[1] Matt. xi. 28–30.   [2] John v. 14.

ογερητε'	επ[	]ρωμε'	πωϩ επεκ-
ⲙ̄ⲙⲁⲩ' ϩⲓϫⲙ̄	ⳁⲕⲁⲓ[	] ⲛ̄ⲧⲉ-	ⲕⲣⲟ̄' · ⲉⲩ-
ⲡⲕⲁϩ' ⲛ̄ϭ̄ⲟⲩ-	ⳙⲙ[	]ⲉⲓ	ⳁ ⳙⲁⲛⲡⲱϩ'
ⳁⲁ̄ⲣ̄ⲥ̄' ⲉϫ̄ⲙ̄ⳙⲟ-	ⳁⲕⲁⲛ[	]ⳙ'	ϫⲉ' ⲉⲡⲉⲕⲣⲟ̄
ⲣ̄ⲡ̄' ⲛ̄ⲡⲟⲉⲓⳙ'	ⲧⲡ[	] ⲉⲣⲟϥ'	ⲙⲟⲃⲛⲉ' ·
ⲛ̄ⲧⲉϭⲗⲟϭⲥⲉ ·	?	]ⲅ	
ⳁⲧⲁⲓ ϩⲱⲱϥ'-	ⳁ ⲙ[	ⲡ]ϫⲟⲓ ·	ⳁ ⳙⲁⲩⲉⲓ ϫⲉ'
ⲧⲉ ⲑⲉ' ⲙ̄ⲡⲣⲱ-		]ⲉ̄ ·	ⲉϩⲣⲁⲓ ϩⲙ̄-
margin		]ⲧⲟⲩ'	margin

Fol. 3. *Recto.* . . . desiring to repent (μετανοεῖν) he hath the type (τύπος) of a ladder, the foot thereof fixed upon the earth, its head reaching up to heaven and its steps[1] raised one (above) the other. Like as a man lifteth his foot from the earth and setteth it upon the first step of the ladder, even thus the man . . . . .

Verso. . . . others[2] stay in the water, hanging upon the ship; others sit on the outside of (?)[3] the ship; others stand upon the ship and have not found place to sit, until they attain unto the shore. But (δέ) when they attain unto the shore and the ship is in port, they come (+ δέ) up from (?) [the ship . . . . .

Fol. 4. → *Recto.*

↑ *Verso.*

ⲛ̄ · ⲟⳗⲛ ⲉⲩ-	ϩⲓⲧⲉ' · ⲁⲕ-
ϩⲙⲟⲟⲥ' ⲕⲁ-	ⳁⲧⲱⲟⲩⲛ̄' ϫⲉ-
ⲗⲱⲥ' ⲙ̄ⲡ-	ⲉⲓⲛⲁⲉⲥⲕⲣⲁ-
ⲛⲉⲧϩⲙ̄ⲙⲟ-	ⲧⲉⲩⲉ' ⲙ̄ⲙⲟⲓ
ⲟⲩ' ⲛ̄ⲥⲉⲉ̄ⲓ	ⲛ̄ⲧⲁⲙⲉⲧⲁ-
ⲧⲏⲣⲟⲩ' ⲉϫⲙ̄	ⲛⲟⲉⲓ · ⲛ̄ⲧ̄-
ⲡⲉⲧⳙⲟⲩ-	ⲥⲟⲟⲩⲛ̄' ⲁⲛ'
ⲱ̄ⲟⲩ' ⲛ̄ⲥⲉ-	ϫⲉⲛ̄ⲛⲁⲱ̄ⲛ̄ϩ'

ϩ[|]ⲓⲕⲟⲥ [a]

[a] ⲕⲟⲥⲙⲓⲕⲟⲥ, ⲕⲗⲏⲣⲓⲕⲟⲥ, ϩⲁⲓⲣⲉⲧⲓⲕⲟⲥ ?

---

[1] ⲡⲟⲉⲓⳙ is a new word.
[2] The preceding column too dealt with the shipwreck : ϫⲟⲓ is legible.

[3] I can find no instance of ϩⲙⲟⲟⲥ so constructed. Brit. Mus. *Gk. Cat.* iv, no. 1609 is too uncertain ; Crum, *Ostr.* no. 351 still more so.

ογϫⲁⲓ̈ ⲧⲏ-	ⲥⲉ[	]ϣⲁⲣⲉ-	ϣⲁⲛⲧⲕ̄ⲣ̄-
ⲣⲟⲩ · ⲧⲁⲓ̈-	ⲟⲩ[	]ⲕⲏ	ϩ̄ⲗ̄ⲗⲟ' ⲛ̄ⲅⲙⲉ-
+ⲧⲉ θⲉ' ⲙ̄ⲡⲉ-	ⲥⲓ[	ⲟ]ⲩⲁ ⲉⲓ	ⲧⲁⲛⲟⲉⲓ ·
ⲧⲟⲩⲛⲁϭⲉ'	ⲧ[	?	+ⲙⲏ ⲁⲕⲥ̄ⲙ̄ⲛ̄
ⲉⲩⲃ̄ⲗ̄ⲃⲓⲗⲉ'	ⲁⲅ[	]ⲉϥ-	ⲇⲓⲁθⲏⲕⲏ
ⲛ̄ⲟⲩⲱⲧ'	θⲉ[	[. ⲣϩ̄ⲗ̄ⲁⲟ'ᵃ ⲡϥ̄-	ⲙ̄ⲡⲙⲟⲩ'
ϩ̄ⲙⲡⲉϥⲥⲙⲁϩ'	ⲟⲛ[	[ⲉⲥⲕⲣⲁ]ⲧⲉⲩⲉ'	ⲁⲛ' ϩ̄ⲛ̄ⲧⲉⲕ-
ⲉⲧⲉⲡⲁⲓ̈-	ϫⲁ[	[ⲛ̄ⲙⲟ]ϥ ⲛ̄ⲥⲉ-	ⲙ̄ⲛ̄ⲧⲕⲟⲩⲓ̈ ·
ⲡⲉ ⲟⲩⲙⲉ-	?	]ⲥ ⲉⲣⲟϥ'	+ⲟⲩⲣⲱⲙⲉ' ⲉϥ-
ⲣⲟⲥ' ⲛ̄ⲙⲉ-	ϫ[	]ⲉⲥⲕⲣⲁ-	ⲣ̄ⲛⲟⲃⲉ' ⲉϥ-
ⲧⲁⲛⲟⲓⲁ' ·	ⲕⲁ[	[ⲧⲉⲩⲉ ⲁⲗ]ⲗⲁ' ⲟⲩ-	ⲕⲱ' ⲛ̄ϩⲧⲏϥ'
+ϣⲁⲣⲉⲙ̄ⲡⲧ-	ϩⲁⲥ[	[ⲙⲛ̄ⲧⲁ]ⲧⲥⲟⲙ'	ⲉⲡⲛⲁ' ⲙ̄ⲡⲛⲟⲩ-
ϣⲁⲛϩⲧⲏϥ'	+ⲉⲣⲟ[	ⲡ]ⲥⲱⲙⲁ'	ⲧⲉ' ⲉϥϫⲱ'
ⲙ̄ⲡⲛⲟⲩⲧⲉ'		ⲥ]ⲛⲁⲩ'	ⲙ̄ⲙⲟⲥ' ϫⲉ-
ⲧⲁϩⲟⲟⲩ'		?	margin
ⲧⲏⲣⲟⲩ' ⲛ̄-		]ⲓⲁ	
margin		margin	

ᵃ ⲉϥⲉⲣ- or ⲉϥⲛⲁⲣ-.

Fol. 4. Recto. . . . they remaining (*lit.* sitting) placidly (καλῶς) with them that are in the water, and all come on to dry-land and are all saved. This is the manner of him who shall find a single grape in his cluster,[1] that is to say, a portion (μέρος) of repentance (μετ.). God's pitifulness reacheth all of them . . . . .

Verso. . . . when] he [shall] grow old and be temperate (ἐγκρατεύειν) and they . . . him . . . be temperate (ἐγκ.). But (ἀλλά) [it is] an impossi-[bility that ? the] body (σῶμα) . . . two (?) . . . . .

. . . torment and didst arise (saying,) ' I will be temperate (ἐγκ.) and will repent (μετ.).' Thou knowest not that thou shalt live till thou be old and (then) repent (μετ.). Hast thou (μή) established a covenant (διαθ.) with death[2] in thy youth ? A man that, sinning, turneth his thoughts to God's mercy, saying, ...

[1] *Cf.* Isa. lxv. 8 (Sa'id. *ed.* Schleifer).   [2] *Cf.* Isa. xxviii. 15, 18.

Fol. 5. ↑ p. ⲓⲉ.   → p. ⲓⲋ.

ⲓ̅ⲥ̅ ✝ ⲭ̅ⲥ̅

margin   margin

[ⲉⲓϣⲁ]ⲛⲙⲟⲩ´	+ⲛ̅ⲟ̄ⲏⲧⲟⲩ ⲉϥⲟ̄
[ⲉⲣⲉⲡⲛ]ⲁⲛⲧ´	ⲙ̄ⲙⲁⲧⲟⲥ´·
[ⲛ̄]ⲛⲟⲩⲧⲉ´ ᵃ	ⲡⲁⲓ̈ ⲛ̄ⲧⲓⲙⲓⲛⲉ´
[ⲛ̄]ⲁ̄ⲣⲟⲩⲛⲁ´	ⲉϥϣⲁⲛⲙⲟⲩ´
[ⲛ̄]ⲛ̄ⲙⲁⲓ̈ ⲛ̄ϥ-	ⲙ̄ⲡⲁⲧϥⲙⲉ-
[ⲕⲱ´] ⲛⲁⲛⲟⲃⲉ´	ⲧⲁⲛⲟⲉⲓ · ϥ̄ⲛⲁ-
[ⲉⲃ]ⲟⲗ ⲛ̄ϥⲥⲱ´	+ⲕⲁⲧⲁⲛⲧⲁ´
[. .]ⲟⲩⲉϩ ᵇ ⲛⲟ-	ⲉⲁ̄ⲙ̄ⲛⲧⲉ´ ⲙ̄-
[ⲃⲉ] ⲉϫ̄ⲛⲛⲉϥ-	ⲡⲉⲥⲛⲧ´· ⲡⲙⲁ´]
[ⲛⲟ]ⲃⲉ ⲛ̄ϥ-	+ⲉⲧⲉⲙ̄ⲛⲗⲁⲁⲩ
[ⲧ̄ⲙ̄] ⲙⲉⲧⲁ-	ⲛ̄ⲟⲩϭⲟⲉⲓⲛ´
ⲛⲟⲉⲓ · ⲡⲁⲓ̈	ⲛ̄ϩⲏⲧϥ̄· [ⲟⲩ-]
ⲛ̄ⲧⲉⲓⲙⲓⲛⲉ´	+ϫⲉ ⲡⲛⲟⲩⲧⲉ
ⲟ̄ ⲛ̄ϣⲙⲙⲟ	ⲛⲁⲣⲡ[ⲙⲉ]ⲉⲩⲉ
ⲉⲡⲛⲁ´ ⲙ̄ⲡⲛ̄-	ⲁⲛ´ ⲛ̄[ⲛⲉⲧ-]
ⲩⲧⲉ´ ⲙ̄ⲡⲁⲛ-	ϩⲓⲛⲙⲁ´ ⲉ[ⲧⲙ̄-]
[ⲧⲟⲕⲣⲁ]ⲧⲱⲣ´	ⲙⲁⲩ´ ϣⲁⲉ-
[. . . .]ⲡⲕⲟⲥ .	ⲛⲉϩ · ⲟⲩⲭⲣⲏⲥ-
	ⲧⲓⲁⲛⲟⲥ [ⲉϥ-]
	[ⲛⲁ]ⲝⲓⲥ[

Column (right page, p. ⲓⲋ):

ⲧⲉ ⲛ̄ⲧⲁϥⲁⲁⲥ´·	ⲫⲩⲗ[ⲁⲕⲧⲏ-]
+ⲟⲩⲭⲣⲏⲥⲧⲓⲁ-	ⲣⲓⲟⲛ [
ⲛⲟⲥ´ ⲉϥⲛⲁϫⲓ	ⲛⲟⲩⲙ[
ⲥⲟⲗ´ ⲉ̄ⲛⲗⲁⲁⲩ´	ⲛ̄ⲥⲉ[
ⲛ̄ϩⲱⲃ´ ⲛ̄ⲟⲩ-	ⲉϫⲱϥ´ [
ⲭⲣⲏⲥⲧⲓⲁⲛⲟⲥ´	ⲟⲩⲛⲉ[
ⲁⲛ´ⲡⲉ· ⲟⲩ-	ⲉ̄ϥ´· ⲛ̄ [ⲉϥ-]
+ⲣⲱⲙⲉ ⲉϥⲟ̄-	ⲛⲁⲃⲱ[ⲕ
ⲣ̄ⲕ´ ⲙ̄ⲡⲣⲁⲛ´ ⲙ̄-	ϩⲟⲗⲱ[ⲥ´
ⲡⲛⲟⲩⲧⲉ´ ⲛ-	ⲉⲡⲙⲁ´ [ⲛⲟⲩ-]
ⲛⲟⲩϫ´ ⲉϥⲧⲁ-	ⲣⲉϥⲙ[ⲟⲩⲧⲉ]
ⲕⲉ´ ⲙ̄ⲙⲟϥ ⲛ̄-	ⲛ̄ ⲟⲩⲣⲉϥ-
ϩⲁϩ ⲛ̄ⲥⲟⲡ´	ⲕⲁ ⲟⲩⲛⲟⲩ´·
ⲡⲛⲟⲩⲧⲉ ⲛⲁ-	+ⲡⲁⲓ̈ ⲛ̄ⲧⲉⲓ-
ⲧⲁⲕⲟϥ´ ⲛ̄ϥⲣ̄	ⲙⲓⲛⲉ´ ⲁⲩ-
ϭⲣⲱϣ´ ᶜ ⲙ̄ⲡⲟⲉⲓⲛ´	ⲟⲩⲱ´ ⲉⲩⲕⲱ
[ⲙ̄]ⲡⲁⲧϥⲙⲟⲩ·	ⲙ̄ⲙⲟϥ´ ⲕ[ⲁ-]
[+ⲟⲩⲭ]ⲣⲏ[ⲥ]ⲧ[ⲓⲁ-]	ϩⲏ[ⲩ
[ⲛⲟⲥ	

ᵃ Perhaps too little, but grammar forbids ⲙ̄ⲛⲛⲟⲩⲧⲉ.   ᵇ Should be ⲉϥⲟⲩⲉϩ.

ᶜ So copy, but must be ϭⲣⲱϩ.

Fol. 5. P. 15. ...'If I] die, the merciful God shall have mercy with me and forgive my sins,' and he continueth adding sin to his sin and repenting (μετ.) not; such an one as this is estranged from the mercy of God Almighty (παντοκρ.) .....

... therein, being a magician (μάγος). Such an one as this, if he die ere he have repented (μετ.), shall reach (κατανταν) the nether hell,[1] the place

[1] *Cf.* Ps. lxxxv. 13.

where no light is, neither (οὐδέ) shall God remember them that are in that place for ever.   A Christian (χρ.) that shall . . . . .

P. 16 (*last of a quire*).   . . . that he hath done.   A Christian (χρ.) that shall lie in anything is not a Christian.   A man that sweareth by God's name falsely destroyeth himself many times.   God shall destroy him, and he shall be in want of bread ere he die.   A Christian . . . . .

. . . amulet (φυλακτήριον) . . . . shall go (?) . . . at all (ὅλως) to the place of a wizard or (ἤ) a soothsayer, such an one hath already been stripped [of baptism (?)][1] . . . . .

Fol. 6.   → p. ⲓⲍ.   ↑ p. ⲓⲏ.

ⲓ̅ⲥ̅ ✝ ⲭ̅ⲥ̅

]ⲟⲩϭⲓ-	✝ⲉⲛϣⲁⲛⲣⲡⲉ-	ⲕⲁⲗⲱⲥ ⲛ̅ⲡⲓⲥ-	ⲧⲓⲥⲙ[ⲁ
[ⲙⲉ ⲉ]ⲥⲡⲟⲣ-	ⲟⲃⲏⲩⲉ' ⲛ̅ⲙⲟⲩ'	ⲧⲉⲩⲉ' ⲉⲡⲙⲟⲩ'	ϥⲉⲧ[ⲧⲉϥ-]
[ⲛⲉⲩ]ⲉ' ⲉⲩⲛ̅-	ⲛ̅ⲃⲁⲡⲧⲓⲥⲙⲁ	ⲛ̅ⲓⲥ̅' ⲙⲛ̅ⲧⲉϥ-	ⲥϥⲣⲁ[ⲅⲓⲥ]
[ⲧⲥ ϩ]ⲁⲓ̈ ⲁⲩ-	ⲉⲓⲉ ⲕⲁⲗⲱⲥ	ⲁⲛⲁⲥⲧⲁⲥⲓⲥ̅:	ⲉⲃⲟⲗ [ϩⲏⲧ-]
]ⲡⲉ ⲁⲛ'	ⲁⲛϫⲓ ⲛ̅ⲃⲁⲡ-	✝ⲁⲕϫⲓ ⲛ̅ⲃⲁⲡ-	ⲧⲉϩⲏ[ⲉ
]ⲓ ⲉⲃⲟⲗ'	ⲧⲓⲥⲙⲁ' ⲛ̅-	ⲧⲓⲥⲙⲁ ⲁⲕ✝	ⲡⲱϩ' ⲉ[
[ϩⲛ]ⲧⲙⲛ̅ⲧ-	✝ⲡⲣ̅ⲧⲣⲉⲛϣⲟⲩ-	ⲡⲉⲭ̅ⲥ̅ ϩⲓⲱ̅ⲱⲕ'	ⲉⲧⲙ[
[ⲭⲣⲏ]ⲥⲧⲓⲁ-	ϣⲟⲩ' ⲛ̅ⲙⲟⲛ'	ⲉⲕϣⲁⲛⲕⲁ-	ⲛ̅ⲥⲉⲡ[
[ⲛⲟⲥ]' ⲁⲛⲟⲕ'	ϫⲉⲁⲛⲫⲟⲣⲉⲓ	ⲁⲕ' ⲕⲁϩⲏⲩ ⲛ̅-	ⲗⲁⲁⲩ [ⲛ̅ⲙⲁ-]
[ⲅⲣⲏ]ⲅⲱⲣⲓⲟⲥ'	ⲛ̅ⲡⲉⲥⲭⲏⲙⲁ'	ⲙⲟϥ' ϩⲓⲧⲛ̅-	ⲉⲓⲛ' ⲛ̅[ⲙⲛ̅ⲧ-]
[ⲙⲡ]ⲉⲓϫⲱ'	ⲛ̅ⲡⲓⲥⲧⲓⲥ'	ⲛⲉⲕⲟⲃⲏⲩⲉ'	ⲭⲣⲏⲥ[ⲧⲓⲁ-]
[ⲙⲡⲁⲓ] ⲁⲛϩⲁ-	ⲛ̅ⲧⲏ ⲟ̅ ⲛ̅ ⲧⲡⲓⲥ-	ⲉⲑⲟⲟⲩ' ⲉⲓⲉ	ⲛⲟⲥ' [
[ⲣⲟⲓ ⲙ]ⲁⲅⲁ-	✝ⲧⲓⲥ' ⲉⲥⲟ̅ ⲛ̅-	ⲁⲕⲁⲁⲕ' ⲛ̅ⲁⲣ-	✝Ⲟ̅ⲩⲟ[ⲓ ⲛⲁⲕ]
[ⲁⲧ ⲁⲓ]ⲙⲟⲩ-	ⲁⲣⲧⲟⲛ'· ⲧⲡⲓⲥ-	ⲧⲟⲛ' ⲉϣⲁⲩ-	ⲉⲩⲧⲙ[ⲟ̅ⲛ]
[ϣ]ⲧ' ϩⲛ̅ⲛⲟ-	ⲧⲓⲥ' ⲉⲥ̅ⲛ̅ⲛⲉ-	✝ⲙⲟⲩⲧⲉ' ⲉϩⲟ̅	ⲡⲙⲁⲉ[ⲓⲛ
[ⲙ]ⲟⲥ' ⲛ̅ⲧⲁ-	ⲟⲃⲏⲩⲉ' ⲥⲟ̅	ⲛⲓⲙ ⲉϥⲛⲁⲣ	ⲛ̅ⲙⲟ[ⲩ]
[ⲛⲉ]ⲛⲉⲓⲟⲧⲉ'	ⲛ̅ⲁⲣⲧⲟⲛ'·	ⲁⲥ' ⲛ̅ⲥⲉⲧⲁ-	ⲛ̅ⲡⲉⲭ̅ⲥ̅ [ϩⲓ-]
[ⲉ]ⲧⲟⲩⲁⲁⲃ'	✝ⲕⲁⲗⲱⲥ ⲛ̅ⲡⲓⲥ-	ⲕⲟ̅' ϫⲉⲁⲣⲧⲟⲛ'·	ⲱ̅ⲱⲕ' ⲉ-
[ⲛⲁ̅ⲡⲟⲥⲧⲁ-	ⲧⲉⲩⲉ' ⲉⲡⲛⲟ̅-	✝ⲉⲩⲧⲙ̅ⲙ̅ⲡⲛ̅ⲥ-	ⲛⲉⲥⲉⲫ̅ⲣⲟⲥ-]

[ⲗ]ⲟⲥ ⲕⲁⲛⲱ-   ⲧⲉ'· ⲛ̄ⲕⲉ- | ⲣⲃⲏⲩⲉ' ⲛ̄ⲡⲃⲁⲡ-   ⲡⲉ' ⲝⲉ[ⲕ-]
[ⲛ]ϊ̈ⲍⲉ ⲛ̄ⲙⲟ-   ⲍⲁⲓⲙⲟⲛⲓⲟⲛ' | ⲧⲓⲥⲙⲁ' ⲁⲕ-   ⲛⲁⲣⲟⲩ [
[ⲟⲩ ⲛⲛⲉ]ⲧⲛⲁ-   ⲣⲱⲟⲩ ⲟⲛ' | ⲧⲁⲕⲟ̄ ⲛ̄ⲡⲃⲁⲡ-
   ⲡⲓⲥⲧⲉⲩⲉ' | ⲧⲓⲥⲙⲁ · ⲥⲉ-
   [ⲁ]ⲩⲱ' ⲥⲉⲥⲧ[ⲱⲧ'] | [ⲛⲁ]ⲕⲁⲁⲕ' ⲕ[ⲁⲣⲏⲩ]

Fol. 6. P. 17 (*first of a quire*). . . . a woman that fornicateth (πορνεύειν), she having an husband . . . . out from Christianity (-χρηστιανός). I, Gregory, I have not said this of myself alone ; I have studied (?) the laws (νόμ.) which our fathers the apostles (ἀπ.) did fix (κανονίζειν) [for them ?] that should . . . . .

. . . If we do the deeds of baptism (βάπτισμα), then (is it) well (καλῶς) that we have received baptism (βάπ.). Let us not boast ourselves that we wear (φορεῖν) the habit (σχῆμα) of faith (πίσ.), and (then) find faith barren (ἀργός). 'Faith without works is barren (ἀρ.).'[1] (It is) well (καλῶς) thou believe (πιστεύειν) in God ; the devils (δαιμόνιον) also believe and tremble[2] . . . . .

P. 18. (It is) well (καλῶς) thou believe (πιστ.) in the death of Jesus and His resurrection (ἀνάστ.). Thou hast received baptism (βάπτ.) and hast clothed thee with Christ. If thou strip thyself of Him through thy evil deeds, then hast thou made thyself barren (ἀργός), every vessel that is becoming old and perished being called barren (useless ἀρ.). If thou do not the deeds of baptism (βάπ.), thou hast destroyed baptism : thou shalt be stripped . . . . .

. . . wipe off its (?) seal (σφραγίς) from the brow . . . . . and they . . . no sign of Christianity (-χρ.). Woe [unto thee], if the sign of Christ's death be not [found] upon thee, which is His cross (στ.). For what wilt thou do ? . . . . .

Fol. 7. ↑ p. ⲓ̄ⲍ̄.   → p. ⲕ̄.

        margin   margin
   ⲧⲕ̄ ⲉⲧⲃⲉⲛⲉⲕ-   ⲉⲣⲟⲟⲩ' ⲝⲉ-
   ⲣⲃⲏⲩⲉ' ⲉⲑⲟ-   ⲛⲉⲧⲧⲁⲕⲟ̄
   ⲟⲩ' · ⲧⲡⲓⲥⲧⲓⲥ'   ⲏ̄ ⲛⲉⲛⲧⲁⲩ-   +ⲣ[

---

[1] Jas. ii. 20.   [2] *Ib.* 19.

]ⲉⲧⲁ	+ⲉⲭ̄ⲡⲛⲉⲟⲃⲏⲅⲉ'	ⲧⲁⲕⲟ · ⲛ̄ⲧⲟⲕ'	ⲏ[
]ⲉⲣⲉ-	ⲥⲟ̄ ⲛ̄ⲁⲣⲧⲟⲛ' ·	+ⲟⲱⲟⲕ' ⲉⲕ-	ⲧ[
]ⲉ	+ⲁ̈ⲓ̈ⲭⲟⲟⲥ' ⲛ̄ⲕⲉ-	ϣⲁⲡⲉⲙⲙⲉ'	ⲡ̄[
]ⲉⲡⲉⲕ-	ⲥⲟⲡ' · ⲭⲉⲉϣⲁⲅ-	ⲭⲉⲁⲕⲣⲁⲧ-	ⲉⲣ[
]ⲉⲕ-	ⲙⲟⲩⲧⲉ' ⲉⲟⲛⲟ̄	ϣⲁⲅ' ⲛ̄ⲥⲁ'ⲥⲁ'	+ⲱ ⲁ[ⲕⲁϣⲁ-]
]ⲟⲱϣ'	ⲛⲓⲙ' ⲉϥⲛⲁⲣ	ⲛⲓⲙ' · ϭⲉⲡⲏ	ⲟⲙ [
[ⲉⲃⲟⲗ] ⲭⲉⲁⲡ̄ⲧ̄-	ⲁⲥ ⲛ̄ⲥⲉⲧⲁⲕⲟ̄	ⲡⲱⲧ' ⲉⲣⲁⲧϥ	ⲟⲓⲟⲑ [ⲙ̄ⲡⲉ-]
[ⲟⲩⲭⲣⲏⲥ]ⲧⲓⲁ-	ⲭⲉⲁⲣⲧⲟⲛ' ·	ⲙ̄ⲡⲉⲑⲛⲥⲓ-	ⲑⲏ[ⲥⲓⲁⲥⲧⲩ-]
[ⲛⲟⲥ ⲟⲱ]ⲱⲧ	+ⲉⲓⲧⲉ' ⲟⲛⲟ̄ ⲛ̄-	ⲁⲥⲧⲩⲣⲓⲟⲛ' ·	ⲣ[ⲓⲟⲛ
[ⲁⲓⲭⲓ] ⲙ̄ⲡⲃⲁⲡ-	ⲟⲙⲏⲛⲧ: ⲉⲓ-	+ⲡⲱϫⲧ ⲡⲛⲉⲕ-	ⲥⲁⲟⲱ[ⲟⲕ]
[ⲧⲓ]ⲥⲙⲁ'	ⲧⲉ' ⲟⲛⲟ̄ ⲟⲣⲁⲧ'	ⲣⲙⲉⲓⲟⲟⲩⲉ'	ⲉⲃⲟⲗ' [ⲛⲛⲉⲕ-]
[ⲉⲡ]ⲣⲁⲛ' ⲙ̄-	ⲉⲓⲧⲉ' ⲛⲟⲩⲃ'	ⲟⲓⲑⲏ ⲙ̄ⲡⲉ-	ⲛⲟⲃⲉ' [ⲡⲛ̄ⲥ̄-]
[ⲡ]ⲉⲭ̄ⲥ̄ · ⲁⲓⲭⲓ	+ⲉⲥϣⲁⲛϣⲱ-	ⲭ̄ⲥ̄ · ⲟⲓⲟⲩⲉ'	ⲧⲙⲕ[ⲧⲟⲕ]
ⲡⲉⲕⲥⲱⲙⲁ'	ⲡⲉ ⲛ̄ⲥⲉⲣⲁⲥ	ⲉⲟⲟⲩⲛ' ⲟⲛ̄ⲧⲉⲕ-	ⲉⲣⲟⲟⲩ [ⲁⲅⲱ]
[ⲛ̄]ⲛⲟⲩⲧⲉ'	ⲛ̄ⲥⲉⲧⲁⲕⲟ̄	ⲙⲉⲥⲟ̄ⲛⲧ' ·	+ⲁⲛⲟⲕ' [ϯⲛⲁ-]
[ⲙⲛ̄]ⲡⲉⲕⲥⲛ̄ϥ̊'	+ϣⲁⲅⲟⲩⲟⲧϣⲟ[ⲩ]	ⲉⲕⲭⲱ' ⲙ̄ⲙⲟⲥ	ϣⲡ̄ ⲧⲱ[ⲣⲉ]
ⲛ̄ⲁⲭⲟⲟⲥ	ⲛ̄ⲕⲉⲥⲟⲡ' ⲛ̄-	ⲭⲉⲁⲓ̈ⲣⲛⲟⲃⲉ'	ⲛⲁⲕ' ϫ[ⲉⲛ-]
]ⲧ .	ⲥⲉⲁⲁⲩ' ⲛ̄ⲃⲣ̄-	ⲡϫⲟⲉⲓⲥ'	ⲛⲉⲕ[
	⟨sic⟩ ⲃⲉ' ⲛ̄ⲥⲉⲗⲟ̄	ⲕⲱ' ⲛⲁⲓ̈ ⲉⲃⲟⲗ'	
	ⲉⲩ[ⲙ]ⲟⲩⲧⲉ	ⲛ̄ⲛⲟⲃⲉ'	
	margin	ⲙ̄ⲡⲁⲟⲟⲩ'	
		ⲛ̄ϯⲛⲁⲟⲩⲱⲟ	
		[ⲁⲛ ⲉⲧⲟⲟ]ⲧ	

Fol. 7. P. 19. . . . thou . . . cry out, 'I too am a Christian (χρ.); I have received baptism (βάπ.) in the name of Christ; I have received Thy divine body (σῶμα) [and] Thy blood . . . . . shall say . . . . .

. . . thee because of thy evil deeds. Faith without works is barren (ἀργός).[1] I say once more that every vessel that is becoming old and perished is called useless (ἀργ.), be it (εἴτε) vessel of bronze or (εἴτε) vessel

[1] Jas. ii. 20.

of silver or (εἴτε) gold. If so be that they grow old and perished, they are molten again and made new and cease to be called

P. 20. perishable or (ἤ) perished.[1] Thou likewise, if thou know that thou art useless altogether (*lit.* on every side), hasten, flee unto the altar (θυσιαστήριον); pour forth thy tears before Christ; beat thy breast, saying, 'I have sinned; Lord, forgive me the sins of the past (*lit.* of behind); I will not continue ' . . . . .

. . . hast] groaned . . . before the altar (? θυσ.) . . . departed far from [thy] sins [and tu]rned not again unto them, I it is will go surety for thee, that thou do [not . . .

Fol. 8.　→ *Recto,*ᵃ p. ?　　　↑ *Verso*, p. ?

	margin		margin	
	† ⲁⲅⲁⲡⲏ̄' ⲛⲁⲩ'		ⲉⲡⲉⲥⲏⲧ'	
	ⲣ̄ⲭⲣⲓⲁ' ⲁⲛ'·		ⲉⲝ̄ⲙ̄ⲡⲟⲉⲓⲕ'	
]ⲡ̄ⲛ̄°	+ⲟⲩⲛ̄ⲑⲟⲉⲓⲛⲉ'		ⲙ̄ⲛ̄ⲡⲡⲟⲗⲏ-	
	ⲉⲩ†ⲡⲣⲟⲥ-		ⲣⲓⲟⲛ' ⲡ̄ϥⲥⲱ-	+ⲉ[
	ⲫⲟⲣⲁ' ⲉⲡⲏⲓ̈		ⲧⲙ̄ ⲛ̄ⲥⲱⲟⲩ'	
]ⲙ̄ⲙ̄	ⲙ̄ⲡⲛⲟⲩⲧⲉ'		ⲡ̄ϥⲉⲓ'· ⲉⲓⲝⲉ-	ϩ[
]ⲡⲛ̄ⲩ°	ⲉⲣⲉⲡⲉⲩϩⲏⲧ'		+ⲣⲟⲕ' ⲛ̄ⲧⲟⲕ'	ⲉⲓ[
[ⲧⲉ . ϣⲙ̈]ϩⲁⲗ'	ϭⲛ̄ ⲁⲣⲓⲕⲉ'		ⲱ̄ ⲡⲗⲁⲓ̈ⲕⲟⲥ'	ⲧⲁ[
]ϩⲱ	ⲉⲣⲟⲟⲩ' ⲝⲉ-		ⲙ̄ⲡⲣ̄ⲕⲣⲓⲛⲉ	ⲉⲣ[
]ⲕⲟⲩ	ⲛⲉⲧⲛ̄†		ⲛ̄ⲛⲉⲧⲉⲣⲉ-	+ϣⲁ[
]ⲡⲛⲁ'	ⲡⲣⲟⲥⲫⲟⲣⲁ'		ⲡⲛⲟⲩⲧⲉ'	ⲟϩ[
	ⲛⲁⲩ' ϩⲉⲛⲣⲉϥ-		ⲥⲱⲧⲙ̄' ⲉⲣⲟ-	ⲧ̣[
	ⲣ̄ⲛⲟⲃⲉ'ⲛⲉ'		ⲟⲩ'· ⲕⲁⲛ' ϩⲉ̄-	ⲧ̣[
ⲗ]ⲁⲁⲩ' ⲛⲁ-	ⲛ̄ⲧⲉϥϩⲉ' ⲉⲧⲉ-		+ⲣⲉϥⲣ̄ⲛⲟⲃⲉ'-	ⲧⲙ̣[
[ⲛⲟ]ⲩϩⲙ̈' ⲡⲣⲱ-	ⲛⲁⲉⲧⲟⲥ'ⲛⲉ'		ⲛⲉ' ⲙ̄ⲛ̄ⲧⲁⲕ-	ⲧⲉⲧⲱ[

ᵃ The traces of pagination here might be $\overline{\Lambda}$ and a second letter; not $\overline{\Lambda}$ and $\overline{\Lambda\alpha}$, since these would not, by rights, fall upon the same leaf.

[1] *Lit.* 'they that perish or that have perished'. It is not easy to reproduce this in idiomatic English.

[ⲙⲉ] ⲛ̄ⲥⲁⲧⲁ-	ⲉⲧⲟⲩⲁⲁⲃ'	ϩⲱⲃ' ⲛ̄ⲧⲟⲕ'	ⲛ̄ⲓ̈ⲉϩⲉ[ⲕⲓⲏⲗ]
[ⲥⲁ]ⲡ̄ⲏ̄ · ⲧⲁ-	ⲛ̄ⲕⲗⲏⲣⲓⲕⲟⲥ	ⲛ̄ⲧⲁⲩⲧⲁⲛ-	ⲉⲓ ⲉϫⲛ̄[ⲧⲏⲩ-]
[ⲥⲁⲡ]ⲏ̄ · ⲙⲉⲥ-	+ⲛⲁⲓ̈ ⲉϣⲁⲩ-	ϩⲟⲩⲧⲕ̄' ⲁⲛ'	ⲧⲛ̄' · ⲉ[ⲣⲉ-]
[ϣⲓ]ⲛⲉ' ⲛ̄ⲥⲁ-	ϫⲟⲟⲥ' ⲙ̄ⲡⲏⲩ°-	ⲉⲣⲟⲟⲩ' ⲉⲧⲣⲉⲕ-	+ⲡⲉⲥⲛⲟ[ϥ ⲙ-]
[ⲛ]ⲉⲧⲉⲡⲟⲩⲥ-	ⲧⲉ' ϩⲓⲧⲙ̄-	ⲡⲣⲉⲥⲃⲉⲩⲉ'	ⲡⲟⲩⲁ' [ⲡⲟⲩⲁ']
[ⲛⲉ ·] ⲟⲩⲛ̄-	ⲡϣⲁϫⲉ' ⲛ̄-	ϩⲁⲡⲉⲩⲛⲟⲃⲉ'	ⲛⲁⲉⲓ ⲉ[ϫⲛ-]
[ϩⲟⲉⲓⲛ]ⲉ ⲉⲩ-	ⲧⲉⲩⲧⲁⲡⲣⲟ	ⲁⲗⲗⲁ ⲛ̄ⲧⲁⲩ-	ⲧⲉϥ[
]ⲛ̄ ⲉⲣⲉ-	ⲛ̄ⲙ̄ⲙⲁⲧⲉ' ϫⲉ-	ⲧⲁⲛϩⲟⲩⲧⲟⲩ'	+ⲉⲧ[
	ⲕⲁⲧⲁϩⲓⲟⲩ	ⲉⲛⲉⲧⲛ̄ⲯⲩ-	
	ⲛ̄ⲙ̄ⲙⲟⲕ' ⲁⲙ-	ⲭⲏ̄' ⲉⲧⲣⲉⲩ-	
	[ⲟⲩ]		

Fol. 8. *Recto.* . . . nought shall save (?)[1] a man except charity (ἀγάπη). 'Charity seeketh not the things that are her own.'[2] There are [some] do . . . . .

. . . to whom charity (ἀγ.) is given that need (-χρεία) it not. There are some do make offering (προσφορά) at the house of God, whose heart accuseth them (saying,) 'Those unto whom we give offerings (πρ.) are sinful men like unto us,' that is, the holy eagles (ἀετός)[3] the clergy (κληρικός), that do say unto God, with the mere words of their mouth, 'Be favourable (καταξιοῦν), come

(*Verso*) down upon the bread and the cup (ποτήριον),' and He heareth them and doth come. I say unto thee,[4] O layman (λαικός), judge (κρίνειν) not them whom God heareth,[5] even (κᾶν) be they sinful men : thou hast nought (to do with that). Hast thou been entrusted with them, that thou shouldest intercede (πρεσβεύειν) for their sins? Rather (ἀλλά) have they been entrusted with your souls (ψυ.), that they may . . . . .

. . . to (?) Ezekiel [shall] come upon you.[6] The blood of [each] one shall come u[pon] his [[7] . . . . .

---

[1] If so, ⲛⲉϩⲙ is required. But this scribe is not very accurate.   [2] I Cor. xiii. 5.

[3] Cf. *Can. Athanas.* p. 16, where the same simile is used. A sermon on Epiphany (Paris 131⁴, 114 = MS. of Br. Mus. no. 257 &c.) refers to flapping (ⲧⲁⲁⲧⲉ) their wings around the body

(σῶμα) '.

[4] *V.* p. 65 note.

[5] The difference achieved by the varying preposition is between mere *hearing* here and *acquiescing, obeying* in the preceding sentence.

[6] V. Ezek. iii. 18.

[7] ? 'hand'; *cf.* Ezek., *l. c.*

Fol. 9. ↑ *Recto.*   → *Verso.*

ⲍⲉ [ⲙ̄ⲡⲉϥϫⲟ-]

ⲟⲩ]ⲕⲟⲩⲛ̄   ⲟⲥ' ⲍⲉ[ⲁⲕⲁϩ-]   ]ϥⲧⲁ-   ⲙⲁ[

[ⲁⲧⲉ]ⲧⲛ̄ⲉⲓ-   ⲉⲣⲁⲧⲕ̄ [ⲛ̄ⲥⲁ-]   ]ϥⲥⲙⲟⲩ'   ϯⲛⲁⲛⲟ[ⲩ ⲅⲁⲣ]

ⲙⲉ ᵃ ⲱ̄ ⲛⲁ-   ϩⲃⲟⲩ[ⲣ ⲙ̄ⲡϩⲏ-]   ]ⲣ' · ⲉⲓⲉ   ϯ' ⲁⲅⲁⲡⲏ [

ⲙⲉⲣⲁⲧⲉ' ⲍⲉ-   ⲕⲉ' · ⲁ[ⲗⲗⲁ]   [ⲛ̄ⲥ]ⲱⲧⲙ̄' ⲁⲛ'   ⲛⲟⲩⲁ' ⲛ̄ϭ[ⲟⲩⲟ]

ⲧⲉⲧⲉⲣⲧ[.]   ϯ[ⲁ]ϥϫⲟⲟⲥ ᵈ   [ⲍⲉϣⲁ]ⲣⲉⲡⲉⲧ-   ⲉⲣⲟⲥ' ⲉⲕ[ϣⲁⲛ-]

ⲟⲙ̣ⲡⲟⲩⲁ   [ⲍⲉ]ⲁⲕⲁϩ'-   [ϯ ⲛ]ⲟⲩϩ[ⲛⲕⲉ]'   ϫⲓ ⲛ̄ⲧⲟ[ⲟⲧ ᵉ

]ⲙⲟϥ'   [ⲉⲣ]ⲁⲧⲕ̄ ⲛ̄ⲥⲁ-   ϯ ϩⲁⲧ' ⲉ[ⲙⲏ]-   ⲛ̄ⲕⲟⲧ[

] ⲙ̄ⲙⲟϥ' ·   [ⲟ]ⲩⲛⲁⲙ' ⲙ̄-   ⲥⲉ' ⲙ̄ⲡⲛ[ⲟⲩ-]   ϯⲉⲓⲉ ⲛ[

] ⲉⲧϭⲓⲝ'   ⲡⲟⲏⲕⲉ' ·   ⲧⲉ' · ⲉⲓⲉ [ⲉⲓ-]   ϩⲁⲙ[

[ⲙ̄ⲡⲉ]ⲭ̄ⲥ̄ ⲓ̄ⲥ̄ ·   ϯ[ⲉ]ⲡⲉⲓⲇⲏ ⲣⲱ-   ⲥⲱⲧⲙ̄ ⲁⲛⲟⲕ   ⲍⲉ[

[ⲡⲉⲛ]ϫⲟⲉⲓⲥ ᵇ   ⲙⲉ' ⲛⲓⲙ' ⲉϥϯ   ⲍⲉⲉϥ ⲟⲥⲱⲛ   ⲧⲉ' ⲧ[

]ⲥⲱⲧⲙ̄   ϩ[ⲛ̄]ⲧⲉϥϭⲓⲝ   ⲁⲧⲉⲧⲛⲁⲁ[ⲥ]   ⲁⲩ · [

]ⲡⲉⲓⲁ ᶜ   [ⲛⲟⲩ]ⲛⲁⲙ'   ⲛⲟⲩⲁ' ⲛ̄[ⲛ]ⲉⲓ-   ⲥ[

[ⲉϥϫⲱ] ⲙ̄ⲙⲟⲥ'ϯϩ[ⲙ̄ⲡ]ⲧⲣⲉϩ̄ⁿ⁻   ⲕⲟⲩⲓ [ⲁⲛⲟⲕ]   ⲉⲕ[

[? ⲛ̄ⲧⲉⲓ]ϩⲉ   ⲕⲉ ⲥⲟⲟⲩⲧⲛ̄   ⲡⲉⲛⲧ[ⲁⲧ]ⲉⲧⲛ-   ϯⲉⲓ[ⲉ

]ⲟⲩ   ⲉⲃⲟⲗ ⲛ̄ⲧⲉ[ϥ-]   ⲁⲁⲥ' ⲛ[ⲁⲓ]   ⲍⲉ[

margin   ϭⲓⲝ' ⲉϫⲓ ·   [ϯⲉ]ⲧⲃⲉⲡⲁⲓ ⲉⲕ-   ⲉ[

                margin   ϣⲁⲛⲣⲟⲩⲡⲉⲧ-   ⲁ[

                          ϩⲟⲟⲩ' ⲛ̄ⲟⲩ-   margin

ᵃ Or ⲙⲡⲉⲧⲛⲉⲓⲙⲉ.   ᵇ This reading unlikely if the stop after ⲓ̄ⲥ̄ is correct. *Cf. vo.*, col. 1, ll. 3, 4 ⲉⲓⲉ.   ᶜ ? ⲁⲁ]ⲅⲉⲓⲁ.   ᵈ Or ⲁ[ⲗⲗⲁ ⲛ̄][ⲧⲁϥ-.   ᵉ Or ⲛ̄ⲧⲟⲕ.

Fol. 9. *Recto.* . . . Do ye then not (οὔκουν) know, O my beloved, that . . . . the hand of Christ Jesus [our] Lord . . . . . hear David (?), speaking thus, ...

. . . [He hath not] said, 'Thou hast stood at the left of the poor,' but (ἀλλά) he said,[1] 'Thou hast stood at the right of the poor.' Since (ἐπειδή) every man that giveth with his right hand, when the poor stretcheth forth his hand to receive . . . . .

---

[1] Ps. cviii. 31. But no text or version that I can find reads 2nd pers. thus, for 3rd.

Verso. ... bless(ing ?) ... Dost thou then not hear that[1] 'He that giveth unto a poor (man), lendeth at usury unto God ? ' I indeed do (?) hear that[2] 'Inasmuch as (ἐφ' ὅσον) ye have done it unto one of these little ones, it is unto me ye have done it.' Wherefore if thou do evil unto a (?) . . . . .

... [? For (γάρ)] it is better to give charity (ἀγ.) than if thou receive from (?)[3] . . . . .

Fol. 10. → *Recto.*   ↑ *Verso.*

margin   margin

Recto		Verso	
	ⲙⲛⲧ' ⲛ̄ⲅⲟⲗⲟ-	ⲕⲁⲛ' ⲟⲩⲣⲙ̄[ⲙⲁⲟ-]	
	ⲕⲟⲧⲓⲛⲟⲥ'	ⲡⲉ' ϣⲁϥⲧⲁ-	
	ⲛ̄ⲁⲥⲁⲡⲏ ⲧⲣ̄ⲣⲟ-	ⲁϥ' ⲛⲁϥ · ⲁϥ-	
	ⲣⲟⲙⲡⲉ' ⲟⲩⲁ'	†ⲧⲱⲟⲩⲛ̄' ⲛ̄-	
	ⲕⲁⲧⲁ ⲟⲩⲟⲉⲓϣ ·	ⲡⲉⲓϩⲟⲟⲩ' ⲁϥ-	
	†ⲁϥⲥⲱⲧⲙ̄'	ⲁⲡⲁⲛⲧⲁ' ⲉⲩ-	
	ⲉⲡⲁⲅⲗⲟⲥ'	ⲛⲟϭ' ⲛ̄ⲣⲙ̄ⲙⲁⲟ	
	ⲉϥϫⲱ' ⲙ̅ⲙ̅ⲥ̊	ϩⲛ̄ⲧⲡⲟⲗⲓⲥ'	
]ⲁⲧ-	ϫⲉⲙⲉⲣⲉⲧⲁ-	ⲁϥⲙⲟⲟϣⲉ'	
[ⲁⲡⲏ ⲁ]ⲗⲗⲁ'	ⲧⲁⲡⲏ' ϣⲓⲛⲉ'	ⲉⲣⲟϥ' ⲛ̄ϩⲱⲡ'	
]?	ⲛ̄ⲥⲁⲛⲉⲧⲉ-	ⲁϥⲧⲁⲁϥ'	
	ⲛⲟⲩⲥⲛⲉ ·	ⲛⲁϥ' · ⲙ̄ⲡ-	
	†ϣⲁϥⲧⲱⲟⲩ[sic]	†ⲛ̄ⲥⲁⲧⲣⲉϥ-	
]ⲥ	ⲉϩⲧⲟⲟⲩⲉ'	ⲧⲁⲁϥ ⲛⲁϥ'	[
ⲛ̄ϥⲣ̄ⲭⲣⲓⲁ'	ϩⲙ̄ⲡⲉϩⲟⲟⲩ'	ⲁϥⲥⲟⲩⲱⲛϥ̄' ·	†ⲁϥⲥⲟ[
[ⲁⲛ] ⲥⲱⲧⲙ'	ⲉⲧϥ̄ⲛⲁ†-	†ⲁϥϭⲱ' ⲉϥⲁⲓ-	ⲟⲛ' · ⲁ[ⲩⲱ]
ⲧⲁⲧⲁⲙⲟⲕ'	ⲁⲅⲁⲡⲏ ⲛ̄-	ⲁⲕⲣⲓⲛⲉ' ϩⲙ̄-	†ⲉⲣⲉⲡⲉⲓ[ⲙⲉ-]
[ⲙ]ⲡⲉⲓϩⲱⲃ'	ϩⲏⲧϥ̄' ϣⲁϥ-	ⲡⲉϥϩⲏⲧ'	ⲉⲩⲉ' † [ⲙⲙ-]
[ⲛ̄]ϣⲟⲩⲣ-	†ⲃⲱⲕ' ⲉⲃⲟⲗ'	ϫⲉⲟⲩⲣⲙ̄ⲙⲁⲟ̄-	ⲙⲁϥ' · ϩ[ⲟ-]
[ϣⲏ]ⲣⲉ' ⲛ̄-	ϩⲙ̄ⲡⲉϥⲏⲓ'	ⲡⲉ ⲡⲁⲓ̈ ⲡⲁ-	†ⲙⲟⲓϣ[ⲥ
[ⲙⲟϥ ·] ⲛⲉⲩ-	†ⲡϣⲟⲣⲡ̄' ⲛ̄-	ⲣⲁⲣⲟⲓ̈ · ⲁⲛⲟⲕ'	ⲁϥ† [ⲡⲉϥ-]

[3] Or 'if thou thyself receive.'

---

[2] Matt. xxv. 40. Note the reading.

[ноүр]шаеʼ   ршаеʼ етϥ-   [+]етр̄хрıаʼ п̄-   оү[оı
]нс·̣   нааꙥанта   ẍı агапн̄ʼ п̄-   [
            ероϥʼ кан   тоотϥ ·

† що-]   [о]үѳнкеʼп[еʼ]   [+]п̄п̄п̄сшс [
    margin   margin

Fol. 10. *Recto.* ... hath [not] need (χρεία). Hearken and I will tell thee this thing, worthy of wonder. There was a man . . . . . ? was wont to give] three *solidi* (ὁλοκ.) in charity (ἀγάπη) yearly, one at (κατά) a time. He heard Paul saying,[1] 'Charity (ἀγ.) seeketh not the things that are her own.' He would arise in the morning on the day whereon he should do charity (ἀγ.), and would go forth from his house; the first man that he should meet (ἀπαντᾶν), whether (κἄν) he were a poor man, (*Verso*) or (κἄν) a rich, he would give it (*sc.* the *solidus*) unto him. He arose that day and met (ἀπ.) a great rich man of the city (πόλις) and he went toward him stealthily and gave it unto him. After that he had given it unto him he knew him, and stayed doubting (διακρίνειν) in his heart (saying), 'This man is richer than (παρά) I. It is I have need (χρεία) to receive charity (ἀγ.) at his hands.' Afterwards . . . . .

... and these thoughts contended with him. Likewise (ὁμοίως[2]) he betook himself (?) . . . . .

Fol. 11. → *Recto.*   ↑ *Verso.*

    margin   margin

]с̣о[ẍетг̄еннс[ıсʼ]   епıаʼ · ẍе-   [
] еросʼ аϥ-   п̄ашⲩ̈снсʼ   +пıаʼ етеп̄п̄-
            +каı гарʼ п̄ке-   нолосʼ п̄п̄-
            еıо̄теʼ п̄таү-   параѳасıсʼ ·
            ẍпе лшⲩ̈-   +пеẍаϥʼ ẍе-
            снсʼ п̄поү-   п̄лон п̄-
            щшпеʼ ϩп̄-   теıϩеʼ ан’-
            тг̄еннсıсʼ   те тпара-
            [. .]ѧпетшш   ѳасıс [
            ]тнр̄с̄   +е. ас п̄т[

-----
[1] 1 Cor. xiii. 5.   [2] Ὅμως 'however' would seem more suitable.

Fol. 11. *Recto.* ... the Genesis (γέν.) of Moses. For (καὶ γάρ) the parents too that begat Moses were not in Genesis, but (? ἀλλά) all that .....

Verso. ... to (?) whom? 'Where there is not law, there is not transgression.' He said, 'Nay[1]; the transgression (παράβασις) is not of this sort .....

Fol. 12. → *Recto.*   ↑ *Verso.*

ⲧⲥ̅’ ⲁⲛⲡⲉ	+[. . .]ⲛⲛⲟⲃⲉ ·
+ⲉⲧⲃⲉⲡⲁⲓ̈	ⲉⲧⲃⲉⲭⲉⲁⲩ-
ⲁⲡⲁⲅⲗⲟⲥ’	ϯ ⲡⲛⲟⲙⲟⲥ’
ⲱϣ ⲉⲃⲟⲗ’	ⲛⲁϥ’ ⲁϥⲡⲁⲣⲁ’-
ϫⲉⲡⲙⲁ’ ⲉⲧⲉ-	ⲃⲁ’ ⲙ̅ⲙⲟϥ ·
ⲙ̅ⲡ̅ⲛⲟⲙⲟⲥ	+ⲡⲙⲁ’ ⲉⲧⲉ-
ⲙ̅ⲡ̅ⲡⲁⲣⲁⲃⲁ-	ⲙ̅ⲡ̅ⲛⲟⲙⲟⲥ’
ⲥⲓⲥ’ · ϩⲟⲙⲟⲓ-	ⲙ̅ⲡ̅ⲡⲁⲣⲁⲃⲁ-
+ⲱⲥ’ ⲟⲛ’ ϩⲣⲟⲩ-	ⲥⲓⲥ · ⲉⲓⲥ ⲟⲩ-
ⲃⲏⲛ’ ⲛ̅ⲧⲁϥ-	+ⲏ̅ⲣ̅ ⲛⲉⲧⲛⲁ-
ⲉⲛⲕⲟⲧⲕ̅	ϣⲱⲡⲉ’ ⲙ̅-
ⲙ̅ⲡ̅ⲑⲁⲙⲁ[ⲣ] *sic*	ⲙⲟⲛ’ ⲁⲛⲟⲛ’
ⲑⲓⲙⲉ’ ⲙ̅[ⲡⲉϥ-]	ⲛⲉⲭⲣⲏⲥⲧⲓ̈-
ⲉⲓⲱⲧ [ⲁⲅⲱ]	[ⲁⲛ]ⲟⲥ’ · ⲉⲓⲥ
ⲁ̣ⲃ̣ⲓⲙⲉⲗ[ⲉⲭ]	[ⲛ]ⲉⲩⲁⲅⲅⲉⲗⲓ-
ⲛ̅ⲧⲁϥⲉ[ⲡⲓ-]	ⲟⲛ’ ⲁⲩⲧⲁⲁϥ’
ⲑⲩⲙⲉⲓ̄’ · [ⲁⲅⲱ]	ⲉⲧⲟⲟⲧ̅ⲛ̅ ·
+ⲡⲕ’ⲉⲥⲉ[ⲉⲡⲉ]	[ⲉ]ⲓⲥ ⲛⲉⲥⲃⲟ-
ⲛ̅ⲧⲁϥ[	[ⲟ]ⲩⲉ’ ⲛ̅ⲛⲉⲛ-
+ ?	[ⲉⲓ]ⲟⲧⲉ ⲉⲧⲟⲩ-
	[ⲁⲁ]ⲃ’ ⲛⲁⲡⲟⲥ-
	[ⲧⲟⲗⲟⲥ

(margin) ... *(margin)*

Fol. 12. *Recto.* ... not ... it. For this cause did Paul cry out, 'Where there is not law, there is not transgression (παρ.). Likewise (ὁμοίως) also

[1] Or 'Verily'.

Reuben, when he lay with Thamar,[1] his father's wife, [and] Abimelek, when he coveted [2] (ἐπιθυμεῖν), and the rest, when they . . . . .

   Verso. . . . sin, because the law (νόμ.) hath (had?) been given him and he hath (had?) transgressed (παραβαίνειν) it. 'Where there is not law, there is not transgression (παρ.).' Lo, how much shall not be ours,[3] we Christians (χρ.)? Lo, the Gospels (εὐ.) have been given unto us; lo, the teachings of our holy fathers the apostles (ἀπ.) . . . . .

Fol. 13.   → *Recto* (?).   ↑ *Verso* (?).

ноχоγ ñса'-			пωн а[ппе ·]
ʙoλ' ᵹ̄ᵹ̄ᵹ̄ωⲟⲛ ·		]пωⲟγ	+алнѳⲱс'
+oγōⲉ̄ı · oγōı	ϣа[	]псⲱⲙⲉ'	намерате'
oγн̄р̄'нⲉ п̄-	ⲉχ[	]таас̄ϥ'	ⲉретᵹ̄пнꙮⲩ-
ᵹıсⲉ' ⲉтсⲉ-	ⲥıн[	]аγϥı	тⲉ' к̄ⲱ' нан'
ⲉт' ⲉроⲛ ·	+апо[	]oγ' аγ-	ⲉʙoλ' ᵹ̄п̄-
+ⲉϣχⲉ аγⲙⲟγ-	ᵹıⲥ[	]χⲉᵹ̄-	oγа' ñoγⲱт'
oγ̄т̄ ᵹ̄паї	нан[	]аᵹᵹⲉ'	ᵹ̄нтⲉıᵹⲉнеа'
ñтаγⲥ̄ñт̄ϥ	oγⲟ[	] . . . γ	наoγχаı
ⲉϥⲥ̄λϣⲉ' ᵹ̄п̄-	п̄т[	]пⲉⲉγ [a]	ⲉнколаⲥıⲥ'
тⲥⲱϣⲉ ·	ⲟϣ[	ñа]ϣ ñⲥ̄т̄	ᵹ̄пϣнрⲉ'
+ⲉıⲉ oγⲙⲟγ'	ⲟ꙳'[	[пⲉтна]таᵹⲟ̄'	ᵹ̄пноγтⲉ ·
ñаϣ' ñⲥⲟт'	тᵹ̄[	]ⲟλ' χıн-	+пⲙа' ⲉтⲉᵹ̄п̄-
пⲉтната-	oγ[	[ᵹтооγ]ⲉ' ϣа-	номос ᵹ̄п̄-
ᵹⲟⲛ' · oγōı	ⲉт[	[роγᵹⲉ] ᵹ̄ᵹ̄н-	параʙаⲥıⲥ' ·
+oγⲟ̄ⲉ̄ı χⲉтⲛ̄-	пра[ⲛ ᵹ̄пноγ-]	[ⲛпⲉ] ⲉϣχⲉ-	+ⲉпⲉ ᵹ̄пⲉıⲉı
фoрⲉı ñoγ-	тⲉ[	]oγ'	таϣаχⲉ'
ⲥхнⲙа' ñ-		]γ' р̄ⲱ'	ᵹ̄пⲛкос-
аᵹᵹⲉλıкⲟⲛ'			ⲙⲟⲥ' нⲉᵹ̄н̄-
анᵖ нⲉᵹʙнγⲉ'			ноʙⲉ' ⲉрⲟoγ'
			margin

         [a] Perhaps o]ꙟ[рп]ⲙⲉⲉγ[ⲉ.

[1] A mistake for Bilhah; *v.* Gen. xxxv. 22 (21). Yet palaeographically ʙaλλa and ѳaⲙa[ᵖ] might well be confused.

[2] Gen. xx. 2.

[3] I suppose this to mean, 'How great punishments shall not be ours?'

Fol. 13. *Recto* (?). . . . cast them forth from us. Woe, woe! How great are the troubles that await us. If they slew this (man) whom they had found gathering wood[1] in the field, what manner of death, then, is it shall overtake us? Woe, woe! For we wear (φορεῖν) an angelic (ἀγγελικός) habit (σχῆμα) and have done the deeds [of . . . . .

Verso (?). . . . the garden . . . . What manner of [remembr]ance (?) [is it shall] overtake us? . . . . . .[2] from . . . till . . ., da[ily.] If . . . . that are] not ours (?). Verily (ἀληθῶς), my beloved, unless God forgive us, there shall not a single one from this generation (γενεά) be saved from the punishment (κόλασις) of the Son of God. 'Where there is not law, there is not transgression.' 'If[3] I had not come and talked with the world (κόσ), they had been guilty of no sin' . . . . .

No. 10.

From a Sermon, treating here of repentance, as exemplified by Nebuchadnezzar. Repentance is apostrophized similarly in a sermon by Theophilus (Budge, *Copt. Hom.* 69).

Fol. 1. → *Recto.*

ⲧ[
ϣ[
ⲙ̄ⲡⲉⲣ[
ⲭⲱⲣⲓⲥ [
ⲥⲱⲧⲙ [ⲉⲧⲙⲉⲧⲁⲛⲟⲓⲁ]
? [
ϩⲣⲁⲓ ϣⲁⲧ[
ⲛ̄ⲛⲉⲧⲡⲏ[ⲧ ⲉ]ⲣⲁⲧⲥ
ⲥⲱⲧⲙ ⲉⲧⲙⲉⲧⲁⲛⲟⲓⲁ
ⲧⲉⲧⲥⲱⲧⲉ ⲉⲃⲟⲗ ⲛ̄-   ⲉ[
ⲛⲉⲛⲧⲁⲅⲣⲁⲁⲥ ϩⲛ̄-   ϩⲟ[

↑ *Verso.*

]ⲧⲉⲧⲛ-
]ⲁ
]ⲧⲥ
]ⲁⲗ ⲙⲙ-
]ⲛⲧ . . ⲧ
]ⲣ
[. .]ⲛ . ⲣⲟ . ⲙ .
[. .]ⲁⲩ . ⲛ . . ⲁⲓ ϥ-
]ⲃⲟ .   [. .]ⲧⲟ[ⲗ]ⲙⲏⲣⲟⲥ̄
] ?   ⲉⲓ ⲟⲩⲱ[ⲛ]ϩ ⲉⲃⲟⲗ
]ⲟⲥ ⲉⲓ   ⲛ̄ⲛⲉⲛⲧⲁⲕϣⲱ-

---

[1] Num. xv. 30 (32). ϭⲗϣⲉ in Zoega, 337 = συλλέγειν ξυλα in Σ Ɔ. ⲟϩ, ⲟϥ. xxix. 11 ≈ ξυλοκόπος, also Zoega 487 *ult.*

[2] Perhaps 'We lie (ϫⲓϭⲟⲗ) from morn till

[3] John xv. 22. Note the reading.

ⲧⲕⲁⲕⲓⲁ · ⲥⲱⲧⲙ   ⲕ[   ]ⲁⲅⲣⲟⲗ-   ⲡⲉ ⲛ̀ϩⲏⲧⲟⲩ ⲙ-
ⲉⲧⲙⲉⲧⲁⲛⲟⲓⲁ ⲉⲧⲟ   ⳾ ⲧⲙⲉⲧⲁⲛⲟⲓⲁ   [ⲗⲟ ⲟ̅ⲛⲛⲉⲩⲛ]ⲟⲃⲉ   ⲙⲟⲛ ⲛⲛⲉⲥϣⲱ-
ⲛϣⲃⲏⲣ ⲉⲛⲁⲅⲅⲉ-   ⲧⲣ[ⲛ]ⲕⲉⲥⲟⲡ   ⲡⲉ · ⲁⲗⲗⲁ ⲉⲓ̈ⲧⲁ-
ⲗⲟⲥ ⲙ̅ⲡⲛⲟⲩⲧⲉ   ϩ̅[[⳾ ⲧⲙⲉⲧⲁⲛⲟ]ⲓ̈ⲁ   ⲙⲟ ⲛⲟⲩⲟⲛ ⲛⲓⲙ
⳾ ⲧⲙⲉⲧⲁⲛⲟⲓ̈ⲁ ⲡⲟ-   ⲫ[   ]ⲉⲛ   ⲉⲧⲟⲩⲱϣ ⲉⲱ-
ⲉⲓ̈ⲕ ⲛⲕⲁⲑⲁⲣⲱ̅ⲛ   ⲟⲩ[ⲡⲛ]ⲧ ⲉⲣⲁⲧⲥ   ⲛϩ ⲛⲕⲉⲥⲟⲡ ϭⲓ̈-
[ⲉ]ⲧⲥⲁⲁⲛϣ ⲛ[....   ⲡⲟ̣[   ]ⲡⲛ ..   ⲧⲛⲧⲙⲉⲧⲁⲛⲟⲓ̈ⲁ
       ]ⲏⲩ[[.]ⲧⲛⲛⲉ[
                                                             ϣ[

Fol. 1. *Recto*. ... Hearken [unto Repentance (μετ.) .... them that betake themselves to her. Hearken unto Repentance, she that cleanseth (*lit.* wipeth out) such as are old in wickedness (κακία). Hearken unto Repentance, that is a fellow unto the angels (ἄγγ.) of God. O Repentance, pure (καθαρός) bread which nourisheth .....

... O Repentance, ...

Verso. ...that] are grown old [in their] sins ... once more. [O Repentan]ce ..... flee unto .....

... bold (τολμηρός), whilst I show forth the state that thou wast in. Nay; so shall it not be. Rather (ἀλλά) I tell every one that would live again through Repentance .....

Fol. 2. ↑ *Recto*.   → *Verso*.

     margin   margin

ⲁⲁϥ [[.....] ⲙⲛⲛⲁ-
ⲛⲁⲓ̈ · ⲁ[ⲧⲉⲧⲛ-]   [..]ϭⲟⲙ ⲙ̅ⲡⲛⲟⲩ-
ⲥⲱⲧⲙ ⲉⲡⲥⲟ-   ⲧⲉ ⲁⲩⲱ ⲁϥⲡⲱⲧ
ⲡⲥ ⲛ̅ⲇⲁⲛⲓ̈ⲏⲗ   ⲉⲣⲁⲧⲥ ⲛ̅ⲧⲙⲉⲧⲁⲛⲟ[ⲓ-]
ⲉⲧⲃⲉⲧⲭⲟⲩⲧⲟⲩⲉ   ⲁ · ⲁϥⲟⲩⲱⲛϩ ⲉ-
ⲡⲣⲟⲙⲡⲉ ⲛ-   ⲃⲟⲗ ⲛ̅ⲧⲉϥⲙⲛ[ⲧⲁⲧ-]
[ⲧⲁⲩ]ϩⲟⲣⲓⲍⲉ ⲙ-   ϭⲟⲙ · ⲁⲩⲱ [
[ⲙⲟⲥ ⲛ]ⲁϥ ⲉⲛ-   ⲥⲙ̅ⲛ[
[.....]ⲧⲟⲩⲥ   ⲙ[

Fol. 2. *Recto.* . . . [Ye] have heard the prayer of Daniel concerning the one and twenty years[1] that had been fixed (ὁρίζειν) for him . . . . .

Verso. . . . power of God, and he betook himself unto Repentance (μετ.) and displayed his weakness. And . . . . .

Fol. 3. ↑ *Recto.*　　　　　　　　　→ *Verso.*

margin		margin
а]ϥтрєтоι-		ϫ ι -]
к[ογ]ⲙⲉⲛⲏ ⲧⲏⲣⲥ		ⲧϥ [ⲉⲃⲟⲗ[a] ϩⲙ-]
ⲟⲩⲱϣⲧ ⲛⲁϥ		ⲡⲙⲁ ⲉⲧϥⲟⲧⲡ
ϩⲱⲥ ⲛⲟⲩⲧⲉ ⲁⲩ[ⲱ]		ⲉϩⲟⲩⲛ ⲉⲣⲟϥ
ⲡⲁϊ ⲛⲧⲉϊⲙⲓⲛ[ⲉ]		ⲁϥϯ ⲛⲁϥ ⲙ-
ⲛⲧⲉⲣⲉⲡⲉϥϩⲏ[ⲧ]		ⲡⲉϥⲉⲟⲟⲩ ⲛ-
ⲉⲛϣⲟⲧ ⲉⲣⲟϥ		ϣⲟⲣⲡ ⲁⲩⲟⲡϥ
ⲛⲟⲉ ⲙⲡϩⲏⲧ		ⲙⲛⲛⲉϥⲉⲓⲟⲧⲉ
ⲛ[		ⲁⲧⲉⲧⲛⲛⲁⲩ ⲱ
		[ⲛⲁⲥⲛⲏⲩ] ϫⲉⲟⲩ-

[a] Or ⲛⲧϥ ⲉϩⲣⲁⲓ.

Fol. 3. *Recto.* . . . caused all the world (οἰκουμένη) to worship him as (ὡς) God. And the aforesaid (king), after that his heart had been hardened, like the heart of . . . . .

Verso. . . . he brought ?] him [forth from] the place wherein he was confined and gave unto him his former honour, and he was reckoned unto his fathers. Ye have seen, O [my brethren ?,] how . . . . .

Fol. 4. ↑ *Recto.*　　　　　　　→ *Verso.*

margin　　　　　　　　　　　　　margin

ϫⲉ[ⲛⲧⲟⲕ ⲡⲭⲟ-]　　　　　ⲟⲩ̄ sic

]ⲛⲟⲩ　ⲉⲓⲥ ⲡ[　　　　　ⲙ]ⲛ̄ϭⲟⲙ

　　ⲥⲉ ⲛϣⲁⲛⲟⲧⲛϥ　　ⲙⲙⲟⲓ ⲉϭⲱϣⲧ

　　ⲁⲩⲱ ⲛϩⲁⲣϣ　　　ⲉϩⲣⲁⲓ ⲉⲧⲡⲉ ⲉⲧ-

　　ϩⲏⲧ ⲉⲛⲁϣⲉ　　　ⲃⲉⲡⲁϣⲁⲓ ⲛ[ⲛⲁ-]

　　ⲡⲉⲕⲛⲁ · ⲉⲕϯ　　ϫⲓⲛϭⲟⲛⲥ [ϩⲛ-]

　　ⲙⲉⲧⲁⲛⲟⲓⲁ ⲛⲛ̄-ᵃ　ⲟⲩⲙⲉ ⲁⲓϯ ϭⲱ-

　　ⲣⲉ[ϥⲣ]ⲛⲟ[ⲃⲉ] ⲧⲏ-　ⲛⲧ ⲛⲁⲕ ϯⲥⲟⲡ[ⲥ]

　　ⲣⲟ[ⲩ　　　　　　ⲙⲙⲟⲕ ⲉⲓ̈ⲙ[

　　　　　　　　　　ϩⲛⲟⲩⲙⲏⲛ[ϣⲉ

ᵃ A 3rd ⲛ precludes the proposed restitution.

Fol. 4. *Recto.* . . . (saying,) [Thou] Lord, . . . merciful and longsuffering, whose mercy is great. Thou givest repentance (μετ.) unto all sinners (?) . . . . .

Verso. . . . I am not able to look up to heaven by reason of the multitude of my iniquities. Verily I have angered Thee. I entreat Thee, . . . -ing with many . . . . .

Fol. 5. ↑ *Recto.*　　　　　　　→ *Verso.*

margin　　　　　　　　　　　　　margin

ⲙⲙⲟϥ ϩⲱⲧⲧⲏⲩ-　　ϣⲁϥϣⲱ · ᵃ ⲉⲙⲁⲩ

　ⲧⲛ ϫⲉⲛϩⲟⲥⲟⲛ　　sic ⲧ

　ⲉⲣⲉⲡⲣⲙⲙⲁⲟ ϫⲓ̈　　ⲛⲁⲗⲁⲁⲩ ⲛⲉⲧ-

　ⲛϩⲣⲁϥ ϩⲛⲛⲉⲓ̈ϫⲓ̈　ⲡⲱ —

　ϩⲣⲁϥ ⲧⲏⲣⲟⲩ —　　)Ⲡⲣⲙⲙⲁⲟ ϩⲱⲱϥ

margin　)ϣⲁⲣⲉⲟⲩϭⲉ ϣⲱ-　ⲉϥⲧⲛⲧⲱⲛ ⲉⲩ-

　ⲡⲉ ⲉⲣⲟϥ ⲉⲧⲉⲧⲁⲓ̈-　ⲛⲟϭ ⲛϫⲟⲓ ⲉⲣⲉⲡⲉϥ-　]ⲕⲉ

　ⲧⲉ ⲑⲁⲛ [ⲙ]ⲡⲉϥⲁ-　ⲁⲅⲉⲓⲛ ϩⲟⲣϣ ⲉⲙⲉϥ-　]ⲁⲧ

　ϩⲉ ⲛϥϯ ⲟⲥⲉ ⲙⲡⲉϥ-　[. . . . .] ϩⲛⲗⲁⲁⲩ　　　]ⲕ

　ⲱⲛϩ ⲧⲏⲣϥ —　　[ⲙ]ⲙⲁ ⲉⲓⲙⲏⲧⲉⲓ

　)Ⲟⲩⲛ ϩⲟⲉⲓⲛ ϩⲛⲛ-　ϩⲛⲡⲡⲉⲗⲁⲅⲟⲥ

　　　　　sic　　　　　ⲉⲧϣⲏⲕ ⲉϣⲁϥ-

　ϩⲁⲗⲁⲁⲧⲉ ⲙⲡⲕⲟⲥ-　ⲕⲓⲛⲁⲩⲛⲉⲩⲉ ⲛⲟⲩ-

　[ⲙ]ⲟⲥ ⲉⲣⲉⲛⲉⲩ[　　. ⲡ . ⲙⲱⲉᵇ ⲛⲥ[

ᵃ ϩⲱⲛ or ϩⲱⲗ.　　　　ᵇ ? ⲙⲏⲛϣⲉ.

Fol. 5. *Recto.* . . . ye also. For whilst (ὅσον) the rich man disporteth himself in all these sports, evening cometh upon him, which is the end of his lifetime, and he doth forfeit his whole life. There be some of the birds of the world (κόσ.) whose . . . are . . . . .

Verso. . . . will draw nigh (*or* fly) there, without any burden. But the rich man is like unto a great ship, whose freight ís heavy, (so that) it doth not . . . anywhere, except (εἰμήτι) in the deep sea (πέλαγος) and is in danger (κινδυνεύειν) of a . . . . .

No. II.

From a Sermon, treating here of charity and of the Good Samaritan.

→ *Recto.*

[ⲡⲧ]ⲙⲉⲣⲉ[ⲡⲉⲧⲟⲓ-]
ⲧⲟⲩⲱⲟⲩ [ⲛ̄ⲧⲉⲕ-]
ⲅⲉ ⲉϥⲧⲁⲙ[ⲟ ⲙ-]
ⲟⲛ ϫⲉϣϣ[ⲉ ⲉϯ]
ⲣ̄ⲧⲏⲕ̄ ⲉϫⲛ̄[ⲟⲩⲟⲛ]
ⲛⲓⲙ ⲉⲧⲕ̄ⲛⲁⲛⲁⲩ
ⲉⲣⲟⲟⲩ ϩⲛ̄ⲛⲉⲅⲁ-
ⲗⲁⲥⲕⲏ̄ ϩⲓⲧⲛ̄ⲛⲉⲓ-
ⲧⲟⲗⲏ ⲅⲁⲣ ⲉⲕ-
ⲓⲁⲟⲩⲱⲡ̄ⲅ̄ ⲉⲃⲟⲗ
ⲥⲉⲕⲙ̄ⲙⲉ ⲙ̄ⲡⲭⲟ-
ⲓⲥ ⲡⲉⲕⲛⲟⲩⲧⲉ
ⲙ̄ⲡⲉⲕϩⲏⲧ ⲧⲏⲣϥ̄
ⲃⲟⲗ ϫⲉⲉⲓⲛ̄ ϩⲁⲟ
ⲩ̄ϣⲁⲛ̄ⲛⲁⲩ ⲉⲟⲩⲁ̄
ⲉϣⲟⲟⲡ ϩⲛ̄ⲟⲉⲛ⁻ *sic*
.]ᵃ ⲉⲩⲟϣ′ ⲉⲓⲧⲉ
ⲩϣ]ⲱⲛⲉ ⲉⲓⲧⲉ ⲟⲩ-

ⲡⲧⲩ[ⲡⲟⲥ ⲙ̄ⲡⲟⲩⲏ-]
ⲏ̄ⲃ ᵇ ⲙ̄[ⲛ̄ⲡⲗⲉⲅⲓ-]
ⲧⲏⲅ̄ ⲛ[
ⲡⲉⲛⲧⲁⲩ[
ⲙ̄ⲉⲓ ⲙ̄ⲡ[
ⲉⲁⲩⲛⲁⲩ ⲉⲣ[ⲟϥ ⲁⲩ-]
ⲥⲁⲁⲧϥ̄ ⲙ̄ⲡⲟ[ⲩϣⲛ-]
ϩⲧⲏⲩ ϩⲁⲣⲟϥ [ⲟⲩ-]
ⲁⲉ ⲙ̄ⲡⲟⲩⲙ[ⲟⲩⲣ]
ⲛ̄ⲡⲉϥⲥⲁϣ [

↑ *Verso.*

]. ⲁⲉ ⲙ̄[
]. . ⲙ̄ⲡⲡ̄ⲁ-ᵈ
[ⲧⲟⲭ]ⲉⲩⲥ′ ⲁⲩⲱ ⲁϥ-
[ϩⲱ]ⲛ ⲉⲧⲟⲟⲧϥ̄
ϫⲉϥⲓ ⲡⲉϥⲣⲟⲟⲩϣ
ⲕⲁⲗⲱⲥ ⲡⲉⲧⲕ̄-
ⲛⲁϫⲟϥ′ ⲉⲃⲟⲗ ⲉⲣⲟ̄ϥ
ⲉⲓ ϣⲁⲛⲕⲧⲟⲓ ϯⲛⲁ-
ⲧⲁⲁϥ ⲛⲁⲕ ·
ⲁⲕⲛ̄ⲁⲩ ⲱ ⲡⲙ̄ⲉⲣ[ⲓⲧ]
ⲉⲧⲙ̄ⲛⲧϣⲁⲛϩ̄ⲧ[ⲏϥ]
ϫⲉϣⲁⲥϫⲱⲕ [ⲉ-]
ⲃⲟⲗ ϩⲓⲧⲛ̄ⲟⲩϩⲏⲣ
ⲛ̄ϩⲱⲃ · ⲟ[ⲩⲛⲟϭ]
ⲛ̄ⲕⲉⲫⲁⲗ[ⲁⲓⲟⲛ-]
ⲧⲉ ⲧⲙ̄ⲛⲧ[ϣⲁⲛ-]
ϩ̄ⲧⲏϥ ϣⲁⲝ[

] ?
]. ϩⲓⲧⲛ̄-
[ⲧⲙ̄ⲛ̄ⲧϣⲁ]ⲛϩ̄ⲧⲏϥ
[ⲉⲧⲛ̄ϩⲏⲧϥ̄]ⲧⲡⲉ ᶜ
]ⲉⲁϥⲙⲟⲩⲣ
[ⲛ̄ⲛⲉ]ϥⲥⲁϣ ⲁϥ-
[ⲡⲱ]ϩⲧ̄ ⲛ̄ⲟⲩⲛⲉϩ
[ⲙ̄ⲛ̄]ⲟⲩⲏⲣⲡ̄ ⲉϩⲣⲁⲓ
[ⲉϫ]ⲱϥ ⲁϥⲧⲁⲗϥ̄
[ⲉϫ]ⲙ̄ⲡⲉϥⲧⲃⲛⲏ
[ⲙ̄]ⲙⲓⲛ ⲙ̄ⲙⲟϥ

margin

margin

ᵃ ⲛ[ϣⲟⲧ], if the space would permit it, parenthetically, or ⲡⲉ[ⲭⲁϥ ϫ]ⲉ-. *V.* Luke x. 33, 34.

ᵇ *V.* Luke x. 31 ff.   ᶜ Or ⲡⲉ[ⲭⲁϥ],
ᵈ Probably ⲡⲁ̄ = ⲡⲁⲛ.

Recto. ... and thou] love thy neighbour as thyself,'[1] while he telleth us, 'Thou oughtest to give heed to every [one] whom thou seest in trouble (ἀνάγκη).'[2] For (γάρ) by means of these commandments (ἐντολή) shalt thou make manifest that thou dost love the Lord thy God with all thy heart. Because many there be that, when they see one in heavy difficulties (?), whether (εἴτε) an illness or (εἴτε) a . . . . .

... the manner (τύπος) of the priest and the Levite . . . ., when they had beheld him, they passed him by; they had not pity on him, neither (οὐδέ) did they bind up his wounds . . . . .

Verso. ... through the compassion that was in him, sai[th? he,] having bound up his wounds, he poured oil and wine upon him and set him upon his own beast . . . . .

... the innkeeper (πανδοχεύς). And he bade him, saying, 'Take well (καλῶς) care of him; whatever thou spendest, when I shall return, I will give it thee.' Thou hast seen, O beloved, by how many means (*lit.* things) compassion may be fulfilled. Compassion is a great matter (κεφάλαιον) . . . . .

No. 12.

Apparently from a Dialogue or ἐρωταπόκρισις concerning the interpretation of various passages in the Gospels.[3] The problems are stated by Anatolius (tolerably certain, *v.* fol. 2 *ro.*) and Militius (3 *ro.*, uncertain, for Meletius?), and solved by Ba . . . . (perhaps Bachius[4]). The bible texts incidental are for the most part paraphrased or loosely quoted. The sequence in foll. 2 and 3 is certain; the position of fol. 1 doubtful.

Fol. 1. ↑ *Recto.*

]ϫⲉ[ⲕ-]
ⲁⲥ ⲛϩⲟ]ⲅⲟ ⲛⲧⲉ-   ϥϫⲱ ⲙ[ⲙⲟⲥ]
[ⲛϩⲃⲏ]ⲅⲉ [a] ⲙⲡⲁ-   ϫⲉⲡⲉⲧⲛ[ⲁⲛⲟⲩⲥⲥ]

[a] My copy]ⲛⲉ.

→ *Verso.*

]ⲛϩⲁⲙ . [b   ⲛⲁ[
ⲙ]ⲡⲉⲕϭⲟ̄ ⲉⲃⲟⲗ   ⲡⲉⲛ[
[ϩⲙ]ⲡⲙⲁ ⲉⲧⲙⲙⲁⲩ   ⲡⲉⲡⲟⲥ[

b ⲉⲓⲱ ⲙ]ⲡⲉⲕ- or ⲉⲓⲁ]ⲡⲉⲕ-.

[1] Matt. xix. 19, xxii. 39, or Mark xii. 31.

[2] *Lit.* 'their troubles'.

[3] The literature of such dialogues is described by R. Nachtigall in *Arch. f. Slav. Philol.* xxiii, xxiv; Berendts in *T. u. U.*, N. F. xi. 34 ff.; and Heinrici in the Leipzig *Abhandl.*, Phil. hist. Kl., xxviii. But I have found nothing resembling the present fragments, either in names or contents.

[4] The obvious Basilius seems too long for the gap, fol. 2 *ro.*, l. 1, though not for *ib. vo.*, l. 8. Bachius is the name (1) of a writer of sermons (Zoega cclxv) and ? of an encomium on James the Persian martyr (to be presumed from the words quoted by Zoega cclxiv. The martyr's relics were in Egypt; *v. Synax.*, 27th Hathor); (2) of a priest in Palestine who converts a Samaritan in a λόγος of Pseudo-Cyril of Jerusalem (Brit. Mus. Or. 6799, abstract in *Synax.*, 17th Thot).

ειωτ ογωπ̅ϩ̅	ⲉⲡⲉϥⲥⲟⲛ [ⲉⲓⲕⲏ]	[ⲁⲅ]ⲱ ⲕⲛⲁⲛⲁⲩ ⲉ-	ⲡⲕⲁϩ ⲙⲡϣ[ⲟ-]
ⲉϐⲟⲗ ϩⲣⲁⲓ ⲛϧⲏⲧ-	ϥⲟ ⲛⲉⲛⲟⲭ[ⲟⲥ ⲉⲧⲉⲕ-]	[ϐⲟⲗ]· ϯϫⲱ ⲙⲙⲟ̅ⲥ̅	ⲣ̅ⲡ ⲛⲥⲟⲡ ⲙ[ⲛ̅-]
ⲧϥ̅· ⲟⲛⲧⲱⲥ ϯ-	ⲣⲓⲥⲓⲥ [	[ϫⲉ]ⲥⲓⲗⲱ-	ⲛⲥⲱⲥ ⲛⲅ[ⲓⲅⲁⲥ]
ⲁⲡⲟⲣⲉⲓ ⲉⲓϫⲱ	ⲟⲛ ϫ[ⲉ	[ϩⲁⲙⲡⲉ] ⲧⲉⲕⲕⲗⲏ-	÷ ⲙ̅ⲛⲥⲱⲥ [ⲡⲕⲁ-]
ⲙ̅ⲡⲉⲓϣⲁϫⲉ	ⲛⲟⲩ[	[ⲥⲓⲁ ⲙ̅]ⲙⲟⲟⲩ ⲟⲛ	ⲧⲁⲕⲗⲩⲥⲙⲟⲥ
[ⲉ]ⲣⲉⲡⲛⲟⲩⲧⲉ ⲣⲙ̅ⲉᵃ	ⲡⲕⲁ[	[ⲉⲧⲉⲙⲙⲟ]ⲟⲩ ⲙ̅-	÷ ⲙ̅ⲛⲥⲱⲥ ⲟ[ⲛ]
[ⲣ]ⲙ̅ⲛⲧⲣⲉ ϧⲁⲡⲉⲓ-	ⲛ[	[ⲡⲃⲁⲡⲧⲓⲥ]ⲙⲁ	ⲡⲕⲁϩ ⲛⲧⲁϥ[ϫⲱ-]
ⲣⲱⲙⲉ ϫⲉⲙ̅ⲡⲉ-	ϧ[	[ⲉⲧⲟⲩⲁⲁⲃ]ⲡⲉ	ⲣ̅ϭ ⲙ̅ⲡⲙⲉϩ-
[ⲡ]ⲁⲓ ⲣⲛⲟϐⲉ ⲟⲩ-	[	]	ⲥⲟⲡ ⲥⲛⲁⲩ [ⲙⲛ̅-]
ϫⲉ ⲙ̅ⲡⲉⲛⲉϥⲉⲓ-	ϫⲉ[		ⲛⲥⲱⲥ ⲡⲛ[ⲟⲙⲟⲥ]
ⲟⲧⲉ ⲉⲓⲣⲉ	ϫⲁ[	]ⲛⲛⲟⲩ-	ⲛⲧⲁϥⲧⲁⲅⲟ[ϥ]
Ⲡⲉϫⲉ ⲁⲡ[ⲁ] ϐⲁ-	ⲛⲉⲛⲉ[	[ⲧⲉ]ϫ ⲟⲩⲱ-	ⲙⲙⲱⲩⲥ[ⲏⲥ]
	ⲧⲁⲩϫ[	[ⲛϩ ⲉϐ]ⲟⲗ ϩⲛ̅-	ϩⲓϫⲙ̅ⲡⲧⲟ[ⲟⲩ]

ᵃ Possibly ⲣⲱ.

Fol. 1. Recto. . . . rather that the works (?) of my Father may be manifested in him.'[1] Verily (ὄντως) I am perplexed (ἀπορεῖσθαι) when I say these words, God Himself (?) testifying concerning this man that ' Neither did this (man) sin nor (οὔτε) did his parents do (so).' Apa Ba[. . . .] said [. . . . . saying,[2] ' He that shall be [wroth] against his brother without cause (εἰκῆ), is in danger of the judgement (ἔνοχος, κρίσις) . . . . .

Verso. . . . wash] thy face there and thou shalt see.'[3] I say . . .[4] Siloam is the church (ἐκκλ.). The waters are [the wate]rs of [holy baptis]m (βαπ.)[5], manifested in . . . . the earth, the first time; afterward the giants (γίγας)[6]; afterward the flood (κατακλυσμός); afterward the earth that was peopled for the second time; afterward the law (νόμος) that He committed unto Moses upon the mount . . . . .

[1] *Cf.* John ix. 3.

[3] *Cf.* John ix. 7.

[4] Some particle or ' to thee '.

[5] *Cf.* Cyril's interpretation in Lagarde, *Catenae,*

[6] Gen. vi. 4.

Fol. 2. → *Recto.*   ↑ *Verso.*

Пєхє а[па ҕ
хєптаγ[

]єн
]трєпщо-

] ⲙⲛⲟⲩⲡⲓⲥ-   ⲱⲥ ⲣⲱ[ⲙⲉ ·
[ⲟⲩ ⲣⲏ]ⲣⲡ ⲛ̄ⲏⲛⲧⲉ   ⲧⲱⲁ-]

[ⲧⲓⲥ ⲛ̄ⲟⲩⲱⲧ ⲉⲥ-   ÷Пєхє ап[атⲟ-]
[ⲭⲏ]ⲙⲙⲟⲛ ⲉⲣⲉ-   ⲗ̄ⲓ̈ⲗⲁⲓⲁ

[ⲭⲏⲕ] ⲉⲃⲟⲗ ⲟ̄ⲙ-   ⲗⲓⲟⲥ хєⲙ[
[ⲝⲉ]ⲛⲟⲩⲙⲟⲟⲩ   ⲣⲏⲙⲁⲥ ᵃ[

[ⲡ]ϣⲱϣ ⲛⲁⲧ-   ⲛ̄ⲧⲁⲥⲧⲣ[ⲉⲡⲙⲟ-]
[ⲛ̄]ⲧⲟⲟⲧϥ ⲉϥⲣⲱⲃ   ⲙⲙⲁⲩ [

[ⲣ̄ⲛⲟ]ⲃⲉ ⲛⲁⲧⲥⲕⲁⲛ̄-   ⲟⲩ ⲣⲏⲣⲡ [
[ⲛⲟ]ⲏⲧⲟⲩ ·   ⲟⲛ ⲛ̄ⲓ̅ⲥ̅ ⲙ̄[ⲛⲛⲉϥ-]

[ⲍⲁⲗ]ⲓ𝔷ⲉ · ⲛⲁ̈ⲡⲉ   ⲉ̈ⲓⲣⲉ ⲱ[ⲥ ⲣⲱ-]
[Пє]хє апа ⲃⲁ-   ⲙⲁⲑⲏⲧⲏⲥ ⲉⲧ̣ϣⲉ·

[ⲛⲉⲟ]ⲃⲛⲏⲅⲉ ⲛ̄ⲧⲁⲡⲏⲅ̄-   ⲙⲉ хє[ⲛ̄ⲱⲥ ⲛ̄ⲟⲩ-]
[. . .]ⲥ хєⲙⲙⲟⲛ̄   ⲗⲉⲉⲧ ⲛ̄[ⲉⲓⲟⲧⲉ ᵇ]

[ⲧⲉ ⲟ̄]ⲩⲟⲛⲟⲩ ⲉⲃⲟⲗ   ⲧⲉ · ⲡⲉ[хⲉ апа]
[ⲛⲧⲉⲓ]ⲟⲥ ⲁⲛⲧⲉ   ÷Ꙃⲉ ⲛ̄ⲧϣⲉ[ⲗⲉⲉⲧ]

[ⲙ̄]ⲡⲉⲛⲉⲓ̈ⲱⲧ ⲁ-   ÷Ⲃⲁ[хⲉⲛ-]
ⲥⲱ[ⲧ̄ⲙ ⲉⲣⲟⲓ̈   ⲛⲉⲩⲧⲧⲉ[ⲛⲏⲥⲛⲉ]

[ⲍⲁ]ⲙ ⲡⲉхⲉ апа-   ⲧⲁ[ϥ
†ⲱⲧⲏϥ ⲁⲩⲱ   ⲙⲙⲁⲣⲓ̈ⲁ [ⲧ̄ⲙⲁⲁⲩ]

[Ⲧⲟⲗ]ⲓ̈ⲟⲥ хⲉⲙ-   ⲱⲟ[ⲥ
]ⲡ̄хⲟⲣⲏ-   ⲛ̄ⲓ̅ⲥ̅ ⲁⲩⲱ [ⲛ̄ⲣⲱ-]

[ⲛⲛⲁ]ⲩ ⲛ̄ⲧⲁⲩⲧⲉ-   ÷Пⲉ[хⲉ
[ⲅⲉⲓ ⲛ̄]ⲡⲉ̄ⲡⲛ̄ⲁ   ⲙⲉ ⲉⲧⲙⲙⲁⲩ

       margin   margin

ᵃ For ⲥ perhaps ⲟ or ⲱ.   ᵇ Or ⲣⲱⲙⲉ.

Fol. 2. *Recto.* ... with a single faith (πίσ.), perfect in equality, sinless and without offence (σκανδαλίζειν). These are the things that God revealed unto our father A[da]m '.[1] Ana[tol]ius said, '.....

... A[pa B .....] said, 'They [2] ..... as (ὡς) man.' An[ato]lius said, 'At [the time] when He caused the water become wine,[3] [did He] do (this) as (ὡς) man or (?) [as (ὡς)] God?' [Apa] Ba[.....] said, '.... [He] did .... as (ὡς) .....' ..... said, '

Verso. ... wherewith [He?] cause[d?] the water become wine; or hath He times (*or* seasons) in His hand,[4] wherewith He worketh?' Apa Ba...s said, 'Nay, not thus is it ..... heard one ..... [payeth] heed? (and) ... furnisheth (χορηγεῖν [5]) the Spirit (πν.) .....

[1] Space scarcely allows ⲁ[ϩⲣⲁⲟⲁ]ⲙ, but is Adam probable?

[2] One is tempted to read хⲉⲛⲧⲁϥ[, 'He ...

[3] *Cf.* John ii. 1 ff.

[4] *I.e.* 'at His disposal'. Perhaps a reference to some accusation of magical processes.

[5] Perhaps χορηγός preferable. Πνεῦμα could not be subject unless there were space for ⲛⲟⲓ.

. . . Ga]li[lee . . . . there . . . . . also Jesus and His disciples (μαθ.) to the marriage. But (δέ) the [parents ¹ ?] of the bride were kinsmen (συγγενής) of Mary [the mother] of Jesus, and the people there . . . . .

1.

ol. 3. ↑ *Recto.*   → *Verso.*

margin   margin

] ετвεπαϊ αϛ-	αвολος ноҳ̣ҳ̣[ε]	[п]ҳαϩε ҳωκ	р̄п εγωн[ε н̄-]
ϲоо]ϲ нαϲ ҳεϫ-	нϩрооγ ϫ̄нϫ̣ϫ̣[ε]	εвολ ϫ̄пϊраϲϫοϲ	τεκογερн[τε]
ια]τεταογноγ	ноγϣн нατογ-	нϊϫ απҳαϩε ҳϊ-	÷ пεҳε ῑϲ н[αϛ ҳε-]
ι ¹] пεҳε ϫ̄ϊλ̄ϊ-	ωϫ нατϲω	τ̄ϥ εϩογн ετпο-	ннεκп[ιραϩε]
ϲ] ҳεεноγ-	Ν̄τερεπαϊαво-	λιϲ ετογααв ѳ̄ϊ-	ϫ̄пҳо[ειϲ πεκ-]
оϣ] ω. пεпεϊ-	λοϲ ειϫε ҳεαϛ-	ελн̄ϫ αϛταλοϛ	ноγτ[ε αγω]
от ε]τρεκвωλ	ϩκ̄в αϛϯ πεϛογ-	εҳϫ̄πτп̄ ϫ̄-	пҳоειϲ πεκ-
ιαн] ϫ̄πεϊκε-	оεϊ εροϛ εϛҳω	прпε · πεҳαϛ н̄αϛ	ноγτ[ε πετκ-]
нт]нϫα εϛҳω	ϫ̄ϫοϲ ҳεεϣ-	ҳεεϣҳε н̄τοκ-	нαϣλ[н̄λ εροϛ ·]
ϫ̄ϫоϲ] ҳεντερε-	ҳεντοκπε [πε-]	πε пϣнρε ϫ̄-	÷ λγω н̄[τερεϛ-]
ϲ̄ ει εϩр]αϊ ϩϫ-	χ̄ϲ αϫ̄ϲ εнει[ω-]	пноγτε но̄κ̄	ҳωκ [εвολ н̄-]
ϫοογ] ϫ̄пнϲα-ᵃ	πε ϫαρογροειϊ	επεϲнτ ϫ̄ϫ̄	πϊρα[ϲϫοϲ нϊϫ]
. . .]пвап-	÷ Пεҳε ῑϲ н̄αϛ ҳ[ε-]	πεϊϫα · ϛϲнϩ	πεҳ[ε ῑϲ нαϛ]
ιϫα . .]αϛ	ϫερεрωϫε ωн[ϩ]	ϭαρ ҳεϛнαϩωн	ҳεϲα[ϩωκ επα-]
]ҳϊ	εοεϊκ ϫαγααϛ	ετοотογ н̄πεϛ-	ϩογ ϫϫοϊ]
?	αλλα εϣαҳε н̄[ϫ̄]	αϭϭελοϲ ετвн-	п[ϲαταнαϲ ·]
	[ε]τннγ εвολ ϩϫ-	нтκ нϲεϛϊτκ	λ[
	τ[τα]про ϫ̄пн[ογτε]	εҳн̄нεγϭ[ιҳ]	?
пαϊ-]	[λγ]ω н̄τερ[ε-]	ϫнпот[ε нϫ̄ҳω-]	
margin		margin	

ᵃ Perhaps ϫ̄пнϲα[τρεϛ]ҳι ͷ.

¹ Or 'people'. This tradition referred to in F. Robinson, *Ap. Gosp.*, 165.

Fol. 3. *Recto.* ... Wherefore He said unto her,[1] 'Not yet is my hour [come].' Mili[tius?] said, 'We des[ire], O our father, that thou wouldest explain [unto us] this other question (ζήτημα?), when he[2] saith, 'When [Jesus was come] up from [the water], after that [He had had?] baptism (βάπτισμα) ..... take (took?) .....

... the] devil (διάβ.)[3], forty days and forty nights, neither eating nor drinking. When the devil (διάβ.) knew that He was an hungered, he betook him unto Him, saying, 'If thou art the Christ, say unto these stones that they may become bread.' Jesus said unto him, 'Man useth not to live by bread alone, but (ἀλλά) by every word that cometh forth from the mouth of God.' And when

(*Verso*) [the] enemy had fulfilled every temptation (πειρασμός)[4], the enemy brought Him in unto the holy city (πόλις) Jerusalem and set Him upon the wing of the temple. He said unto Him, 'If thou it is art the son of God, cast thyself down from hence. For (γάρ) it is written, He shall bid His angels (ἄγγ.) concerning thee, and they shall bear thee upon their hands, lest at any time (μήποτε) thou dash against a stone thy foot.' Jesus said unto him, 'Thou shalt not tempt (πειράζειν) the Lord thy God, [and] the Lord [thy] God [it is to whom] thou shalt pray.'[5] And when he had fulfilled [every] temptation (πει.), [Jesus] said [unto him], 'Withdraw [thyself be]hind [me.] [Satan .....

No. 13.

Fragments of a version from the Greek of anecdotes embodied by John of Maiuma in his Πληροφορίαι, whereof hitherto only a Syriac translation was known.[6] That this Coptic text is not a translation of the latter is clear from divergences in detail which even its dilapidated condition allows us to recognize.[7] The former existence of a Coptic version of the *Testimonies* is known from its occurrence in a 6th or 7th century book list,[8] and its mention in the *Antiphonary.*[9] As in both these the work is definitely ascribed to Peter the Iberian, it may be assumed that John's collection was made from one already existing, and due to that saint himself.

[1] John ii. 4.
[2] *I. e.* the evangelist. *Cf.* Matt. iii. 16.
[3] *Cf.* Matt. iv. 2-4.   [4] *Cf.* Luke iv. 13.
[5] ϣⲙ̅[ϣⲉ 'serve' (Matt. iv. 10) would be preferable.
[6] *Ed.* Nau in *Patr. Or.* viii (1). Our passages are parallel with the end of cap. xxvi and beginning of xxvii (= *l.c.*, pp. 67, 68). Fol. 2 is not identified; it seems to be absent from John's collection.

[7] *Recto*: 'blessed Timotheus', 'his treatises'; *Verso*: 'rank', 'to-day'.
[8] *V.* my *Coptic Ostr.*, no. 459: 'The Pler. of Apa Peter the Iberian'.
[9] *V.* Rylands *Catal.*, p. 212. The context is: 'Those that would forsake the treachery of Chalcedon, let them take the Book of Testimonies (ϫⲱⲙ ⲛ̅ⲧⲉ ⲛⲓⲙⲉⲧⲙⲉⲑⲣⲉ) of Peter and the συντάγματα of Timothy the ὁμολογητής and the Letters of Severus.'

Fol. 1. → *Recto.*

margin

ⲁⲩ]ⲱ ⲁⲓⲥⲟⲧⲙⲉ[ⲥ]
]ⲥⲟⲟⲩⲛ ⲙ̄ⲙⲟϥ
]ⲃⲉ ⲉⲡⲁⲣⲭⲓⲉⲡ[ⲓ]-
ⲟⲡⲟⲥ ⲁⲡⲁ ⲧⲓⲙⲟ]ⲑⲉⲟⲥ · ⲉⲧⲓ ⲇⲉ ⲟⲛ
]ⲟⲩⲁ̄ ⲛ̄ⲛⲉⲛⲧⲁⲩ-
ⲛ]ⲥⲩⲧⲕⲉⲗⲗⲟⲥ
ⲛⲥⲉⲟ]ⲩⲡⲏⲣⲉⲧⲉⲓ ⲙ̄-
ⲟⲩ ⲉϥϧⲛ̄ⲧ]ⲉϩⲱⲣⲓⲥⲧⲉⲓⲁ · ⲉⲧⲃⲉ-
ϩ]ⲱⲥ ⲉⲁϥⲉⲓⲙⲉ ⲉⲧ[
ⲡ]ⲙⲁⲕⲁⲣⲓⲟⲥ ⲧⲓⲙⲟⲑ[ⲉⲟⲥ]
ⲛ̄ϩⲁ]ϩ ⲛ̄ⲥⲟⲡ ϩ̄ⲛ̄ⲛⲉϥ[ⲉⲡⲓⲥ-]
ⲗⲏ ⲁⲩⲱ ϩ]ⲛ̄ⲛⲉϥⲕⲉⲥⲩⲛⲧⲁ[ⲅⲙⲁ]
ⲧⲥⲩ]ⲛϩⲟⲇⲟⲥ ⲛ̄ⲭⲁⲗⲕ[ⲏⲇⲱⲛ]
]ⲱ[

↑ *Verso.*

margin

[ⲍ]ⲏⲛⲱⲛ · ⲛ[ⲧⲡⲁ-]
ⲗⲁⲓⲥⲧⲓⲛⲏ ⲛ[
ⲡⲉⲛⲙⲁⲕⲁⲣⲓ[ⲟⲥ ⲛⲉⲓⲱⲧ   ϩⲁ-]
ϩⲧⲏϥ ⲭⲉⲁⲟⲩ[ⲁ ⲉⲡⲉϥⲣⲁⲛⲡⲉ ⲡⲉ-]
ⲧⲣⲟⲥ, ⲉⲩⲥⲭⲟⲗ[ⲁⲣⲓⲟⲥⲡⲉ ϩⲙ̄ⲡⲉϥ-]
ϫⲓⲱⲙⲁ · ⲡ[
ⲡⲟⲟⲩ ⲛⲉⲓⲙⲉ [ⲛ̄ⲛⲉⲥⲧⲱⲣⲓⲟⲥ
ⲡⲉ · ⲁⲩⲱ ϯ[ϯ̄[ⲧⲥⲩⲛϩⲟⲇⲟⲥ]
[ⲛ̄]ⲭⲁⲗⲕⲏⲇⲱⲛ ⲙ̄ⲡ[ⲣ̄ⲣⲟ ⲙⲁⲣ-]
[ⲕⲓ]ⲁⲛⲟⲥ · ⲁⲩⲱ ϩⲁϩ [ⲛ̄ⲥⲟⲡ
[. .]ⲁⲓϯ ⲟⲩⲃⲉⲛⲉⲧⲕ[ⲁⲧⲏⲅⲟⲣⲉⲓ ⲙ̄-]
[ⲙⲟ]ⲟⲩ · ⲙ̄ⲡⲛ̄ⲥⲱⲥ [
[ⲟⲩ]ϣⲏ ⲉⲟⲩⲁ̄ ⲉϥⲁⲙ[
]ⲧⲏ[

Fol. 1. Recto. ... and I heard it .... knew him ..... to the arch[bishop Apa Tim]otheus. And while (ἔτι δέ) yet .... one of them that had ..... *syncellus*[1] .... and had] served (ὑπηρετεῖν) [him while he was in] exile (ἐξορίστία). Wherefore ..... since (ὡς) he had known the ....., the blessed (μακ.) Timotheus[2] ..... many a time in his [epistles (ἐπ.) and] also in his treatises (σύνταγμα) ..... the synod (σύνοδος) of Chalcedon .....

Verso. ... the king] Zeno ..... Palestine .... our blessed (μακ.) [father] .... with him,[3] saying, 'One [whose name was Pe]ter, being a σχολ[άριος in his] rank (ἀξίωμα) ..... to-day, I loved [Nestorius] ..... And I ..... of Chalcedon and ..... [the king Mar]cian. And many [times] ..... I opposed them that did ac[cuse] (κατηγορεῖν) them. Afterwards ..... night, one that .....

---

[1] This is accented in the MS. - a very rare feature in Coptic (*e.g.* Brit. Mus. Pap. v, *ed.* Winstedt, *Coptic Texts*, 1910, p. 175).

[2] Or 'Timotheus' might (with preceding ⲙ̄ⲙⲟϥ) be subject of 'known'.

[3] *I.e.* in his presence.

Fol. 2. ↑ *Recto* (?).　　　　→ *Verso* (?).

]ppo ⲑⲉⲟ[ⲇⲟⲥⲓⲟⲥ　　　　]ⲙⲟ [

]ⲁⲱ ⲛ̄ⲣ̣[a　　　　　　ⲁ]ⲩⲱ ⲛⲧ[

]ⲁϥ b ⲭⲉⲉϥ[　　　　　ⲛ]ⲧⲁϥⲱ[

　]ⲉ ⲛ̄[　　　　　　　]ⲁⲡⲟⲥⲧⲟ[ⲗⲟⲥ

　]ⲧⲟ[　　　　　　　ⲭ]ⲡⲟⲓ̈ⲡⲉ ⲡ̣[

　　　　　　　　　　　　?

　　　　　　　　　　　　]ⲁⲣ[

a ⲛ]ⲁⲱ ⲛⲣ̣[ⲉ, or ⲛ]ⲁⲱⲛⲣ̣[ⲧⲏϥ, or ⲁⲡ]ⲁⲱ.　　　b ⲡⲉⲭ]ⲁϥ, or ⲡⲉⲭⲁϥ ⲛ]ⲁϥ, or
ⲭⲟⲟⲥ ⲛ]ⲁϥ.

Fol. 2. *Recto*. ... king Theo[dosius .... in what manner [1] (?) .....
said?] unto him, '.....

Verso. ... and .... he had ..... apostles (ἀπ.) .....

No. 14.

This is presumably from apocryphal Acts, in which Andrew plays a part;
but it is difficult to say to which story it belongs. Passages on pp. 70, 73-
75 of Bonnet's *Acta Apost. Apocr.* ii[1] relate to sea voyages, and the last of
them to the appearance of Christ as a ship's master, whom the apostle
accosts[2]; but none of these is sufficiently like to be identified with what
is discernible here.

Sequence of *Recto* and *Verso* is uncertain.

Fol. 1. ↑ *Recto* (?).　　　　→ *Verso* (?).

　　　　ⲉⲧⲉⲛ[　　　　　]ⲃ̣ⲓ̣ⲥ ⲟⲛ-

]ⲛⲛ̣-　　ⲁⲛ ⲛ[ⲕⲛ-]　　]ⲛⲉ ⲥ　　ⲙⲁ[

] ⲡⲣⲟⲥ　　ⲁⲩⲛ[ⲟⲥ ⲛⲑⲁ-]　　]ⲛⲣⲁⲣⲧ　Ⲏⲧ[

]ⲉⲕⲁⲥ ⲟⲩ a　ⲗⲁⲥⲥⲁ　　]ϯⲃⲱⲕ　　ⲛ[

] ⲛϭⲓ ⲙ̄-　Ⲋⲑⲉⲗⲡⲓⲥ ⲛ-　　]ⲡ̣ ⲉⲡⲙⲁ　　ⲭ . [

[ⲙⲁⲑⲏ]ⲧⲏⲥ　ⲧⲁⲩⲣⲁϥ[b　　] ⲙⲡⲉⲓⲛ c　　ⲑⲏ[

a Perhaps ⲭ]ⲉⲕⲁⲥ ⲉⲩ[ⲉ-.　　b This cannot be correct. Perhaps ⲛ[ⲛⲉⲛ]ⲧⲁⲩ-, followed
by a Greek verb.　　c ? ⲛⲓ[ϥⲉ ⲛ].

[1] Several alternatives are possible here.　　　(= *Mélanges Asiatiques* x), p. 156; Ethiopic in
[2] *Cf.* the Coptic in Guidi's *Frammenti*, pp. 55,　　Budge, *Contendings* ii. 189, 270, 374.
56 (Nota iv); Lemm, *Kopt. Apokr. Apost.*

[ϣⲁⲛⲧⲟ]ⲩⲡⲱϩ	ϫⲉ ⲉⲧⲉⲁ[ⲛⲟⲛ-]	]ⲣⲏⲧ ϫⲉ-	ⲧⲕⲁ[
ⲉ[ⲧⲡⲟ]ⲗⲓⲥ ⲉⲧⲟⲩ-	ⲡⲉ ⲛⲧⲁ[ⲛⲕⲱ]	[ⲕⲁⲥ] ⲉⲩⲉⲟⲩϫⲁⲓ	?
ⲛⲁⲃⲱⲕª ⲉⲣⲟⲥ	ⲛ[ⲥ]ⲱⲛ [ⲛⲑⲉⲗ-]	]ⲛⲟϭ ⲛⲥⲟ-	ⲡⲕ[
ϫⲉⲕⲁⲥ ⲛⲛⲉⲩ-	ⲡⲓⲥ ⲙⲡⲉⲛ[	]ⲉⲣ ?	ⲡϫⲟⲓ ⲉⲧⲙ[ⲣⲱ]
ϣⲧⲟⲣⲧⲣ ⲛⲑⲁⲗ-	ϫⲉⲕⲁⲥ ⲉⲛⲉⲭ[ⲡⲟ]	? ?	ⲡⲉ ? [
ⲗⲁⲥⲥⲁ·	ⲛⲁⲛ ⲛⲧⲉⲕ-	ⲛϭⲓ ⲁⲛⲇⲣⲉⲁⲥ	Ⲡⲉϫⲁϥ ϫⲉⲉⲓ-
Ⲁϥϣⲗⲏⲗ ⲛⲧⲉⲓ-	*sic* ϩⲗⲡⲓⲥ ⲉⲧⲉ-	ⲉⲓⲥ ϩⲏⲏⲧⲉ ⲁⲩ-	ϫⲉⲣⲟⲛ ⲛⲧⲟⲕ
ϩⲉ ⲉϥϫⲱ ⲙ-	ⲧⲱⲛⲧⲉ		ⲡⲛⲉⲉϥ ⲙ-
ⲙⲟⲥ ϫⲉⲧⲱ-	ⲡⲁ[		ⲡϫⲟⲉⲓⲥᵇ ⲁⲧⲁ-
ⲃⲟ ⲙⲙ[ⲟⲛ			]ⲧⲉⲕ-

ª My copy has ⲓⲧⲟⲩ-.   ᵇ Or ⲡϫⲟⲉⲓ. But the form ϫⲟⲓ above makes this unlikely.

Recto (?). . . . so that (?) the disciples (μαθ.) should . . . [until] they reached the city (πόλις) whither they were going, so that they might not disturb[1] the sea (θάλ.). Thus did he pray, saying, 'I beseech [Thee' . . . . .

. . . 'the perils (κίνδυνος) of the sea (θάλ.). The hope (ἐλπίς) of them that have[2] (?) . . ., that is [us] who have [forsaken] . . . . . the hope (ἐλ.) of th[is? world] . . ., so that we may [get] for ourselves Thy hope (ἐλ.) which is Thine' . . . . .

Verso (?). . . . I go [to . . .] the place . . . ., so that they be saved . . . . Andrew [said,] 'Behold,' . . . . .

. . . the ship to the sho[re (?) . . . . . He said, 'I say (?) unto thee,[3] thou sailor of the Lord,[4] my . . . hath . . . . . thy' . . . . .

No. 15.

The date in the title and the words of fol. 1 point to the martyrdom of Mark the Evangelist. We have, therefore, it may be assumed, an Encomium upon him. Those known in Greek, whereof the initial words are published, do not appear to correspond with this text.[5]

[1] Grammar demands this. The subject may be 'winds', or the like, in the earlier, lost part of the sentence.

[2] This assumes an emendation of my copy.

[3] A doubtful locution ; *v.* Steindorff, *Gram.*²
4⁵ , also no. 9 above, l. 8 ɓɓ., ᴅᴀᴛᴏ., no. 183,
1. Peyron 47 and Stern § 26 took it for εἴγε.

But Mk. v. 41 (σοὶ λέγω) confirms Steindorff's suggestion. In Bo. it appears as ⲁⲓϭⲉⲣⲟⲕ ⲛⲟⲟⲕ (*Test. Abr.*, Rendic. 1900, 164, 10), but also ϫⲉ-, *CSCO.*, vol, 41. 17, 47.

[4] 'Of the ship' is less likely.

[5] *v.* the Bollandist inventories. Fragments of Coptic texts, *v.* Br. Mus., nos. 299, 300.

Fol. 1. ↑ *Recto.*   → *Verso.*

Recto:

, ⲁⲗⲕⲉ ⲙ̅ⲡⲉ[ⲃⲟⲧ ⲡⲁⲣⲙⲟⲩⲧⲉ]

ϛ ϩⲛⲟⲩⲉⲓⲣⲏ[ⲛⲏ ⲛ̅ⲧⲉ ⲡⲛⲟⲩⲧⲉ]

ϛ ϩⲁⲙⲏⲛ

· ——— · · · ——— · ·

· ——— · · · ——— · ·

Ϯⲭⲣⲉⲱⲥⲧⲉ̄ⲓ   ⲧⲁⲃ[

ⲛⲁⲕ ⲱ̄ ⲡⲣⲁⲅⲓ-   ⲅⲁⲣ !

ⲟⲥ ⲙⲁⲣⲕⲟⲥ ⲛ̄ⲟⲩ-   ⲥⲁⲣ[

ⲛⲟϭ ⲛ̄ⲭⲣⲉ-   ⲕⲁ[

ⲱⲥ̄ · ϯϩⲟⲙⲟⲗⲟ-   ⲡⲱ[

ⲅⲉ̄ⲓ ϫⲉϯⲭⲣⲉ-   ⲅⲁⲣ [

ⲱⲥⲧⲉⲓ ⲛⲁⲕ   ⲡⲙ[

ⲛ̄ⲟⲩϩⲟⲟⲩ̄ ⲁⲛ̄   ⲉⲣ[

ⲟⲩⲇⲉ̄ ⲥⲛⲁⲩ   ⲡⲣ[

ⲁⲗⲗⲁ̄ ⲙ̄ⲡⲉⲓ-   ⲡ . [

ⲟⲩⲟⲉⲓ̈ϣ ⲧⲏ-   · ⲱ[

ⲣ̄ϥ ⲙ̄ⲡⲁⲱ̄ⲡⲧⲟ̄   ?

ⲧⲁⲧⲁ̣[

ⲱⲥ[

ⲙ̅ⲙⲡ̄[

ⲛϩⲉⲛⲛ[

margin

Verso:

]ϫⲱ

ⲁⲩ ⲛ̅ⲥⲉⲁⲡⲁⲧⲏ

ⲧⲏⲣⲟⲩ ϩⲁⲑⲏ

ⲛ̄ⲛⲉⲓⲟⲩⲟⲉⲓ̈ϣ

ⲡ̅̄ ϛⲀϥϫⲟⲟⲩ̄

] ⲁⲩⲱ̄ ϫⲉ ⲉⲣⲁⲕⲟⲧⲉ

]ϭⲱⲧⲡ̄ ⲙ̅ⲙⲁⲧⲉ ⲁⲛ

]ⲡⲟⲗⲩⲙⲉ̄ⲓ ⲁⲗⲗⲁ ⲁϥϫⲟ-

]ⲕⲉ ⲟⲩⲛ̄ ⲟⲛ ⲉⲧⲉ-

]ⲧⲡⲓⲥ ⲭⲱⲣⲁ ⲛ̄ⲕⲏⲙⲉ

]ⲛⲉ ⲉⲧⲗⲟϥⲉ ϩⲁ-

? ⲑⲏ ⲙ̅ⲡⲟⲟⲩ

] . ⲥⲟ̄ ϩⲓⲧⲛ̄ⲡⲗⲓⲃⲉ

]ⲉⲡ . ̄ ⲛ̄ⲛⲉⲓϩⲱ-

]ⲟⲗ . ⲗⲟⲛ ⲛⲓⲙ̅

]ⲥⲁϥ ⲡⲉⲧⲛⲁϣⲡⲓ-

]ⲁ ⲑⲉ ⲛ̄ⲛⲓⲗⲁⲟ[ⲥ

]ⲁ̄ . . . ⲧⲏⲡⲉ ⲉ-

]ⲁⲓ̣ [ⲕⲁ]ⲧⲁⲫⲣⲟ[ⲛⲉⲓ

ⲛ̄ⲛⲁⲓⲙⲱⲛ

margin

Fol. 1. *Recto.*   . . . on] the last day of the month [Parmoute].   In peace (εἰρ.) [of God].   Amen :—

I owe (χρεωστεῖν) thee, O holy (ἅγ.) Mark, a great debt (χρέως).   I confess (ὁμολογεῖν) that I owe (χρ.) thee not one day nor (οὐδέ) two, but rather (ἀλλά) all the (*lit.* this) time of my life, that I may . . . as (? ὥς) . . . . .

Verso.   . . . conquer . . . contend (πολεμεῖν) . . . . .

. . . all,[1] before this age (*lit.* these times).   And (δέ) He sent thee not to

---

[1] The preceding word perhaps ἀπάτη for ἀπατᾶ(ν) 'deceive'.

Rakote (Alexandria) alone, but (ἀλλά) He sent thee also to the land (χώρα) of Egypt, that was mad until to-day, with the madness of the idols (εἴδ.).[1] Who shall be able to persuade (πείθειν) the peoples (λαός) . . . to despise (καταφρονεῖν) the demons (δαίμων) . . . . .

Fol. 2. ↑ *Recto* (?).   → *Verso* (?).

[πα]ϩⲣⲉ ⲉⲣⲟⲟⲩ   ⲉϣ[ⲙⲡ[ⲉⲩⲁⲧⲧⲉ-]
ϩⲛⲧⲉϥⲡⲁⲥ-   ⲛⲉ[   ]ⲭ̄ⲙ̄   ⲗⲓⲟⲛ ⳪[
ⲥⲉ · ⲛⲉϯⲛⲁϣⲟⲟ-   ]ϥ   ⲁϥϫⲓϣⲏⲡⲉ
ⲟⲥⲟⲩ ϩⲛⲛⲁ̄-   ⲛϭⲓ ⲡⲭⲁⲭⲉ
ⲥⲟⲧⲉ̄ ϥⲛⲁ-   ⳼Ⲁϥⲙⲟⲩ ⲙⲉⲛ̄
ⲧⲁⲗⲥⲟⲟⲩ ϩⲙ̄-   ⲅⲁⲣ ⲁⲗⲗⲁ̄
ⲡⲉϥϣⲁϫⲉ̄   ⲡⲉϥⲙⲟⲩ ⲡⲣⲟ̄-
ⲛⲉϯⲛⲁϭⲓ-   ⲧⲣⲉⲡⲉ̄ ⲛⲟⲩ-
ⲧⲟⲩ̄ ⲉⲛⲉⲥⲡⲏ̄-   ⲙⲏ̄ⲛϣⲉ ⲁⲩⲣ̄-
ⲗⲁⲓⲟⲛ ⲛⲕⲁ-   ⲙⲁⲣⲧⲩⲣⲟⲥ
ⲕⲉ ϥⲛⲁⲣⲟⲩⲟ̄-   ⲁϥϩⲱⲡ ⲙⲉ̄
ⲉⲓⲛ̄ ⲉⲣⲟⲟⲩ̄   ϩⲁⲡⲕⲁϩ̄ ⲁⲗ̄-
ϩⲛⲧⲗⲁⲙ̄ⲡⲁⲥ   ⲗⲁ ⲛⲉϥⲕⲗⲟⲙ
ⲙⲡⲉ[ⲩ]ⲁⲧⲧⲉ̄-   ⲣⲟⲩⲟⲉⲓⲛ̄ ⲙ-
ⲗ̄[ⲓⲟⲛ .]ϥ ⲛ̄-   ᵒ
ⲧ[ⲙⲏⲛⲉ̄ ⲛϩⲟⲩⲟ
⳼Ⲁϥ[ⲉⲧⲁⲥ[ⲧⲣⲁⲡ]ⲏ̄
⳿ⲥⲓ[   ]
                                         ] ?
        margin   ⲥ]ⲱⲙ̄ⲁ̄

                                        margin

Fol. 2. *Recto* (?). . . . 'give] healing[2] unto them by his spittle.[3]   Them that I shall wound with my darts he will make whole with his word ;

---

[1] *Cf.* εἰδωλομανία.   [2] The devil *loq.*   [3] A reference to the healing of Anianus' hand.

them that I shall lead into dark caverns (σπήλαιον), he will enlighten with the lamp (λαμπάς) of the gospel (εὐαγ.)'[1] . . . . .

Verso (?). . . . of (?) the gospel (εὐαγ.) . . . the enemy was shamed. He died indeed (μὲν γάρ), yet (ἀλλά) his death incited (προτρέπειν) a multitude and they became martyrs (μάρτυρος). He was (+ μέν) hidden below the earth, yet (ἀλλά) do his crowns[2] shine forth daily, more than the li[ghtning] (ἀστραπή) . . . . body . . . . .

No. 16.

From the Martyrdom of Philotheus of Antioch. The story was apparently similar to that abbreviated in the *Synaxarium*, 16th Tubah.[3] Other remnants of the Saʿidic version are among the copies of papyri made by A. des Rivières[4] and in a Borgian MS.,[5] Brit. Mus., no. 330 being another copy of the latter passage. His Martyrdom appears in a 6th or 7th century library catalogue.[6] It is presumably this martyr[7] who is invoked, with other Antiochene military saints, upon grave stelae[8] and in the diptychs.[9] He too appears once as a dragon slayer.[10] The Encomium, attributed to Severus of Antioch, for the building (? بنيان) of his church and 'invention' (ظهور) of his relics, on the 16th Abib, appears to relate various miracles, but no facts.[11]

→ *Recto.*

]ɴλ[

ϣʜρε] κοⲩⲓ ⲁε ⲟⲛ[

[. .]ρⲓⲧε [a] ⲛⲣⲟⲙⲡⲉ ⲉⲡⲉϥⲣⲁⲛ[ⲡⲉ ⲫⲓⲗⲟⲑⲉⲟⲥ]

[a] One might more easily emend to ϣⲓⲧⲉ than ⲙⲛⲧⲉ which Ar. requires.

[1] *Cf.* the phrases in Paris 129[14], f. 136 (encom. on Mark): ⲕⲁⲓ ⲅⲁⲣ ϩⲁⲑⲏ ⲙⲡⲁⲧⲉⲙⲁⲣⲕⲟⲥ ⲉⲓ ⲛⲉⲙⲡϩⲟⲟⲩ ϣⲟⲟⲡ ⲉⲡⲧⲏⲣϥⲛⲉ ⲟⲛⲕⲛⲙⲉ ⲁⲗⲗⲁ ⲟⲩⲟⲩϣⲏⲡⲉ ⲉⲥⲙⲛ ⲉⲃⲟⲗ ⲛⲧⲉⲣⲉϥⲉⲓ ⲁⲉ ⲛϭⲓ ⲙⲁⲣⲕⲟⲥ ⲡⲟⲩⲟⲉⲓⲛ ⲁⲡϩⲟⲟⲩⲁⲣⲭⲉⲓ . . . *Cf.* here the very similar phraseology in the Encomium of Severus (9th cent.), *ed.* Bargès, p. 6.

[2] Those granted to martyrs for their virginity, piety, sufferings &c.

[3] Forget, i. 213 = Wüstenfeld, *Synax.* 241; Amélineau, *Actes*, 193.

[4] Munich, Landesbibl., MS. Copt. no. 3, fragg. lxxiv–lxxvii. The first fragment gives the calf's name, ⲥⲙⲁⲣⲁⲅⲁⲟⲛ, with the epithet ⲛϣⲟⲩ-

ⲙⲉⲣⲓⲧϥ = ἀγαπητός.

[5] *Ed.* Balestri, *Sacr. Bibl. Fragm.*, xxxix ff.

[6] *Recueil*, xi. 133.

[7] And not him of Oxyrhynchus (Hyvernat, *Actes*, 100). Philotheus of Dronkah (Forget, *Synax.* ii. 100) suffered in A.D. 1380.

[8] Quibell-Thompson, *Saqqara*, no. 203. *Cf.* Clédat, *Baouit*, i, pl. xxxi.

[9] Tuki's *Theotokia*, 41; Cairo *do.* 289; Leyden Museum, MS. copte no. 41; Brit. Mus. no. 865.

[10] *Bull. Soc. Nat. d. Antiq. de France*, 1898, Novembre = G. Lefebvre, *Rec. des Inscr.*, no. 778.

[11] Paris, MS. arabe 153, 243b, almost wholly illegible.

Ⲛⲉϥⲉⲓⲟⲧⲉ̈ ⲍⲉ ⲛⲉⲣⲉⲛϩⲉⲗ[ⲗⲏⲛⲉ ⲉⲩⲥⲟⲟⲩⲛ]

ⲁⲛ ⲙ̄ⲡⲛⲟⲩⲧⲉ· ⲁⲗⲗⲁ ⲉⲩ[ϣⲙ̄ϣⲉ ⲛⲟⲩ-]

ⲙⲁⲥⲉ ⲛⲁⲙⲭⲟⲣⲧⲟⲥ ⲁ̣[*sic*

ⲛⲉϥⲉⲓⲟⲧⲉ ⲉⲓⲣⲉ̈ ⲙ̄ⲙⲟⲟⲩ ⲙ̄[

ⲛⲁϥ ⲙ̄ⲙⲏⲛⲉ ϣⲟⲙⲛ̄ⲧ ⲛ̄ϣ[ⲓ [ⲛⲥⲁⲙⲧ ⲉⲩⲟⲩ-] *sic*

ⲱϣⲙ̣̄ ⲛ̣[. . .] ⲛ̄ⲛⲉϩᵃ ϩⲛ̄ⲟϩ̣ᵇ

Ⲧⲣⲉϥⲛ̣[. . . ⲉ]ⲃⲟⲗ ⲛϩⲏⲧⲟⲩ ⲁⲩⲱ [

]ⲛⲥ[ⲟ]ϭⲛ ⲛ̄ϣⲟⲙⲛ̄ⲧ ⲛ̄ⲥⲟⲡ

]ⲛⲉϥⲥⲱ ⲉⲃⲟⲗ ϩⲛ̄ⲟⲩⲏⲣ[ⲡ

] ⲙ̄ⲛⲟⲩϩⲣⲱⲥⲁⲧⲟⲛ· ⲁⲩ[ⲱ

]ⲛⲏⲩⲉ . . . [

]ϣⲟⲙ̣· ⲁⲩⲱ ⲕ[ⲉ

]ⲛⲉ ⲁⲩⲱ . [

] ⲛ̄ⲛⲟⲩⲃ· ⲁⲩⲱ [

] . ⲧⲉ[

ᵃ The constant phrase is ⲟⲩⲟϣⲙ̄ ϩⲙⲉϩ (*e. g.* Lev. vii. 12, ix. 4), rarely ϩⲛ̄ⲟⲩϩⲉϩ (ii. 4). My copy makes either of these difficult here.   ᵇ ? ϩⲓϩⲣⲱ[ⲥⲁⲧⲟⲛ, following Ar. بزيت وسيرج .

↑ *Verso.*

]ⲛ̣ⲟ̣ . ⲙⲟ : ⲛⲉ . [

ⲛⲉϥⲙⲁⲁ]ⲍⲉ ⲥⲓⲧⲉ ⲟ ⲛ̄ⲑⲉ [ⲛ̄

ⲧ]ⲉϥⲧⲁⲡⲣⲟ̇ : ⲉⲣⲉⲛⲉϥⲟⲩⲉⲣⲏ[ⲧⲉ]

ϩⲉⲛⲥⲧⲩⲗ]ⲗⲟⲥ ⲛ̄ⲛⲁⲧ· ϩⲓⲭⲛ̄ϩⲉⲛⲃⲁⲥⲓⲥ̣

ⲉⲩⲧⲁ]ϫⲣⲏⲩ· ⲉϥⲟ ⲛ̄ⲙ̄ⲣⲁϣ ⲛⲁⲡⲁ-

[ⲑⲟⲥ   ]ⲙ̄ⲙⲛ̄ⲧⲥⲁⲓ̈ⲛ ⲛ̄ⲙ̄ ⲛ̄ⲑⲉ ⲛ̄-

[ⲓⲱⲥⲏⲫ   ]ⲕⲛⲙⲉ ⲉϥⲟ ⲛ̄ⲙ̄ⲣⲁϣ ⲛ̄ⲛⲁⲩ ⲛ̄ⲙ̄

]ⲛ̄ⲛⲉϥϩⲙ̄ϩⲁⲗ ⲙ̄ⲛⲛⲁⲡⲉϥ⳽ⲏ̄ⲓ· ⲙⲛ̄-

ⲛ̣̄]ⲉⲧϩⲓⲃⲟⲗ· ⲛⲉⲩⲙⲉ [ⲙⲙ]ⲟϥ ⲧⲏⲣⲟⲩ ⲉⲧ-

[ⲃⲉ   ]ⲡⲉϥⲥ̣ⲟ̣ⲩⲣⲟⲧ ⲙ̄ⲙⲛ̣ⲉⲥ . [. . . .] ⲛⲉⲣⲉⲛ .

]ϥ ⲙ̄ⲙⲏⲛⲉ ⲛⲉⲧⲉ̣[. . . . . .]ⲛ̄ⲧⲉ

]ⲍⲙⲡⲙⲁⲥⲉ ⲥⲉⲛⲉⲅⲟⲩⲁ[ⲩϥ

]ⲛ ⲉϥϫⲱϭⲉ [ⲙⲙⲟ]ⲥ [

]ⲡⲉ ᵃ ⲡⲛⲟⲩⲧⲉ ⲛⲧ[ⲡⲉ

]ⲛⲛⲉⲧⲛϩⲏ[ⲧⲟⲩ

ϣⲁϫⲉ ⲛϭⲓ ⲡϣⲏⲣ[ⲉ ϣⲏⲙ

]ⲙ[.]ⲙⲩⲥⲧ[ⲏⲣⲓⲟⲛ

ᵃ ? ⲛⲧⲟⲕ]ⲡⲉ.

Recto. ... But (δέ) a young boy ..... [of] ...[1] years, whose name was [Philotheus]. And (δέ) his parents [were] pag[ans (ἕλλην), knowing] not God, but rather (ἀλλά) [worshipping (?) a] grass-eating (-χόρτος) calf ..... that his parents did, [giving ?] him daily three measures [of flour] kneaded [with ?] oil .....[2] they ... from them and .... of ointment three [times daily. And] he used to drink of ..... wine and ... and rose-wine (ῥόσατον). And .... summer and another .... and .... of gold. And .....

Verso. ... his[3] two ears were like .... his mouth, while his feet were ..... pillars (στῦλος) of silver upon bases (βάσις) of ..... firmly fixed ; and he was mild and good (ἀγαθός) [and adorned with] every beauty, even as [Joseph[4] ...] Egypt, being mild[5] at all times [toward] his servants and those of his house and ..... those without. They used all to love him be[cause of his] joyous ... and his .... him (?) daily .... upon (?) the calf, for they loved [him ?] .... saying (?), ...[6] the God of [heaven and earth and all] that are in [them] ..... the boy ..... [his ?] words (?) .... mysteries (μυστ.) .....

No. 17.

From the Martyrdom of Philotheus. Nothing parallel to the incidents here related is found in the *Synaxarium's* abbreviated story. It will be observed that Brit. Mus. no. 330 (*v.* above) gives Raphael as the angel who attended the saint. The last of A. des Rivières' fragments (lxxvii) tells of the emperor's dismay at the destruction of his gods.[7]

[1] It is difficult to read 'ten' with Ar.; 'nine' were more possible.

[2] Perhaps here 'and rose-wine'. This would, here and below, = Ar. 'sesame oil'. *Cf.* the mixture described by Lane, *Mod. Eg.* (1836), ii. 274.

[3] *I.e.* Philotheus.   [4] *Cf.* Gen. xxxix. 6.

[5] The epithet applied to Moses (= πραΰς), Num. xii. 3.

[6] Perhaps ' Art thou the God?' *Cf.* Arabic.

[7] 'Thou hast destroyed', he says, 'the great god that gave me victory and hast enchanted my three generals and all my army. By the might of the Romans, I will cause thy flesh to ...'

Fol. 1. → *Recto.* ↑ *Verso.*

margin margin

]ⲉⲅⲣⲁⲫⲁⲏⲗ	[. .]ⲏⲡ[	ⲍⲓⲟ]ⲕⲗⲏ [ ]	ⲁⲙ[ⲟⲟ]ⲩ [. .]
ⲓⲁⲡ]ⲅⲉⲗⲟⲥ ⲁϩ-	[. .]ⲉⲓⲡ[	]ⲁⲙ[. .]	ⲧⲟⲩ ⲉⲓ ⲉϩⲣ[ⲁⲓ ⲉ-]
ⲣ]ⲁⲧϥ ⲛⲥⲁⲟⲩ-	ⲙⲛⲧⲯ[ⲓⲥ ⲛ-]	]ϥⲙ . ⲧ	ⲡⲉⲑⲉⲁⲧⲣ[ⲟⲛ]
ⲁ] ⲁ̄ⲙⲟϥ ⲛ̄-	ⲧⲟⲩⲱⲧ [	]ⲁϥϯ ⲣ .	ⲛ̄ⲥⲉⲁⲇⲉⲣ[ⲁⲧⲟⲩ]
]ⲙⲙⲏ ⲡⲉ-	[.]ⲉⲁ . ⲙ[	] ⲍⲉ[ⲉ]ⲓⲥ [	ⲙ̄ⲡⲉⲙⲧⲟ [ⲉⲃⲟⲗ]
ⲍⲁϥ] ⲉϩⲟⲩⲛ ϭⲡ̄-	[.]ⲡ[.]ⲕⲉ[	[. . . .]ⲟ[. .]ⲉⲁⲛ	ⲙ̄ⲡⲣⲁⲥⲓⲟⲥ ᵇ
ⲍⲓⲟ]ⲕⲗⲏ [ⲍ.ⲉ]ⲱ̄	ⲛ̄ⲟⲩ[.]ⲏ[. .]ⲧ	. ⲉ[. . ⲡ]ⲣⲙϩⲁⲗ	ⲫⲓⲗⲟ[ⲑ]ⲉⲟⲥ ϩ[ⲛ̄ⲟⲩ-]
ⲉ]ⲑⲩⲣⲓⲟⲛ ⲉ-	ⲧⲁϩ[ⲟ]ⲓ̈ ⲛ . ⲉⲓⲙ	ⲙ̄ⲡ[ⲛⲟⲩ]ⲧⲉ	ⲛⲟϭ ϩⲣⲟⲧ[ⲉ ⲁⲅⲱ]
ⲟⲟ]ⲩ · ⲉⲉⲓⲉϩⲉ̄-	ϩ̄ⲛⲟⲩϭⲉⲡⲏ ·	[ⲫ]ⲓⲗ[ⲟⲑ]ⲉⲟⲥ	ⲡⲉⲭⲁⲩ ⲧⲏ[ⲣⲟⲩ]
]ⲁⲡⲉ ⲡⲉⲕ-	ⲧ[ⲁ]ⲣⲉⲧⲥⲟⲙ ⲙ̄-	ϩ̄ⲛⲟⲩϭⲉⲡⲏ ·	ⲛ̄ⲑⲉ ⲉⲃⲟⲗ [ϩⲛ̄ⲟⲩ-]
] ⲛ̄ⲧⲉⲓϩⲉ	ⲡⲁⲭⲟⲉⲓⲥ ⲟⲩⲱ-	ⲁⲅⲱ ⲛ̄ⲧⲉⲩⲛⲟⲩ	ⲧⲁⲡⲣⲟ ⲛ̄[ⲟⲩⲱⲧ]
ⲡ]ⲉⲓⲙⲛ-	ⲡⲣ̄ [ⲉ]ⲃⲟ[ⲗ] ϩⲛ̄-	ⲁⲩϭⲟϭⲟⲩ [ⲉ]ⲡⲉ-	ⲍⲉⲉⲓⲥ ϩⲏⲛⲧⲉ
ϣⲉ . .] . . ϩⲁ	ⲧⲙⲏⲧⲉ ⲙ̄ⲡⲉⲓ-	ⲥⲏⲧ ϩⲓϫⲛ̄ⲡⲉⲩ-	ⲁⲛⲉⲓ ⲡ[ⲣⲙϩⲁⲗ]
. . . . ⲉ . ⲛⲁ	ⲙⲏⲏϣⲉ · ⲁⲅⲱ	ⲃ[ⲁ]ⲥⲓⲥ ⲍⲉⲉⲛⲉⲅⲣⲁ-	ⲙ̄ⲡⲛⲟ[ⲩⲧⲉ ⲍⲉ-]
]ⲙⲟⲣ-	ⲁⲡⲉⲧⲟⲩⲱⲧ	ⲫⲁⲏ[ⲗ ⲡⲁ]ⲣⲭⲁⲥ-	ⲁⲕⲙⲟⲩ[ⲧⲉ ⲉⲣⲟⲛ]
]ⲟϥ	ⲡⲱⲧ [ϩⲛ̄]ⲟⲩϭⲉ-	ⲅⲉⲗⲟ[ⲥ	⟩ⲛ̄ⲧ[ⲉ]ⲣⲉ[
	ⲡ[ⲏ . . .]ⲧ ⲙ̄-		
	ⲙⲟ[ϥ . . .]ⲛ ᵃ ⲉ-	ⲉⲃⲟⲗ	
	ⲡⲣ̄ⲡⲉ	]ⲛ̄ϭⲓ	
	ⲉϩⲟⲩ[ⲛ		

ᵃ ? ⲉϩⲟⲩ]ⲛ ⲉ-. ᵇ Space for ⲁⲡⲁ.

Fol. 1. *Recto.* . . . Raphael the angel (ἄγ.) standing be[side] him . . . He said unto Diocletian,[1] 'O evil beast (θηρίον), are then . . . . . thy (*pl.*) . . . like this . . . . . this mul[titude (?)] . . . . .

. . . 'nineteen idols [2] . . . . quickly, that the power of my Lord

[1] Here (as in *PSBA*. xxxii. 246 ff.) always 'Dioclê', a form due presumably to the ⲍⲓⲟⲕⲗⲏ/ frequently used in Saʿidic dated colophons (Brit. &c.) and represented in Arabic as ﺩﻳﻮﻗﻠﺲ (Sever.

Ashm. in *Patr. Or.* vi. 126, 127).

[2] Diocletian is usually given seventy idols: Hyvernat, *Actes*, 78, 202; Winstedt, *Theodore*, pp. 16, 120 &c.

may be manifested in the midst of this multitude.' And the idol ran quickly . . . . . in (*or* into) the temple . . . . .

   Verso. . . . Diocletian . . . . [saying,[1]] 'Lo . . . . the servant of God Philotheus quickly.' And straightway they leapt down from their pedestals (βάσις), for the archangel (ἀρχάγ.) Raphael was . . . . .

   . . . then . . . . . come in unto the theatre (θέατρον) and stood before Saint (ἅγιος) Philotheus[2] in great fear [and] they all said, as if with a [single] voice, 'Lo, we are come, servant of God, [for] thou didst call [us.]' When . . . . .

Fol. 2. ↑ *Recto.*   → *Verso.*

margin   margin

]аѧтє	[. .ⲙⲉⲱ[	[. .]ⲡ︦ⲣ︦ⲣⲟ [	ⲁⲗⲗ[ⲁ] ⲡⲉ[ⲧⲟⲩⲛⲁ
ⲭ]ⲟⲉⲓⲥ · ⲁⲛⲛⲁⲩ	ⲛ[ⲣ]ⲟⲕⲣⲟ[ⲩ ⲟ︦ⲡ︦-]	[. . .]ⲣⲉⲛ[	ⲭ[ⲁ]ⲣⲓⲍⲉ ⲛⲧ[ⲟⲟ-]
[ⲉ]ⲛ︦ⲭⲣⲓⲥⲧⲓⲁⲛⲟⲥ	ⲟⲩⲥⲁⲧⲉ [ϣⲁⲛⲧ-]	[. . .]ⲡⲓϣⲁⲭⲉ[	ⲧⲓ ϣⲁⲛⲕⲱ[ⲕ]
]ⲣⲓⲑⲛ ⲱ︦	ⲟ[ⲩ]ⲱⲝⲡ̄ [	[. . .]ⲛⲥⲓ ⲛ̄ⲙⲁ[ⲧⲟⲓ]	ⲉⲃⲟⲗ · ⲛ̄ⲡⲟⲩ[ⲉⲥ-]
] ⲟ︦ⲡ︦ⲟⲉⲙⲙⲁ	[. .]ⲧ[.]ⲕ[	[. . . .]ⲥ · ⲙⲡⲱ	ⲥⲁϩⲛⲉ [ⲛ̄ⲡ︦-]
]ⲛ̄ⲡⲛ︦ . . ⳓⲉ	ⲛ̄ⲧⲛ[ⲟ]ⲭⲥ	[. . . . .] · ⲉⲧⲉⲩ-	ⲣ︦ⲣⲟ ⲁⲥⲉⲫⲣ[ⲁⲧϭⲉ]
]ⲓⲁ ⲉⲥ[ⲟ] ⲛ̄ⲟⲉ *sic*	ⲉⲑⲁⲗ[ⲗ]ⲁⲥⲥⲁ]	ⲁ[. . .] ⲛⲁⲥ ⲕⲁⲧⲁ	ⲛ̄ⲙⲁ[ⲟ]ⲥ ϩⲙ̄[ⲡⲣⲁⲛ]
[ⲛⲟⲩⲕ]ⲟⲩⲓ[a] ϣⲏⲣⲉ	ϩⲱⲥⲧⲉ ⲉ[ⲧⲙ̄]ⲧⲣ[ⲉⲩ-]	ⲧⲕ[ⲉⲗ]ⲉⲩⲥⲓⲥ ⲛ̄-	ⲛ̄ⲡⲉⲭ︦ⲥ︦ · ⲡ[ⲉⲭⲁⲥ
] . ⲉⲧⲟⲛⲁⲙⲛ̄ⲧⲏ	[ϩ]ⲉ ⲉⲡⲉ[ⲥ]ⲕⲉⲥⲱⲙ[ⲁ]	ⲡ︦ⲣ︦ⲣⲟ ⲁⲩⲭⲟⲟⲥ][b]	ⲭⲉⲡⲁⲭⲟⲉⲓⲥ ⲓ︦ⲥ︦
[ⲛ̄ⲣⲟⲙ]ⲡⲉ · ⲡⲉ-	[ϩ]ⲟⲗⲱⲥ ⲉⲕⲱⲧ	ⲛⲁⲥ ⲛⲥⲓ ⲛ̄ⲙⲁ[ⲧ]ⲟⲓ	ⲡⲉⲭ︦ⲥ︦ · ⲉϣ[ϫⲉ
[ⲭⲉ ⲁ]ⲓⲟⲕⲗⲏ ⲉϩⲟⲩⲛ	ⲉⲣⲟⲥ ⲛⲟ[ⲩ]ⲙⲁⲣⲧⲩ-	ⲭⲉⲧⲛ[ⲟ]ⲩⲱϣ *sic* ·	ⲡⲁⲓⲡⲉ ⲡⲉⲕ[ⲟⲩⲱϣ
[ϩ︦ⲙ︦ⲣ]ⲱⲙⲁⲛⲟⲥ	ⲣⲓⲟⲛ ⲭⲉⲥⲉⲛⲁ-	ⲉⲧⲥⲟ︦ ⲉⲣⲟⲕ ⲉⲧⲃⲉ-	ⲉⲧⲣⲁⲭⲱⲕ [ⲉ-]
[ⲛ̄ⲙⲛ̄]ⲉⲥⲛⲟϭ ⲧⲏⲣⲟⲩ	ⲕⲱⲧ ⲉⲣⲟⲟⲩ ⲛⲟⲩ-	ⲡⲉⲛⲥⲁ ⲱ︦ ⲫⲓⲗⲟ-	ⲃⲟⲗ ⲛ̄ⲡⲁ[ⲁⲧⲱⲛ
[ⲭⲉ] . . ⲡⲉⲕ-	ⲙⲁⲣⲧⲩⲣⲓⲟⲛ ϩ︦ⲙ︦	[ⲑ]ⲉⲟⲥ · ⲁⲗⲗⲁ ⲧⲏ︦ⲣ-	ϩ︦ⲛ︦ⲧⲉⲓⲕⲟⲗ[ⲁⲥⲓⲥ]
[. . .]ⲡⲁⲓ]ⳋⲉⲥⲓⲥ	ⲑⲁⲛ · ⲛ̄[	[. . .]ⲧⲥ[c] ⲛ̄ⲧⲕⲉ-	ⲧⲁ[ⲓ] ⲉⲓⲉ [d
]ⲥ ⲛⲁⲥ	ⲛ̄ⲧ[	[ⲗⲉⲩⲥⲓⲥ ⲛ̄ⲡ︦ⲣ︦ⲣⲟ	?
	ⳓ[	]ⲉⲛ	
	ⲃⲟⲗ ⲛ̄[	]ⲭⲉⲙⲛϣ-	
	[.]ⲟⲩ[		

---

  [a] Or [ⲙⲛⲓⲕ].   [b] My copy does not admit of ⲡⲉⲭⲁⲩ.   [c] There should be space for
[ϩⲟⲧⲉ ϩⲏ]ⲧⲥ.   [d] My copy allows ⲧⲁⲉⲓ ⲉ[.

      [1] Raphael *loq.* ?   [2] Possibly 'the saintly [Apa] Ph.'

Fol. 2. Recto. ... 'lord. We beheld the Christians ($\chi\rho$.) ... before .....
in places ...., he being like unto a youth[1] ... of about fifteen years.'
Diocletian said unto Romanus and all his great (men), '..... thy (?) ...
[com]mand (? $\kappa\epsilon\lambda\epsilon\nu\sigma\iota\varsigma$[2]) ... to him .....

... burn them[3] [in] fire, [until they] cease .... then cast [him
in]to the sea ($\theta\alpha\lambda$.), so that ($\omega\sigma\tau\epsilon$) they may not even find (?) his body ($\sigma\hat{\omega}$.)
at all ($\delta\lambda\omega\varsigma$), to build for it a shrine ($\mu\alpha\rho\tau\upsilon\rho\iota\upsilon\nu$)'; for a shrine ($\mu$.) shall be
built for them at the last .....

Verso. ... the king .... this word ... the so[ldiers?] ....
their ... according to ($\kappa\alpha\tau\alpha$) the command ($\kappa\epsilon\lambda\epsilon\nu\sigma\iota\varsigma$) of the king. The
soldiers [said] unto him, 'We would spare thee for thy beauty's sake,
O Philotheus, but ($\alpha\lambda\lambda\alpha$) we [fear?] the com[mand ($\kappa\epsilon\lambda$.) of the kin]g .....

... but ($\alpha\lambda\lambda\alpha$)'whoso is delivered ($\chi\alpha\rho\iota\zeta\epsilon\sigma\theta\alpha\iota$) unto us, we fulfil the king's
bidding.' He signed ($\sigma\phi\rho\alpha\gamma\iota\zeta\epsilon\iota\nu$) himself in Christ's [name] and said, 'My
Lord [Jesus] Christ, if this be Thy [will], that I should finish my [fight
($\alpha\gamma\omega\nu$)] in this torture ($\kappa\delta\lambda\alpha\sigma\iota\varsigma$), and that I go (?)[4] .....

No. 18.

From the Martyrdom of Psate, bishop of Psoi (Ptolemais).[5] The same
incident, of the devil, in the guise of a serpent, inspiring the young Diocletian, then still known as Agripidos,[6] is found in the *Synaxarium*.[7] The
only new feature is the name of the saint's native village.[8]

[1] Or 'this youth'.

[2] Or possibly 'instruction, chastisement', $\pi\alpha\iota\delta\epsilon\upsilon\sigma\iota\varsigma$.

[3] The *number* of this and several following pronouns is quite uncertain.

[4] Or possibly 'then' (*apodosis*) .....

[5] *Synax.*, 27 Kihak. The name is as often Psote. Fragments of the text: Brit. Mus. no. 347; Winstedt in *PSBA.* xxxii. 195, 246, 283.

[6] Written ⲁⲕⲣⲓⲡⲡⲓⲧⲁ Zoega 60 = Winstedt, *Theod.* 57, *Synax. l. c.* Aḳribîdâ, Ethiop. (*CSCO.*, vol. 37, 133) Agripâdâ, ⲁⲅⲣⲓⲡⲓⲇⲟⲥ (*CSCO.*, vol. 42, 36), Balaizah frag. (Petrie, *Gizeh* 41) ⲁⲅⲣⲓⲡⲓⲧⲟⲥ.

[7] Basset p. 456. The Copts had also a befitting legend of the persecutor's miserable end: Joh. Nikiou 418, *CSCO.*, vol. 38, 80; *B. Kopt.*

[8] Doubtless منجوج Mangûg, opposite Psoi (Menshîyah). In our fragment ⲧⲙⲟⲩ- is scarcely possible, though most such names have the article (ⲧⲙⲟⲩⲡⲥⲣⲏⲥⲉ, ⲧⲙⲟⲩⲡⲁⲣⲓ, ⲧⲙⲟⲩⲡⲣⲁⲥⲉ), rarely not (Μουναχθη). The full form, though without gen. ⲛ-, is in ⲧⲙⲟⲩⲓ-ⲟⲩⲃⲁⲥⲧⲓ (Brit. Mus. no. 529). Mangûg is 'in the district of ابسو' (Amél. *Géog.* 238), in a Cairo *Synax.* (my copy) ابسو ابصاى, though transcribed in another (Forget ii. 270) ⲡⲥⲱ, *i.e.* ⲡⲥⲟⲓ. Note that either ⲡⲥⲱⲟⲩ, Zoega 34 (= *CSCO.*, vol. 41, 11), should be read ⲡⲥⲱⲟⲩⲛ, to agree with ابصونة, *Synax.* 5 Mechîr (Forget i. 452), now باصونة, S. of Marâghah (probably the same too as ⲡⲥⲟⲟⲩⲛ, *Miss.* iv. 737); or that

l. c. is right in reading this as ابصاى.

→ *Recto.*　　　　　　　　　　↑ *Verso.*

Recto		Verso	
	[. . .]ⲱ ⲛⲟⲩⲉϣ-	ⲙⲡⲟⲣ[ϣⲓⲣⲉ]	
	[ϭ]ⲱⲗⲡ ⲉⲃⲟⲗ	ⲙⲙⲁⲡⲉ[ⲃⲁⲗ-]	
	[ⲙ]ⲡⲉⲩⲃⲓⲟⲥ ⲉ-	ⲡⲉ ⲡⲁⲓ ⲉ[ⲧⲉ-]	
	[. . . .]ⲏⲩ	ϣⲁⲩⲙⲟ[ⲩⲧⲉ]	
	[ⲡⲁⲓⲕ]ⲁⲓⲟⲥ ⲙⲛ	ⲉⲣⲟϥ ϫⲉ[ⲁⲕⲣⲓ-]	
	[ⲡⲁ]ⲇⲓⲕⲟⲥ ·	ⲡⲓⲧⲁ ·	
] ⲛⲟⲩⲱⲧ	[.]ⲙⲡⲉⲩⲥⲉⲃⲏⲥ	Ⲁⲡⲛⲟⲩⲧⲉ ϭ[ⲱ-]	ⲡⲉϫⲁ[ϥ ⲛⲁϥ]
] ⲉϣⲁⲩ-	[ⲙⲛ]ⲡⲁⲥⲉⲃⲏⲥ	ⲗⲡ ⲉⲃⲟⲗ ⲛ[ⲟⲩ-]	ϫⲉⲡⲁ[ϣⲏⲣⲉ]
[ⲙⲟⲩⲧ]ⲉ ⲉⲣⲟϥ	]ⲟⲩⲥⲙⲟⲧ ⲛ-	ϩⲱⲣⲱ[ⲙⲁ	ⲁⲕⲣⲓ[ⲡⲓⲧⲁ]
[ϫⲉ]ⲙⲟⲩⲛϭⲟⲩϭ	ⲧⲉⲓⲙⲓⲛⲉ ·	ⲑⲁⲩⲙⲁⲥⲉ ⲡ[ⲡⲉ-]	ⲁⲟⲩⲱ[ⲛ ⲛⲧⲉⲕ-]
]ϩⲣϣⲓⲣⲉ	[Ⲁ]ⲥϣⲱⲡⲉ ⲇⲉ	ⲧⲟⲩⲁⲁⲃ ⲁⲡ[ⲁ]	ⲧⲁⲡⲣ[ⲟ
	ⲛⲟⲩϩⲟⲟⲩ ⲁ-	ⲯⲁⲧⲉ ⲁϥ-	
	ⲡϣⲱⲥ ⲕⲁⲁⲩ	ϭⲱϣⲧ ⲁϥⲛⲁⲩ	
	ⲙⲡⲉⲥⲛⲁⲩ	ⲉⲡⲉⲓⲛⲟϭ ⲛ-	
	ϩⲁϩⲧⲛⲓⲧⲃ-	ⲇⲣⲁⲕⲱⲛ ⲛ-	
	ⲛⲟⲟⲩⲉ ⲁϥ-	ϩⲟϥ ⲛⲕⲁⲙ[ⲉ]	
	ⲃⲱⲕ ⲉⲡⲉϥ-	ⲉϥⲛⲕⲟⲧⲕ [ϩⲁ-]	
	ⲛⲓ ⲁϥⲛⲕⲟⲧ[ⲕ]	ⲧⲁⲡⲉ ⲛⲁⲕ[ⲣⲓ-]	
	ⲙⲡⲉϩⲟⲟⲩ ⲉ-	ⲡⲓⲧⲁ ⲡⲕ[ⲟⲩⲓ	

Recto. . . . the] same [village], which they call Mouṅgouṅ . . . youth (? youths) . . . . .

. . . without displaying their life (βίος) . . . . . the just (δίκ.) and the unjust (ἄδικος), . . . the godly (εὐσεβής) and the ungodly (ἀσεβ.), in a fashion such as this. It befell, on a day, that the shepherd left them both with the beasts and went to his house and lay down, [that] day . . . . .

Verso. . . . and the goat-herd boy, him that was called [Akri]pita. God revealed a vision (ὅραμα) . . . wonder (? θαῦμα)[1] . . . the holy Apa Psate beheld and saw this (*sic*) great black dragon (δράκων) serpent lying beneath the head of the boy (?) Ak[ri]pita . . . . .

. . . He said [unto him], 'My [son] Akri[pita], open [thy] mouth' . . . . .

---

[1] I cannot offer a satisfactory reading here.

No. 19.

The Martyrdom of Apa Moui seems to be otherwise unrecorded, though the name, sometimes with 'Apa' prefixed, is frequent.[1] He appears to have suffered at Alexandria, presumably just before his companion, Apa Herwoj,[2] here mentioned. The story is apparently narrated by a certain Pĝôl,[3] in presence of other 'saints'; but this narrative again is embedded in an Encomium, pronounced at the martyr's shrine upon his festival day.

Fol. 1. → *Recto.*

ⲗⲁⲕⲏ ᵃ ⲛ[ⲣⲁⲕⲟ-]
ⲧⲉ· ⲁⲥⲱϣ ⲉⲃ[ⲟⲗ]
ϫⲉⲡⲣⲁⲅⲓⲟⲥ ⲉ[ⲧⲟⲩ]ⲁⲁⲃ
ⲡϣⲏⲣⲉ ϣⲏⲙ ⲛⲁⲫⲟ[ⲁⲣ-]
ⲧⲟⲥ· ⲃⲟⲏⲑⲉⲓ ⲉⲧⲁⲙⲛⲧⲁⲧ-
ⲣⲱⲙⲉ· ⲛⲥⲡⲁⲣⲁⲕⲁⲗⲉⲓ
ⲙⲡⲉⲭ̅ⲥ̅ ⲛϥ̅ⲭⲁⲣⲓⲍⲉ ⲛⲁⲓ ⲛ-
ⲟⲩϣⲏⲣⲉ· ⲙⲙⲟⲛ ⲉⲓⲥ ⲟⲏⲏ-
ⲧⲉ· ⲉⲓⲥ ⲡⲉⲙⲕⲁϩ· ⲛϩⲏⲧ
ⲛⲙⲙⲁⲓ̈ ⲛ̅ⲣⲟⲅⲟ· ⲉⲟⲩⲁ· ⲉϥ-
ϩ̅ⲛⲟⲩⲛⲟϭ ⲛⲉϩⲱⲣⲏⲥ-
ⲧⲓⲁ· ⲟⲛⲧⲉⲩⲛⲟⲩ ⲇⲉ

↑ *Verso.*

[ⲁⲩⲱ ⲁⲥ]ϣⲱⲡⲉ ⲁⲡⲛⲏ̊ⲩ-
[ⲧⲉ ⲥⲙⲟⲩ ⲉ]ⲣⲟⲥ ⲁⲥⲱ· ⲁⲥⲭⲡⲟ·
[ⲛⲟ]ⲩϣⲏⲣⲉ [ⲁ]ⲥⲙⲟⲩⲧⲉ· ⲉⲡⲉϥ-
[ⲣⲁ]ⲛ ⲛ̅ⲡⲣⲁⲛ ⲛ̅ⲡⲙⲁⲣⲧⲩ-
[ⲣⲟ]ⲥ ⲉⲧⲟⲩⲁⲁⲃ· ⲁⲡⲁ ⲙⲟⲩⲓ̈:
ⲁⲥϣⲱⲡⲉ ⲇⲉ ⲡⲉϫⲁϥ· ⲙ̅ⲛ-
ⲛ̅ⲥⲁⲧⲣⲉⲡϩ̅ⲛⲥⲉⲙⲱⲛ
ϣⲓⲛⲉ ⲛ̅ⲥⲱϥ ⲕⲁⲧⲁ ⲡⲟⲣ-
ϩⲓ̈ⲛⲟⲛ· ⲁϥϣⲁϫⲉ· ⲙ̅ⲡⲙⲁⲣ-
ⲧⲩⲣⲟⲥ ⲉⲧⲟⲩⲁⲁⲃ· ⲉϥϫⲱ ⲙ̅-
ⲙⲟⲥ ϫⲉⲟⲩⲛⲉ ⲛⲉⲓ̈ⲟⲣⲃⲏⲅⲉ· ⲉ-
ⲧ̅ⲕⲉⲓⲣⲉ ⲙ̅ⲙⲟⲟⲩ ϩ̅ⲛⲧⲉϥⲫⲩⲗ-

ᵃ ⲫⲩⲗ]ⲗⲁⲕⲏ.

[1] With ⲁⲡⲁ, Brit. Mus. nos. 1027, 1228; *Saqqara* no. 73; without, Brit. Mus. no. 1102; Gayet pl. lviii; Hall *Copt. and Gr. Texts*, 113; Rylands no. 122 &c. Krall no. viii cites Μούη (whence?), *cf.* ᾿Αμμῶης of the *Apophthegmata.* The بمويه of *Synax.*, 20 Bâbeh = ⲁⲙⲟⲓ (*Mus. Guim.* xxv. 327). Μωβεῖ *Vit. Pachom.* § 72 is أموى in the Cairo edition 136 (*v.* Appendix below), though in Paris MS. 261, f. 218 أمون.

[2] Reading uncertain. A martyr thus named, ـا.ؤ.د. 16 Kihak. His church, at ? Aphrodito, *Pap. Gr. Byz.* (J. Maspero) no. 67094. Scarcely the saint هروة Abû Sâlih, 90 b = Makrizi,

Churches no. 31 ماروطا (?ظا), with church at Sumustâ. The name Ὀρουόγχιος, ᾿Αρ- (*v.* Brit. Mus. no. 1028) is particularly frequent in Aphrodito documents (*v.* Brit. Mus. *Gr. Pap. Cat.* iv). Abû 'l-Barakât's Calendar (Paris arabe 203, f. 258 v.) transcribes this رواخياس.

[3] Whether this is Shenoute's predecessor, and the latter same as the ⲡϫⲟⲗ جول of certain Diptychs (Cairo *Theotokia* 82, Leyden MS. no. 41, named with the martyrs ⲕⲗⲟϫ Coluthus and ⲕⲁⲩ) we cannot tell; nor whether ⲡϭⲱⲗ invoked on stelae (Petrie *Memphis* i, pll. lill, livᵛ; *Ann. au Serv.* viii. 83) is distinct from these.

ⲈⲦⲘ̅ⲘⲀⲨ ⲀⲠⲘⲀⲢⲦⲨⲢ[ⲟⲥ]
ⲉⲧⲟⲩⲁⲁⲃ ϣ̅ⲡ̅ⲧ̅ⲏ̅ϥ̅ ⲉϫⲱ[ⲥ]
ⲁϥⲥⲙⲟⲩ' ⲉⲣⲟⲥ ⲁⲥⲟⲩϫⲁⲓ̈
ⲁⲥⲃⲱⲕ ⲉⲡⲉⲥⲏ̅ⲓ̈ ⲉⲥϯ ⲉⲟ[ⲟⲩ]
ⲙ̅ⲡⲛⲟⲩⲧⲉ' ⲙ̅ⲡⲙⲁⲣ-
ⲧⲩⲣⲟⲥ ⲉⲧⲟⲩⲁⲁⲃ ·
                margin ⟩

ⲗⲁⲕⲏ · ⲁⲩⲱ ϩ̅ⲛ̅ⲟⲩⲛⲟϭ ⲛ̅-
ⲑⲩⲙⲟⲥ' ⲁϥⲕⲉⲗⲉⲩⲉ ⲉⲧⲣⲉⲩ-
ⲃⲁⲥⲁⲛⲓⲍⲉ ⲙ̅ⲡⲡⲉⲧⲟⲩⲁⲁⲃ'
ϩ̅ⲛ̅ϩⲉⲛⲃⲁⲥⲁⲛⲟⲥ' ⲉⲩⲟϣ'
ⲙ̅ⲛ̅ϩⲉⲛⲕⲟⲗⲁⲥⲧⲏⲣⲓⲟⲛ'
ⲉⲛⲁϣⲱⲟⲩ ⲉⲁϥⲧⲁⲗⲟϥ'[a] ⲉ-
                margin

_____

[a] Apparently not ⲉⲁⲩ-; therefore ⲁϥϭⲓⲧⲉ in next line.

Fol. 1. *Recto.* . . . 'prison (φυλακή) of [? Rako]te (Alexandria) and she cried out, "Holy (ἅγιος) saint, un[blemish]ed (? ἄφθαρτος [1]) youth, help (βοηθεῖν) my forlornness, and entreat (παρακαλεῖν) the Christ that He grant (χαρίζειν) me a child. Verily behold, grief is mine (*lit.* is with me) more than (were I) one in distant (*lit.* great) exile (ἐξοριστία)." And (δέ) thereupon the saintly martyr (μάρτυρος) had pity upon her and blessed her, and she was made whole and went unto her house, giving glory unto God and the saintly martyr (μαρ.).[2]

(*Verso.*) [And it] befell that God [blessed] her and she conceived and bare a son, and called his name (as) the name of the saintly martyr (μαρ.). Apa Moui. But (δέ) it befell,' said he, 'after that the *praeses* (ἡγεμών) had required him in (κατά) his turn (ὄρδινον), that he spake with the saintly martyr (μαρ.), saying, "What be these things which thou doest in the prison (φυλ.)?" And in great wrath (θυμός) he bade (κελ.) them torment (βασανίζειν) the saint with heavy torments (βάσανος) and many punishments (κολαστήριον), and having raised him upon

Fol. 2. → *Recto.*   ↑ *Verso.*
        margin   margin
ⲡϩⲉⲣⲙⲏⲛⲧⲁ[ⲣⲓⲟⲛ ⲁϥϭⲓⲧⲉ]   ]ⲟⲟⲩ ϩ̅ⲙ̅ⲡⲧⲣⲉϥ-
ⲙ̅ⲙⲟϥ' ϣⲁⲛ[ⲧⲉⲡⲉϥⲥⲛⲟϥ]   ]ⲧⲉϩⲉ' ⲛ̅ϩⲟⲙ̅ⲧ
ϣⲟⲩⲟ ⲉϫⲙ̅ⲡⲕⲁϩ ⲁϥⲕ[ⲉ-]   ⲛⲥⲉⲥⲁϩⲧⲉ ϩⲁⲣⲟϥ ⲛ̅ϥ̅ⲧⲣⲉⲩ-

_____

[1] Sophocles s. v. gives an instance of such a usage.
[2] Presumably no gap between the columns.

ⲗⲉⲅⲉ̄ ⲇⲉ' ⲟⲛ' ⲉⲧⲣⲉⲩϯ' ⲛ̄ϩⲉⲛ-
ⲕⲁⲥⲓⲥ' ⲉⲩⲗⲟⲃϣ̄ ⲉϫⲛ̄ⲧⲉϥϫⲁ-
ⲡⲉ' ϣⲁⲛⲧⲉⲧⲥⲟⲟⲩϩⲉ' ⲛ̄ϫⲱ[ϥ]
ⲕⲱ' ⲉⲃⲟⲗ' ⲙⲛ̄ⲛ̄ⲥⲱⲥ' ⲁϥ-
ⲧⲣⲉⲩϣⲱⲧⲉ ⲛ̄ⲡⲉϥϯⲃⲉ̄
ⲛ̄ⲟⲩⲥⲁⲣ' ⲉϥⲗⲟⲃϣ̄ ⲙⲛ̄ⲛ̄-
ⲕⲉⲃⲁⲥⲁⲛⲟⲥ ⲧⲏⲣⲟⲩ ⲛ̄ⲧⲁϥ-
ϩⲩⲡⲟⲙⲓⲛⲉ' ⲉⲣⲟⲟⲩ ⲛ̄ϭⲓ ⲡϣⲏ-
ⲣⲉ ϣⲏⲙ' ⲛ̄ϫⲱⲱⲣⲉ' ⲗⲟⲓ-
Ⲡⲟⲛ ⲛ̄ⲧⲉⲣⲉϥⲇⲟⲕⲓⲙⲁⲍⲉ
ⲙ̄ⲙⲟ[ϥ] ϩ̄ⲛ̄ϩⲁϩ' ⲛ̄ⲧⲓⲙⲱ-
ⲣⲓⲁ' ⲛ̄ϭⲓ ⲡⲁⲛⲟⲙⲟⲥ ⲛ̄ϩⲏⲅⲉ-
ⲙⲱⲛ' ⲉⲁϥⲉⲓⲙⲉ ϫⲉϥ-
ⲛⲁⲥⲱⲧⲙ̄ ⲛ̄ⲥⲱϥ' ⲁⲛ
ⲉⲟⲩⲥⲓⲁ[ⲍⲉ] ⲛ̄ⲛⲉϥⲉⲓⲇⲱⲗⲟ[ⲛ]
margin

ⲛⲟⲩϫⲉ ⲛ̄ⲛⲉϥϭⲓϫ' ⲉϩⲟⲩⲛ ϩⲁ-
ⲡⲃ̄ⲗϭⲓⲗ ⲛ̄ⲥⲉⲱϣⲉ' ⲉϫⲱϥ· ⲁⲩⲱ
ⲙ̄ⲛ̄ⲥⲁⲧⲣⲉⲩⲡⲱⲧⲉ ⲛ̄ϩⲉ-
ⲙⲟⲩⲥ' ⲉⲃⲟⲗ' ϩⲓⲧⲉϥⲥⲟⲓ ⲛ̄ⲥⲉ-
ϭⲱϣ ⲙ̄ⲙⲟⲟⲩ ϩⲛ̄ⲟⲩⲕⲱϩⲧ̄
ⲙ̄ⲡⲟⲩⲛⲉϥ' ⲙ̄ⲡⲣ̄ⲣⲟⲟⲩϣ'
ⲛⲁϥ' ϩⲟⲗⲱⲥ' ϩⲁⲛⲉⲓⲃⲁⲥⲁⲛⲟⲥ
ϫⲉⲛⲉⲣⲉⲙⲓⲭⲁⲏⲗ' ⲡⲁⲣⲭⲁⲅⲅⲉ-
ⲗⲟⲥ' ⲥⲕⲉⲡⲁⲍⲉ ⲙ̄ⲙⲟϥ' ⲉϥϯ
ϭⲟⲙ' ⲛⲁϥ' ⲁⲩⲱ ⲡⲉⲣⲉⲡⲡⲉⲧ-
ⲟⲩⲁⲁⲃ' ⲁⲡⲁ ϩⲉⲣⲟⲩⲟ[ϫ] ϯ ⲧⲱⲕ
ⲛ̄ϩⲏⲧ' ⲛⲁϥ
Ⲛ̄ⲧⲉⲣⲉϥⲛⲁⲩ ⲇⲉ' ⲛ̄ϭⲓ ⲡϩⲏ-
ⲅⲉⲙⲱⲛ' ϫⲉⲛϥⲛⲁⲥⲱⲧⲙ̄
ⲁⲛ' ⲛ̄ⲥⲱϥ' ⲉⲟ[ⲩⲥⲓ]ⲁⲍⲉ' ⲁϥ-
ϭⲱϣⲧ̄' ⲁϥϯ [ⲛ̄ⲧ]ⲉϥⲁⲡⲟ-
margin

(*Fol. 2. Recto.*) the rack (ἑρμητάριον), [he tortured] him, until [his blood] flowed upon the ground. And (δέ) he bade (κελ.) them moreover set glowing helmets (κασσίς[1]) upon his head, till the crown of his head was loosed. Afterward he caused them to pierce his heels[2] with a glowing awl,[3] besides (*lit.* and) all the other torments (βάσ.) that the brave youth bare (ὑπομένειν). Howbeit (λοιπόν) after the wicked (ἄνομος) *praeses* (ἡγ.) had proved (δοκιμάζειν) him with many punishments (τιμωρία), when he knew that he would not hearken unto him, to sacrifice (θυσιάζειν) unto his idols (εἴδ.)

(*Verso.*) . . . . . as he . . . the cow of bronze and that they should kindle fire beneath it[4]; and he had them lay his (*sc.* martyr's) hands in beneath

---

[1] This torture in Rossi *Pap.* i. v. 28 ; *CSCO.*, vol. 42, 131 (περικεφάλαιον); Budge *St. George*, 24 (*sic* for ⲃⲁⲥⲓⲥ), 91.

[3] Hitherto only ⲥⲁϩϥ (*v.* my *Ostr.*, no. 468).
[4] The cow (*sic* fem.) as here *CSCO., l.c.* 5 ; Budge, *l.c.* 13 (ⲙⲁⲥⲓ), 121. For ⲥⲱϫⲓⲟⲛ,

Actes, 147. For ϩⲱⲧⲉ I read ϫⲱⲧⲉ.

the wheel[1] and press thereon. And after that they had cut out[2] strips from off his back and had boiled them[3] with fire and oil, it caused him not to pay heed[4] at all (ὅλως) under these torments (βάσ.), for Michael the archangel (ἀρχ.) protected (σκεπάζειν) him, strengthening him, and the saintly Apa Herwoj (?) did encourage him. But (δέ) when the *praeses* (ἡγ.) saw how that he would not hearken unto him to sacrifice (θυσ.), he was wroth and gave his sentence (ἀπόφασις).

Fol. 3. ↑ *Recto.*

ϩⲫⲁⲥⲓⲥ· ⲗⲟⲓ[ⲡⲟⲛ· ϩⲙ̄ⲡ-]
ⲧⲣⲉⲡϩⲏⲧⲉⲙ[ⲱⲛ ϯ ⲁⲡⲟⲫⲁ-]
ⲥⲓⲥ· ⲉⲣⲟϥ· ⲁϥ[ϣⲁϫⲉ ⲛ̄ϭⲓ ⲁⲡⲁ]
ⲡⲥⲱⲗ· ⲉⲧⲃⲉⲛϭⲟⲙ ⲙ̄[ⲡⲛⲟⲩ-]
ⲧⲉ· ⲛ̄ⲧⲁⲩϣⲱⲡⲉ ⲉⲃ[ⲟⲗ· ϩⲓⲧⲟ-]
ⲟⲧϥ̄ ⲙ̄ⲡⲉⲧⲟⲩⲁⲁⲃ· ⲁⲡⲁ
ⲙⲟⲩⲓ̈· ⲁⲩⲟⲩⲱϣⲃ̄ ⲛ̄ϭⲓ ⲡⲉ-
ⲧⲟⲩⲁⲁⲃ· ⲉⲩϫⲱ ⲙ̄ⲙⲟⲥ· ϫⲉ
ϩⲁϩ· ⲛ̄ⲥⲟⲡ· ⲁⲡⲉⲭ̅ⲥ̅ ϣⲁϫⲉ
ⲙ̄ⲡⲓⲅⲉⲛⲛⲁⲓⲟⲥ· ⲙ̄ⲡⲉⲭ̅ⲥ̅
ⲛⲁⲙⲉ· ⲉϥϫⲱ ⲙ̄ⲙⲟⲥ ⲉⲛⲥⲱ-
ⲧⲙ̄ ϫⲉⲁⲗⲏⲑⲱⲥ· ⲡⲁⲥⲱ-
ⲧⲡ̄ ⲣⲱⲙⲉ· ⲛⲓⲙ· ⲉϥⲛⲁⲟⲛⲟ-
ⲙⲁⲍ[ⲉ] ⲙ̄[ⲡ]ⲉⲕⲣⲁⲛ· ⲉⲧⲟⲩⲁⲁⲃ·
ⲛ̄ⲥⲉⲭⲟⲟⲥ ϫⲉⲡⲛⲟⲩⲧⲉ ⲙ̄-
ⲡⲙⲁⲣⲧⲩⲣⲟⲥ· ⲉⲧⲟⲩⲁⲁⲃ
ⲁⲡⲁ ⲙⲟⲩⲓ̈ ⲉ]ⲕⲉⲥⲱⲧⲙ̄ ⲉⲣⲟ̄
ϩⲙ̄ⲡⲉⲓ[ϩⲱϣ ᵃ ⲛ̄ⲧⲉⲩⲛⲟ[ⲩ]
margin

→ *Verso.*

[ϯⲛⲁⲥⲱⲧⲙ ⲉⲣ]ⲟⲟⲩ ϩⲛⲟⲩϭⲉ-
[ⲡⲏ ·   (*blank*)
[ⲡⲛⲟⲩⲧⲉ ⲡⲁ]ⲡⲁⲑⲟⲥ· ⲡⲉⲧⲣ-
[ϩⲙ̄ⲙ]ⲉ ⲙⲡⲧⲏⲣϥ̄ ⲱ ⲛⲁⲙⲉ-
[ⲣⲁⲧ]ⲉ· ⲛ̄ⲧⲟϥ· ⲟⲛ ⲧⲉⲛⲟⲩ ⲡⲉ-
ⲧⲣ̄ⲙ̄ⲙⲉ ⲙ̄ⲙⲟⲛ· ⲉⲧⲣⲉⲛ-
ⲃⲱⲕ ⲉⲡⲙⲁⲣⲧⲩⲣⲓⲟⲛ· ⲙ̄-
[ⲡ]ⲙⲁⲣⲧⲩⲣⲟⲥ· ⲉⲧⲟⲩⲁⲁⲃ· ⲁⲡⲁ
ⲙⲟⲩⲓ̈ ⲛ̄ⲧⲛⲟϣ· ⲉⲃⲟⲗ· ϩⲓ-
ⲟⲩⲥⲟⲡ· ϫⲉⲡⲛⲟⲩⲧⲉ ⲙ̄ⲡⲁ-
ⲧⲓⲟⲥ· ⲙ̄ⲙⲁⲣⲧⲩⲣⲟⲥ· ⲙ̄ⲡⲉⲭ̅ⲥ̅
ⲉⲕⲉⲥⲱⲧⲙ̄ ⲉⲣⲟⲛ· ⲡ̄ⲧ̄ϩⲁⲣⲉϩ·
ⲉⲣⲟⲛ· ⲉⲛϭⲟⲣϫ̄ⲥ̄ ⲙ̄ⲡⲇⲓⲁⲃⲟ-
ⲗⲟⲥ· ⲡⲙⲁⲣⲧ[ⲩⲣⲟⲥ] ⲙ̄ⲡⲉ-
ⲭ̅ⲥ̅ ⲉⲕⲉⲥⲟⲟⲩⲧⲛ̄ ⲛⲛⲉⲛϩⲓⲟ-
ⲟⲩⲉ· ⲡ̄ⲧ̄ϩⲁⲣⲉϩ· ⲉⲣⲟⲛ· ⲉⲡⲡⲟ-
ⲗⲩⲙⲟⲥ· ⲉⲑⲏⲡ ⲛ̄ⲧⲉ ⲡⲁⲛ-
ⲧⲓⲕⲓⲙⲉⲛⲟⲥ·
ⲡⲉⲙⲁⲣⲧⲩ[ⲣⲟⲥ ⲉ]ⲧⲟⲩⲁⲁⲃ
margin

ᵃ Or ϩⲙ̄ⲡⲉⲛ[.

[1] The wheel, *CSCO.*, *l.c.* 13, 26, 113, 218; Budge, *l.c.* 113, 178; Rylands *Cat.* no. 94. *Cf.* the remarks of Peeters, *An. Boll.* xxviii. 490, and the text *ib.* xxvi. 27, 28.

[2] *Lit.* 'divide, separate' *Cf.* ⲥⲱⲗⲡ ⲉⲃⲟⲗ.

CSCO., *l.c.* 73.

[3] *Sc.* the places thus bared.

[4] The same phrase, Zoega 361. *Cf.* Brit. Mus. no. 344, ⲛ̄ⲥⲙⲉⲗⲉⲓ ⲛⲁⲓ ⲁⲛ.

(Fol. 3. *Recto.*) Howbeit (λοιπόν), as the *praeses* (ἡγ.) [gave senten]ce (? ἀπ.) upon him, [Apa] Pgôl [spa]ke[1] concerning the mighty (works) of God that had come about through the saintly Apa Moui. The saints made answer saying, 'Many a time did Christ talk with the truly noble one (γενναῖος) of Christ, saying, whilst we heard, "Of a truth (ἀληθῶς), my chosen one, every man that shall pronounce (ὀνομάζειν) thy saintly name and say, God of the saintly martyr (μαρ.) Apa Moui, do Thou hear us in this (*or* our) need; straightway

(*Verso.*) [I will hear] them quickly." '

[The] good (ἀγαθός) God, He that guideth all, O my beloved, He it is also that now guideth us, that we should go to the shrine (μαρτύριον) of the saintly martyr (μαρ.) Apa Moui, and that we should cry out together, 'God of Christ's holy (ἅγιος) martyr, do Thou hear us and preserve us from the snares of the devil (διάβ.). Martyr of Christ, do Thou make straight our ways and preserve us from the hidden war (πόλεμος) of the adversary (ἀντικείμενος).' This saintly martyr

Fol. 4. ↑ *Recto.*

   margin

ετη[ρ]ϣα ν[αϥ ⲙ̅ⲡⲟⲟⲩ ⲟⲩ-]
ⲕⲟⲩ̈ⲓ̈ⲡⲉˊ ϩ̅ⲧ[ϩⲏⲗⲓⲕⲓⲁ ⲁⲗ-]
ⲗⲁˊ ⲟⲩⲛⲟϭⲡⲉˊ ϩ̅ⲧⲥⲟⲫⲓⲁ [ⲛ̅-]
ⲁⲗⲏⲑⲓⲛⲟⲛ · ⲁⲩϫⲟⲟⲥ ⲇⲉ ⲟⲛ ª
ⲭⲉϩⲁϩ ⲛ̅ⲥⲟⲡˊ ⲁⲡⲉⲡ̅ⲡ̅ⲁ̅ ⲙ̅[ⲡⲭⲟ-]
ⲉⲓⲥ ⲧⲟⲣⲡ̅ϥ ⲉⲛⲉⲡⲟⲩⲅⲁⲛⲓⲟ[ⲛ]
ⲙ̅ⲡⲟⲩⲟⲉⲓⲛˊ ϩⲓⲧⲛ̅ⲡⲉϥⲧⲃ̅-
ⲃⲟˊ · ⲁⲩⲱ ⲁⲩϯ ⲛⲁϥˊ ⲙ̅ⲡⲉϥ[ⲱ-]
ⲧⲓⲥⲙⲁˊ ⲛ̅ⲉⲡⲏⲅⲉˊ ϩⲓⲧⲛ̅-
ⲧⲛⲟϭ ⲛ̅ⲁⲩⲛⲁⲙⲓⲥˊ ⲉⲧⲙⲟⲟ-
ϣⲉˊ ⲡ̅ⲉⲙⲁϥˊ ⲛ̅ⲟⲩⲟⲉⲓϣˊ
ⲛⲓⲙˊ ⲉⲓⲧⲁˊ ⲙ̅ⲡ̅ⲥⲁⲛⲁⲓ̈
ⲛ̅ϯⲛⲁⲕⲁ ⲣⲱⲓ̈ ⲁⲛˊ ⲉⲡⲣ̅ⲡⲙⲉ-

→ *Verso.*

[ⲛ̅ϣⲁ ⲉⲧⲧⲁⲉⲓ]ⲏⲩ ⲛ̅[ⲧ]ⲉⲡⲁ-
[ⲑⲗⲏⲧⲏⲥ ⲛ̅ⲅ̅ⲉ]ⲛⲛⲁⲓⲟⲥˊ ⲡⲁⲣⲁ-
[ⲕ]ⲁⲗⲉⲓ ⲙ̅ⲡⲛⲟⲩⲧⲉˊ ⲡⲁϩⲟⲣⲁ[ⲧⲟⲥ]
ⲛ̅ϥⲕⲁ ⲛⲉⲛⲛⲟⲃⲉˊ ⲛⲁⲛˊ ⲉⲃ[ⲟⲗ·]
ⲁⲛⲉⲓ ⲉⲡⲉⲕⲙⲁⲣⲧⲩⲣⲓⲟⲛˊ ⲱ
ⲡⲉⲛⲧⲁϥⲡⲁⲣⲁⲇⲓⲇⲟⲩ ⲙ̅-
ⲡⲉϥⲥⲱⲙⲁˊ ⲉⲡⲙⲟⲩ ⲉⲧⲃⲉ-
ⲓ̅ⲥ̅ ⲡⲱⲛϩ ⲛ̅ⲟⲩⲟⲛ ⲛⲓⲙˊ ⲡⲁ-
ⲣⲁⲕⲁⲗⲉⲓ ⲙ̅ⲡⲉⲭ̅ⲥ̅ ⲡⲣ̅ⲣⲟˊ ⲛ̅-
ⲛⲁⲓⲱⲛˊ ⲛ̅ϥⲭⲁⲣⲓⲍⲉˊ ⲛⲁⲛˊ
ⲙ̅ⲡⲕⲱˊ ⲉⲃⲟⲗˊ ⲛ̅ⲛⲉⲛⲛⲟⲃⲉˊ
ϯⲡⲁⲣⲁⲕⲁⲗⲉⲓ̈ ⲇⲉ ⲙ̅ⲙⲱⲧⲛ̅
ⲱ ⲛⲁⲙⲉⲣⲁⲧⲉˊ ⲙⲁⲣⲛ̅ⲥⲟ-

---

[1] The sense involved by my reading here is scarcely acceptable.

ⲉⲩⲉ' ⲛ̄[ⲡⲙ]ⲁⲣ[ⲧⲩⲣ]ⲟⲥ [ⲉⲧⲟⲩ-]
ⲁⲁⲃ' ⲡⲁⲓ ⲉⲧⲡ̄ⲣ̄ϣⲁ' ⲛⲁϥ
ⲙ̄ⲡⲟⲟⲩ ⲙⲁⲣⲛ̄ⲥⲱⲟⲩϩ
Ⲱ ⲛⲁⲙ[ⲉⲣⲁ]ⲧⲉ ⲉⲡⲉⲓⲛⲟϭ
margin

ⲡϫ̄ ⲙ̄ⲡϩⲁⲅⲓⲟ[ⲥ ⲙⲙⲁ]ⲣ[ⲧⲩ-]
[ⲣⲟⲥ] ⲙ̄ⲡⲉⲭ̄ⲥ̄ ⲁⲡⲁ ⲙⲟⲩⲓ ⲛϥ̄-
ⲣϩ̄ⲙ̄ⲙⲉ ⲙ̄ⲙⲟⲛ' ϩ̄ⲙ̄ⲡⲉⲡⲉ-
ⲗⲁⲅⲟⲥ' ⲉⲧⲙ[ⲉϩ] ⲛ̄ϣⲧⲟⲣⲧ[ⲣ]
ⲉⲧⲉⲡⲉⲓⲕⲟⲥ[ⲙⲟⲥⲡⲉ] ⲁⲩ[ⲱ]
margin

(Fol. 4. *Recto.*) that we celebrate [to-day], little he is in [age (ἡλικία)], but (ἀλλά) great in the true wisdom (σοφία, ἀληθινός). And (δέ) they said[1] also (?), ' Many a time did the spirit (πν.) of the Lord catch him up to the celestial (places ἐπουράνιον) of light, because of his purity ; and he was given the baptism (φώτισμα) of heaven, because of the great power (δύναμις) that went with him at all times.' Then (εἶτα) furthermore, I will not keep silence regarding the commemoration of the saintly martyr (μαρ.), him that we celebrate to-day. Let us gather, O my beloved, to this great [and honou]red

(*Verso.*) festival], and may the noble champion (ἀθλητής, γενναῖος) entreat (παρακαλεῖν) the invisible (ἀόρατος) God that He forgive us our sins. We are come unto thy shrine (μαρτύριον), O thou that didst give thy body (σῶμα) over (παραδιδόναι) unto death for the sake of Jesus, the life of every one ; entreat thou (παρακ.) the Christ, the king of the ages (αἰών[2]), that He grant (χαρίζειν) us the forgiveness of our sins. But (δέ) I beseech (παρακ.) you, O my beloved, let us pray the holy (ἅγ.) martyr (μαρ.) of Christ, Apa Moui, that he guide us in this sea (πέλαγος) that is full of trouble, namely the world (κόσ.) and . . . . .

No. 20.

From an unidentified Martyrdom. *Recto* shows Christ appearing to several martyrs, in prison or under torture together ; *verso*, a single martyr, healed after torture.

→ *Recto.*

[. . . .]ⲡⲱⲕ
[. . . . .]ⲧⲛ ⲛ̄

margin

margin

↑ *Verso.*

ⲛⲧ[ⲉⲩⲛⲟⲩ]
ⲁϥⲧ[ⲱⲟⲩⲛ]

---

[1] *I.e.* the saints, or = ' it was said '.   [2] *Cf.* 1 Tim. i. 17.

[ⲧⲱ]ⲧⲛ̄ ⲭⲣⲟ ⲛ̄-
[ⲙ]ⲱⲧⲛ̄ ⲱ̄ ⲛ̄-
ϣⲟⲉⲓⲭ ⲛ̄ϫⲱ-
ⲱⲣⲉ ⲛⲉⲛ-
[ⲧ]ⲁⲩⲅⲩⲡⲟⲙⲓ-
ⲛⲉ ⲛ̄ⲙⲙⲁⲓ
ϩⲛ̄ⲛⲁⲡⲓⲣⲁⲥ-
ⲙⲟⲥ · ⲉⲃⲟⲗ ϫⲉ-
ⲛ̄ⲛ̄ⲥⲁⲕⲉ-
ⲕⲟⲩⲓ̈ ⲧⲉⲧⲛⲁ-
ⲟⲩⲱⲙ ⲛ̄ⲧⲉ-
ⲧⲛ̄ⲥⲱ ⲛ̄ⲙ-
ⲙⲁⲓ̈ ϩⲓϫⲛ̄[ⲧ]-
ⲧⲣⲁⲡⲉ[ⲍⲁ ⲛ-]
ⲧⲁⲙⲛ̄[ⲧⲉⲣⲟ]
ⲁⲩⲱ ⲛ̄[
    margin

margin | margin

ⲉϩⲣⲁⲓ ⲉϥⲟ[ⲩ-]
ⲟϫ ⲧⲏⲣϥ̄ ⲉ-
ⲙ̄ⲡⲗⲁⲁⲩ ⲛ̄-
ⲡⲱⲗϩ ϩⲓⲱ-
ⲱϥ ⲉⲣⲉⲛⲉϥ-
ⲙⲉⲣⲟⲟϭⲉ
ⲟⲩⲟϫ · ⲙ̄ⲛ-
ⲛⲉϥⲟⲃϩⲉ ⲁϥ-
ϯ ⲉⲟⲟⲩ ⲙ̄ⲡ-
ⲛⲟⲩⲧⲉ · ⲉϥ-
ϫⲱ ⲙⲙⲟⲥ ϫⲉ-
[ⲁϥⲟ]ⲩⲱⲛ̄ϩ ⲉ-
[ⲃⲟⲗ ⲉϫ]ⲱⲛ ⲛ̄-
[ϭⲓ ⲡⲟ]ⲩⲟⲉⲓⲛ
    margin

Recto. . . . 'you (?). Hail to you, O mighty champions, that have endured (ὑπομένειν) with me in my trials (πειρασμός)! For after yet a little (while) ye shall eat and drink with me at the table (τρά.) of my kingdom.'[1] And . . . . .

Verso. . . . Forth[with] he a[rose] all whole, with no wound upon him, his cheeks being whole and his teeth.[2] And he gave glory to God, saying,[3] ' The light [of Thy countenance] hath been displayed upon us ' . . . . .

---

[1] Luke xxii. 30.
[2] This might recall the martyrdom of Philo-theus (*v.* Wüstenfeld, *Synax.* 242, 21 ff.), but the
script here does not appear to be that of Nos. 16 or 17.
[5] Ps. iv. 6.

No. 21.

From an unidentified Martyrdom, as it would appear from fol. 2.

Fol. 1. → *Recto.*   ↑ *Verso.*

	ⲉⲙ[	]ⲡⲉⲓ	
	ⲡⲛⲟⲩ[ⲧⲉ	]ϭⲱϣⲧ̄	· ⳯⳨[
	ϭⲱⲡ̄ⲧ [	] ϩⲓⲣⲁⲧⲕ̄	ⲉϥⲉ[
	⳯ϥⲟⲧⲟⲩ ⲉⲃ[ⲟⲗ]	[ⲧⲉ]ⲛⲟⲩϭⲉ ⲉⲓⲥ	ⲧⲙⲛ[
] ⲙⲙⲟ-	ⲁⲕⲃⲱⲕ ⲟⲩ[ⲛ	[ⲡ]ⲭⲟⲉⲓⲥ ⲁϥ-	ϫⲉⲟⲩ[ⲟⲓ] ⲛⲁⲕ
ⲟⲩ ⲙⲡⲟⲩⲣⲱ	ⲁⲕϣⲱⲡⲉ	[ⲧ]ⲛⲛⲟⲟⲩⲕ	ⲡϫⲁϫⲉ ⲙ̄-
ϣⲉ ⲉⲣⲟⲕ	ϩⲛ̄ⲛⲉⲓⲣⲱ-	ϣⲁⲣⲟⲓ̈ · ⲁ-	ⲡⲛⲟⲩⲧⲉ
ⲁⲗⲗⲁ ⲁⲕⲃⲱⲕ	ⲙⲉ ⲛ̄ϭⲛⲁϣ[ⲧ̄	[ⲛ]ⲁⲩϭⲉ ⲧⲉⲛⲟⲩ	ⲙⲛ̄ⲡⲉ ⲙⲛ̄-
ⲟⲛ ⲉⲛⲟⲩ · [	ϣⲁⲛⲧⲉⲛ[	[ϯⲛ]ⲟⲉⲓ̈ ⲡⲉⲧⲛ-	ⲡⲕⲁϩ ⲉⲕⲛⲁ-
ϫⲛ̄ⲏ · ⲛ̄	?	?	ⲣⲟⲩ ⲉ[·]ϣⲁⲛ-
	margin	margin	

Fol. 1. *Recto.* . . . 'them. They sufficed thee not, but (ἀλλά) thou didst go also to' . . . . .[1] . . . 'God . . . wrath . . .; blotting[2] them out. Thou didst go, then (? οὖν), and wast in these men and didst grow strong, until' . . . . .

Verso. . . . 'behold . . . toward thee.[3] So now, lo, the Lord hath sent thee unto me. See then, now, [I ?] know (? νοεῖν) your' . . . . .
. . . 'he shall . . . ., woe unto thee, enemy of God and heaven and earth! What wilt thou do when' . . . . .

Fol. 2. ↑ *Recto.*   → *Verso.*

ϣⲁⲛ[ⲧⲱ]ⲙⲉ ⲉ-		ⲛ̄ⲧⲉⲣⲟⲩⲉⲓ ⲇⲉ
ⲣⲟⲟⲩ ⲥⲉⲛⲁⲛⲟ-		ⲉⲡⲉϣⲧⲉⲕⲟ
ⲉⲓⲛ ⲛ̄ϭⲓ ⲛ̄ⲥⲛ̄-	]ⲩⲧ	ⲁⲩⲧⲱϩⲙ̄ ⲉ-

---

[1] This may be a place or personal name, beginning with ⲛⲟⲩ-, less probably with plur. art. ⲛ-; or a word such as σύντεχνος.

[2] Reading ⲉϥϥⲟⲧⲟⲩ.

[3] ϩⲓⲣⲁⲧ- is rare. In Josh. ii. 5 = ὀπίσω ('follow after'), similarly in Budge *Homilies*, p. 16 ('towards'), and Pap. Bruce 239.

те ⲙ̄ⲡⲉϣⲧⲉ-		]ⲏ ⲡ̄ⲙ̄ⲙ̄-	ⲡⲣⲟ ⲁϥⲟⲩⲱ̄
ⲕⲟ ⲙ̄ⲛ̄ⲛ̄ⲥ̄ⲛ̄-	ⳅ[	]ⲏ	ⲛ̄ⲧⲉⲩⲛⲟⲩ
ⲧⲉ ⲙ̄ⲡⲕⲁϩ· ⲉ-	ⲏ[	]ⲡ̄ⲙ̄ⲙ̄	/ Ⲡⲙ̄ⲛⲏϣⲉ ⲁⲉ
sic ⲛⲉⲛⲧⲁⲩⲉⲛⲧⲁⲩ-	ⲏ[	]ⲏ	ⲡ̄ⲣⲱⲙⲉ ⲉⲧ-
ⲛ̄ⲧ[ⲟⲩ] ⲉ[ⲃ]ⲟⲗ ⲛ̄-	ⲡⲁ[	?	ⲣⲟⲉⲓⲥ ⲁⲩⲣⲟⲉ
ⲥⲉϣ[ⲁⲁ]ⲧⲕ̄ᵃ· ⲟⲩ̄	ⳅⲙ̄·	]ⲉϥ-	ⲛ̄ⲡⲉⲧⲙⲟⲟⲩⲧ
ⲡⲉⲧⲕⲙⲉⲉⲩⲉ	ⳤ[	ⲍ̄ⲧ	ⲛ̄ⲧⲉⲣⲉϥⲉⲓ
ⲉⲣⲟϥ·	ⲉ[		ⲁⲉ ⲉϩⲟⲩⲛ ⲛ̄-ᶜ
/ Ⲗ̄ϥⲟⲩⲱϣⲃ̄ ⲛ̄ᵇ	?		
margin		margin	

ᵃ My copy gives as alternative ⲙ[. .]ⲡⲕ, so ? ϣⲟⲡⲕ or ϣⲟⲁⲡⲕ (*cf.* Ps. cxxxviii. 10), or ⲙⲟⲟⲩⲧⲕ.   ᵇ ⲛ̄ϭⲓ.   ᶜ ⲛ̄ϭⲓ.

Fol. 2. Recto. . . . 'if [they? he?] shut (the door) upon them, shall the foundations of the prison and the foundations of the earth tremble at the things they have (*or* that have been) brought forth, and require (? them) of thee[1]? What thinkest thou?' . . . . . answered . . . . .

Verso. . . . And (δέ) when they had come to the prison, they knocked at the door and straightway it opened. But (δέ) the multitude of men that kept watch were as if dead. And (δέ) when . . . had come in . . . . .

No. 22.

From the beginning of a Martyrdom. Diocletian's gods are enumerated and a part of the edict is to be read, whereby he ordered their worship.[2] Some 20 goddesses were named in the space of this fragment; may we conclude that the complete list gave 35, since in the passages usually parallel to this the 70 deities are divided equally into male and female?[3] I know of no other Coptic martyrdom showing a like list of names. If we assume the text to be a translation, there is no need to seek for egyptianized forms of the divinities.

[1] This sentence is not necessarily interrogative, but the following question makes it likely. An alternative reading allows 'and they slay thee', which would show that the person addressed is not the devil, as fol. 1 *vo.* might suggest.

[2] Similar edicts: *CSCO.*, vol. 42, 80, 157, 200.

[3] *Cf. op. cit.* 200; Hyvernat *Actes*, 78, 201.

→ p. ⲧ̄.

margin

ⲧⲁ]ⲣⲑⲉⲙⲓⲥ

ⲧ]ⲃⲉⲣⲥⲉⲫⲱ-

[ⲏⲏ   ]ⲁⲭⲏ, ⲧⲥⲩⲗⲏ-

[ⲏⲏ   ]ⲕⲏ · ⲑⲉⲗⲗⲁⲥ

] ⲧⲕⲁⲗⲗⲓⲟⲡⲏ

] · ⲧⲉⲣⲩⲛⲓⲥ ·

]ⲁⲧⲏ · ⲧⲡⲟⲛ-

]ⲛⲱ · ⲧⲓⲛⲙⲉ-ᵃ

[ⲥⲓⲥ   ] · ⲛ · ⲧⲅⲩⲣⲁ

]ⲓⲥ · ⲧⲁⲩⲣⲁⲛⲟⲥᵇ

ⲛ]ⲁⲓⲛⲉ ⲛ̄ⲣⲁⲛ

ⲛⲟⲩ]ⲧⲉ ⲛ̄ⲥϩⲓⲙⲉ

ⲇⲓⲟⲕⲗⲏⲧ]ⲓⲁⲛⲟⲥ ⲇⲉ ⲡ-

[ⲣⲣⲟ   ]ⲡ ⲉⲃⲟⲗ ⲛ̄[

]ϩⲓⲣⲙ̄[

]ⲁⲧ[

↑ p. ⲇ̄.

margin

ⲡⲣⲉⲥⲃ[ⲩⲧⲉⲣⲟⲥ · ⲉⲓⲧⲉ ⲇⲓⲁ-]

ⲕⲟⲛⲟⲥ · ⲉⲓ[ⲧⲉ ⲁⲛⲁⲅⲛⲱⲥ-]

ⲧⲏⲥ · ⲉⲓⲧⲉ [ⲣⲙ̄ϩⲉ · ⲉⲓⲧⲉ]

ϩⲙ̄ϩⲁⲗ · ⲉⲓ[ⲧⲉ

ⲟⲩⲥⲓⲁⲍⲉ · [ⲛⲟⲩ-]

ⲧⲉ ⲁⲩⲱ ⲡ[ⲉⲧⲛⲁϫⲟⲟⲥ]

ϫⲉⲁⲛ̄ⲅ̄ⲟⲩⲭ[ⲣⲏⲥⲧⲓⲁⲛⲟⲥ]

ⲉⲩⲉⲁⲛⲙⲉⲅ[ⲉ ⲙ̄ⲡⲉϥ-]

ⲙⲟⲩ ϩⲛ̄ⲧⲥ[ⲏϥⲉ · ⲛ̄ⲧⲱⲧⲛ]

ⲇⲉ ⲧⲏⲣⲧⲛ̄ [ⲛⲁϫⲓⲱⲙⲁ-]

ⲧⲓⲕⲟⲥ ⲙ̄ⲡ[

ⲥϩⲁⲓ̈ ⲉⲣⲏⲥ[

ⲧⲏⲣⲟⲩ ⲕⲁ[ⲧⲁ ⲙⲁ

. . .] ϫⲉⲕⲁ[ⲥ

. . . .]ⲛⲁⲩ[

]ϫⲉ[

margin   margin

ᵃ ⲉ altered from (or to ?) ⲏ.   ᵇ Or -ⲁⲥ.

(p. 3.) . . :, Artemis, ..., Persephone, . . . achê, Selene, . . . kê,[1] Thellas,[2] . . . ., Calliope, ..., Erinys, . . . atê,[3] Pon . . ., . . . nô, Nemesis, ... n,[4] Hera, . . .,[5] Dyranos,[6] . . . . . These are the names [of . . . god]desses . . . And (δέ) [Diocle]tian the [king . . . . .

(p. 4.) '. . . whether] presbyter (πρεσ.) or (εἴτε) deacon (διάκονος) or (εἴτε) reader (ἀναγ.) or (εἴτε) freeman [or (εἴτε)] slave or (? εἴτε) . . . . . sacrifice (θυσιάζειν) . . . . . god(s ?). And whoso [shall say], I am a Ch[ristian (χρ.),

---

[1] k uncertain. Nike, Ananke?

[2] Assuming ⲧ the article. But perhaps misspelt (for ⲑⲉⲗ-), so 'Hellas'. The name may have continued into next line.

[3] a uncertain. Hekate (even Aphrodite) too

short for space, which may have held two names.

[4] n uncertain.

[5] Themis ? (or in l. 1, for Artemis).

[6] Or Dyranas. After this probably another name.

his] death shall be adjudged ($\delta\eta\mu\epsilon\acute{\nu}\epsilon\iota\nu$[1]) with the s[word].   But ($\delta\acute{\epsilon}$) do ye all, [offici]als ($\dot{\alpha}\xi\iota\omega\mu\alpha\tau\iota\kappa\acute{o}s$) of . . . . ., write[2] to the south, [to] all . . . in turn ($\kappa\alpha\tau\alpha$-) . . . . ., so that . . . . .'

No. 23.

Perhaps from a Martyrdom.   The sequence of *recto* and *verso* are doubtful.

→ *Recto.*

margin

[. .] a[ɣⲱ] ⲡⲁⲛⲟⲩ-
ⲧⲉ ⲉⲕⲉⲭⲓ ⲙⲟⲉⲓⲧ
ϧⲏⲧ ϧⲓⲛⲉ̈[ϧ]ⲓⲟⲟⲩⲉ
ⲧⲏⲣⲟⲩ ⲉϯⲛⲁⲃⲱⲕ
ⲛϧⲏⲧⲟⲩ ⲭⲉⲛ[. .]
ϣⲁ ⲙⲡⲟⲗⲩⲙⲟⲥ
ⲉⲧϧⲏⲡ ϧⲙⲡⲭⲁ-
ⲭⲉ ⲉϧⲟⲩⲛ ⲉⲓⲧⲉ ϧ[ⲓ]
[. .]ᵃˡ aⲗ . . . [
[. . .]ⲡ ϣⲁⲡⲁ[
[. . a]ɣⲱ ⲡ[

↑ *Verso.*

]ⲧⲉϥ   ⲉϣϣⲱⲙ[
]ⲧ   ⲟⲩⲛᵃ ϧⲁⲣⲟϥ ⲁϥⲛ-
          ⲕ[ⲟⲧ]ⲕ ⲁϥⲱⲃ̄ϣ
          ⲁⲅⲱ ⲛⲧⲉⲩⲛⲟⲩ
          ⲉⲓⲥ ⲡϣⲏⲣⲉ ⲛⲧⲙ[ⲛⲧ-]
          ⲁⲅⲁⲑⲟⲥ ⲁϥⲧⲱ-
          ⲟⲩⲛ ⲁϥ[ⲁ]ⲗⲉ ⲉⲭⲛ-
          ⲟⲩⲕⲗⲟⲟⲗⲉ [ⲛⲟⲩⲟ-]
          [ⲉⲓ]ⲛ ⲙⲛⲙ[
          [. ⲁ]ⲣ̄ⲭⲁⲅⲅ[ⲉⲗⲟⲥ]
          [. . .]ⲡⲉⲛ[

margin

ᵃ Perhaps ⲧⲱ]ⲟⲩⲛ.

Recto.   . . . '[and] my God, do Thou guide me upon all the ways wherein I shall go; for (?) . . . . . hidden war ($\pi\acute{o}\lambda\epsilon\mu os$) with the enemy within,[3] or ($\epsilon\check{\iota}\tau\epsilon$)' . . . . .

Verso.   . . . bear (?) it (? him), and he lay down and slept.   And straightway, behold, the Son of Goodness (-$\dot{\alpha}\gamma\alpha\theta\acute{o}s$[4]) arose and mounted upon a cloud [? of ligh]t . . . . . archangel[s?] . . . . .

[1] Or ?[the publicly executed]: cf. δημ...
[2] Or ['this] rescript'.
[3] The text, as I have read it, scarcely allows of

this.   After ϣⲁ, ⲡ[ⲟⲗ] seems impossible

[4] *Cf.* Rossi ii. IV. 65, 'Son of Compassion,' as epithet of Christ.

No. 24.

Life of (or Encomium on) Pachomius. There is little to guide us as to the sequence either of leaves or pages here, if indeed all nine fragments belong to one MS. The order I have adopted is merely tentative. Pachomius' name occurs only in foll. 7 and 9, but 4, 5, and 6 may, with much probability, be claimed for the same subject. As to the remainder it is impossible to feel any certainty; they might be from parenetic introductions to or digressions from known incidents of the history. Certain incidents (foll. 6 *ro.*, 9 *vo.*) are only conceivable as part of this Life if we assume a widely different or much amplified recension to be at the base of our text.[1] It must however be confessed that the reading of scarcely a phrase but is open to question.

Fol. 1.   ↑ *Recto.*   → *Verso.*

margin   margin

[. . .]ⲧⲓⲙⲉ	ⲣⲟ ⲛⲁ̣ⲓ̣ⲧᶜ·[	[ⲡⲉⲧ]ⲥⲟⲟⲩⲛ̄ⲡ̄ϥᵈ ⲁⲩ-	ⲛ̄ⲧⲟϣ [
[. . .]ⲡ̄ⲣ̄ⲣⲟ ⲛⲁ-	ⲉⲧⲟⲩⲁⲁⲃ ⲡ̄[ⲣⲟ-]	[ⲧⲟ]ⲣ̄ⲡ̄ϥ ϣⲁ-	ⲧⲉϥⲡⲁ̣[ⲧⲣⲓⲥ]
[ⲧⲁ]ⲁⲥᵃ ⲛⲁⲩ ϣⲁⲛ-	ⲧⲣⲉⲡⲉ ⲙ̄ⲙ̣[ⲟ-]	[ⲧ]ⲙⲉϩϣⲟⲙⲧⲉ	ⲇⲉ ⲡⲁⲗⲏ[ⲑⲓ-]
[.]ⲁⲧⲥⲟ ⲛⲉⲩϯ	ⲟⲩ · ⲙ̄ⲡⲉ̣[	[ⲛ̄]ⲡⲉ · ⲁⲩⲉⲓⲥ	ⲛⲏ · ⲟⲩⲥⲩ[ⲙⲡⲟ-]
[ⲙ]ᵇ ⲉⲧ̄ⲙ̄ ⲉⲃⲗⲁⲡ-	ⲛ̄ⲣⲁϩ ⲛ̄ⲥ[ⲟⲛ	[. .]ⲛ̄ⲧⲉⲭⲁⲣⲓⲥ	ⲗⲓⲧⲏⲥⲡⲉ ⲛ̄[-]
[ⲧ]ⲉⲓ ⲙ̄ⲙⲟⲟⲩ	ⲉⲧ[ⲥ-]	[ⲙ̄ⲡ]ⲛⲟⲩⲧⲉ ⲛ̄-	ⲓⲉⲣⲟⲥⲟⲗⲩⲙ[ⲓ-]
[ϩ]ⲛ̄ⲗⲁⲁⲩ ⲍⲉⲛ̄-	ⲃ̄ⲱ̄ [	]ⲛⲉ	ⲧⲏⲥ ⲛ̄ⲧⲉ
ⲛⲉⲡⲣ̄ⲣⲟ̄ ⲥⲱ-	ⲉⲧ[	]ϩⲉⲛ-	ⲧⲙⲉϩⲥⲁϣ[ϥⲉ]
ϣⲧ ⲉⲣⲟⲟⲩ · ⲟⲩ-	ⲛ̄ϩ[	ⲡⲣ]ⲟⲥ ⲑⲉ	ⲙ̄ⲡⲉ · ⲧⲉⲕ[ⲕⲗⲏ-]
[ⲧ]ⲉⲓ̈ⲙⲛⲉ ⲥⲁⲣ-	ⲡ[	]ϭ̄ⲙ̄-	ⲥⲓⲁ ⲛⲁⲙⲉ ⲛ̄[ⲛ-]
ⲡⲉ ⲡⲃⲓⲟⲥ ⲛ̄-			ϣⲣ̄ⲡⲙ̄ⲙⲓⲥ[ⲉ]
ⲛⲉⲧⲟⲩⲁⲁⲃ [			[ⲉ]ⲧⲟⲛ̄ⲙ̄ⲡ[ⲏⲩⲉ]
[. . .]ⲛⲁⲣⲁ[			[.]ⲁϥϣ[

ᵃ Or ⲕⲁⲁⲥ.   ᵇ Apparently not space for [ⲙⲉ]. In 4 perhaps [ⲧ]ϥⲧⲥⲟ.   ᶜ Perhaps ⲡⲉ for ⲣⲟ.   ᵈ This cannot be correct: either ⲛⲉⲧⲥⲟⲟⲩⲛ ⲉⲁⲩ- (*v.* Bible text) or ⲡⲉⲧⲥⲟⲩⲱⲛϥ ⲁⲩ-.

---

[1] That it is already far removed from the primary recensions of the Life may be gathered from the mere citation of the Psalms by P., before his conversion (fol. 8).

Fol. 1. *Recto.* ... village (?) ..... the king shall grant (?) them, that he would spare their villages and not injure ($\beta\lambda\acute{a}\pi\epsilon\iota\nu$) them in aught, lest the king should behold them. For ($\gamma\acute{a}\rho$) such is the life ($\beta\acute{\iota}os$) of the saints .... [the] king shall (?) ... saints (?) exhort ($\pi\rho\sigma\tau\rho\acute{\epsilon}\pi\epsilon\iota\nu$) them to ... oftentimes ..... instruction ...

Verso. ... God it is] knoweth. He was caught up to the third heaven.[1] Give ... the grace ($\chi\acute{a}\rho\iota s$) of God .... according as ($\pi\rho\acute{o}s$) .... nome. But ($\delta\acute{\epsilon}$)· his true fatherland ($\pi\alpha\tau\rho\acute{\iota}s$, $\dot{a}\lambda\eta\theta\iota\nu\acute{o}s$) (was that) he was a fellow citizen ($\sigma\upsilon\mu\pi\sigma\lambda\acute{\iota}\tau\eta s$), one of Jerusalem ($\acute{\iota}\epsilon\rho\sigma\sigma\sigma\lambda\upsilon\mu\acute{\iota}\tau\eta s$) of the seventh heaven, the true church ($\acute{\epsilon}\kappa\kappa\lambda$.) of the first-born that are in heaven[2] ...

Fol. 2.　↑ *Recto.*　　　　→ *Verso.*

ⲙ̄ⲡⲣ[	]ϥ̄
ⲱ ⲡ[ⲇⲓⲁⲃⲟ-	]ⲙⲡⲉϥ-
ⲗⲟⲥ ⲛ̄ⳅ̄ⲝ[ⲟⲟⲥ	] .. ⲉⲛⲛⲁ-
ⲝⲉⲁⲛⳇ̄ⲟⲩ[ⲥⲟⲟ-	[ⲛ]ⲟⲩⲝⲉ ⲙⲙⲁⲩ̑
ⲡⲉ ⲛ̄ϯⲙ[a	[ⲛ̄ⲥ]ⲁⲛⲃⲟⲗ ⲛ̄-
ⲁⲛ ⲙ̄ⲡⲉ[	[ⲙⲟ]ⲛ ⲝⲉⲛⲁ-c
ⲙ̄ⲡⲁⲝⲟ[ⲉⲓⲥ	] . ⲛϩⲟ ⲉⲣⲟϥ
ⲉⲓⲟⲧ[b	]ⲉ̄ ⲉⲙⲁⲩ
ⲧ[	]ⲛ̄
	]ϩ

a ⲙ[ⲉⲓⲛⲉ] is tempting, but a verb is equally probable.　b Perhaps ⲥ for ⲟ.　c Perhaps ⲡⲁ- for ⲡⲁ-.

Fol. 2. *Recto.*[3] Do not ....., O Devil ($\delta\iota\acute{a}\beta$. ?)[4], saying, I am not a thief (?) of this (sort) ..... my Lord (?) ...

Verso. ... we (?) will cast death forth from us, for ....

---

[1] 2 Cor. xii. 2. The words do not coincide with Ciasca's text. *Cf.* the similar words used in Am...

[2] *Cf.* Heb. xii. 23. Such phrases, as to heavenly citizenship, are used by martyrs under trial, *e. g.* Hyvernat *Actes*, 197.

[3] Scarcely a word can be read here with certainty. If not disposed, perhaps ... ⲗⲟⲥ seems still less suitable.

Fol. 3. ↑ *Recto.*[a]

margin
[ⲡⲛⲟ]ⲩⲧⲉ † ⲛⲟ-
[ⲙⲟⲥ] ⲙ̣ⲡⲉϥ-[b]
]ⲛⲧⲁϥ-
]ϩⲉⲛ-
ⲛ̄]ⲛⲟⲩⲃ
ⲁ]ⲗⲗⲁ
ϫ]ⲟⲓ̈ⲥ̣

→ *Verso.*

margin
ⲙ̄ⲡϫⲁ[ϫⲉ
ⲛⲁⲉⲓⲣ̣[
ⲡⲉϥⲧ[
ⲥ̣ⲓ̣ⲛ[
ⲙ . [
ⲛⲧ[
ⲧⲕ[

[a] I am not sure that this fragment does not rather belong to No. 21. [b] Perhaps ⲁⲡⲉϥ-.

Fol. 3. *Recto.* . . . God gives laws (*νόμος*) to (?) his . . . . which he had . . . . golden . . . But (*ἀλλά*) . . . Lord (?) . . .

Verso. . . . the enemy . . . will (*fut.*) . . . his . . .

Fol. 4. ↑ *Recto.*

]ⲣ̣ⲟⲕ
[ⲧⲁϩⲉ]ⲗⲡⲓⲥ
[ϫⲓⲛⲉⲓϫⲓ] ⲉⲕⲓⲃⲉ
[ⲛ̄ⲧⲛ̄ⲧⲁ]ⲙⲁⲁⲩ
[ⲁⲓⲛⲟϫⲧ] ⲉⲣⲟⲕ
[ϫⲓⲛⲉⲓϩ]ⲛ̄ⲧⲟⲟⲧⲉ

ⲣⲟⲥ ϭⲛ̄ ⲗ[ⲁⲁⲩ]
ⲙ̄ⲙⲁ ϩⲣⲁⲓ̈ [ⲛ̄ϩⲏ-]
ⲧϥ̄ · ⲡⲉⲓ̈ⲡ̣[ⲉ-]
Ⲧⲟⲩⲁⲁⲃ ⲇ[ⲉ]
ⲛⲉϥⲡⲣⲟⲕⲟ-
ⲡⲧⲉ ϩⲛ̄ⲑⲩⲗⲓ-
ⲕⲓⲁ · ⲛⲉⲩⲛ̄
Ⲟⲩⲣ̄ⲡⲉ ⲇⲉ ⲙ̄-
ⲡⲣ[ⲏⲥ] ⲙ̣̄ⲡϯ-
ⲙⲉ ⲛ̄ⲟⲩⲕⲟⲩⲓ̈
ⲧⲁⲭⲁ ⲉϣⲁⲩ-
ⲧⲏⲛⲟⲟⲩ ⲛ̄-
[ⲛ̄]ⲕⲟⲩⲓ̈ ⲛ̄ϣⲏ-
[ⲣⲉ ⲉ]ⲧⲣⲉ̣ⲩⲣ̄ϩⲱⲃ
[ⲛ̄ϩ]ⲏⲧϥ̄ ϩⲱⲥ

→ *Verso.*

[. . .]. ϩⲙ̄ⲡⲙⲟ-
[ⲟⲩ]. ⲛⲁⲓ̈ ⲉⲧⲉ-
[ϣ]ⲁⲩⲙⲟⲩⲧⲉ ⲉ-
[ⲣ]ⲟⲟⲩ ϫⲉⲛ̄ⲧⲁⲓ̈-
ⲣⲉ · ϩⲁϩⲧⲛ̄ⲙ̄-
ⲡⲟⲛⲇⲏⲥ ⲇⲉ ⲛ̄-
ⲧⲁⲩⲥⲙⲓⲛⲉ ⲛ̄-
ⲛ̄ϫⲱⲱⲙⲉ ⲛ̄-
ⲛ̄ϩⲉⲗⲗⲏⲛ ⲉ-
ϣⲁⲩⲙⲟⲩⲧⲉ ⲉ-
ⲣⲟⲟⲩ ϫⲉⲛ̄ϣ[ⲏ-]
ⲣⲉ ⲙ̄ⲡⲟⲥⲓ[ⲇⲱⲛ]
ϩⲙ̄ⲡⲉϩⲟⲟ̣[ⲩ
ⲟⲩⲛ̄ⲛ̄ⲧ̣[
ⲙ̣̄ⲡ[

Ⲁⲩⲱ̣[
ⲛⲁ[
ⲛ̄ⲟ]
ⲧⲁ[
Ⲡⲉ[

Fol. 4. Recto (cf. AS. § 2). . . . Thou[1] art my hope (ἐλπίς) since I took the breast of my mother : I cast myself upon Thee since I was in the womb . . . . . [not] find any place therein.[2] But (δέ) this saint advanced (προκόπτειν) in age (ἡλικία). And (δέ) there was a temple, a little to the south of the village. Now (τάχα[3]) they would send boys to work therein, as (ὡς) . . .

Verso. . . . in the water, which are called 'sprites?'[4], but (δέ) by the authors (ποιητής) that have composed the books of the Greeks (ἕλλην) they are called 'the children of Poseidon'.[5] On the day therefore (οὖν) when . . .

Fol. 5.   ↑ *Recto.*   → *Verso.*ᵃ

margin   ⳋ   ⲁ̄

ϩⲓⲧⲙⲡⲉϥⲉⲓⲟⲧⲉ	ⲧⲉ ⲛ[	ⲛ̄]ⲧⲉⲣⲟⲩ-	ⲙ̄ⲡⲛⲟⲩⲧⲉ ϩⲟⲧⲡ
ⲉⲃⲟⲗ ϫⲉϩⲉⲛ-	ⲛ̄ⲧⲉ[	]ⲛⳓⲓ ⲛ̄-	ⲁⲛ ⲙ̄ⲡⲛⲉϥϣⲏ-
ⲥⲡⲟⲩⲁⲁⲓⲟⲥⲛⲉ	ⲉⲡⲣ̄[ⲡⲉ	[ⲧⲁⲗⲁⲓ]ⲛⲱⲣⲟⲥ	ⲣⲉ· ⲟⲩⲁⲧϭⲟⲙ ⲅⲁⲣ-
ϩ̄ⲡⲧⲙ̄ⲛⲧ-		]ⲩ	ⲡⲉ ⲉⲧⲣⲉⲛ̄ⲗⲏⲥ-
ϩⲉⲗⲗⲏⲛ· ⲙ̄-			ⲧⲏⲥ ϥⲓ ⲛ̄ⲙ̄ⲙⲁⲩ
ⲡⲟⲩⲉⲓⲙⲉ ⲇⲉ ⲉ-			ⲙ̄ⲡⲟⲛⲏⲃⲥ ⲉⲧ-
ⲧⲙⲉⲣⲓⲥ ⲛ̄ⲓ̈ⲁ-			ⲙⲟⲩϩ ⲉⲡⲙⲁ ⲉ-
ⲕⲱⲃ ϫⲉⲛⲟⲩ-			ⲧⲟⲩⲛⲁϫⲓⲟⲩⲉ
ⲧⲉⲓ̈ⲙⲛⲉ ⲁⲛ[ⲛⲉ]		]ⲉϥ	ⲛ̄ϩⲏⲧϥ̄· ⲁⲗⲗⲁ
ϫⲉⲡⲉⲛ[			ϣⲁⲩⲃⲱⲕ ϩ̄ⲛ-
[. . .]ⲧⲛ̄[			[ⲟⲩⲕ]ⲁⲕⲉ ϫⲉⲛ̄-
[. .]ⲙ· ⲁϥ[			[ⲛⲉⲩ]ⲧⲁϩⲟⲟⲩ
			]ϩⲉ[
			]ⲧϭⲟⲙ[

ᵃ The ⳋ above line 1 in different ink. Quires thus indicated in Rossi, i. II. 10, 36; ii. IV. 96. The ⲁ̄ indicates the last leaf of first quire.

[1] Ps. xxi. 9, 10. Perhaps ⲛ̄]ⲧⲟⲕ[ⲡⲉ, though no MS. of the Psalm reads thus.

[2] Or 'in him'.

[3] Τάχα with some such meaning in F. Robinson *Ap. Gosp.* 182, *PSBA.* xxv. 273 (= Syr.

715; Crum *Copt. Ostr.* no. 290.

[4] Taking ⲛⲧⲁⲓⲣⲉ for an incorrect plur. of ⲛⲟⲩⲧⲉ (v. Erman *ÄZ.* xxxiii. 47, Griffith *ib.* xxxviii. 88). This is supported by the 'name' ⲉⲛⲧⲁⲓⲣ, *Pistis* 376. But ⲧⲁⲓⲣⲉ may be a descriptive name, with ⲛ- of plur. reference to *Mém. Inst. Eg.* ii. 407.

Fol. 5. *Recto* (*cf.* AS. § 2). by his parents; for they were zealous (σπουδαῖος) in paganism (-ἔλλην) and (δέ) they knew not the portion (μερίς) of Jacob, that it is not of this sort.[1] For our . . .[2] . . . . to the temple (?)[3] . . .

Verso. when the wretched (ταλαίπωρος *pl.*) . . . . . had . . .

. . . the gods were[4] not content with their children. For (γάρ) it is impossible that thieves (λῃστής) should take with them the lamp that lighteth the place where they would thieve; rather (ἀλλά) they go in darkness, lest they be caught . . . . . authority . . .

Fol. 6.   → *Recto.*[a]   ↑ *Verso.*

margin

Ⲋ̄

Ⲉⲧⲓ ⲇⲉ ⲟⲩⲛ ⲉⲩ-	ⲛⲧⲡⲟ[ⲗⲓⲥ	ⲕⲁ]ⲕⲉ ⲛ̄ⲡⲉ-	ⲡⲛⲟⲩⲧⲉ ⲉⲩ-
ⲟⲩⲛⲡⲏ̈ ⲛ̄ϭⲓ	ⲉ[	]ⲡⲉϩⲟⲟⲩ ⲧⲏ-	ϣⲓⲛⲉ ⲛ̄ⲥⲁ-
ⲛⲉⲧⲟⲩⲁⲁⲃ· ⲁϥ-	ⲁ[	[ⲣϥ]]ⲩ	ⲡⲟⲩϫⲁⲓ̈ ⲛ̄ⲣⲱ-
ϣⲱⲡⲉ ⲛ̄ϭⲓ ⲡϣⲏ-	?[	]ⲟ̣	ⲙⲉ ⲛⲓⲙ· ϩⲙ̄
ⲣⲉ ⲛ̄ⲧⲥⲱⲛⲉ ⲙ̄-	ⲧ[	]?	Ⲡⲉϩⲟⲟⲩ ⲇⲉ ⲟⲩⲛ
ⲡⲉⲩⲉⲓⲱⲧ· ⲁⲩ-	[	]?	ⲛ̄ⲧⲁϥⲣ̄ⲣ̄ⲣⲟ·[sic]
ⲧⲱⲟⲩⲛ ⲁⲩⲃⲱⲕ		]ⲩ	ⲛ̄ϭⲓ ⲡⲁⲩⲧⲟⲩⲥ-
ⲉϩⲟⲩⲛ ϩⲱⲥ ⲉⲩ-			ⲧⲟⲥ ⲛ̄ⲣⲉϥϫⲣⲟ
ⲛⲁϭⲙ̄ ⲡⲉϥ[ϣⲓ-]			[ⲕ]ⲱⲥⲧⲁⲛⲧⲓ-
ⲛⲉ[· ⲁ]ⲩⲱ ϩ[ⲙ̄ⲛ-]			[ⲛⲟ]ⲥ· ϩⲓⲧⲛ̄ⲡⲟⲩⲟ̈ⲓ-
[ⲧⲣⲉ			[ⲕⲟⲛⲟⲙⲓⲁ ⲛ̄ⲧⲉ]
			[ⲡⲛⲟⲩⲧⲉ

[a] The first of quire 2.

Fol. 6. *Recto.* While yet therefore (ἔτι δὲ οὖν) the saints were in the house, their father's sister's son fell sick. And they arose and went in, as if (ὡς) they would visit him. And as they (?) . . .
the city (? πόλις) . . .

[1] Jer. ⲭ. 16.
[2] 'Our father Pahôm' possible but improbable.
[3] Refers ? to temple whither his parents took the child.
[4] Tense uncertain.

: *Verso* (*cf.* AS. § 2). dark (?) all (?) the day . . .

: God, seeking the salvation of every man. And so (δὲ οὖν) on the day when the victorious[1] Augustus (αὔγουστος), Constantine, became king, by [God's] providence (οἰκονομία) . . .[2]

Fol. 7. → *Recto.*   ↑ *Verso.*

margin   margin (*page no. here ?*)

Recto		Verso	
пепростаτ-	εγϭωϣ[τ ϧн-]	]мептас- sic	ϧн εβολ ϫε-
ма ϫε ѝτεроγ-	тϥ ѝπρ[ро ·]	]оγαϧωм	оγскеос наї
ѝτϥ ернс ϧπ-	Ϲτι оγн[	† пеϥоγоï	ѝсωτнπе
кнме · αγ†	пе ω[	]коγï ϧπѝ-	Ѝток ϫе πα-
пеγоï επ̇α-	α[	θε]βαïсᵇ ѝ-	ϧωм поλε-
рнс ѝкнме ·	π[	]εε	меï ѝπѝ-
Αγω ѝτεроγϭω-	π[	ѝ]тереϥ-	ϫαϫε εθнπ
πε ѝϧαϧ κατα	ϫ[	]α	ετеѝβαρβα-
ма · αγϭωπε	ϫ[	]αϥ	роске ѝλαï-
ϧωωϥ ѝπα-			мωносᶜ ѝтак-
ϧωм ϧιτѝѝ-ᵃ			ϭ[о]τπογ ϧιτѝ-
ноϭ ѝπ[			[πε]с†ос · ѝ†-
[.]ε · ετϥ[			

ᵃ Perhaps пноϭ. But п- with ммнϣε (*cf.* Bo.) is unlikely.   ᵇ Perhaps р for ϧ.   ᶜ о erased.

Fol. 7. *Recto* (*cf.* AS. § 3). And (δέ) when they had brought the order (πρόσταγμα) southward in Egypt, they betook them to the southern part of Egypt. And after they laid hold on many in various (κατά) places, they laid hold also on Pahôm, because of the great (*pl.*) number (?) that[3] . . . . which waited for the king. Thus while (ἔτι οὖν) . . .

Verso. . . . which had . . . . . an eagle[4] . . . went . . . . . little in the (*pl.*) . . . .[5] . . . . . after it (he ?) had . . .

[1] *Cf.* ὁ τὰ πάντα νικῶν (Brit. Mus. Gk. Cat. ii. 328, iii. 253; P. Amh. no. cxl &c.). Νικηφόρος = ⲛⲁⲭⲣⲉ seems to be applied only to martyrs (*v.* Crum-Steindorff, *Kopt. Rechtsurk.* i, Index).

[2] *Cf.* Am. 342.

[3] *Cf.* Bo. 5 *infra.*

[4] 'Eagle' (*ahôm*) possibly in reference to Pahôm, whose name is compounded with that word.

[5] 'Thebais' just possible.

... before (him ? it ?) ; for he is unto me a chosen vessel (σκεῦος).[1] But (δέ) thou,[2] Pahôm, fight (πολεμεῖν) with the hidden foes, which are the barbarous demons (βάρβαρος, δαίμων), whom thou hast overcome by the cross (σταυρός) ; and do thou ...

Fol. 8. ↑ *Recto.*   → *Verso.*

margin   margin

[.]ⲁⲡⲥⲁϩ ⲡⲁⲩ-   ϭⲓⲥⲛⲟϥ [. . ⲁ̅-]   [. . . .]ⲛⲁⲕⲗⲏ-   ⲏ ? ? [
[ⲗ]ⲟⲥ ⲡⲗⲁⲥ ⲙ̅-   ⲡⲉⲡⲙ[ⲁⲕⲁ-]   [ⲣⲟⲛ]ⲟⲙⲉⲓ̈ ⲛ̅-   ⲕⲣⲓⲥⲓⲥ ⲁⲩ[ⲍⲁ-]
ⲡⲉⲥϯⲛⲟⲩϭⲉ   ⲣⲓⲟⲥ ⲣ̅[[ⲧⲙ]ⲡⲧⲉⲣⲟ ⲙ̅-   ⲛⲉ ϩⲣⲁⲓ̈ ⲛ̅ϩⲏⲛ-
ⲭⲉⲙ̅ⲡⲧⲣⲉϥ-   ⲉⲟⲩⲁϣϥ̅ [ⲛ̅ⲥⲱ-]   [ⲡ]ⲛⲟⲩⲧⲉ· ϩⲉⲛ-   ⲧϥ̅ ⲛ̅ⲑⲉ ⲛ̅ⲟⲩ-
ⲣ̅ϩⲛⲁϥ ⲛ̅ϭⲓ   ⲟⲩ ⲛ̅ϭ[[ⲥⲁⲣⲍ] ⲅⲁⲣ ϩⲓⲥ-   ϣⲏⲛ ⲉⲩⲧⲥⲟ
ⲡⲛⲟⲩⲧⲉ ⲡⲁⲓ̈   ⲛⲉ ⲛ̅ⲛ[[ⲛⲟϥⲛⲉ] ⲧⲏⲣⲟⲩ   ⲙ̅ⲙⲟϥ ϩⲛ̅ϯ
⟩ⲛ̅ⲧⲁϥ ⲡⲟⲣⲭ̅ⲧ   ⲧⲉ· [   ]ⲡⲁⲡⲟⲥ-   ⲱⲧⲉ ⲛ̅ⲧⲡⲉ·
ⲉⲃⲟⲗ ⲭⲓⲛⲉⲓ̈ϣ̅ⲡ   ⟩ⲅⲁⲣ ⲙ[ⲧⲟⲗⲟⲥ[b] ⲉ]ⲧⲟⲩⲁⲁⲃ ⟩ⲁϥⲙⲉⲕⲙⲟⲩⲕϥ̅
ϩⲛ̅ⲧⲉ ⲛ̅ⲧⲁⲙⲁ-   ⟩ⲧⲟϥ[[. . .ⲧⲁ]ⲙⲟⲛ[c]   ϩⲣⲁⲓ̈ ⲛ̅ϩⲏⲛⲧϥ̅
ⲁⲩ· ⲉⲟⲩⲉⲛ̅ϩ ⲡⲉϥ-   ⲭⲉ[[ⲭⲉⲣⲱⲙ]ⲉ ⲛⲓⲙ   ⲛ̅ⲧⲉⲓ̈ϩⲉ ⲉϥ-
ϣⲏⲣⲉ ⲉⲃⲟⲗ ⲛ̅-   ϩ[   ]ⲉϥ-   ⲧⲁⲅⲟ̅ ⲛ̅ⲧⲉⲥⲙⲏ
ⲛ̅ϩⲉⲑⲛⲟⲥ· [ϩⲛ̅-]   ]ⲛⲥⲁ-   ⲉⲧⲟⲩⲁⲁⲃ ⲭⲉ-
[ⲧ]ⲉⲩⲛⲟⲩ ⲙ̅[ⲡⲓ-]   ⲙⲁⲧⲥⲁⲃⲟⲓ̈ ⲧⲁ-
[ⲟⲩⲁϩⲧ ⲉⲥⲁⲣⲍ][a]   [ⲣ̅]ⲡⲉⲕⲟⲩⲱϣ

[a] Hence we see that a full column had 14 or 15 (*cf.* fol. 4) lines. [b] Perhaps capital ⲧ. [c] Perhaps ⲧⲁⲙⲟ ⲙ]ⲙⲟⲛ.

Fol. 8. *Recto.* ... according to (?) the teacher, Paul, the tongue of perfume [3]: 'When it pleased God, who set me apart since I was in my mother's womb, to reveal His Son unto the heathen (ἔθνος) ; immediately I [followed not flesh] and blood,' ..... the blessed one (μακάριος) did not ... to follow after them .... For (γάρ) ...

Verso. ... shall inherit (κληρονομεῖν) the kingdom of God.'[4] For (γάρ) they are all flesh (σάρξ) and blood ; [For ?] the holy apostle (ἀπ.) [hath]

[1] Acts ix. 15.
[2] Perhaps a development of the Spirit's words, Bo. 8.
[3] Gal. i. 15, 16 (*om.* ' and called me through His grace ').
[4] *Cf.* 1 Cor. xv. 50.

told us : 'Every man (?) . . . . discernment ([? διά]κρισις) increase [1]
(? αὐξάνειν) in him, even as a tree that is watered with the dew of heaven.'
Thus did he meditate within himself, pronouncing the holy words (*lit.* voice) :
'Teach me and I will do Thy will [2] . . .'

Fol. 9.   ↑ *Recto.*   → *Verso.*

        margin   margin

} [. . . .] ⲙⲁⲣⲉ- ⲁϥ ⲛ̄ⲣⲣⲟ [ⲟⲙ-]   [ⲡⲙⲁ]ⲕⲁⲣⲓⲟⲥ ⲁ- ⲕⲁ ⲛ[ⲛ-]
]ⲡ]ⲓⲟⲧⲁ ϩⲱⲱϥ }ⲡⲛⲁⲩ ⲛ̄ⲧ[ⲁⲩ-]   [ⲡⲁ] ⲡⲁϩⲱⲙ ⲟ ⲥⲱⲟⲩ· ⲁⲅⲟⲩ-
ⲕⲁⲧⲁⲣⲅⲉⲓ ⲛ̄-) ⲭⲡⲟϥ ⲟⲩ[ⲛ̄ⲟⲩⲣ-]   [ⲟⲩ]ⲱϩ ϩ̄ⲛ̄ⲟⲩⲣ̄- ⲱϩ ϩ̄ⲛ̄ⲡⲙⲁ ⲉ-
ⲧⲁⲓ ϩ̄ⲛ̄ⲡⲧⲣⲉⲕ- ⲡⲉ ⲛⲧⲁϥ[ϣ̄ⲣ̄-]   [ⲡⲉ] ⲉϥⲧⲁⲙⲟ ⲛ̄- ⲧⲙⲙⲁⲩ ⲉⲧⲃⲏ-
ⲧⲥⲁⲃⲉ ⲛ̄ⲣⲱⲙⲉ ϣⲱⲣϥ [[ⲙⲟ]ϥ ⲭⲉⲛⲉⲛ- ⲛⲧϥ · ⲙ̄ⲡ-
ⲉⲣⲟⲥ · ⲙ̄ⲡⲉⲥ-   [. .]ⲕⲁⲙⲙⲉ ⲛ̄ⲣⲉ }ⲛ̄ⲧⲁⲗϭⲟ[a] ⲛ̄-
}ⲡⲟⲧ ⲉϣⲁⲣⲉⲡⲉ- }ⲋ[[ⲑⲛⲓⲕⲟⲥ] ⲙⲁ)ⲧⲁⲡⲛⲟⲩⲧⲉ
) ⲭⲁⲗⲓⲛⲟⲥ ⲁⲙⲁϩ-) ⲡ[ⲉⲃ̄ⲟⲗ ϩ̄ⲛ̄- ⲭⲁⲣⲓⲍⲉ ⲙ̄ⲙⲟ-
ⲧⲉ ⲉⲭ̄ⲙ̄ⲡⲉⲥ- ⲉ[ϩⲉⲑⲛⲟⲥ ⲟⲩ ⲉⲃⲟⲗ ϩⲓⲧⲟⲟ-
ⲧⲟ ϩ̄ⲛ̄ⲧⲉϥϭⲟⲙ · ⲛ̄[   ]ⲧⲁ- ⲧϥ ⲉⲧⲓ ⲉϥⲟ ⲛ̄-
}ⲭⲉⲕⲁⲥ ⲛ̄ⲛⲉⲛⲱ-   ⲡⲉ]ⲭ̄ⲥ̄ ϩⲉⲑⲛⲓⲕⲟⲥ
) ⲥ̄ⲕ ϩ̄ⲛ̄ⲛ̄ϣ[ⲁϫⲉ]   }ⲛ̄ⲧⲉⲣⲉϥⲱⲥ̄ⲕ̄
ⲁϥⲟⲩⲱϩ ϩ[ⲛ̄   ) [ⲟⲩ]ⲛ̄ ϩ̄ⲛ̄ⲡⲧⲙⲉ
?   ⲟ]ⲩⲁ

.

        [a] ⲛ̄- corrected from ⲡ-.

Fol. 9. *Recto* (*cf.* AS. § 3).   . . . May the . . . . .[3] too bring this to nought
(καταργεῖν), whilst thou teachest it unto men, like as the bridle (χαλινός)
controlleth the horse by its power.   That we may not delay in the story
(*lit.* word), he dwelt in . . . . made him (?) king.   At the time when
he was born, there was a temple [4] that he had destroyed . . .

    Verso.   . . . the blessed (μακ.) Apa Pahôm also (?)[5] dwell in a temple,[6]

[1] Tense uncertain.
[2] Ps. cxlii. 10.
[3] ' the Spirit ' perhaps possible.
[4] All quite uncertain as to number and person
of pronouns.

[5] Tense of verb uncertain.
[6] Presumably the ruined Serapis temple.   The
name by which this seems elsewhere to be desig-
nated, ⲡⲙⲁ ⲙ̄ⲡⲉⲥⲧⲉⲣⲡⲟⲥⲉⲓⲛ (*Miss.* 535), is,
I think, merely a deformed reproduction of
ⲡⲙⲁ ⲙ̄ⲡⲉⲥⲣⲁⲡⲓⲥⲉⲓⲛ (*q. v. below*).

text ; otherwise ⲟⲛ ' also ' must be omitted.

telling him that it was heathen (*pl.*? ἐθνικός) . . . . . pagans (? ἔθνος) . . . .
Christ . . . . left behind them . . . . . and they dwelt in that place on
account of him (? it) and of the healings that God granted (χαρίζειν) by his
(? its) means,[1] while yet (ἔτι) he was pagan (ἐθνικός).　So (οὖν) when he had
continued in the village . . .

No. 25 (called, in Appendix and elsewhere, SaX).

The history of Pachomius and Theodore.　That this MS. did not form
part of No. 24 is evident from the following considerations : (1) the divergent
spelling of the name Pachomius, (2) the absence of the paragraph-mark
such as used by no. 24, (3) the abnormal forms here of certain letters,
e.g. ϰ,[2] (4) the usually greater number of letters in a line in the present MS.,
(5) finally, the entire dissimilarity between the texts of no. 24 and of Am.,
a version based, as will be shown, strictly upon the present text.

A column of our text is 23 cm. high, and has 26–28 lines.　Of the 32 foll.
here preserved, in greater or less completeness, only three still show pagination (foll. 2, 4, 5).　Were it not therefore for the uninterrupted text of
Am., it might have been impossible to assign any plausible sequence to the
fragments, which I found dispersed throughout the whole collection of
papyri.　As it is, however, a few of them fortunately show the junctures,
upon one and the same leaf, of two paragraphs of AS. (foll. 9 *vo.*–10 *ro.*,
11 *ro.*, 12 *ro.*, 13 *ro.*, 18 *vo.*, 24 *vo.*, 25 *vo.*, 26 *vo.*) ; and it is thence evident
that, not only is the new text verbally identical with Am., but that in
arrangement of paragraphs they likewise agree.　This should suffice to
justify the assignment of the remaining paragraphs to positions relatively
such as they hold in Am.　The latter offers no parallels to the text of foll. 1,
2, 7, 29, 32.　The absence (scarcely fortuitous) of quire-numbers prevents
us from using the relative sequence of *horizontal* and *vertical* fibres as a
further guide to the sequence of the leaves.　Leaves, the continuity of whose
text allows of no doubt as to their order,[3] show the simple sequence *hv, vh,
hv, vh.*

The practical identity of the two texts SaX and Am. can scarcely be
doubted by any one who will compare the parallel passages (observing at
the same time the alterations to the French translation which I have given
in the notes).　The text of Am. is, in no instance, materially longer than
that of the corresponding Sa. passage ; whereas the latter shows, often
enough, phrases, nay whole paragraphs, lacking from the parallel Arabic.
These are proof enough that, as would be expected, the younger is abridged
from the older text.

[1] *Sc.* the temple's ?
[2] Palaeographical features do not otherwise
afford very cogent arguments here (*cf.* facsimiles).
[3] *E.g.* foll. 8–14, 16–22.

The chief interest of this new addition to the Coptic recensions is genea-
logical: we now see clearly the source whence Am. was derived. It has
been long recognized that Am. neither translates immediately any of the
Sa. versions hitherto known[1] nor Bo. which is derived from certain of these.
Am. neither follows them (except intermittently) in paragraph sequence nor
in details of phraseology or vocabulary. With our present text, on the
contrary, it agrees in both these particulars; as to the last, with often
surprising closeness. The new text is of course too fragmentary to allow
of our assuming that it alone was the immediate source translated by Am.[2]
Prof. Ladeuze has called attention to portions of the latter which appear to
be derived from Bo.,[3] *i. e.* ultimately from one of the other Sa. versions.

Fol. 1.   → *Recto.*[a]   ↑ *Verso.*

```
                    ]ⲙ · ⲁϥ-        ⲥⲧⲉⲣ[ . . . . . ]
                    ]ϥ̄ ⲛ̄ⲟⲩ-        ⲭⲱ ⲙ̄ⲙⲟⲥ ⲭⲉ-
                  ⲕⲟⲩ̈ⲓ ⲛ̄ⲧⲙⲛⲧⲉ     ⲡⲉⲧⲥⲡⲁⲧⲁⲗⲁ’
                  ⲛ̄ⲛⲉϥⲙⲁⲑⲏⲧⲏⲥ     ⲭⲓⲛⲧⲉϥⲙⲛ̄ⲧ-      ⲧⲟ[
. . . . . . ] . ⲁⲁⲩ     ⲉϥⲭⲱ ⲙ̄ⲙⲟⲥ ⲭⲉ-    ⲕⲟⲩ̈ⲓ ⲛⲁⲣⲟⲩϩⲁⲗ ·    ⲉⲧⲉ[
. . . . . ]ⲉ̈ⲓⲙⲉ-       ⲡⲉⲧⲛⲁϣⲱⲡ’ ⲉ-      ⲧⲉⲛⲟⲩϭⲉ ⲡⲉⲥⲛⲏⲩ,    ⲁⲁⲥ · [
. . . . . ] ϥⲛⲁⲩ       ⲣⲟϥ’ ⲛ̄ⲟⲩϣⲏⲣⲉ ϣⲏⲙ   ϣⲏⲣⲉ ϣⲏⲙ’ ⲛⲓⲙ    ⲉⲛϣⲁⲁ[
ⲉⲡⲭⲟ]ⲉⲓⲥ ⲙ̄ⲡⲧⲏ-        ⲛ̄ⲧⲉⲓⲣⲉ ⲉϩⲣⲁ̈ⲓ ⲉⲭⲙ̄-  ⲙ̄ⲡⲛⲉⲛⲧⲁⲩⲣ-       ⲛ̄ⲟⲁϩ ⲛ̄ⲥⲟⲡ [ⲙⲁ-]
ⲣϥ] ⲡϣⲏⲣⲉ ⲙ̄ ▸        ⲡⲁⲣⲁⲛ . ⲉϥϣⲱⲡ’      ⲛⲟϭ ⲉⲣⲟⲟⲩ ϩⲛ̄ⲟⲩⲑⲉⲛ-  ⲣ̄ⲧⲁⲙⲟⲟⲩ [ⲭⲉ-]
ⲓⲛ]ⲟⲩⲧⲉ ⲉⲁϥⲥⲁ-        ⲙ̄ⲙⲟ̈ⲓ ⲉⲣⲟϥ · ⲉⲧⲃⲉ-   ⲗⲓⲕⲓⲁ, ⲉⲛⲧⲁⲡⲭⲟ-    ⲡⲛⲟⲩⲧⲉ ⲉⲛ-
ⲟ]ϩ ⲉⲧⲃⲉⲡⲉⲩ-        ϩⲉⲛⲕⲉⲕⲟⲩ̈ⲓ ⲍⲉ ⲉ-     ⲉⲓⲥ ⲉⲓⲛⲉ ⲙ̄ⲙⲟⲟⲩ    ⲧⲁϥⲧⲁⲙⲟⲟⲩ
ⲁⲓ̈ · ⲙⲁⲗⲓⲥⲧⲁ ⲍⲉ     ⲁⲩⲭⲡⲟ’ ⲛⲁⲩ ⲛ̄ⲟⲩ-    ⲉϩⲟⲩⲛ ϣⲁⲣⲟⲛ, ⲉ-    ⲁⲩⲱ ⲉⲧⲃⲉⲧⲡ[ⲉ]
ϩⲛ ⲉⲛⲥⲱⲧⲙ̄ ⲉⲣⲟϥ      ⲡⲣⲟϩⲁⲓⲣⲉⲥⲓⲥ ⲉⲥ-     ⲡⲉⲭⲡⲟ’ ⲛ̄ⲕⲉⲥⲟⲡ .    ⲟⲛ ⲙ̄ⲡⲛⲕⲁϩ’ ⲙ[ⲛ̄-]
ϥ]ⲙ̄ⲡⲉⲩⲁⲅⲅⲉⲗⲓⲟⲛ      ϩⲟⲟⲩ, ϩⲛ̄ⲧⲉⲩⲙⲛ̄ⲧ-     ⲙⲁⲣⲛ̄ⲥⲡⲟⲩⲍⲁⲍⲉ     ⲡⲣⲏ’ ⲙ̄ⲛⲡⲟⲟϩ [
ⲭⲉ]ⲙ̄ⲡⲣⲕⲱⲗⲅⲉ ⲛ̄-

            margin                                  margin
```

[a] The position of this fol. is hypothetical. It is assumed to precede that placed next (pp.
63, 64).

[1] Nor the lost Sa. represented by Av. *V.*   figure in SaX. But not all MSS. of Am. include
Appendix.   it (*v.* Appendix).

[2] I assume, from our foll. 1, 2, that the Palla-   [3] Ladeuze, *Étude Gén.*, 33 n.
dian version of the Rule (Am. 366–369) did not

Fol. 1. (The proper positions of this and the next 2 foll. are uncertain.)

Recto. . . . he saw (? seeth) the Lord of all, the Son of God, having become flesh (σάρξ) for our salvation. But (δέ) above all (μάλιστα) too we hear Him in the Gospel (εὐ.) saying,[1] 'Forbid (κωλύειν) not . . . . .

. . . He . . . a little one in the midst of His disciples (μαθ.), saying,[2] 'Whoso shall receive a young child such as this in my name receiveth me.' But (δέ) as for the young that have gotten for themselves an evil resolve (προαίρεσις), in their[3] . . . . .

Verso. . . . saying,[4] 'Whoso liveth wantonly (σπαταλᾶν) from his youth shall be a servant.' Now therefore, brethren,[5] every young child and such as are greater than they in age (ἡλικία), whom the Lord hath brought in unto us for the second birth, let us be zealous (σπουδάζειν) . . . . .

. . . we . . . . . many times, let us tell them how that God it was did create them. And concerning the heaven also and the earth and the sun and the moon . . . . .

Fol. 2.　↑ p. ⲍⲅ̄　　　　　　　　　→ p. ⲍⲁ̄

	margin		margin	
]ⲉⲥⲱ	Ⲧⲥⲃⲱ̄ naⲩ ⲛ̄ⲟⲩ[ⲟ-]	ⲙ̄ⲡⲉϥⲟⲩⲱϣ' ⲉ-	ⲡ[
]ⲅⲉ ⲛ̄-	ⲉⲓϣ ⲛ̄ⲙⲉ' ⲉⲧⲣⲉ[ⲩ-]	[ⲃ]ⲟⲗ ⲟ̄ⲙⲡⲉϥⲛⲟⲙⲟⲥ·	ⲉⲩ[
]ϥⲧⲁ-	ⲥⲙⲟⲩ ⲉⲡⲉⲛⲧⲁϥ-	ⲙ̄ⲡⲛ̄ⲕⲱⲧ' ⲉⲛⲧⲁ-	ⲉⲃⲟ[
ⲉ]ⲩϣⲁ̄	ⲧⲁⲙⲓⲉ naⲓ̈ ⲧⲏⲣ[ⲟⲩ]	ⲉⲓⲧⲁⲁⲩ ⲛⲏⲧⲛ̄ ⲉ-	ⲙⲧ[
] ⲡⲣⲟⲥ	ⲁⲝⲛ̄ⲱⲝⲛ̄· ⲉⲓⲧⲉ	ⲃⲟⲗ' ⲛ̄ⲟ̄ⲏⲧϥ̄ ϫⲉ-	ⲉⲧ[
ⲟⲩⲟ]ⲉⲓϣ	ⲟ̄ⲛⲧⲉⲩⲧⲁⲡⲣⲟ	̄ⲣ sic ⲕⲁⲥ ⲉⲛⲛⲁⲙⲉⲣⲉ	ⲟⲟⲩ[
]ⲓ ⲙⲟ̄ᵃ	ⲉⲓⲧⲉ ⲟ̄ⲙⲡⲉⲩϩⲏⲧ	ⲡϫⲟⲉⲓⲥ ⲡⲉⲛⲛⲟⲩ-	ϫⲉ[
]ϥⲏⲧ'	ⲉⲩϫⲱ' ⲙ̄ⲙⲟⲥ ϫⲉ-	ⲧⲉ ⲉⲃⲟⲗ ⲟ̄ⲙⲡⲉⲩϩⲏⲧ' ˢⁱᶜ	ⲡⲛ[
ⲟ]ⲩϥ	ⲕⲥⲙⲁⲙⲁⲁⲧ' ⲡϫⲟ-	ⲧⲏⲣϥ̄ ⲙ̄ⲡⲧⲉⲩ-	ⲧⲁϥ[
]ⲁⲙ	ⲉⲓⲥ ϫⲉⲕⲁⲥ ϩⲱⲟⲩ	ⲯⲩⲭⲏ ⲧⲏⲣⲥ̄ ⲙ̄ⲡ-	ⲱⲛ[
]⸵.	ⲉⲩⲉϣⲱⲡⲉ ⲛ̄ϣⲏ-	ⲡⲉⲩⲙⲉⲉⲩⲉ ⲧⲏⲣⲟⲩ	ⲁⲩ[

ᵃ Line over ⲙ not certain.

[1] ? Matt. xix. 14.
[2] Matt. xviii. 5.
[3] An abstract, ? ' youth '.
[4] Prov. xxix. 21. So Ciasca ; LXX κατα-σπαταλᾷ.
[5] I assume that this and the next fragment are

from instructions given by Pachomius, corresponding perhaps to Am. 372 ff. Evidence for the independent existence of the Pachomian Rule is given by the book catalogue, *Rec.* xi. 133, no 31 (the βίος there figures as no. 34).

]єоє	ρε ⲛ̄ⲗⲁⲅⲉⲓⲁ· ⲡⲁⲓ̈	ⲙ̄ⲡⲉⲩϭⲟⲙ ⲧⲏ-	ⲉⲧ[
]ⲛ̄ϩⲁϩ,	ⲉⲧϫⲱ ⲙ̄ⲙⲟⲥ ϫⲉ[†-]	ⲣⲥ̄· ⲁⲩⲱ ⲉⲧⲣⲉⲩⲙⲉ-	ⲟⲩⲧ[
]ⲟⲛ	ⲛⲁⲥⲙⲟⲩ ⲉⲡϫⲟⲉⲓ[ⲥ]	ⲣⲉ ⲡⲉⲧϩⲓⲧⲟⲩⲱⲟⲩ	ⲉⲣⲉ[
ⲉ]ⲧⲃⲉ-	ⲛ̄ⲟⲩⲟⲉⲓϣ̈· ⲛⲓⲙ· ⲛ̄-	ⲛ̄ⲧⲉⲩϩⲉ· ⲉⲧⲣⲉⲩ-	ⲁⲩ[
]ⲛ	ⲟⲩⲟⲉⲓϣ̈· ⲛⲓⲙ· ⲉⲣⲉ-	ⲉⲓⲙⲉ ϩⲛ̄ⲟⲩⲱⲣⲝ̄	ⲟ· [
]ⲧ	ⲡⲉϥⲥⲙⲟⲩ ϩⲛ̄ⲣⲱⲓ̈·	ⲉⲛⲉⲛⲧⲁⲩⲥϩⲁⲓ̈ⲥⲟⲩ	ⲉ[ϣ]
]ⲕⲉ	ⲙ̄ⲡ̄ⲛ̄ⲥⲱⲥ ⲇⲉ ⲟⲛ ⲉ-	ϩⲙ̄ⲡⲉ ⲡ̄ⲛ̄ⲁ̄ ⲉⲧⲟⲩ-	ⲥ[
]	† ⲛⲁⲩ ⲛ̄ϩⲉⲛⲯⲁⲗ-	ⲁⲁⲃ· ϫⲉⲕⲁⲥ ⲉⲩ-	[
	ⲙⲟⲥ ⲛ̄ⲁⲡⲟⲥⲧⲏ-	ϣⲁⲛϩⲁⲣⲉϩ· ⲉⲡⲉⲩ-	
	ⲑⲟⲩⲥ· ⲁⲩⲱ ⲟⲛ ⲉⲧ-	ⲥⲱⲙⲁ· ⲉϥⲟⲩⲁⲁⲃ	
	[ⲣⲉⲩ]ϫⲓ ⲉⲃⲟⲗ ϩⲛ̄ⲡⲕⲉ-	ϫⲓⲛⲧⲉⲩⲙ[ⲛ̄ⲧ-]	
	[ϫⲱ]ⲱⲙⲉ ⲛ̄ⲧⲉⲅⲣⲁ-	ⲕⲟⲩⲓ̈, ⲥⲉⲛⲁϣ[ⲱ-]	
	[ⲫⲏ] ⲉⲧⲟⲩⲁⲁⲃ· ⲁⲩⲱ	ⲡⲉ ⲛ̄ⲣ̄ⲡⲉ· ⲙ̄[ⲡϫⲟ-]	
	[ⲙ̄ⲡ̄]ⲛ̄ⲥⲱⲥ ⲉⲧⲥⲁⲃⲟ	ⲉⲓⲥ ⲁⲩⲱ ⲛ̄ϥ̄ⲟ̄[ⲩⲱϩ]	
	[ⲛ̄ⲛ̄]ⲕⲟⲩⲓ̈ [	[ϩⲣⲁⲓ̈ ⲛ̄ϩ]ⲏⲧⲟ[ⲩ	

Fol. 2. P. 63. . . . 'Teach them at all times that they bless Him that created all these things, without ceasing, whether (εἴτε) with their mouths, or (εἴτε) with their heart, saying, Blessed art thou, Lord, that they also may become children of David, who saith,[1] I will bless the Lord at all times; at all times His blessing is in my mouth. And (δέ) afterwards too, (see) that (thou) give unto them Psalms (to learn) by heart[2] (ἀπὸ στηθοῦς); and moreover, that they get (by heart) from the other books of holy scripture (γραφή). And afterwards, (see) that (thou) teach the young . . . . .

P. 64. . . . and His will, from out His law (νόμος), and the rules that I have given you therefrom, that they[3] shall love the Lord our God with all their heart and all their soul (ψυ.) and all their thoughts and all their strength; and that they should love their neighbour as themselves; that they may know of a surety the things that have been written of the Holy Spirit (πν.), so that, if they keep their body (σῶ.) pure from their youth, they shall become temples of the Lord and He shall [dwell with]in [them . . . . .

[1] Ps. xxxiii. 1.
[2] Cf. Ladeuze, 291 *inf.*; Butler, *Laus. Hist.*
[3] Corrected from 'that we'. Cf. Luke x. 27.

Fol. 3. ↑ *Recto* (?).   → *Verso* (?).

[ογω]ϣ [ⲁⲛ ⲛⲧⲉⲣⲉϥⲁⲛ-]   [. .]ⲁⲛ ⲛϥⲧⲱϣ ᵃ ⲙ̄[

[ⲁⲛⲕ]ⲁⲍⲉ ⲍⲉ ⲙ̄ⲙⲟϥ   ⲙⲟ [ⲙ̄ⲡⲗⲁⲁⲩ ⲙ̄ⲙ̄[ⲛⲧ-]

[ⲟⲛ] ⲉϫⲓⲧⲟⲩ · ⲡⲉ[ϫ]ⲁϥ ⲛⲁϥ   ⲁⲧⲥⲱⲧⲙ̄ ⲙ̄ⲡⲛ̄-

[ϫⲉⲡ]ⲛⲟ' · ⲁⲩⲱ ⲡⲉϫⲁϥ ⲉ-   ⲥⲱⲥ · ⲁⲩⲱ ⲁⲥϣⲱ-

[ϩⲟⲩ]ⲛ ⲉϩⲣⲁϥ' ϫⲉⲟⲩ'ⲡⲉ   ⲡⲉ *sic* ⲁⲥϣⲱⲡⲉ ϫⲓ[ⲛ-]

[ⲡⲉⲓ]ϣⲁϫⲉ ⲛⲧⲁⲛ-   ⲡⲉϩⲟⲟⲩ ⲉⲧⲙ̄ⲙⲁ[ⲩ]

[ϫⲟⲟ]ϥ' ϫⲉⲡⲛⲟ . ⲉⲁⲕϯ   ⲉϥϣⲁⲛⲛⲁⲩ ⲉⲡ-

[ⲙⲁ] ⲛϩⲏⲧⲕ̄ ⲛⲟⲩⲍⲁⲓ-   ⲉⲧⲙ̄ⲙⲁⲩ ⲉϥⲙ[ⲟⲟ-]

[ⲙⲟⲛⲓ]ⲟⲛ ⲙ̄ⲙ̄ⲛⲧⲁⲧ-   ϣⲉ ϩⲛ̄ⲑⲉⲛⲉⲉ[ⲧⲉ]

[ⲥⲱⲧ]ⲙ̄ · ⲕⲁⲛ ⲉϣϫⲉ ⲛ̄ⲕ-   ϣⲁϥϣⲱⲡⲉ [ⲛϥ̄ⲕⲁ]

[ⲟⲩⲱϣ ⲁ]ⲛ ⲉϫⲓⲧⲟⲩ · ⲁ-   ϫⲱϥ ⲉⲡⲉ[ⲥⲏⲧ ⲛⲉ-]

[ϫⲓⲥ ϫⲉⲛϯ]ⲟⲩⲱϣ ⲁⲛ   ⲣⲉⲡⲉϥⲃⲁ[ⲗ' ϯ ⲣⲙ̄ᵇ-]

[ⲧⲉⲛⲟⲩ ⲙ]ⲟⲛⲟⲛ ϫⲓⲧⲟⲩ   ⲉⲓⲏ · ⲛ . [

[ⲛ̄ⲥⲕⲁⲁⲩ ⲉϩ]ⲣⲁⲓ · ⲙⲟ-   ⲉⲩⲙⲛ . [

[ⲛⲟⲛ   ⲧⲁϥϫ[

margin   margin

ᵃ Perhaps ⲥⲱϣ (ⲥⲱϣⲙ).   ᵇ Perhaps more in gap; ⲟⲛ or ϫⲉ?

Fol. 3. *Recto* (v. Am. 396). ... I] wish [not.'] But (δέ) [after that he had] constrained (ἀναγκάζειν) him [again] to take of them, he said unto him, 'I will not.' And he said unto him,[1] 'What is [this] word that thou hast [said], I will not, having given [place] in thyself to a demon (δαιμόνιον) of disobedience [2]? If so be (κἄν) thou [wishest] not to take of them, say, [I] wish not [now][3]; but (μόνον) take them [and lay ? them] down. But (μόνον) ...

Verso.[4] ... and he determined (?)[5] ..... no disobedience thereafter. And it befell from that day, if he saw that (brother) walking in the monastery, he would be ashamed and bend down his head, his eyes shedding tears ...

[1] ⲉϩⲟⲩⲛ ⲉϩⲣⲁϥ, of earnest or angry talk, *e.g.* Num. ix. 7, Josh. ix. 12, Brit. Mus. no. 342 ϥⲉ, Rossi *Nuov. Cod.* 89, Budge *Homil.* 127.

[2] So Am., not 'pécher'.

[3] Am. should be 'And if it be that thou wishest not to take (thereof), say, I wish (for it) not now, and take and use (? eat) a little; then lay it down'.

[4] This is not in Am.

[5] Perhaps 'despised'.

Fol. 4. ↑ p. r̅i̅a̅ [a]

margin

ϣⲉ [b] ⲁⲛ ⲟ̅ⲛ̅ⲛⲉⲩ-　　　　　ⲙ̅ⲡϫⲟⲉⲓⲥ · ⲁⲩⲱ
ⲡⲣⲁⲍⲉⲓⲥ ⲙ̅ⲡ̅ⲛ̅ⲕⲱ-　　　　ⲉϥⲁⲩⲍⲁⲛⲉ ⲟ̅ⲛ̅ⲡⲉ-
ⲣ̅ϣ̅ ⲛ̅ⲧⲉⲩⲧⲁⲡⲣⲟ'　　　ⲥⲃⲟⲟⲩⲉ' ⲉⲧϥ̅ⲥⲱⲧⲙ̅
ⲧ̅ⲡⲟⲩⲟ̅ⲛ̅ⲡ̅ ⲉⲃⲟⲗ' ϫⲉ-　　ⲉⲣⲟⲟⲩ ϩⲓⲧⲟⲟⲧϥ̅
ⲙ̅ⲡ̅ⲙ̅ⲙⲉⲣⲓⲧⲟⲩ　　　　ⲙ̅ⲡⲉⲛⲉⲓⲱⲧ' ⲡⲁ-
ⲕⲁⲧⲁ ⲑⲉ ⲉⲧⲥⲛ̅ϩ ·　　　ϩⲱⲙ̅' ⲉϥⲙⲟⲟϣⲉ' ⲕⲁ- *sic*
ϫⲉ[ⲡⲉ]ⲧⲏⲛ[ⲩ ϣⲁⲣ-]　　ⲧⲁ ⲡⲉϥϭⲓⲛⲉ ⲁⲩⲱ
[ⲟⲓ ⲉⲛϥ]ⲙ̅[ⲟ]ⲥⲧ[ⲉ ⲁⲛ]　　ⲕⲁⲧⲁ ⲧⲉϥϭⲣⲉ ·
[ⲙⲙⲟ]ⲟⲩ · · ⲥⲛⲉϥ　　　　ⲛⲉⲥⲛⲏⲩ ϫⲉ ⲛ̅ⲧⲉ-
[· · ·]ⲉⲛⲁⲣⲁⲛ ⲙ̅-　　　ⲣⲉⲩⲛⲁⲩ ϫⲉϥϯ · · ⲧ [c]
[ⲙⲟⲟⲩ · ·]ⲛⲉⲣⲙⲉ

[a] Sir H. Thompson has discovered a fragment with part of this text in the binding of Br. Mus. Or. 7024 (4), and this allows me to fill some lacunae.

[b] ⲙⲟⲟ]ϣⲉ.　　　　　　　　　　[c] Not ⲟⲩⲱ. Perhaps ⲉⲑⲏ.

→ p. r̅i̅b̅

margin

ϣⲗⲏⲗ' ⲡ̅ⲙ̅ⲙⲁⲩ,ⲡⲉ　　　ⲛⲁⲩ ⲉⲡⲉⲛⲧⲁϥⲧⲁ-
ⲛ̅ⲧⲉⲓϩⲉ ⲟ̅ⲛ̅ⲣ̅ⲉⲛⲡ̅ⲙ̅-　　ⲙⲓⲟⲓ, ⲟⲩⲡⲉ ⲡ̅ϩⲛⲩ
ⲉⲓⲟⲟⲩⲉ ϣⲁⲛⲧϥ̅ϯ　　　ϫⲉⲁⲩϫⲡⲟⲓ ⲉⲡⲉⲉⲓ- *sic*
ⲙ̅ⲧⲟⲛ ⲛⲁⲩ ⲛ̅ϭⲓ　　　ⲕⲟⲥⲙⲟⲥ · ⲛⲉⲛⲁ-
ⲡϫⲟⲉⲓⲥ ⲉⲃⲟⲗ' ϩⲓ-　　ⲛⲟⲩⲥ ⲅⲁⲣ ⲛⲁⲓ̈ ⲉⲛⲉ-
ⲧⲟⲟⲧϥ̅ · ⲁⲩⲱ ⲁⲥ-　　ⲙ̅ⲡⲟⲩϫⲡⲟⲓ · ⲡⲉ-
Ϣⲱⲡⲉ ⲛ̅ⲧⲉⲣⲉϥ-　　　ϫⲁϥ ⲛⲁ[ϥ] ϫⲉⲁϫⲓⲥ
ⲉⲓ' ⲉϩⲟⲩⲛ, ⲉⲛⲉⲥⲛⲏⲩ　　ⲉⲣⲟⲓ̈ ϫⲉⲉⲕⲟⲩⲉϣ
ⲛ̅ⲧⲁⲣⲭⲏ ⲟ̅ⲛ̅ⲧⲉϥ-　　ⲛⲁⲩ ⲉⲣⲟϥ' ϩ̅[ⲙ̅ⲡⲉⲓ-]
ⲙ̅ⲡ̅ⲕⲟⲩⲓ̈ ⲁϥϯ　　　　ⲙ[ⲁ · ·]ⲉ[
ⲛⲉⲧⲟⲙⲟⲥⲓ' ⲉⲛⲉⲛ-　　　· · ⲛ̅

[ⲉⲓⲱⲧ

Fol. 4. P. 111 (v. Am. 402[1]). ... walk not in their deeds (πρᾶξις) and the entreaties of their mouths, we show that we love them not, as (κατά) it is written,[2] 'Whoso cometh unto me and hateth them not . . . . . my name . . .

... the Lord,[3] and (he) growing (αὐξάνειν) in the instructions that he heard from our father Pahômius,[4] walking after (κατά) his likeness and according to (κατά) his manner. And (δέ) the brethren, when they saw that he ...

P. 112. ... he would] pray[5] with them thus, with tears, until the Lord gave them rest by his means. And[6] it befell that when he came in to the brethren, at the beginning (ἀρχή[7]), in his boyhood, he betook him to our [father Pahômius ...

... see Him that created me, what profit is there that I have been begotten into this world (κόσμος)? For (γάρ) it would have been good for me if I had not been begotten.' He said unto him, 'Tell me, dost thou desire to see Him in this world (*lit.* place) ...

Fol. 5. → p. ρ̄ῑ̄γ̄

margin

ⲛ̄ⲏⲣⲟⲛ ⲛ̄ⲑⲉ ⲉⲧ-
ⲥⲛ̄ϩ' ϩⲙ̄ⲡⲉⲩⲁⲅ'ⲅⲉ-
ⲗⲓⲟⲛ ϫⲉⲛⲁϊⲁⲧⲟⲩ
ⲛ̄ⲛⲉⲧⲟⲩⲁⲁⲃ' ϩⲙ̄-
ⲡⲉⲩϩⲏⲧ' · ϫⲉⲛ̄ⲧⲟ-
ⲟⲩ ⲛⲉⲧⲛⲁⲛⲁⲩ, ⲉ-
ⲡⲛⲟⲩⲧⲉ · ⲉϣⲱ-
ⲡⲉ ϭⲉ ⲉⲣϣⲁⲛⲟⲩⲙⲉ-
ⲉⲩⲉ ⲛ̄ϫⲱ[ϩ]ⲙ̄ ⲁⲗⲉ'
ⲉϩⲣⲁⲓ̈ ⲉϫⲙ̄ⲡⲉⲕϩⲏⲧ'.
[ⲏ ⲟⲩⲙⲟ]ⲥⲧⲉ ⲉϩⲟⲩⲛ
[ⲉⲡⲉⲕⲥⲟⲛ] ⲏ̄ ⲟⲩ-
      ]ⲛ ⲏ̄ ⲟⲩⲫ'-
[ⲑⲟⲛⲟⲥ   ] . ⲱⲣⲁ

ϭⲙ̄ϭⲟⲙ' ⲉⲣⲟⲕ · ⲕⲁⲣ-
ⲡⲟⲥ ⲛⲓⲙ' ⲉⲧⲥⲛ̄ϩ
ϩⲛ̄ⲛⲉⲅⲣⲁⲫⲏ ⲙⲉ-
ⲗⲉⲧⲁ ⲙ̄ⲙⲟⲟⲩ ϩⲙ̄-
ⲡⲉⲕϩⲏⲧ' ⲁϫⲛ̄ⲱ̄-
ϫⲛ̄ · ⲉⲕⲧⲱϣ'ⲙ̄ⲙⲟⲕ
ⲙ̄ⲙⲓⲛ ⲙ̄ⲙⲟⲕ' ⲉⲙⲟ-
ⲟϣⲉ ⲛ̄ϩⲏⲧⲟⲩ · ⲛ̄-
ⲑⲉ ⲉⲧⲥⲛ̄ϩ ϩⲛ̄ⲛⲥⲁ-
ϊⲁⲥ ϫⲉⲧⲉⲧⲛ̄ⲯⲩ-
ⲭⲏ' ⲛⲁⲙⲉⲗⲉⲧⲁ' ⲛ̄-
ϩⲟⲧⲉ ⲙ̄ⲡϫⲟⲉⲓⲥ
ⲁⲩⲱ ⲛⲁϊ ⲧⲏⲣⲟⲩ
[ⲛⲁ]ⲱϫⲛ ⲛ̄ϩⲏⲧⲕ̄

---

[1] The sequence does not continue as in Am. *Cf.* Bo. 49, 50.   [2] *Cf.* Lu. xiv. 26.   [3] *V.* Am. 406.

[4] Here and once again written Pahôm. Elsewhere in this MS. Pahôme, *i. e.* Pahomius, as Makare = Macarius, Ammône = Ammonius &c.

The form Pahôme in *Miss.* iv. 607 (*sic*), Hall *Copt. and Gk. Texts* p. 143. *Cf.* ⲡⲁϩⲱⲙⲓ, Br. Mus. no. 1252.

[5] *V.* Am. 407.   [6] *V.* Am. 402.

[7] *Cf.* ἀρχή in Br. Mus. Cat. p. 97 *a*, p. 168 *a*.

↑ p. р͞і͞а

margin

ⲁⲏⲥⲓⲥ ͣ ⲅⲁⲣ ⲁⲡⲭⲟ-　　　　ⲏⲓ ⲉⲅⲛ̄ⲧⲁⲥ ⲙ̄ⲙⲁⲩ
ⲉⲓⲥ ⲕⲁⲗⲥ ⲟ͞ⲙⲡⲣⲱ-　　　ⲙ̄ⲡⲉⲥⲣⲟʼ ⲉⲧⲉⲡⲣ̄ⲛⲧʼ-
ⲙⲉ ⲙ̄ⲡⲁⲅⲧⲉϩⲟⲩ-　　　ⲡⲉ · ⲁⲅⲱ ⲛ̄ⲑⲉ ⲟⲛ ⲙ̄-
ⲥⲓⲟⲛ · ⲙ̄ⲛ̄ⲧⲁⲓⲁ-　　　　ⲡⲣⲟʼ ⲉⲅⲛ̄ⲧϥ̄ ϣ[ⲟ]ϣ̄ⲧ
ⲕⲣⲓⲥⲓⲥ · ⲙ̄ⲛ̄ⲧⲁⲓⲥ-　　　ⲙ̄ⲙⲁⲩ ϩⲓⲕⲗ̄ⲗⲉ · ϩⲓ-
ⲑⲏⲥⲓⲥ · ⲙ̄ⲛ̄ⲧⲙ̄ⲛ̄ⲧ-　　　ⲙⲟⲭⲗⲟⲥ ϩⲓⲉⲡⲱʼ ϩⲓ-
ⲥⲁⲃⲉ · ⲛ̄ⲑⲉ ⲅⲁⲣ ⲛ̄-　　　ⲱⲣ͞ϫ ⲛⲓⲙ · ⲧⲁⲓ-
ⲙ̄ⲙⲉⲗⲟⲥ ⲙ̄ⲡⲥⲱ-　　　ⲧⲉ ⲑⲉ ⲙ̄ⲡⲁⲅⲧⲉϩ-
ⲙⲁ ⲉⲧⲟⲩⲟⲡ͞ⲅ ⲉⲃⲟⲗʼ　　ⲟⲩⲥⲓⲟ[ⲛ] ⲙ̄ⲛ̄ⲧⲥⲩ-
ⲉϣⲁϥⲣⲟⲟⲃʼ ⲛ̄ϩⲏ-　　　ⲛⲉⲓⲁⲏⲥⲓⲥ · ⲙ̄ⲛ̄-
ⲧⲟⲩ ⲛ̄ϭⲓ ⲡⲣⲱⲙⲉ　　　ⲧⲁⲓⲥⲑⲏⲥ[ⲓⲥ ⲙ̄ⲛ̄-]
ⲡⲟⲩⲁ ⲡⲟⲩⲁ ⲕⲁⲧⲁ　　ⲧⲁⲓⲁⲕ[ⲣⲓⲥⲓⲥ ⲙ̄ⲛ̄-]
ⲧⲉϥⲭⲣⲓⲁ　? 　　　　ⲧⲙ̄ⲛ̄ⲧ[ⲥⲁⲃⲉ
　　　　　　　　　　　　　ⲉⲧ[

ͣ ⲥⲩⲛⲉⲓⲁⲏⲥⲓⲥ.

Fol. 5. P. 113 (*v.* Am. 402, *cf.* Bo. 50). . . . wicked (? πονηρόν [1]), as it is written in the Gospel (εὐαγγ.),[2] 'Blessed are the pure in heart, for they it is shall see God.' If then an impure thought rise up in thy heart, [or] hatred toward [thy brother], or ἤ) . . . . . or (ἤ) envy (φθόνος) . . .

. . . have power over thee,[3] every fruit (καρπός) that is written in the scriptures (γραφή), meditate (μελετᾶν) them in thy heart without ceasing, resolving of thyself to walk therein, as it is written in Esaias,[4] ' Thine heart shall meditate (μελ.) the fear of the Lord '; and all these things shall cease from thee . . .

[1] A slight change would allow of reading 'all '.

[2] Matt. v. 8.

[3] Text hence as Am., not Bo. The former should read (402 *ult.*) 'And if thou wouldest that all the thoughts should diminish in thee and not have power over thee, so meditate in thy heart, without ceasing, always, the good fruit written in the scriptures. And do thou be of steadfast mind and sure in all steadfastness, that thou be careful to walk therein, to the extent of thy power ; and thus shall the evil thoughts decrease in thee, little by little, and shall grow weak, like the spider '. (The last word due to confusion in meanings of χαλ.τω [τ.)

[4] xxxiii. 18.

P. 114. ... For [1] (γάρ) the Lord hath placed the conscience (συνείδησις) in man, and free-will (αὐτεξούσιον) and judgement (διάκρισις) and understanding (αἴσθησις) and knowledge. For (γάρ) even as the members (μέλος) of the body (σῶμα) that are visible, wherewith man worketh, each according to (κατά) his need ...

... a] house that hath its door, which is the heart. And further, like as the door hath key and bolt and chain (μοχλός) and ..... [2] and every surety, even thus it is with free-will (αὐτ.) and conscience (συν.) and judgement (διακ.) and wisdom ...

Fol. 6.   ↑ *Recto.*

[є]ϣⲱ[ⲡ]є ⲙєⲛ єⲣє-
ⲡⲣⲱⲙє о' ⲛ̄ⲁⲧ-
ⲥооⲩⲛ ⲙ̄ⲡⲛоⲙ̊с̄
ϣⲁⲥⲧоⲃєϥ ⲝⲉⲙ̄-
ⲡєїϩⲱⲃ' ⲛⲁⲛоⲩϥ
ⲁⲛ· ϩоєⲙⲉ ⲙєⲛ
ϣⲁⲥⲣ̄ⲙ̄ⲛ̄ⲧⲣⲉ ⲛⲁⲩ
ⲕⲁⲧⲁ ⲡⲥооⲩⲛ ⲙ̄-
ⲡϩⲏⲧ'· ⲝⲉⲕⲛⲁⲣ̄-
ⲛоⲃє єⲡⲝоєⲓⲥ єⲕ-
ϣⲁⲛⲉⲓⲣⲉ ⲙ̄ⲡⲁї·
ϩⲉⲛⲕоⲟⲩⲉ ⲇⲉ оⲛ
ϣⲁⲥⲣ̄ⲙ̄ⲛ̄ⲧⲣⲉ ⲛⲁⲩ
ⲝⲉⲉⲩϣⲁⲛⲧⲁϩоⲕ'
ⲕⲛⲁⲕⲓⲛⲁⲩⲛⲉⲩⲉ·
+
ⲏ̄ ⲛ̄ⲧоϥ ⲥⲉⲛⲁⲙо-[a]

ⲕⲛоⲙⲟⲥ]
єⲧⲥⲏϩ є[
ⲙ̄ⲛ̄ⲥⲁⲡⲧ[ⲱⲃⲉ̄]
ⲛ̄ⲧєⲛⲉⲓⲙⲉ ... [b]
єⲧⲥ̄ⲧⲱⲃⲥ̄ ⲙ̄ⲙ[оϥ]
ⲛ̄ϩⲏⲧϥ ϣⲁϥⲧⲁ-
ⲕⲉ' ⲧⲉϥⲥⲩⲛⲉⲓⲇⲏ-
ⲥⲓⲥ ⲙ̄ⲙⲓⲛ ⲙ̄ⲙ[оϥ]
ⲡ̄ϥ̄ⲣоⲕϩ̄ϥ̄ ϩⲱ[с]
єⲧⲙ̄ⲧⲣⲉⲥⲧоⲃ[с̄ϥ]
ⲝⲓⲛⲡєїⲛⲁⲩ · [ⲛ̄-]
ⲑⲉ єⲧⲥⲏϩ єⲧⲃⲉ[ⲛ̄-]
ⲕооⲩⲉ ⲛ̄ⲧєïⲙⲓ[ⲛⲉ]
ⲝⲉⲉⲣⲉⲧⲉϥⲥⲩⲛ[єⲓ-]
ⲇⲏⲥⲓⲥ ⲣоⲕϩ̄ϥ̄ є[ⲣооⲩ]

<hr>

[a] Perhaps ⲙо[оⲩⲧⲕ.

[b] Perhaps ⲛ̄ⲧⲉⲓⲙⲓⲛⲉ ⲡⲁⲓ.

[1] Am. should be, 'For the Lord hath set conscience in all men, and free-will and judgement and perception (حس) and knowledge. For conscience pricketh a man by reason of evil and saith to him, That which thou hast done is evil &c.'

[2] єⲡⲱ, *v. Aeg. Z.* xxxvi. 147. Rylands no. 252 shows that it is attached to the door; perhaps the lock.

→ *Verso.*

]ⲛϣⲁϫⲉ ⲇⲉ
[. . .]ⲓ̈ϭⲉ ⲡⲁⲩⲗⲟⲥ
ⲉⲧⲃⲉⲛⲁⲓ̈ ⲛ̄ⲧⲉⲓ̈-
ⲙⲓⲛⲉ ⲉⲧⲣⲉⲩⲉⲓ̈ ⲉ-
ϩⲟⲩⲛ, ⲉⲩⲙⲉⲧⲁⲛⲟⲓⲁ
ⲉⲃⲟⲗ ϫⲉⲙ̄ⲡⲟⲩⲥⲟⲩ-
[ⲛ̄]ⲡⲛⲟⲙⲟⲥ· ϣⲁϥ-
[ⲥ]ⲏϩ ⲛ̄ⲧⲉⲓ̈ϩⲉ ϫⲉ-
ⲉⲣⲉⲡⲉⲛϩⲏⲧ ϭⲉϣ-
[ϭ]ⲱϣ ⲉⲃⲟⲗ ϩⲛ̄ⲥⲉⲩ-
ⲛⲉⲓⲇⲏⲥⲓⲥ ⲛⲓⲙ
[ⲙ̄]ⲡⲟⲛⲏⲣⲟⲛ, ⲁⲩⲱ
[ⲉⲣⲉ]ⲡⲉⲛⲥⲱⲙⲁ
[ϫⲟ]ⲕⲙ̄ ϩⲛ̄ⲟⲩⲙⲟⲟ[ⲩ]

[ⲟⲩ]ⲏⲧⲟⲩ ⲛⲟⲙⲟⲥ [ϩⲓ-]
ⲛ̄ⲧⲉⲩⲥⲩⲛⲉⲓ[ⲇⲏ-]
ⲥⲓⲥ· ϥⲧⲁⲙⲟ ⲙ̄-
ⲙⲟⲛ ⲛ̄ⲧⲉⲓ̈ϩⲉ ⲛ̄ϭⲓ
ⲡⲕⲏⲣⲩⲍ ⲙ̄ⲡⲉⲩ-
ⲁⲅⲅⲉⲗⲓⲟⲛ ϫⲉϩⲟ-
ⲧⲁⲛ ⲅⲁⲣ ⲛ̄ϩⲉⲑⲛⲟⲥ
ⲉⲧⲉⲙⲙ̄ⲛ̄ⲧⲟⲩ-
ⲛⲟⲙⲟⲥ ⲫⲩⲥⲉⲓ ⲥⲉ-
ⲉⲓⲣⲉ ⲛ̄ⲛⲁⲡⲛⲟⲙⲟⲥ
ⲛⲁⲓ̈ ⲉⲙⲙ̄ⲛ̄ⲧⲟⲩ-
ⲛⲟⲙⲟⲥ ⲥⲉϣⲟⲟⲡ
ⲛⲁⲩ ⲛ̄ⲛⲟⲙⲟⲥ ⲙⲁⲩ-
ⲁⲁⲩ· ⲛⲁⲓ ⲉⲩⲧⲥⲁ-
ⲃⲟ ⲙ̄ⲙⲟⲕ ⲉⲡϩⲱⲃ
ⲙ̄ⲡⲛⲟⲙⲟⲥ ⲉϥⲥⲏϩ
ϩⲛ̄ⲡⲉⲩϩⲏⲧ, ⲉⲣⲉ-
ⲧ[ⲉⲩⲥⲩⲛⲉⲓⲇⲏⲥⲓⲥ]

Fol. 6. *Recto* (v. Am. 403). Now (μέν) if the man be ignorant of the law (νόμος), it (*sc.* conscience) prompteth him, (saying), This thing is not good. Some indeed (μέν), it testifieth to them according to (κατά) the knowledge of the heart, (saying), Thou wilt sin against the Lord if thou do this ; while (δέ) others again, to them it testifieth, If thou be discovered, thou shalt be in danger (κινδυνεύειν), or (ἤ) indeed, they will [? slay thee . . . . .

. . . laws (νόμος)] that are written . . . after the prompting (?) of this sort (?) wherewith it hath prompted him, he will destroy his own conscience (συν.) and sear it, so that (ὡς) it shall not thenceforth prompt him, as it is written concerning others of this sort,[1] ' Their conscience being seared for [them ']

Verso (not in Am.). . . . but (δέ) the words ; . . Paul concerning such as these, that they should come in unto repentance (μετάνοια) because they

---

[1] 1 Tim. iv. 2.

have not known the law (νόμος). It is written thus,[1] 'Our hearts being sprinkled from all evil conscience (συν. πονηρός) and our body (σῶμα) washed with [pure] water . . . . .

. . . they [have] a law (νόμος) through their conscience (συν.). Thus doth the herald (κῆρυξ) of the Gospel (εὐαγ.) tell us,[2] 'For when (ὅταν γάρ) the Gentiles (ἔθνος), that have not law (νόμος), by nature (φύσει) do the (things) of the law, these, having not law, are a law unto themselves. These teach thee (*sic*) the work of the law written in their heart, their [conscience . . . . .

Fol. 7.　→ *Recto.*

margin

]ⲙⲟⲕ ⲟⲩϩⲓⲏ
ⲛϩⲟⲟ. ⲁ[. .]ⲅⲣⲱ
ⲙ̅ⲃⲉⲏ[.].[. .]ⲁⲩ ⲁⲛ
ⲛϭⲓⲅ . . [ⲁ̅ⲡ]ⲡ̅ⲥⲁ-
ⲛⲁⲓ̈ [ⲟⲛ] ⲛ̅[ⲧⲉ]ⲣⲉϥⲁⲓ-
ⲥⲟⲁⲛⲉ ⲛ̅ⲛⲉ[ϩ]ⲙⲟⲧ'
ⲉⲧⲉⲣⲉⲡϫⲟⲉⲓⲥ ⲉⲓⲣⲉ
ⲙ̅ⲙⲟⲟⲩ ⲡ̅ⲙⲙⲁϥ ⲛ̅-
ⲑⲉ ⲉⲧⲉⲣⲉⲁⲅⲉⲓⲁ'
ϫⲱ ⲙ̅ⲙⲟⲥ ϫⲉⲓ̈ⲛⲁ-
ϯ ⲟⲩ' ⲛ̅ϣⲃ̅ⲃⲓⲱ ⲙ̅-
ⲡϫⲟⲉⲓⲥ ⲉⲡⲙⲁ ⲛ̅ⲛⲉ̅-
ⲧⲁϥⲁⲁⲩ ⲛⲁⲓ̈ ⲧⲏ-
ⲣⲟⲩ · ⲁⲩⲱ ⲛ̅ⲑⲉ ⲟⲛ
ⲉⲧϥ̅ⲇⲓⲁⲕⲣⲓⲛⲉ ⲙ̅ⲡ-
ⲧⲉϥⲯⲩⲭⲏ ⲙ̅ⲙⲓⲛ
ⲙ̅ⲙⲟϥ ϩ̅ⲛ̅ⲟⲩⲁⲓⲥⲑⲏ-
ⲥⲓⲥ ⲉϥϫⲱ ⲙ̅ⲙⲟⲥ ϫⲉ-
ⲧⲁⲯⲩⲭⲏ ⲥⲙⲟⲩ ⲉ-
ⲡϫⲟⲉⲓⲥ · ⲁⲩⲱ ⲛⲉⲧⲙ̅-

ⲛⲉ̅ ⲉⲃⲟⲗ' ⲛ̅ⲛⲟⲩⲁ[ⲛⲟ-]
ⲙⲓⲁ ⲧⲏⲣⲟⲩ · ⲡⲉ[ⲧ-]
ⲧⲁⲗϭⲟ' ⲛ̅ⲛⲟⲩϣ[ⲱ-]
ⲛⲉ ⲧⲏⲣⲟⲩ · ⲡⲉ[ⲧ-]
ⲥⲱⲧⲉ ⲙ̅ⲡⲟⲩ[ⲱⲛϩ]
ⲉⲃⲟⲗ' ϩ̅ⲙ̅ⲡⲧⲁⲕ[ⲟ]
ⲡⲉⲧϯ ⲡⲟⲩⲕⲗ[ⲟⲙ]
ⲉϫⲱ̅ ⲛ̅ⲛⲁ' ϩⲙ̅[ⲛ̅ⲧ-]
ϣⲁⲛϩⲧⲏϥ · [ⲡⲉⲧ-]
ⲧⲥⲓⲟ' ⲙ̅ⲡⲟⲩⲟⲩ[ⲱϣ]
ⲛ̅ⲁⲅⲁⲑⲟⲛ · ϫⲉ[ⲕⲁⲥ]
ϫⲉ ⲉⲛⲉⲉⲓⲙⲉ ϫ[ⲙ-]
ⲙⲉⲗⲟⲥ ⲛ̅ⲧⲉ[ⲯⲩⲭⲏ-]
ⲛⲉ ⲛⲉⲛⲧⲁⲛϣ[ⲣ̅ⲡ-]
ϫⲟⲟⲩ ⲕⲁⲧⲁ ⲡϣⲁϫ[ⲉ]
ⲛ̅ⲁⲅⲉⲓⲁ' ϩ̅ⲙ̅ⲡⲧⲣ[ⲉϥ-]
ⲡⲣⲟⲧⲣⲉⲡⲉ ⲛ̅ⲧⲉ[ϥ-]
ⲯⲩⲭⲏ ⲉⲥⲙⲟⲩ ⲉⲡϫ[ⲟ-]
ⲉⲓⲥ ⲉϥⲡⲣⲟⲧⲣⲉⲡ[ⲉ]
ⲟⲛ ⲛ̅ⲛⲉⲥⲕⲉⲙⲉⲗⲟⲥ

[1] Heb. x. 22.　　　　　[2] Rom. ii. 14.

ⲡⲁⲥⲁⲛϩⲟⲩⲛ ⲧⲏ-
[ⲣ]ⲟⲩ ⲥⲙⲟⲩ ⲉⲡⲉϥ-
[ⲣⲁⲛ' ⲉ]ⲧⲟⲩⲁⲁⲃ· ⲧⲁ-
[ⲯⲩⲭ]ⲏ ⲥⲙⲟⲩ ⲉⲡϫⲟ-
[ⲉⲓⲥ ⲁⲩⲱ ⲙ̄]ⲡⲣ̄ⲣⲡⲱ-
[ⲃϣ ⲛ̄ⲛⲉϥⲧⲱ]ⲱⲃⲉ
[ⲧⲏⲣⲟⲩ· ⲡⲉⲧⲕⲱ̄]

ⲉⲧⲟ̄ ⲛ̄ⲟⲩⲁ' ⲛ̄ⲟⲩⲱⲧ
ⲛ̄ⲙⲙⲁⲥ. ⲏ . ⲅⲏ ?
ⲛⲉⲙ ⲉϥϫⲱ ⲙⲙⲟⲥ
ⲉⲧⲃⲏⲧⲟⲩ ϫⲉ[ⲛⲉ-]
ⲧⲙ̄ⲡⲁⲥⲁⲛϩⲟⲩⲛ
ⲧ[ⲏⲣⲟⲩ ⲥⲙⲟⲩ ⲉⲡⲉϥ-]
ⲣⲁⲛ' ⲉⲧⲟⲩⲁⲁⲃ· [ⲟⲩ]
ⲙⲟⲛⲟⲛϭⲉ ϫⲉⲉⲣ[ⲉ-]

margin

↑ *Verso.*

margin

ϯⲁⲓⲥⲑⲏⲥⲓⲥ ϣⲟⲟⲡ
ϫⲉⲉⲣⲉⲡⲣⲱⲙⲉ ⲙ̄ⲡⲓ-
ⲥⲧⲟⲥ ⲁⲓⲥⲑⲁⲛⲉ ⲛ̄-
[ϩⲏ]ⲧⲥ̄ ⲛ̄ⲧⲉⲭⲁⲣⲓⲥ
[ⲙ̄]ⲡϫⲟⲉⲓⲥ ⲁ[ⲗⲗ]ⲁ ⲉ-
[ⲧⲣ]ⲉϥⲁⲓⲥⲑⲁⲛⲉ ϩⲛ
[ⲛ̄]ⲙⲡⲉⲧⲛⲁⲛⲟⲩϥ
[.. ᵃ]ⲉⲧⲟⲩ[ⲉⲓ]ⲣⲉ ⲙ̄ⲙⲟ-
[ⲟⲩ]. ϫᵇ [ϩ]ⲓⲧⲙ̄ⲛ̄-
[. . . . .] ⲙ̄ⲡⲛⲟⲩⲧⲉ·
[ⲉϥϭⲛ̄]ⲁⲣⲓⲕⲉ ⲅⲁⲣ
[ⲉ]ϩⲟⲉⲓⲛⲉ ⲉⲙⲡⲟⲩ-
ⲁⲓⲥⲑⲁⲛⲉ ⲛ̄ⲡⲉϩ-
ⲙⲟⲧ' ⲧⲏⲣⲟⲩ ⲉⲛ-
ⲧⲁϥⲁⲁⲩ ⲛ̄ⲙⲙⲁⲩ
ⲛ̄ϭⲓ ⲡⲉⲛⲧⲁϥⲥⲁ-
ⲛⲟⲩϣⲟⲩ ⲉϥϫⲱ ⲙ̄-
ⲙⲟⲥ ϫⲉⲁⲛⲟⲕ ⲅⲁⲣ

ϩⲏⲧ ⲧⲙ̄ⲛ̄ⲧ[ⲥⲁ-]
ⲃⲉ ⲇⲉ ⲕⲁⲧⲁ ⲡⲛⲟⲩⲧⲉ
ⲉⲧⲣ[ⲉ]ⲡⲣⲱⲙⲉ ⲥⲟⲩ-
ⲛ̄ ⲡ[ⲉⲧ]ⲣ̄ⲁⲛⲁϥ' ⲧⲏ-
ⲣϥ̄ ⲙ̄[ⲡ]ϫⲟ[ⲉⲓ]ⲥ ⲙ̄ⲡ-
ⲡⲉϥ[ⲟⲩ]ⲱϣ ⳨ ⲛ̄ ⲛ̄-
ⲧⲟϥ ⲡϥ̄ⲥⲟⲩⲛ̄ ⲡⲉ-
ⲧⲟⲩⲛⲁϭⲟⲗⲡϥ̄ ⲛⲁϥ
ⲉⲃⲟⲗ' ϩⲓⲧⲟⲟⲧϥ̄ ⲛ̄ⲑ-
ⲉ ⲉⲧⲥⲛϩ ϫⲉϩⲱⲃ
ⲛⲓⲙ' ⲉⲧⲉⲧⲛ̄ⲙⲉ-
ⲉⲅⲉ ⲉⲣⲟⲟⲩ ⲛ̄ⲕⲉⲥ-
ⲙⲟⲧ, ⲡⲁⲓ ⲡⲛⲟⲩⲧⲉ
ⲛⲁϭⲟⲗⲡϥ̄ ⲛⲏⲧⲛ̄
ⲉⲃⲟⲗ'· ⲕⲁⲓ ⲅⲁⲣ' ⲇⲁ-
ⲛⲓⲏⲗ ⲛ̄ⲧⲉⲣⲉϥ-
ϭⲱⲗⲡ ⲉⲣⲟϥ ⲛ̄ⲧⲣⲁ-
ⲥⲟⲩ ⲙ̄ⲡⲉⲥⲕⲉ-

ᵃ ? ⲛⲁⲓ.   ᵇ ? ⲉⲃⲟⲗ.

пєϣϣєпє[a] єтрєγ-   ⲃⲱⲗ' ⲛ̅ⲧⲉⲩϣⲏ ⲛ̅-
ⲥⲩⲛ̅ϩⲓⲥⲧⲁ ⲙ̅ⲙⲟⲓ̈   ϭⲓ ⲡⲭⲟⲉⲓⲥ . ⲁϥ-
ϩⲓⲧⲟⲧⲧⲏⲩⲧⲛ̅ ·   ⲥⲙⲟⲩ ⲉⲣⲟϥ' ⲉϥϫⲱ
ⲁγⲱ ⲙ̅ⲛ̅ⲛ̅ⲥⲁⲧⲁⲓ-   ⲙ̅ⲙⲟⲥ ϫⲉⲡⲉⲧϯ
ⲥⲑⲏⲥⲓⲥ ϣⲁⲥⲟⲩⲱ-   ⲛ̅ⲧⲥⲟⲫⲓⲁ ⲛ̅ⲛ̅[ⲥⲟ-]
ⲛ̅ϩ̅ ⲉⲃⲟⲗ' ⲛ̅ϭⲓ ⲧⲉϥ-   ⲫⲟⲥ · ⲁγⲱ ⲧ[ⲙ̅ⲛ̅ⲧ-]
ⲙ̅ⲛ̅ⲧⲥⲁⲃⲉ ⲙ̅ⲛ̅-   ⲥⲁ[ⲃⲉ
[ⲧ]ⲉϥⲙ̅ⲛ̅ⲧ[ⲣⲙ̅]ⲛ̅-   ⁻.[

margin

[a] *Cf.* Woide, Balestri (less correct).

Fol. 7. (*The right position of this fol. is uncertain.*)

Recto. ...a... road ..... not ..... Thereafter [again?], after he hath recognized ($αἰσθανέσθαι$) the mercies that the Lord doeth with him, even as David saith,[1] 'What shall I give in exchange unto the Lord, in place of all the (things) that He hath done unto me?' And like too as he doth argue ($διακρίνειν$) with his own soul ($ψυ.$), in understanding ($αἴσθησις$), saying,[2] 'My soul, bless the Lord, and all (things) that are within me, bless His holy name. My soul, bless the Lord, and forget not all His requitals. Who forgiveth thee all thy iniquities ($ἀνομ.$), who healeth all thy diseases, who redeemeth thy life from destruction, who setteth a crown upon thee of mercy and compassion, who satisfieth thy desire with good-things ($ἀγαθός$).' And ($δέ$) so that[3] we may know (?) that it is the members ($μέλος$) of the [soul ($ψυ.$)] whereof we have already spoken,[4] according to ($κατά$) the words of David, when he doth exhort ($προτρέπειν$) his soul ($ψυ.$) to bless the Lord, exhorting ($πρ.$) besides its members ($μέλ.$) also, that are one with it ....., saying of them, 'All (things) that are within me, [bless His] holy name.' For not only ($οὐ μόνον$) (is it so) that

Verso. the understanding ($αἰσ.$) doth exist in order that the believing ($πιστός$) man may recognize ($αἰσθανέσθαι$) thereby the grace ($χάρις$) of the Lord, but ($ἀλλά$) that he may also recognize ($αἰσ.$) the benefits that are done him by God's ..... For ($γάρ$) some He blameth, in that they have not recognized ($αἰσ.$) all the graces that He who nourished them hath done

[1] Ps. cxv. 3.
[2] Ps. cii. 1-5.
[3] The uncertainty of the conjunction renders the logic of the sentence obscure.
[4] *V.* Am. 403 *infra*. If that were the passage here referred to, the position given to this leaf would be justified.

with them saying,[1] 'For (γάρ) I ought to have been commended (συνίστα-σθαι) of you.' And after the understanding (αἰσ.), his knowledge is displayed and his wisdom.

But (δέ) knowledge according to (κατά) God (is) that man should know all that is pleasing to the Lord and His will, or (ἤ) else that he know that which shall be revealed unto him by Him, as it is written,[2] 'Every thing whereof ye shall think otherwise, this shall God reveal unto you.' For (καὶ γάρ) Daniel, after that the Lord had revealed unto him the dream and also its interpretation, at night, blessed Him saying,[3] 'He that giveth wisdom (σοφία) unto the wise (σοφός) and knowledge . . . . .

Fol. 8.   → *Recto.*

margin

ⲧⲁˈᵃ ⲉⲣⲟⲥ ⲝⲉⲁⲩⲧⲁⲙⲟⲓ
[ⲝ]ⲉⲥⲣⲓⲙⲉ ⲁⲩⲱ ⲥⲙⲟ-
ⲕⲟ ⲛ̄ϩⲏⲧ · ⲙⲏⲡⲟ-
ⲧⲉ ⲛ̄ⲧⲥⲱⲧⲙ̄ ⲡ̄ⲧ̄-
ϭⲏⲡ ⲟ̄ⲛ[ⲡⲉ]ⲕⲟϩⲏⲧ ·ᵇ
ⲁⲛⲟ[ⲕ ⲇⲉ] ⲡⲁⲓⲡⲉ
ⲡⲁ[ⲟⲩⲛⲟ]ϥ [ⲉⲕ]ϣⲁⲛ-
ϣⲱ[ⲡⲉ] ⲉⲕ[ⲧⲁ]ⲝⲣⲏⲩ
[ⲉⲝ̄ⲛ̄ⲛⲉ]ⲛⲧ[ⲟⲗ]ⲏ ⲧⲏ-
[ⲣⲟⲩ ⲛ̄]ⲡⲱⲛϩ · ⲁⲩⲱ
[. .ᶜ ⲡⲉ]ⲡⲓⲥⲕⲟⲡⲟⲥ
[. . . . .ᵈ ⲉ]ϩⲁⲓ̈ ϣⲁⲣⲟ[ⲛ]

ϩⲟⲟⲩ ⲉϥⲛⲁⲃⲱⲕ ⲉ[ⲩ-]
ⲙ̄ⲁ̄ ⲡⲃⲟⲗˈ ⲛ̄ⲧⲥⲟⲟⲩ[ⲉ̄]
ⲉⲣϩⲱⲃˈ ⲛ̄ⲛⲉⲥⲛⲏ[ⲩ]
ⲁⲩⲝⲓⲧ̄ⲥ ⲉϩⲣⲁⲓ̈ . . .
ⲉⲩⲝⲉⲛⲉⲡⲱⲣ ⲉⲥ-
. ⲉ . . ⲧᵉ [ⲧⲁ-]
ⲃⲛ̄ⲛⲥⲉ ⲉⲩⲝ[ⲱ ⲙ̄-]
ⲙⲟⲥ ⲛⲁⲥ ⲝ[ⲉⲉⲓⲥ ϩⲏ-]
ⲛⲧ[ⲉ] ⲛ̄ⲧⲟ[ϥ]
ⲛ[

ᵃ ⲁⲡⲁⲛ]ⲧⲁ.   ᵇ Perhaps ϭⲟⲧϩ ⲛⲡⲉⲕⲟϩⲧ.   ᶜ Apparently not ⲟⲛ.   ᵈ Scarcely
space for ⲡⲉⲛⲧⲁϥ.   ᵉ Adjective or participle referring to ⲝⲉⲛⲉⲡⲱⲣ.

↑ *Verso.*

margin

ⲙ̄ⲡⲉⲟⲩⲟⲉⲓϣˈ · ⲛ̄ⲑⲉ
ⲅⲁⲣᵃ ⲉⲧⲙ̄ⲙⲟⲟϣⲉ ⲛ̄-

ⲧⲉⲛⲟϭⲉ ᵛⁱᶜ ϯⲛⲁⲧⲁ-
ⲙⲱⲧⲛ̄ ϩⲙ̄ⲡⲁⲓ̈ ⲉ-

ᵃ [ⲩⲕ]ⲁⲛⲉ-, which I at first read, is difficult to deal with.

[1] 2 Cor. xii. 11.   [2] Phil. iii. 15.   [3] Dan. ii. 21.

[ⲙ]ⲟⲥ ⲅ̄ⲡⲟⲩⲙ̄ⲡⲁⲅⲣⲓ-　　ⲕⲉⲁⲛⲁⲥⲧⲣⲟⲫ[ⲏ]
[ⲟ]ⲥ ϣⲁⲡⲟⲟⲩ· ⲡ̄ⲡⲉⲛ-　　ⲧⲁⲓ ⲉⲧⲡ̄ⲛⲁⲁⲁⲥ, ⲉ-
[ⲣ̄]ϩⲟⲩⲟ ⲁⲛ, ⲡⲁⲣⲁ ⲡⲉⲧ-　　ⲧⲣⲉⲛ[·]ϣ[·]ⲉⲓ′ ⲛ̄ⲟⲩ-
[ⲥⲏϩ ⲛⲁ]ⲛ, ⲅ̄ⲡⲛⲉ-　　ⲕⲟⲩⲓ̈ ⲙⲛ̄[ⲛ̄ⲣ]ⲱⲙⲉ
[ⲅⲣⲁ]ⲫⲏ· ⲛ̄ⲧⲉⲣⲟⲩ-　　ⲉⲧϩ[ⲓⲃⲟⲗ′· ⲛ̄ⲑⲉ ⲉ-
[. . . .] ⲡⲥⲱⲧⲏⲣ′ ⲉ-　　ⲧⲉⲣ[ⲉⲡ]ⲁⲩ[ⲗⲟⲥ ⲝ]ⲱ′
[. . . . .]ⲥⲙ̄ⲛ̄　　ⲙ̄ⲙ[ⲟⲥ ϫⲉⲉ[
　　　　　　　　　　　　　　ϣⲱⲡ′ ⲙ̄ⲛ[
　　　　　　　　　　　　　　ⲛ̄ⲛⲁϩⲣ̄ⲛ[

Fol. 8. *Recto* (*v.* Am. 405). . . . mee]t (ἀπαντᾶν) her ; for I have been told she weepeth and is distressed ; lest (μήποτε) thou shouldest hear and be pricked (?) in thy heart. As for (δέ) me, my joy it is if so be thou art firmly established in all the commandments (ἐντολή) of life. And . . . the bishop (ἐπ.) that (?) did write unto us . . . . .

(*v.* Am. 406) . . . on a] day (that) he should go to a place without the monastery (*lit.* congregation), to work [1] with the brethren. They took her up . . . to a roof, which . . . . . Tabennêse, saying unto her, ' Lo, he [is there . . . . .

Verso (*v.* Am. 406). . . . in time past. For (γάρ) like as [2] we walk in savagery (-ἄγριος [3]) until to-day, let us not do more than (παρά) the things written for us (?) in the Scriptures. After that they had . . . the Saviour (σωτήρ) . . . . .

. . . So now I will tell you herein another (manner of) converse (ἀναστροφή) that we will do, (namely,) . . . go (?) a little with [4] the men that are without, as Paul (?) saith, ...

---

[1] Ac. 33, 12 (= G ⲣ̄ⲗ̄ⲃ b) reads ' they arranged a work outside, with the brethren, that they would do ; and they informed her thereof at Tabennêse and said unto her, ' Lo, he is there with the brethren, working &c.' (Unless واطلعوها عليه refers to bringing her up on to the roof.)　　[2] *I. e.* ? seeing that.

[3] ⲙⲛ̄ⲧⲁⲅⲣⲓⲟⲥ, *e.g.* Steindorff, *Gram.*[2] 55*, *CSCO.* vol. 42 (Sinuth.), 113.

[4] *Cf.* συγκαταβαίνειν.

Fol. 9. ↑ *Recto.*   margin

[ⲙ̄ⲡⲉϥⲙⲁⲑⲏ]ⲧⲏⲥ
[ⲉⲃⲱⲕ ⲡ̄ϭⲧ]ⲱⲗⲙ̄ ⲙ̄-
[ⲡⲉϥⲉⲓⲱⲧ]· ⲁϥ-
[ⲟⲩⲱϣⲃ̄ ⲛ̄ϭⲓ] ⲡⲉⲧ̄ⲙ-
[ⲙⲁⲩ ⲉ]ϥϫ[ⲱ] ⲙ̄ⲙⲟⲥ
[ϫⲉⲙ̄]ⲡϥ̄[ⲕ]ⲁⲁϥ [ⲁ]ⲛ
[ϫⲉ]ⲡϥ̄ⲃⲱⲕ [ⲡϥ̄-]
[ⲧ̄ⲙ̄ⲕⲟ]ⲧϥ̄ ⲛ̄ⲧⲟϥ
[ⲇⲉ ⲡ]ⲉϫⲁϥ ⲛⲁϥ ϫⲉ-
[ϣⲁⲥ]ϣⲱⲡⲉ ⲛ̄ⲧⲉ-
[ⲟⲩⲁ] ⲙ̄ⲡⲟⲟⲩ ⲃⲱⲕ'
[ϣⲁ]ⲛⲉϥⲣⲱⲙⲉ ⲕⲁ-
[ⲧⲁ ⲥ]ⲁⲣⲝ ⲉⲙ[ⲡϥ̄]ⲡⲁ-
[ⲣⲁⲃ]ⲁ ⲛ̄ⲧⲉ[ⲛ̄ⲧ]ⲟⲗⲏ
[ⲙ̄ⲡ]ⲉⲅⲁⲅⲅⲉⲗⲓ[ⲟ]ⲛ·
[ⲡⲉ]ϫⲁϥ ⲛⲁϥ [ϫⲉⲉϣ]
[ϫⲉϥ]ⲛⲁⲧ̄ⲙ̄ⲡⲉⲩϣ[ⲓ-]
[ⲛⲉ] ⲙ̄ⲙⲁⲧⲉⲡⲉ ⲛ̄-
[ⲟⲩ]ⲛⲟⲃⲉ ⲁⲛⲡⲉ· ⲁⲩ-
[ⲱ ⲡⲉ]ϫⲁϥ ⲛⲁϥ ϩⲙ̄ⲡ-
[ⲟⲩ]...ⲅⲥ·ⲧⲁᵃ ϫⲉ-
[ⲧⲁⲓ̈]ⲧⲉ ⲧⲡⲓⲥⲧⲓⲥ
[ⲛ̄ⲡⲣ]ⲱⲙⲉ ⲛ̄ⲧⲁⲃⲓ̄ⲛ-
[ⲛⲏⲥ]ⲉ ⲉⲩϫⲱ ⲙ̄ⲙⲟⲥ
[ϫⲉⲛⲟ]ⲩⲛⲟⲃⲉ ⲁⲛⲡⲉ
[....]ⲥ̄ᵇ ⲛ̄ⲡⲉⲛⲧⲟ-
[ⲗⲏ ⲙ̄ⲡ]ⲉⲅⲁⲅⲅⲉⲗ-
[ⲓⲟⲛ· ⲕⲁⲓ] ⲅⲁⲣ ⲁⲛⲟⲕ

ⲉⲙⲡⲁϯⲉⲓ' ⲉⲡ[ⲉⲓ̈ⲙⲁ']
ⲛⲉⲓ̈ⲁⲧⲱⲛ̄ϫⲉ [ⲕⲁ-]
ⲧⲁ ⲧⲁⲙⲛ̄ⲧⲕⲟⲩⲉ[ⲓ̈]
ϩⲙ̄ⲡ[ⲉ]ⲧⲟⲩⲟⲡⲡ̄ ⲉⲣⲟ[ⲓ]
ϫⲉⲡⲁⲓ̈ⲡⲉ ⲡⲟⲩⲱϣ
ⲙ̄ⲡϫ[ⲟⲉⲓⲥ ⲁ]ⲩⲱ ⲛ̄-
ⲧⲉⲣⲓ[ⲥⲱⲧ]ⲙ ϫⲉⲧⲉ-
ⲧ̄ⲙ̄[ⲟ]ⲟϣⲉ ϩ̄ⲟⲩ-
ⲙ̄ⲛ̄ⲧⲧⲉⲗⲉⲓⲟⲥ ⲕⲁ-
ⲧⲁ ⲡⲉⲛⲧⲟⲗⲏ ⲙ̄ⲡⲉⲩ-
ⲁⲅⲅⲉⲗⲓⲟⲛ ⲁⲓ̈ⲉⲓ' ⲉ-
ⲡⲉⲓ̈ⲙⲁ'· ⲧⲉⲛⲟⲩϭⲉ
ⲛ̄ϯⲛⲁϫⲱ ⲁⲛ ⲁⲗ-
ⲗⲁ ϯⲛⲁⲃ̄[ⲱⲕ] ⲟⲛ ⲉ-
ⲡⲁⲙⲁ ⲉⲛ[ⲧ]ⲁⲓⲉⲓ' ⲛ̄-
ϩⲏⲧϥ̄· ⲁ[ϥϥⲓ̣ ϩⲣⲁϥᶜ
ⲉⲃⲟⲗ' ⲁϥⲣⲓⲙⲉ ⲉϥⲙ[ⲟ-]
ⲕ̄ϩ   ⲛ̄ϩⲏⲧ ⲉϫⲱϥ ⲛ̄-
[ϭⲓ ⲑ]ⲉⲟⲇⲱⲣⲟⲥ· ⲛ̄-
ⲧ[ⲉⲩ]ⲛⲟⲩϭⲉ ⲡⲉⲧⲙ̄-
ⲙ[ⲁⲩ ⲁ]ϥⲃⲱⲕ' ⲉ̣..-ᵈ
ⲡⲉ[ⲛ]ⲉⲓⲱⲧ ⲡⲁϩⲱ-
ⲙⲉ' ⲉϥϫⲱ' ⲙ̄ⲙⲟⲥ [ϫⲉ-]
ⲁⲙⲟⲩ ⲧ̄ⲥ̄ⲗ̄ⲥ̄ⲗ̄ ⲡⲉ[ⲓ-]
ⲕⲟⲩⲓ̈ ⲛ̄ⲥⲟⲡ· ? ᵉ
ⲧⲉ ⲡϥ̄ⲥⲕⲁⲛⲁ[ⲁⲗⲓ-]
[ⲍⲉ·] ⲁϥϫⲱ ⲉⲣⲟϥ [ⲉ-]
ⲡϣⲁϫⲉ ⲉⲛⲧⲁϥϫⲟ-

ᵃ Probably ⲡⲁⲛⲟⲩⲣⲅⲓⲁ (AS. *πανοῦργως*).   ᵇ ⲡⲁⲣⲁⲃⲁ seems impossible.   ᶜ Am.
408, 5 ادار وجهه, through confusion of meanings of ϩⲣⲁϥ.   ᵈ ⲉⲧⲁⲙⲉ, if there were space
enough.   ᵉ Probably ⲙⲛⲡⲟⲧⲉ.

→ *Verso.*   margin

[ⲟⲥ] ⲭⲉⲁⲓ̈ⲥⲕⲁⲛⲇⲁⲗⲓ-   ⲁⲛ ⲓ̈[

[ⲍⲉ] ⲙ̄ⲟⲏⲧϥ· ⲁⲩⲱ   ⲡⲉⲓϣ[ⲁⲭⲉ

ⲛ̄ⲧⲉ[ⲣ]ⲉϥⲉⲓⲙⲉ ⲉⲧ-   [.]ⲙ̄ⲏ[. ⲭⲉⲛⲧⲁⲓ ⲁⲛ-]

ⲡⲁⲛⲟⲩⲅ[ⲅⲓ]ⲁ ⲉⲛⲧⲁϥ-   ⲧⲉ ⲧⲉϥ[ⲡⲓⲥⲧⲓⲥ ⲉⲓ-]

ⲁⲁⲥ ⲟ̄[ⲛ̄ⲧⲙ̄ⲛ̄]ⲧⲣ̄ⲙ̄-   ⲙⲏⲧⲓ̄ ⲛ̄ⲧ[ⲟϥ ⲉϥⲛⲁ-]

ⲛ̄ⲟⲏⲧ [ⲙ̄ⲡⲉ]ⲡ̄ⲡⲁ   [ⲟ̄]ⲙⲟⲗⲟ[ⲅ]ⲉⲓ̈ [ⲛ̄ⲧⲉϥ-]

ⲡⲉⲭⲁϥ [ⲇⲉᵃ ⲛⲁ]ϥ̄' ⲭⲉⲡ̄ⲥ̄-   [ⲧⲁ]ⲡⲣⲟ ⲙ̄ⲙ[ⲓⲛ ⲙ̄-]

ⲥⲟⲟⲩⲛ' ⲁ[ⲛ] ⲭⲉⲟⲩⲧⲱ-   [ⲙ]ⲟϥ ⲭⲉⲡⲉ[ⲧⲛⲁⲃⲱⲕ]

ⲥⲉ ⲛ̄ⲃ̄ⲣⲣⲉ, ⲛ̄ⲛⲉⲕ-   ⲉⲃ̄ⲙ̄ⲡϣⲓⲛⲉ [ⲛ̄ⲛⲉϥ-]

ⲙ̄ⲛ̄ϣⲁ' ⲁⲛ ⲛ̄ϣⲁ-   ⲣⲱⲙⲉ ⲟⲩⲡⲁ[ⲣⲁⲃⲁ-]

ⲭⲉ ⲛ̄ⲙⲙⲁϥ ⲛ̄ⲧⲉⲓ̈-   ⲧⲏⲥⲡⲉ ⲛ̄ⲡ̄[ⲉⲛⲧⲟ-]

ⲣⲉ· ⲟ̄ⲙⲱⲥ ⲙⲟⲩⲧⲉ   ⲗⲏ ⲙ̄ⲡⲉⲅⲁⲩ[ⲅⲉⲗⲓ-]

ⲉⲣⲟϥ [ⲛ̄]ⲧⲁⲡⲓⲑⲉ ⲙ̄-   ⲟⲛ[· ⲉϣⲱⲡⲉ [ⲉⲓ-]

ⲙⲟϥ [ⲛ̄]ⲧⲉⲣⲉϥⲙⲟⲩ-   ϣ[ⲁⲛ]ⲥⲱⲧⲙ̄ [ⲉⲣⲟϥ]

ⲧⲉ [ⲉⲣⲟ]ϥ' ⲡⲉⲭⲁϥ   ⲉϥ[ⲟ̄]ⲟⲙⲟⲗⲟⲅⲉ[ⲓ']

ⲛⲁϥ' [ⲟ̄]ⲱⲥ ⲉϥⲡⲓⲑⲉ   ⲡ[. .].ᵇ ⲧⲟⲧⲉ ϯ[ⲛⲁⲉⲓ-]

ⲙ̄ⲙⲟϥ ⲭⲉⲛ̄ⲡⲣ̄ⲙ̄-   [ⲙ]ⲉ ⲭⲉⲛ̄ⲧⲁⲓ̈ ⲁ[ⲛⲧⲉ]

ⲕⲁⲟ ⲛ̄ⲟⲏⲧ ⲟ̄ⲙ̄ⲡⲓ-   ⲑⲉ ⲉⲧϥ̄ⲡⲓⲥⲧ[ⲉⲩⲉ]

ⲧⲁⲕⲥⲟⲙⲉϥ' [ⲟ̄ⲓⲧⲙ̄-]   [ⲙ̄ⲙ]ⲟⲥ· ⲛ̄ⲧⲉ[ⲣⲉϥ-]

[ⲡⲥⲟⲛ] ⲛ̄ⲧⲁϥ[ϣⲁ]ⲭⲉ   ⲉⲓⲙⲉ ⲇⲉ ⲛ̄ϭⲓ ⲡ[ⲉⲧⲙ̄-]

ⲛ̄ⲙⲙⲁⲕ ⲉ[. . .] ⲉⲉⲓ'   ⲙⲁⲩ [ⲭ]ⲉⲛ̄ϥ̄ⲡⲓ[ⲉⲓ-]

ⲛ̄ⲙⲙⲁⲕ ⲟ̄ⲱ[ⲥ] ⲧⲱ-   ⲑⲉ ⲁⲛ ⲛ̄ϭⲓ ⲡϣ[ⲏⲣⲉ]

ⲥⲉ ⲛ̄ⲃ̄ⲣⲣⲉ· ⲉⲡⲉⲓ ⲛ̄-   ϣⲏⲙ ⲭⲱⲣⲓ[ⲥ ⲟⲟⲙⲟ-]

ⲧⲁⲓ̈ ⲁⲛⲧⲉ ⲧⲉϥⲡⲓ-   ⲗⲟⲅⲓⲁ ⲁϥⲟⲟ[ⲙⲟⲗⲟ-]

ⲥⲧⲓⲥ· ⲛ̄ⲧⲟϥ ⲇⲉ ⲑⲉ-   ⲅⲉⲓ ⲭⲉⲡⲣ[ⲱⲙⲉ ⲉⲧ-]

ⲟⲇⲱⲣⲟⲥ ⲁϥⲟⲩⲱϣⲃ̄   ⲛⲁⲉⲓⲣⲉ ⲙ̄[ⲡⲁⲓᶜ

ⲉϥϫⲱ ⲙ̄ⲙⲟⲥ ⲭⲉⲛ̄ⲡ-   ⲉⲃⲟⲗ ⲛ̄ⲛ̄[ⲉⲛⲧⲟⲗⲏ]

ⲛⲁϣⲡⲓⲑⲉ ⲙ̄ⲙⲟⲓ   ⲙ̄ⲡϫⲟⲉⲓ[ⲥ

           margin

ᵃ ⲇⲉ seems superfluous.   ᵇ Perhaps -ⲅⲉⲓ ⲛ̄ⲧⲉ[ⲓⲟ]ⲉ. Am. ٱلكذا.   ᶜ Scarcely space
for ⲛⲁⲃⲱⲗ or ⲉϥⲃⲱⲗ]. Am. ٱلخلف.

Fol. 9. *Recto* (*v.* Am. 407). . . . suffer His] disciple (μαθ.) [to go and]
bury [his father?'] That (brother) answered, saying, 'He suffered him not,
[lest] he should go [and not] return.' [But (δέ)] he said unto him, [' If it]
befall that one to-day go [to] his kinsfolk according to the flesh (κατά,
σάρξ), he hath not (surely) transgressed (παραβαίνειν) the command
(ἐντολή) of the Gospel (εὐ.)?' He said unto him, ' If he shall but visit
them, it is not a sin.' He said unto him with guile (? πανουργία [1]), 'This
is the faith (πίστις) of the men of Tabennêse, that say, It is not a sin to
transgress (?) the commandments (ἐντ.) of the Gospel (εὐ.). For (καὶ γάρ) I,
ere I came hither, did strive (ἀγωνίζειν), so far as (κατά) my youth (per-
mitted), in what was evident unto me that it was the Lord's will. And
when I had heard that ye do walk in perfection (-τέλειος), according to
the commandments of the Gospel (κατά, ἐντ. εὐ.), I came hither. Now
therefore I will not remain, but (ἀλλά) will go again unto my place whence
I came.' And Theodore lifted up his voice and wept, being grieved for
him. Straightway then that (brother) went to [tell?] our father Pahômius,
saying, 'Come, that we comfort this young brother, lest (? μήποτε) he be
offended (σκανδαλίζειν).' He told him the word that he had said

Verso (*v.* Am. 408, 409). (saying,) ' I am offended (σκαν.) thereat.' And
when he knew the guile (παν.) that he had wrought, by the wisdom of the
Spirit (πνεῦμα), he said (+δέ?) unto him, ' Knowest thou not that he is
a neophyte? It was not meet for thee to speak so to him. Howbeit
(ὅμως [2]) call him and I will persuade (πείθειν) him.' When he had called
him, he said unto him, as if (ὡς) persuading him, ' Be not grieved at that
thou hast heard [? from the brother] that spake with thee . . . . . go with
thee, as a neophyte. For (ἐπεί) this is not his belief (πίστις).' But (δέ)
as for Theodore, he answered saying, ' Thou wilt not be able to persuade
(πείθειν) me,
[3] O, my father with] this word [that thou sayest, that this is not] his
[belief (πίσ.), ex]cept (εἰμήτι) he shall himself declare (ὁμολογεῖν) with his
own mouth that he that shall go to visit his kinsfolk is a transgressor
(παραβάτης) of the commandments of the Gospel (ἐντ. εὐαγ.). If [I] hear
[him] declare (ὁμ.) thus (?), then (τότε) shall I know that not thus doth he
believe (πιστεύειν).' And (δέ) when that (brother) knew (?) that the youth
would not be persuaded without a declaration (πείθειν, χωρίς, ὁμολογία), he
declared (ὁμ.), saying that the man that shall do [this un]doeth (?) the
commandments (ἐντ.)?] of the Lord . . . . .

[1] Am. should be 'said to him in deceit'.
[2] Accented in the text : a rare occurrence.
[3] Gaps filled from Am., although I cannot satisfactorily complete the Coptic text.

Fol. 10. → *Recto.*

[ϣ]ⲱⲡⲉ^a ⲇⲉ ⲟ[ⲛ ⲛ̄ⲧⲉ-]
ⲣⲉ[ϥ]ϩⲉ' ⲉⲕⲉⲥⲟⲛ [ⲛ̄]ϭⲓ
ⲑⲉⲟⲇⲱⲣⲟⲥ ⲉⲣ[ⲉⲡⲉϥ-]
ϩⲏⲧ' ⲗⲩⲡⲉⲓ ⲉ̣[ⲃⲟ]ⲗ'
ⲭⲉⲁϥⲭⲡⲓⲟ[ϥ ⲛ̄ϭ]ⲓ'
ⲡⲉⲛⲉⲓⲱⲧ [ⲡⲁϩ]ⲱ-
ⲙⲉ ⲟ̄ⲛⲟⲩϩ[ⲱ]ⲃ ⲉ-
ⲡⲟⲩⲭⲁⲓ̈ ⲛ̄ⲧ[ⲉϥⲯ]ⲩ-
ⲭⲏ· ϩⲱⲥⲧⲉ ⲉ̣[ⲧⲣⲉ-]
ⲡⲉϥϩⲏⲧ' ⲣⲓⲕⲉ ⲉⲃⲟ[ⲗ]
[ⲉ]ⲧⲣⲉϥⲡⲱⲣ̄ⲝ ⲉⲧ̣[ⲕⲟⲓ-]
[ⲛⲱⲛⲓⲁ^b

                  .
              ]ⲧⲁ
      ⲙⲉⲉ]ⲩⲉ^c ⲭⲉⲧⲁⲓ̈
[ⲟⲛⲧ]ⲉ ⲑⲉ ⲉϥⲙⲟⲕ̄ϩ
[ⲛ̄ϩⲏⲧ] ⲭⲉⲡⲉⲓ̈ⲣⲱ-
[ⲙⲉ ⲛ̄ϣ]ⲛ̄ⲙ̄ⲙⲟ ⲉⲓ
          ]ⲟⲛ' ⲛ̄ⲧⲟϥ
    ⲟⲩ]ⲱϣ' ⲉⲧⲣⲉϥ-
          ]ⲭⲓ ϩⲙⲟⲧ
            ]ⲛ̄ϣⲁ-
[ⲭⲉ   ]ⲙⲟⲥ .

[ⲇⲉ] ⲙⲁⲣ[ⲛ̄ϭ]ⲱ [ⲟⲩⲛ ⲙ̄ⲡⲉ-]
ⲥⲛⲁⲩ ϩⲓⲟⲩⲥⲟⲡ [ⲛ̄-]
ⲧ̄ⲡⲥ̄ⲗⲥ̄ⲗ̄ ⲛⲉⲡⲉⲣ[ⲏⲩ]
ϣⲁⲛ̄ⲧ̄ⲛ̄ϩⲁⲩ ⲉ̣[. . ⲙⲉ-]
ϣⲁⲕ ϥ̄ⲛⲁ[ⲗⲟ
ⲙⲙⲟⲥ ⲉⲭ[ⲡⲓⲟⲛ· ⲉ-]
ϣⲱⲡⲉ [ⲇⲉ ⲉⲛϣⲁⲛ-]
ⲉⲓⲙⲉ ⲭⲉⲛ̣[ϥ̄ⲛⲁ]ⲗⲟ
ⲁⲛ ⲧ̄ⲛⲛⲁⲃⲱⲕ
ⲛ̄ⲧ̄ⲛⲁⲛⲁⲭⲱⲣⲉⲓ'
[ⲛⲁⲛ] ⲉⲕⲉⲙⲁ' ⲛ̄ⲧⲉ-
[. . . .] . ⲧ . . . . . .
[. . . . .]ⲧ . . . ⲉ . . .
ⲧⲉ[. . . . .] . ⲉⲉ ⲛ̄ⲧⲟϥ
ϣⲁ̣ⲭ[ⲉ
ϩⲏⲧ[
ⲡ[
ⲥⲱ[ϩⲩ-]
ⲡⲟⲙ[ⲓⲛⲉ
ⲛ . . [
ⲧ̄ⲙⲁ[
ⲉϥⲛ̣[

---

^a ⲁⲥϣⲱⲡⲉ.   ^b Or ⲧⲥⲟⲟⲩϩⲥ. Size of following gap uncertain, as the two fragments do
not join.   ^c Perhaps ⲉⲧ]ⲃⲉⲭⲉ.

↑ *Verso.*

]ε εμ[.]

]aᵃ a[ⲛ] ⲙ̄ⲡⲉⲛⲉⲓ-
[ⲱ]ⲧ ⲡⲁⲣⲱⲙⲉ ⲅ̄ⲛ̄-
[ⲟⲩ]ⲟⲩⲱⲡⲅ̄ ⲉⲃⲟⲗ·
[ⲅ̄ⲛ̄]ⲡⲁϣⲉ ⲇⲉ ⲛ̄-
[ⲧⲉⲩϣⲏ] ⲛ̄ⲟⲁⲅ ⲛ̄-
[ⲥⲟⲡ ⲛ]ⲉϣⲁϥⲃⲱⲕ'
ⲡ̄ϭⲁⲡⲁⲛⲧⲁ' ⲉⲣⲟϥ
ⲛ̄ⲟⲁⲅ' ⲛ̄ⲥⲟⲡ ⲛϥ-
ⲭ̄ⲱ̄ ⲉⲣⲟϥ' ⲙ̄ⲡ[ⲉⲙ-]
ⲕⲁⲅ' ⲛ̄ⲟ̄ⲏⲧ [ⲙ̄ⲡⲥⲟⲡ ⲉ-]
ⲧⲙ̄ⲙⲁⲩ [ⲁⲩⲱ
ⲉϥⲁ.ⲧ̄[

ⲛⲙ.[   ] ⲉϥ-
[ⲭⲱ ⲙ̄ⲙⲟⲥ ⲭ]ⲉⲃⲟⲏ-
[ⲑⲉⲓ ⲉⲣⲟⲛ ⲱ ⲡⲉ]ⲛⲉⲓ-
[ⲱⲧ   ]a.ⲛ
ⲉⲧⲉⲡ]ⲁⲥⲟⲛ-
[ⲡⲉ ⲛ̄ⲧⲛ̄ⲁⲣⲙⲉ]ⲛ ⲛ̄ⲧⲟ-
[ⲟⲧϥ ⲙ̄ⲡⲁⲓ]ⲁⲃⲟ-
[ⲗⲟⲥ ⲡⲁⲓ ⲉⲧⲉ]ⲗ[ⲟ̄]ⲛⲙ'
[ⲉⲧⲱⲣⲡ ⲛⲛⲉ]ⲛⲯⲩ-

[ⲡⲉⲧ]ⲟⲩⲛⲟ ⲛ[ⲟ̄ⲏⲧⲛ̄]
[ⲟⲩ]ⲛϣⲥⲟⲙ' ⲛ̄[ⲙⲟϥ]
ⲉ[ⲧ]ⲟⲩⲭⲟⲛ ⲁⲩⲱ
ⲙ̄ⲙ̄ⲛⲗⲁⲁⲩ ⲛ̄ⲁⲧ-
ϭ[ⲟⲙ] ⲛ̄ⲛⲁⲟⲣⲁϥ·
ⲁ[ⲩⲱ] ⲁⲥϣⲱⲡⲉ
ⲙ[ⲛ̄ⲛ̄]ⲥⲁⲡⲉ̄ⲃⲟⲧ'
[ⲛ̄ⲟ̄]ⲟⲟⲩ ⲡⲉⲭⲁϥ
[ⲛ̄]ϭⲓ ⲑⲉⲟⲇⲱⲣⲟⲥ ⲉ-
ⲟⲟⲩⲛ ⲅ̄ⲛ̄ⲡⲥⲟⲛ ⲉ-
ⲧⲙ̄ⲙⲁⲩ' ⲭⲉⲙⲁⲣ[ⲛ̄-]

ⲛⲙ[ⲛ̄ⲧⲛ̄-]
ϣⲁⲭⲉ ⲛⲙ[ⲙⲁϥ ⲁⲩⲱ]
ⲉϣⲱⲡⲉ ⲁⲩ[
ϣⲁⲛϣ[ⲱⲡⲉ . . . ⲛ̄ⲙ-]
ⲙⲁⲛ ⲉϥ[
ⲧ̄ⲛ̄ⲛⲁ.[ⲉⲕⲉ-]
ⲙⲁ' ⲛ̄ⲧⲛ̄ⲡⲟⲣⲭ̄ⲛ̄ ⲉⲃⲟⲗ]
ⲉⲣⲟϥ· [ⲉϣⲱⲡⲉ ⲇⲉ]
ⲉϥϣ[ⲁⲛ
ⲅ̄ⲛ̄ⲗ[

margin

ᵃ Should be ⲁⲡⲁⲛⲧ]ⲁ.

Fol. 10. *Recto* (*v.* Am. 409). ... And (δέ) [it] befell again, when Theodore found another brother grieved (λυπεῖν) at heart because that our father Pahômius had reproved him in a matter for the salvation of his soul (ψυ.), so that (ὥστε) his heart was inclined that he should separate from the [community .... 'thought (?), for even so is it also that I am sad at heart. For this stranger ... he ... wish that he ... find grace .....

... let us two stay therefore (οὖν) together and console one another, until we see ... perhaps he will [cease] ... reproving [us. But (δέ)] if we shall know that will not cease, we will go and betake us (ἀναχωρεῖν) elsewhere .....

Verso (*v.* Am. 410). ... not with our father Pahômius openly. But (δέ) in the middle of the night, many a time, he would go and meet (ἀπαντᾶν) him, many a time (*sic*), and tell him of the grief of that [brother] .... [saying,] 'Help (βοηθεῖν) [us, O] our father, ... [who is] my brother,[1] [and? save] us from the devil (διάβ.), that roareth [to devour?] our souls (ψυ.) .....

... [that] dwelleth in [thee] hath power to save us. And there is no impossibility with Him.'[2] And it befell, after the month of days, that Theodore spake to that brother, saying, 'Let us .... [and we] speak with [him. And] if ..... with us, he ....., we will [go else]where and [separate ourselves from] him. [But (δέ) if] he should ..... with .....

Fol. 11. ↑ *Recto.*

ᲙᲘᲜᲢⳓⲩⲛ]ⲉⲧⲟⲥ
[ⲁⲡⲟ]ⲩⲛⲟ𝕲 ᲜᲛⲙⲛ[ⲧ-]
[ⲁ𝕲ⲁ]ⲑⲟⲥ . ϩⲱⲥⲧⲉ
[ⲉⲧ]ⲣⲉⲡⲉⲩϩⲏⲧ' ᲜᲜ-
[ⲧ]ⲟⲛ ⲉⲙⲁⲧⲉ ⲙⲡⲉ-
[ⲥⲛ]ⲁⲩ · ⲁⲩⲱ ⲧⲁⲓ̈-
[ⲧⲉ ⲑⲉ ⲉⲛⲧⲁ𝙲ⲧⲟⲩ-
[ⲭⲟ𝙲] Ნ𝕲ⲓ ⲑⲉⲟⲇⲱ-

ⲉ[
ⲣⲁ̣[ⲕⲟ-]
ⲧ𝙲 ϣⲁⲣ[ⲟⲛ[a]
ⲁⲩⲱ ⲁⲥϣ[ⲱⲡⲉ Ნ-]

[a] *Cf. Miss.* 546, 6. But perhaps here ⲛ]ⲧ𝙲. (*v. verso*).

In gap ⲉⲡⲉⲓⲙⲁ (Am. الى هاهنا) or ⲛⲕⲉⲥⲟⲡ

[1] Am. should be, 'Help us, O our father, me and this one that is my brother, that thou seize us from out the hand of the devil, who would devour our souls. For we are small and feeble in the faith.'

[2] Am. *sic.*

[ⲣⲟⲥ ϩ]ⲛ̄ⲟⲩⲡⲁⲛⲟⲩⲣ-   ⲧⲉⲣⲟⲩⲃⲱ[ⲕ ⲉϩⲟⲩⲛ]
[ⲅⲓⲁ ⲉⲛ]ⲁⲛⲟⲩⲥ·   ⲉⲡⲉϥⲏⲓ̈ [ⲁⲩ
[Ⲟ]ⲩⲁ ⲟ]ⲛ ⲟⲛ̄ⲛⲉⲥ-   ⲧⲁⲓ ⲉⲣⲟϥ [ⲛ̄ϭⲓ
[ⲛⲏ]ⲩ ⲉⲩϣⲏⲣⲉ ϣⲏⲙ’-   ？   ⲙ̄ⲛ̄ⲛ̄-]
[ⲡⲉ ⲉ]ⲁϥⲉⲛⲱⲭⲗⲉⲓ’   ⲥⲱⲥ
[ⲙ̄ⲡⲉ]ⲛⲉⲓⲱⲧ’ ⲡⲁ-   ⲟⲛ̄ⲟⲩ
[ϩⲱⲙ] ⲉϥⲟⲩⲉϣ   ⲭⲉ[ⲉⲩⲛⲁⲟⲩⲱⲙ
[ⲃⲱⲕ ⲉ]ϭⲙ̄ ⲡϣⲓⲛⲉ   ⲁⲩ[ⲱ
[ⲛ̄ⲡⲉϥⲉⲓ]ⲟⲧⲉ· ⲛ̄ⲧⲉ-   ？
[ⲣϥⲉⲓⲙⲉ] ⲇⲉ ⲭⲉⲉϥ-

margin (?)

→ *Verso.*

                         ⲡⲁϩⲱⲙⲉ [ⲁϥⲣ̄ⲟⲩ-]
                         ⲛⲟϭ ⲛ̄ⲟⲩⲟ[ⲉⲓϣ ⲉϥ-]
                         ⲧⲱⲃϩ ⲙ̄ⲡⲭ[ⲟⲉⲓⲥ
              ]ⲙⲁⲩ [a]   ⲉϥⲭⲱ ⲙ̄ⲙⲟⲥ [ⲭⲉ-]
              ] ？   ⲕⲱ ⲛⲁⲓ ⲉⲃⲟⲗ’ ⲭ[ⲉ-]
              ] ？ ⲛⲧⲟϥ   ⲧ̄ϣⲟⲃⲉ ⲁⲛ ⲉⲩ[ⲣⲱ-]
[ⲇⲉ ⲛ̄ⲧ]ⲉⲣⲉϥⲥⲱⲧⲙ̄   ⲙⲉ ⲉⲁϥⲡⲟⲣ[ⲛⲉⲩⲉ]
[ⲉⲛⲉⲓϣ]ⲁⲭⲉ ⲁϥⲣ-   ϩⲙ̄ⲡⲉⲛⲧ[ⲁⲓⲁⲁϥ·]
[ⲡⲙⲉⲉ]ⲩⲉ ⲛⲑⲉ ⲉⲛ-   ⲭⲉⲁⲓⲡⲁⲣⲁ[ⲃⲁ ⲛ̄ⲛ-]
[ⲧⲁϥϣ]ⲁⲭⲉ ⲛ̄ⲙ̄-   ⲛⲟⲙⲟⲥ ⲉⲛ[ⲧⲁⲕⲧⲁ-]
[ⲙⲁϥ ⲛ̄ϭⲓ] ⲡⲉⲛⲉⲓ-   ⲁⲩ ⲉⲧⲟⲟⲧϥ [ⲙ̄-]
[ⲱⲧ’ ⲡⲁϩⲱ]ⲙⲉ ⲉϥ-   ⲡⲉⲕϩⲙ̄ϩⲁⲗ [·]
[ⲭⲱ ⲙ̄ⲙⲟⲥ ⲭ]ⲉⲁⲣⲓ̈   ⲁϥⲥⲱⲧⲙ̄ [ⲡⲁⲣ ⲉ-]
[ⲁⲡⲁⲧⲟⲟⲧⲕ̄] ⲛ̄ⲙ̄-   ⲡⲉⲛⲉⲓⲱⲧ [ⲡⲁ-]
[ⲙⲁϥ ⲉⲧⲣⲉⲕⲉⲛ]ⲉ ⲙ̄-   ϩⲱⲙⲉ ⲛ̄ⲟⲩ[ϩⲟⲟⲩ]
[ⲙⲟⲩ ⲛ̄ⲕⲉ]ⲥⲟⲡ·   ⲉϥⲭⲱ ⲙⲙ[ⲟⲥ ⲭⲉ-]
              ？   ⲭⲙ̄ⲡⲉϩⲟⲟⲩ ⲛ̄ⲧⲁⲓ-]
                         ⲣⲙⲟⲛⲁⲭ[ⲟⲥ ⲛ̄ϩⲏⲧϥ ⲙ̄-]

[a] Perhaps ⲙ̄[ⲙⲁ]ⲩⲁⲓ.

Fol. 11. *Recto* (*v.* Am. 410). . . . prudence (-σύνετός) [and] great goodness (-ἀγαθός), so that (ὥστε) the heart of both of them was greatly quieted. And thus it was that Theodore saved him, by a kindly (*lit.* good) guile (πανουργία). One also of the brethren, that was a youth, importuned (ἐνωχλεῖν) our father Pahôm,[1] wishing to go and visit his parents. But (δέ) when he knew that he . . . . .

. . . return him unto [us hither ?[2]]. And it befell, after that they had gone [in] unto his house, [his people] . . . him. [And] afterwards . . . . . in a . . ., that [they might eat]. And . . . . .

Verso (*v.* Am. 411). . . . But (δέ) he, when he had heard these words, remembered the manner in which our father Pahômius had spoken with him,[3] saying, 'Do thy utmost to bring him (hither) again . . . . .

. . . Pahômius, spent a great while beseeching the Lord, saying, ' Forgive me; for I am not different from a man that hath fornicated (πορνεύειν), in that which I have done. For I have transgressed (παραβαίνειν) the laws (νόμ.) which Thou didst commit unto Thy servant.' For (γάρ) he had heard our father Pahômius, on a day, saying, ' Since the [day whereon I] became a monk (μον.),

Fol. 12.　→ *Recto.*

margin

пелааγ п̄рωⲙе	оγ϶ⲗⲗ[о' ϥ̄ⲡ̄ⲛе-]
п̄ⲕосⲙⲓⲕос ⲛⲁγ	сⲏⲏγ еⲙⲡⲁ[теⲑо]
ероï еïоγⲙⲙ' ⳡ еï-	те ⲙ̄пⳉоеⲓс [ϣⲱ-]
се' ⲙооγ · ⳉеⲕас	пе ⲛ̄϶ⲏⲧϥ · ⲛе-
ереⲡⳉоеⲓс ⳉⲓ еооγ	ⲙ̄пⲁⲧϥⲱ'ⲥⲕⲡе
оⲛ ϶ⲙⲡⲁï · ⲛ̄-	ⳉⲓⲛⲧⲁϥеï' е϶оγ[ⳡ]
[ⲧ]оϥ' ⲁе пеⲛеⲓⲱⲧ'	еⲛесⲛⲏγ · ⲁγ[ⲱ]
пⲁ϶ⲱⲙе' ⲛере-	пⲁï ⲛ̄тереϥсⲱ-
пⳉоеⲓс ϣооп'	тⲙ̄ ⳉеⲛесⲛⲏ[γ]
ⲛ̄ⲙ̄ⲙⲁϥ ϶ⲛ̄϶ⲱⲃ	ⲃⲱⲕ' епесⲏⲧ

---

[1] So ? for usual 'Pahôme'. There is not space for second ⲉ in the text.

[2] Am. should be, 'until thou bring him (back) hither.'

[3] Am. should be, 'Make with him all efforts until thou bring him unto me again. And he stretched forth his hand and did eat with him a little; then he withdrew his hand. And Theodore, by reason of this thing that he had done, in stretching forth his hand to eat, so as to bring back the youth unto our father P., spent &c.'

ⲡⲁⲓ̈ ⲉϥⲉⲓⲣⲉ ⲙ̄ⲙⲟ-
[ⲟ]ⲩ · ⲉϥϯ ⲉⲟⲟⲩ ⲛⲁϥ
[ⲁ]ⲩⲱ ⲉϥⲟⲩⲱⲛⲅ̄
[ⲙ̄]ⲙⲟⲟⲩ · ⲉⲃⲟⲗ · ⲛ̄ⲛⲉ-
[ⲥ]ⲛⲏⲩ ⲧⲏⲣⲟⲩ ⲭⲉ
[ⲟⲩ]ⲁ̂ⲡⲉ ⲅ̄ⲛ̄ⲡⲉϥ-
[ⲅ̄ⲛ̄ϩ]ⲁⲗ̄ ·
[Ⲁⲥϣ]ⲱⲡⲉ ⲇⲉ ⲛⲟⲩ-
[ϩⲟⲟⲩ] ⲉⲧⲣⲉⲩⲣ̄ⲭⲣⲓⲁ
[ⲛ̄ⲕ]ⲁⲑⲁⲣⲓⲍ[ⲉ ⲙ̄-]
[ⲡϣ]ⲏⲓ̈ ⲛ̄ⲑ[ⲉ]ⲡ̄ⲉⲉⲧ[ⲉ]
[ⲁϥ]ⲙⲟⲩⲧⲉ ⲉⲣⲟⲉⲓ-
[ⲡⲉ ⲛ̄]ⲛⲉⲥⲛⲏⲩ ⲉⲧ-
[ϭⲙ̄ϭ]ⲟⲙ̄ · ⲁϥⲃⲱⲕ
[ⲉⲡⲉⲥ]ⲛⲧ̄ · ⲉⲣⲟϥ

ⲉⲡϣⲏⲓ̈ ⲁϥⲕⲣ[ⲙ̄-]
ⲣ̄ⲙ̄ ⲉϥϫⲱ · ⲙ̄ⲙⲟⲥ
ⲭⲉⲡⲉⲓ̈ⲣⲱⲙⲉ ⲟⲩ-
ⲁⲧⲛⲁ̂ⲡⲉ ⲉϥⲙⲟ-
ⲕ̄ϩ̄ ⲛ̄ϣⲏⲣ[ⲉ ⲛ̄-]
ⲣ̄ⲣⲱⲙⲉ · ϩⲱ[ⲥⲧⲉ]
ⲉⲧⲣⲉϥϫⲟⲟⲩ ⲉ-ᵃ
ⲡⲉⲥⲛⲧ̄ · ⲉ[ⲡϣⲏⲓ̈]
ⲙ̄ⲡⲉⲓ̈ⲛ[ⲁⲩ ·]
ⲁⲥϣⲱⲡ[ⲉᵇ ⲛ̄ⲧⲉⲩ-]
ϣⲏ ⲉⲧ[ⲙ̄ⲙⲁⲩ ⲁϥ-]
ⲛⲁⲩ ⲉ[ⲩϩⲟⲣⲁⲙⲁ ⲛ̄-]
ϭⲓ ⲡ[ϩⲗ̄ⲗⲟ · ⲉⲧⲙ̄ⲙⲁⲩ]
ⲉⲁϥ[

ᵃ Probably more here : ϫⲟⲟⲩⲥⲉ ⲉ-?

ᵇ Or ⲁⲥϣⲱⲡⲉ ⲇⲉ.

↑ *Verso.*

margin

ⲟⲩⲁⲅⲅ]ⲉⲗⲟⲥ ⲛ̄-
[ⲧⲉ] ⲡϫⲟⲉⲓⲥ ⲛ̄ⲧⲉⲩ-
[ⲙⲏ]ⲧⲉ ⲉϥⲱϣ · ⲉⲃⲗ
[ⲉ]ϩⲟⲩⲛ ⲉϩⲣⲁⲩ, ⲉϥ-
ϫⲱ ⲙ̄ⲙⲟⲥ ⲭⲉⲓ
ⲡ̄ⲡⲁ ⲉϥⲟⲩⲁⲁⲃ ⲛ[ⲏ-]
ⲧ̄ⲛ · ⲛ̄ⲛⲉⲧⲛ̄ⲣ̄-
ϩⲱⲃ̄ · ⲅⲁⲣ ⲁⲛ, ⲛ̄ⲣⲱ-
ⲙⲉ · ⲁⲗⲗⲁ ⲉⲧⲉⲧⲛ̄-
ⲣ̄ϩⲱⲃ̄ · ⲛ̄ⲡ̄ϩⲙ̄ϩⲁⲗ

ⲭⲉⲉⲣⲉⲡϫⲟⲉⲓⲥ ϥ[ⲓ]
ⲉⲃⲟⲗ ⲙ̄ⲙⲟⲓ̈ ⲙ̄ⲡⲉ-
ⲡ̄ⲡⲁ ⲙ̄ⲙⲛ̄ⲧⲁⲧ-
ⲛⲁϩⲧⲉ ⲭⲉⲁⲓ̈ⲕⲁⲧ[ⲁ-]
ⲗⲁⲗⲉⲓ̈ · ⲙ̄ⲡⲣⲱⲙⲉ
ⲙ̄ⲡⲛⲟⲩⲧⲉ · ⲁⲩⲱ
ⲙ̄ⲡⲓⲡⲓⲥⲧⲉⲩⲉ ϫ[ⲉ-]
ϩⲱⲃ̄ · ⲛⲓⲙ ⲉϥⲉⲓⲣⲉ [ⲙ̄-]
ⲙⲟⲟⲩ · ⲉϥⲉⲓⲣⲉ ⲙ̄ⲙ[ⲟ-]
ⲟⲩ ϩⲛ̄ⲟⲩⲥⲟⲟⲩⲧⲛ̄[·]

ⲙ̄ⲡⲛⲟⲩⲧⲉ· ⲁϥ-
ⲛⲁⲩ ⲇⲉ ⲉⲣⲟϥ ϩⲱ-
ⲱϥ· ⲉϥⲥⲱϣⲧ̄ ⲉ-
ϩⲣⲁⲓ ⲉⲣⲟϥ· ⲉϥϫⲱ
[ⲙ̄]ⲙⲟⲥ ϫⲉⲡⲣⲉϥ-
[ⲕⲣ]ⲙⲣⲙ̄ ⲛ̄ϩⲗⲗⲟ· ⲁⲩ[ⲱ]
[ⲛ̄]ⲁⲡⲓⲥⲧⲟⲥ· ϫⲓ
[ⲡⲛⲁ] ⲛⲁⲕ ⲙ̄ⲙⲛⲧ-
[ⲁⲧⲛⲁ]ϩⲧⲉ ⲁⲩⲱ
[ⲁⲥϣⲱ]ⲡⲉ ⲙ̄ⲡⲛⲁⲩ
[ⲛ̄ϣⲟⲣⲡ] ⲉⲣⲉⲛⲉⲥ-
[ⲛⲏⲩ ⲛ̄ϩⲟⲩ]ⲛ ⲛ̄ⲧⲥⲩ-
[ⲛⲁⲝⲓⲥ ⲉⲩϣⲗ]ⲏⲗ·ᵃ ⲁϥ-
[ⲉⲓ ⲉⲧⲉⲩⲙⲏ]ⲧⲉ ⲁϥ-
[ⲱϣ ⲉⲃⲟⲗ....].

ϩⲉⲣⲉⲡⲉⲥⲛⲏⲩ ⲇⲉ ⲛ[ⲁ-]
ⲃⲱⲕ· ⲉⲩⲙⲁ· ⲉⲱϩ[ⲥ]
ⲛ̄ⲟⲩϣⲏⲙ· ⲡⲕⲁ[ⲙ·]
ⲁⲩⲱ ⲉⲣⲉⲡⲉⲓⲱ[ⲧ]
ⲡⲁϩⲱⲙⲉ ⲡⲙ̄[ⲙⲁⲩ]
ⲛⲉⲁϥⲧⲱϣ· ϫⲉ ⲛ̄[-]
ⲑⲉⲟⲇⲱⲣⲟⲥ ⲉⲧⲃⲉ[-]
ⲟⲩϩⲱⲃ· ϩⲛ̄[
ⲛϥ̄ⲧⲙ̄ⲃⲱⲕ [ⲙ̄ⲡⲛⲉⲥ-]
[ⲛ]ⲏⲩ· ⲛ̄ⲧⲉⲣ[ⲉϥⲉⲓ]
ⲇⲉ ⲉⲃⲟⲗ ⲡⲙ̄ⲙⲁϥ ⲛ̄[-]
ϭⲓ ⲛⲉⲥⲛⲏⲩ [ⲉⲩⲑ-]
ⲡⲟ ⲙ̄ⲙⲟϥ· ⲉⲣ[ⲉ-]
ⲑⲉⲟⲇⲱⲣⲟⲥ ⲛ[ⲙ-]
ⲙⲁⲩ ϩⲱⲱ[ϥ..]

ᵃ Perhaps ⲉϣⲗⲏⲗ, as space is short.

Fol. 12. *Recto* (*v.* Am. 411).   no worldling (-κοσμικός) hath beheld me eating or (ἤ) drinking water,[1] that herein also the Lord might be glorified.' But (δέ) as for our father Pahômius, the Lord was with him in everything he did, glorifying him (Pahômius) and displaying him unto all the brethren for one of His servants.

It befell now (δέ) on a day that they had need (χρεία) to cleanse (καθαρίζειν) the well of the monastery, and he called certain of the brethren that were strong and went down to it . . . . .

. . . an old man among the brethren, in whom the fear of the Lord was not yet; it was not yet long since he had come in among the brethren. And he, when he heard that the brethren had gone down to the well, murmured saying, 'This man is pitiless, distressing the sons of men,[2] in that (ὥστε) he sendeth them down unto the well at this time.' It befell, on that night, that that old man beheld a dream (ὅραμα) . . . . .

[1] Am. differs slightly.

[2] Am. should be ' . . . sons of men '. And as he beheld the brethren working, he beheld an angel of the Lord in their midst, and he crying into their faces (*v.* note on fol. 3), 'Receive ye &c.' Then he beheld him looking up to him, saying to him &c.

Verso (*v.* Am. 412). an] angel (ἄγγ.) of the Lord in their midst, crying out at them, saying, 'Receive unto yourselves a holy spirit (πν.); for (γάρ) ye labour not for man, but (ἀλλά) ye labour for the servant of God.' And (δέ) he beheld him (the angel) likewise, looking up at him, saying, 'Murmuring and faithless (ἄπιστος) old man, receive for thyself a spirit (πν.) of unbelief.' And it befell at morning, the brethren being within the meeting-place (σύναξις [1]), praying, he [came into their] midst and [cried out . . . . .

. . . that the Lord take from me the spirit (πν.) of faithlessness, for I did slander (καταλαλεῖν) the man of God and believed (πιστεύειν) not that everything he doeth, he doth it in uprightness.'

And (δέ) the brethren being about to go to a place, to reap a few reeds, and our father Pahômius being with them, but (δέ) having appointed Theodore concerning a (certain) matter in . . ., and he (Th.) went not [with the] brethren; but (δέ) when the brethren had [gone] forth with [him], speeding him, Theodore being with them also, ...

Fol. 13. ↑ *Recto.*

margin

[. . ⲑ]ⲉⲟⲇⲱⲣⲟⲥ ⲭⲉ-
[ⲁⲗⲉ ⲉ]ⲡⲭⲟⲓ ⲧⲁⲭⲩ·
[ⲁⲩⲱ] ⲧⲟϥ' ⲧⲉⲩ-
[ⲛⲟ]ⲩ ⲡϥⲇⲓⲁⲕⲣⲓ-
[ⲛⲉ ⲗ]ⲁⲁⲩ ⲁϥⲇⲁⲗⲉ' ⲉ-
[ⲡⲭⲟ]ⲓ ⲡϥϥⲓ ⲡⲉϥ-
· [ⲡⲣ]ⲏϣ' ⲙⲙⲁϥ'
[ⲟⲩ]ⲧⲉ ⲡⲉϥⲭⲱⲱⲙⲉ
[ⲉ]ⲧϥⲭⲓ ⲁⲡⲟⲥⲧ-
[ⲟⲟ]ⲩⲥ ϧⲏⲧϥ· ⲁⲩ-
[ⲱ] ⲧⲉⲩⲛⲟⲩ ⲁϥ-
[ⲙ]ⲟⲩ ϧⲙⲡⲉϥϧⲏⲧ'
[ⲉϥⲭ]ⲱ ⲙⲟϥ ⲭⲉ-
[ⲥⲙⲁ]ⲙⲁⲁⲧ' ⲡⲭⲟⲉⲓⲥ

Ⲉϥⲡⲱⲧ ⲇⲉ ϭⲓ ⲡⲉ[-]
ⲉⲓⲱⲧ' ⲡⲁϧⲱⲙⲉ' ⲁⲩ-
ⲱ' ⲛⲉⲥⲛⲏⲩ ⲙⲙⲁϥ·
ⲁϥϭⲱϣⲧ ϧⲛⲛⲉϥ-
ⲃⲁⲗ' ⲁϥⲛⲁⲩ ⲉⲩϭⲱⲗⲡ
ⲉⲃⲟⲗ' ⲉϥⲟ ϧⲟⲧⲉ· ⲁϥ-
ⲛⲁⲩ ⲅⲁⲣ' ⲁⲩⲱ ⲉⲓⲥ ϧⲏ-
ⲛⲧⲉ ϧⲟⲉⲓⲛⲉ ⲙⲉⲛ
ϧⲛⲛⲉⲥⲛⲏⲩ ϧⲛⲣ[ⲱ-]
ⲟⲩ ϧⲉⲛⲑⲏⲣⲓⲟⲛ
ϧⲉⲛⲕⲟⲟⲩⲉ ⲇⲉ ϧⲛⲣ[ⲱ-]
ⲟⲩ ϧⲉⲛⲥⲟⲟⲩ·
ⲁⲩⲱ ϧⲟⲉⲓⲛⲉ ⲉⲩϧ-
ⲧⲙⲏⲛⲧⲉ ⲟⲩⲕⲱ[ϧⲧ]

(= *Miss.* 553, *Mus. Guim.* 105), 88, 92 ; *Miss.* 559 (= *Mus. Guim.* 283 ἐκκλησία), 823 ; *Mus.* Guim. 92 (= *ib.* 218 and our present text), 132, 171. So far as I can ascertain, not thus used outside the Pachomian texts.

[ϫⲉⲁⲕ]ⲗⲁⲁⲧ̅ ⲛ̅ⲧⲉⲡϣⲁ'
ϩⲱ' ⲛ̅ⲣϣⲏⲣⲉ ⲛ̅ⲁⲃ-
ⲣⲁϩⲁⲙ' ϩⲙ̅ⲡϩⲱⲃ
ⲉⲛⲧⲁϥⲁⲡⲁⲛⲧ[ⲁ]
ⲉⲣⲟⲓ ⲧⲉⲛⲟⲩ ⲛ̅ⲑⲉ ⲉⲛ-
ⲧⲁϥⲉⲓ' ⲉⲃⲟⲗ' ϩⲙ̅ⲡⲉϥ-
ⲕⲁϩ' ⲉⲛ̅ϥⲥⲟⲟⲩⲛ ⲁⲛ
ϫⲉⲉϥⲛⲁ̅ ⲉⲧⲱⲛ ·
[ⲗⲩⲱ ⲁⲥ]ϣⲱⲡⲉ ⲛ̅ⲧⲉ-
[ⲣⲟⲩ . .]ⲇ̣ᵃ ⲙ̅ⲡⲱⲛⲛ
[. . . . . . .]ϫⲟϥ'ᵇ ⲉ-

ϩⲉⲛⲕⲟⲟⲩⲉ ⲉ[ⲩ]ϩⲁⲡ[ⲉ-]
[ⲥⲏ]ⲧ ⲛ̅ⲟⲩϣ[ⲱⲙⲉ]
[ⲉⲩⲟ]ⲩⲱϣ ⲉⲉ[ⲓ ⲉϩⲣⲁⲓ]
ⲉⲙⲡⲟⲩⲉϣϭ̅ⲙ̅[ϭⲟⲙ]
ⲁⲩⲱ ⲛ̅ⲧⲟⲟⲩ ⲧⲏ[ⲣⲟⲩ]
sic ⲉⲃⲟⲗ
ⲛⲉⲩⲁϣⲕⲁⲕ ⲉⲩϣ[ⲟ-]
ⲟⲡ' ϩⲙ̅ⲛⲉⲓⲑⲗⲓⲯ[ⲓⲥ]
ⲉⲩϫⲱ ⲙ̅ⲙⲟⲥ ϫⲉ[ⲃⲟ-]
ⲏⲑⲉⲓ ⲉⲣⲟⲛ · ⲛ̅[ⲧⲉ-]
ⲣⲉϥⲛⲁⲩ ⲇⲉ ⲉ[ⲣⲟⲟⲩ]
ⲧ[

ᵃ Apparently not ⲗ]ⲟ nor ⲟⲩ]ⲱ ; ⲕ]ⲁⲙ grammatically difficult.   ᵇ Perhaps ϫⲟⲓ.

→ *Verso.*

margin

ⲉⲃⲟⲗ'ᵃ ⲛ̅ⲧⲉⲧⲛ̅ⲱ ⲛ̅-
ⲕⲁⲙ' ⲉⲧϩⲓϫⲱϥ' ⲛ̅-
ⲧⲙⲛ̅ⲧⲉ' ⲛ̅ⲧⲉϩⲓⲏ[·]
ⲁϥⲁϩ'ⲉ ⲣⲁⲧϥ ⲛ̅ⲧⲉⲩ-
ⲛⲟⲩ ⲁϥⲡⲣϣ ⲛⲉϥ-
ϭⲓϫ' ⲉⲃⲟⲗ' ⲁϥⲁϣ ⲧ̇
ⲕⲁⲕ' ⲉⲃⲟⲗ' ϩⲛ̅ⲟⲩⲛⲟϭ
ⲛ̅ⲥⲙⲏ ⲁϥϣⲗⲏⲗ'
ⲉϥⲉⲡⲓⲕⲁⲗⲉⲓ' ⲙ̅-
ⲡⲛⲟⲩⲧⲉ ⲉⲧⲃⲏⲏ-
ⲧⲟⲩ ⲉⲧⲣⲉⲟⲩⲃⲟⲛ-
ⲑⲉⲓⲁ ϣⲱⲡⲉ ⲛⲁⲩ
ⲉⲃⲟⲗ ϩⲓⲧⲟⲟⲧϥ̅ ·

ⲧⲁϥⲛⲁⲩ ⲉ[ⲣⲟϥ ϫⲉ-]
ⲉϥⲛⲁϣⲱ[ⲡⲉ ⲛ̅-]
ⲛⲉⲥⲛⲏⲩ ⲙ[ⲛ̅ⲛ̅-]
ⲥⲁⲧⲣⲉϥⲛⲕ[ⲟⲧⲕ ·]
ⲛ̅ⲧⲉⲣⲟⲩⲥⲟ[ⲃⲧⲉ ⲇⲉ]
ⲛ̅ⲛⲉⲥⲛⲏⲩ, [ⲉⲧⲣⲉⲩ-]
ⲟⲩⲱⲙ' ⲉⲣⲟⲩϩ[ⲉ·]
ⲁⲩⲱ ⲛ̅ⲧⲟϥ ⲙ̅[ⲡϥ-]
ⲟⲩⲱⲙ · ⲑⲉⲟⲇⲱ[ⲣⲟⲥ]
ⲇⲉ ⲛⲉⲙ̅ⲛ̅ϥϭⲉⲓ[ⲙⲉ-]
ⲡⲉ ⲉⲡⲉⲛⲧⲁϥ[ϣⲟ-]
ⲡⲉ · ⲛⲉⲁϥϫⲟ[ⲟⲩϥ]
ⲅⲁⲣ' ⲙ̅ⲡⲟⲩⲁ'[ϩⲛ̅ⲛⲉ-]

ᵃ ⲁϥⲛⲟⲩϫⲉ] ⲉⲃⲟⲗ : *v.* below.

ⲁⲩⲱ ⲁⲥϣⲱⲡⲉ ⲉⲣ-
[ϣⲁⲛ]ⲡⲟⲩⲁ ⲡ[ⲟⲩ]ⲁ
[ⲛ̄ⲛⲉⲥ]ⲛⲏⲩ ⲉⲓ' [ⲉϫⲱϥ]ᵃ
[ⲉϥⲟⲧ]ⲡ̄ · ⲛⲉϣⲁⲩ-
[ⲡⲟⲩ]ϫⲉ ⲉⲃⲟⲗ' ϩⲱⲟⲩ
[ⲛ̄ⲛ]ⲉⲩⲉⲧⲡⲱ' ⲛ̄-
[ⲥ]ⲉϣⲗⲏⲗ' · ⲁⲩⲱ ⲁϥ-
[ϭ]ⲱ ⲉϥⲙⲏⲛ ⲉⲃⲟⲗ'
[ⲛ̄]ⲧⲉⲓϩⲉ ⲉϥϣⲗⲏⲗ'
[ϣⲁⲛ]ⲧⲉⲣⲟⲩϩⲉ ϣⲱ-
[ⲡⲉ . . . . . .]ϥᵇ

ⲥⲓⲛⲏⲩ ⲛⲟⲩ[ϩⲱⲃ·ᶜ]
ⲁⲩⲱ ⲛ̄ⲧⲉⲣⲉϥⲉⲓ
ⲙ̄ⲡⲛ̄ⲥⲱⲥ' ⲁⲩϫⲱ
ⲉⲣⲟϥ ⲛ̄ⲑⲉ ⲧⲏⲣⲥ̄
ⲉⲛⲧⲁⲥϣⲱⲡⲉ ·
ⲁⲩⲱ ⲟⲛ ⲁⲩⲧⲁⲙⲟϥ
ϫⲉⲙ̄ⲡϥⲟⲩⲱⲙ' ⲉ-
ⲃⲟⲗ' ϫⲉϥⲙⲟⲕϩ̄ ⲛ̄-
ϩⲏⲧ' ⲉϫⲙ̄ⲡϭⲱⲗⲡ
ⲉⲃⲟⲗ' ⲉⲛⲧ[ⲁϥⲛⲁⲩ]
ⲉⲣⲟϥ · ⲛ̄ⲧⲟϥ ϫⲉ]

ᵃ The last of these letters was tailed.
ᶜ Am. Ac. نقش.

ᵇ [ⲡⲉ· ϩⲙ̄ⲡⲧⲣⲉ]ϥ or [ⲡⲉ ⲁⲩⲱ ⲉⲧⲓ ⲉ]ϥ.

Fol. 13. *Recto* (*v.* Am. 412, 413). . . . unto] Theodore, 'Go aboard the boat quickly (ταχύ).' And as for him, he doubted (διακρίνειν) not at all[1] and went aboard the boat and took not his coverlet with him, neither (οὐδέ)[2] his book wherein he learnt by heart (ἀπὸ στήθους). And forthwith he blessed in his heart, saying, 'Blessed art Thou, Lord, for that Thou hast made me also worthy to be a child of Abraham, in the matter that hath happened (ἀπαντᾶν) unto me now, even as he came forth from his country, knowing not whither he went.'[3] [And] it befell, after that [they had ceased?] to load . . . . . the] boat (?) . . . . .

Now (δέ) as our father Pahômius was loading (the boat) and the brethren with him, he looked with his eyes and beheld a terrible revelation. For (γάρ) he beheld and lo, certain of the brethren were in the jaws of wild beasts (θηρ.); others again (δέ) in the jaws of crocodiles; and some were in the midst of a fire, others at the bottom of a cliff, desiring to come up, (yet) not being able. And they all were crying out, being in these tribulations (θλῖψις), and saying, 'Help (βοηθεῖν) us.' And (δέ) when he had seen them (?) . . . . .

[1] Am., asked concerning naught, neither refused, but &c.

[2] his—neither *om*. Am.
[3] Am. *add*. 'even so Thy servant' (*sic*, 413, 1).

Verso (*v.* Am. 413, 414). . . . he cast] down the load of reeds that was upon him, midway in the road,[1] and stood still forthwith[2] and spread forth his hands and cried out with a loud voice and prayed, beseeching (ἐπικα-λεῖν) God[3] concerning them, that help (βοήθεια) might be unto them from Him. And[4] it befell, as each one [of the] brethren came up [to him?] laden (?), they also cast down their loads and prayed. And he stayed, continuing thus to pray, until evening fell. [And while yet (?)] he [prayed . . . . .

. . . the revelation that] he had seen, that it should befall the brethren after he had fallen asleep. But (δέ) after they had made ready for the brethren that they should eat, at even, and as for him (*sc.* Pahômius) he ate not. But (δέ) Theodore had not known of what had befallen, for (γάρ) he had sent [him] with one [from among the] brethren for (?) an [affair?]. And when he afterwards came (back), they told him all the fashion of its happening ; and furthermore they informed him that he (*sc.* P.) had not eaten because he was sad at heart concerning the revelation that [he had beheld.[5] But (δέ)] he (?) . . . . .

Fol. 14.   → *Recto.*

]ⲙ ⲛ[
[ⲉϣⲁⲩ]ⲟⲩⲟⲙⲉϥ ⲛϭⲓ
ⲛⲉⲥⲛⲏⲩ, ⲁϥϫⲟ-
[ⲟ]ⲩ ϣⲁⲣⲟϥ ⲛⲟⲩ-
ⲥⲟⲛ ⲉϥϫⲱ ⲙ̅ⲙⲟ̊ⲥ
ϫⲉⲑⲉⲟⲇⲱⲣⲟⲥ ⲙⲟⲩ-
ⲧⲉ ⲉⲣⲟⲕ · ⲁⲩⲱ ⲛ̅-
ⲧⲟϥ ⲛ̅ⲧⲉⲩⲛⲟⲩ ⲛ̅-
ⲧⲉⲣⲉϥⲥⲱⲧⲙ̅ ⲁϥ-
ⲧⲱⲟⲩⲛ ⲁϥⲉⲓ' ϣⲁ-

[
ⲉ[ⲙ̅-]
ⲡⲉⲑⲉⲟⲇⲱⲣ[ⲟⲥ ⲟⲩ-]
ⲱⲙ' ϩⲱⲱϥ ⲙ̅ⲡ[ⲟⲟⲩ ·]
ⲡⲉϫⲁϥ ⲛⲁϥ ϫ[ⲉⲁ-]
ⲗⲱⲧⲛ̅ ϩⲁⲣⲟϥ [ⲙ̅-]
ⲡ̅ⲧⲣⲉϥⲟⲩⲱⲙ
ⲁⲗⲗⲁ ⲕⲁⲁϥ' ⲙⲁⲣ[ϥ̅-]
ⲣⲓⲙⲉ · ⲁⲩⲱ ⲛ̅ⲧ[ⲟϥ]
ⲛ̅ⲧⲉⲩⲛⲟⲩ ⲁϥϩ[ⲙⲟ-]

[1] Am. *sic.*

[2] Am. *sic.*

[3] Am. *sic.*

[4] Am. should be, 'And each one of the brethren was bearing his load. And when they saw him cast down his load, each one of them

cast down his load also, and stood and prayed. And he stayed continuing thus until the time of evening. And as he prayed, he was informed as to the vision, that it should befall the brethren after his death.'

[5] Am. *sic,* in all this sentence.

ⲣⲟϥ· ⲁϥⲁⲣⲭⲉⲓ, ⲡ-
ϣⲁϫⲉ ⲡⲙⲙⲁϥ
ϩⲧⲣⲉⲛϣⲁϫⲉ ⲛ-
ⲙ̅ⲕⲁϩ' ⲛ̅ϩⲏⲧ' ϩⲱⲥ
ⲉϥϭⲙⲁ[ⲣⲓⲕ]ⲉ' ⲉⲣⲟϥ·
ⲁⲩⲱ ⲁ[ⲡⲉϥϩ]ⲏⲧ'
[ⲙ̅]ⲕⲁϩ ⲁϥⲣⲓⲙⲉ ⲛ-
[ϭⲓ] ⲑⲉⲟⲇⲱⲣⲟⲥ [ⲁ]ϥ-
[ⲉⲓ ⲉ]ⲃⲟⲗ' ϩⲓⲧⲟⲟ[ⲧ]ϥ'
[ⲡⲉ]ϫⲁϥ ⲛⲁϥ ϫⲉ[ⲙ]ⲟ-
[ⲟϣ]ⲉ ϩⲱⲱⲕ' ⲡ̅ϩⲣⲓ-
[ⲙⲉ ⲉ]ϩ[ⲟⲩⲛ] ⲉⲡϫⲟⲉⲓⲥ
[ⲛ̅ⲑⲉ] ⲉⲛⲧⲁⲓⲣⲙⲉ
[ϩⲱ ⲟ]ⲛ ⲁϥⲟⲩⲱ-
[ϣⲃ ⲇ]ⲉ ⲛ̅ϭⲓ ⲟⲩⲁ ϩⲛ̅-
[ⲛⲉⲧ]ⲥⲱⲧⲙ̅ ⲉⲣⲟϥ

ⲟⲥ ⲁϥⲟⲩⲱⲙ' ϩⲛ̅[ⲟⲩ-]
ⲛ̅ⲧⲟⲛ ⲛ̅ϩⲏⲧ·
ⲁⲩⲱ ⲁⲥϣⲱⲡⲉ ⲉ[ϥ-]
ϩⲙⲟⲟⲥ ⲡⲥⲁⲟⲩⲥⲁ [ⲛ-]
ϭⲓ ⲑⲉⲟⲇⲱⲣⲟⲥ ⲙⲁⲩ-
ⲁⲁϥ' ⲉϥⲙⲟⲕϩ̅ ⲛ̅ϩⲏ[ⲧ]
ⲁⲩⲉⲓⲙⲉ ⲛ̅ϭ[ⲓ ⲥ]ⲟⲛ
ⲥⲛⲁⲩ ϫⲉϥⲗⲩⲡⲉ[ⲓ']
ⲁⲩϯ ⲡⲉⲩⲟⲓ̈ ⲉⲣⲟ[ϥ]
ⲡⲉϫⲁⲩ ⲛⲁϥ ϫⲉⲁ-
ϫⲓ ⲟⲩϣⲁϫⲉ ⲉⲣⲟⲛ
ⲛ̅ⲧⲟϥ ⲇⲉ ⲡⲉϫⲁϥ
ⲛⲁⲩ ϫⲉⲧⲉⲛⲟⲩ ⲣⲱ'
ⲁⲛⲟⲕ' ⲉⲧⲣ̅ⲭⲣⲓⲁ ⲛ̅-
ϫⲓ ⲥⲟⲗⲥⲗ̅ ϩⲓⲧ[ⲛ̅-]
ⲟⲩⲁ· ⲡⲉϫⲁⲩ ⲛ[ⲁϥ]
ϫⲉϣⲁⲥϣⲱⲡⲉ

margin

↑ *Verso.*

                   ⲡ]ⲉⲕ-
[ⲙⲕⲁϩ] ⲛ̅ϩⲏⲧ, ⲁⲩⲱ
[ⲁ]ⲛⲟⲛ ⲧ̅ⲛⲛⲁⲥⲗ̅ⲥⲱ-
[ⲗ]ⲕ· ⲛ̅ⲧⲟϥ ⲇⲉ ⲡⲉ-
[ϫ]ⲁϥ ⲛⲁⲩ ϫⲉ ⲛ̅ⲧⲱ-
ⲧ̅ⲛ ⲛ̅ⲧⲉⲧⲛⲁϣ-
ϭⲙ̅ϭⲟⲙ' ⲁⲛ ⲛ̅ⲥⲗ̅ⲥⲱ-
ⲗⲧ̅ ⲙ̅ⲡⲉⲥⲛⲁⲩ· ⲉⲓ-
     ...ⲛ̅ⲧⲓ ⲛ̅ⲧⲉⲟⲙ'
ⲛ̅ⲟⲩⲱⲧ ⲥⲗ̅ⲥⲱⲗⲧ̅

[ⲡ]ⲉ ⲛ̅ϩⲓϫⲓ[ⲱⲧⲏⲥ]
ⲡ̅ϥⲥⲟⲟⲩⲛ ⲁⲛ [ⲛ̅ⲗⲁⲁⲩ]
ⲛ̅ⲧⲟϥ ⲇⲉ ⲁϥⲁⲛ[ⲁⲛⲁ-]
ⲕⲧⲉⲓ, ⲡⲉϫⲁϥ ϫⲉⲡ[ⲉⲛ-]
ⲉⲓⲱⲧ' ⲡⲁϣⲱⲙⲉ ⲛ[ϥ̅-]
ⲥⲟⲟⲩⲛ ⲁⲛ ⲛ̅ⲗⲁⲁⲩ, [ⲁ-]
ⲣⲏⲩ ⲟⲛ, ⲕⲛⲁϫⲟⲟⲥ [ⲉ-]
ⲧⲃⲉⲛ̅ⲁⲡⲟⲥⲧⲟⲗⲟ[ⲥ]
ϫⲉⲛ̅ⲥⲉⲥⲟⲟⲩⲛ ⲁⲛ [ⲛ̅-]
ⲗⲁⲁⲩ· ⲉⲃⲟⲗ' ϫⲉϥⲥⲏ[ϩ]

пϣⲁϫⲉ ⲇⲉ ⲉⲛⲧⲁϥ-　　　ⲉⲧⲃⲏⲏⲧⲟⲩ ϫⲉϩⲉⲛ-
ϫⲟⲟⲩˈ ⲡⲛⲉϥⲥⲟⲟⲩⲛᵃ　　　ϩⲓⲇⲓⲱⲧⲏⲥⲛⲉ ⲛ̄ⲥⲉ-
ⲁⲛ ϫⲉⲟⲩˈⲡⲉ · ⲉⲧⲓ ⲇⲉ　　　ⲥⲟⲟⲩⲛ ⲁⲛ ⲛ̄ⲥⲉϩⲁⲓ ·
ⲉϥϣⲁϫⲉ ⲛ̄ⲙ̄ⲙⲁⲩ　　　ⲛ̄ⲧⲟϥ ⲅⲁⲣ ϥⲃⲱⲗˈ
ⲁϥϭⲱϣ̄ⲧ̄ ⲁⲅⲱ ⲉⲓⲥ　　　ⲉⲣⲟⲛ ⲛ̄ⲙ̄ⲙⲩⲥⲧⲏ-
ϩⲏ[ⲏ]ⲧⲉ ⲉⲓⲥ ⲡⲉⲥⲙⲟⲧˈ　　　ⲣⲓ[ⲟⲛ ⲛ̄ⲛⲉ]ⲅⲣⲁⲫⲏ
ⲛ̄ⲟⲩⲣⲱⲙⲉ ⲁϥϩⲙⲟ-　　　ⲁⲅⲱ [ϥⲧⲁⲙⲟᶜ ⲙ̄-]
[ⲟ]ⲥ ⲉϩⲣⲁⲓ̈ ⲉϫ̄ⲛ̄ⲡⲉϥ-　　　ⲙ̄[ⲟ]ⲛ ⲉ ϩⲉⲛⲥ ϩ ⲁ[ⲓ ⲉⲩ-]
ⲡⲁⲧˈ ⲁϥⲁⲣⲭⲉⲓ ⲛ̄-　　　ⲟ[ⲅⲁⲁ]ⲃ̄ˈ ⲛ̄ⲑⲉ ⲉⲧⲥ[ⲏ ϩ]
ϣⲁϫⲉ ⲛ̄ⲙ̄ⲙⲁϥˈ ⲉϥ-　　　ⲟ[ⲩ ⲙ̄]ⲟⲛⲟⲛ ⲇⲉ ϩ[ⲱ]
ⲟ ⲛ̄ⲑⲉ ⲛ̄ⲛⲉⲧⲥⲟ ϣ ϥᵇ　　　[..]ϥⲥⲟⲟⲩⲛ ⲉ ϩ[ⲟⲩⲉ-]
ⲙ̄ⲡⲉⲛⲉⲓⲱⲧˈ ⲡⲁ-　　　ⲣⲟⲕ · ⲁⲅⲱ ⲙ̄ⲡ[ⲛ̄ⲥⲁ-]
ⲣⲱⲙⲉ ⲉϥⲡⲉⲓⲣⲁⲍⲉ　　　ⲧⲣⲉϥϫⲱ ⲛ̄[ⲛⲁⲓ ⲁ-]
ⲙ̄ⲙⲟϥˈ ⲉϥϫⲱ ⲙ̄ⲙ̄ⲥ̄　　　ⲡⲉⲧϣⲁϫⲉ [ⲛ̄ⲙ̄ⲙⲁϥ]
[ϫⲉ]ⲛⲓⲙ̄ˈⲡⲉ ⲡⲁ ϩ ⲣⲱⲙⲉ ·　　　ϯ ⲑⲉ ⲛⲁϥ ⲉⲧ[ⲣⲉϥⲥⲟⲩ-]
[ⲙⲏ] ⲛ̄ⲟⲩⲣⲱⲙⲉ ⲁⲛ-　　　ⲱⲡϥ̄ ϫⲉⲟⲩⲁϭ[ⲅⲉⲗⲟⲥ-]
　　　　　　　　　　ⲡⲉ ⲛ̄ⲧⲉ ⲡ̄ϫ[ⲟⲉⲓⲥ]

margin

ᵃ So my copy'; should be ⲛ̄ⲛⲉⲩ-.　　　ᵇ So copy; read ⲥⲱ ϣ ϥ.　　　ᶜ Following Am., لِيُعْلِمَ.

Fol. 14. *Recto* (v. Am. 414). . . . which] the brethren [use?] to eat ; and
he sent to him a brother, saying, 'Theodore doth call thee.' And as for
him, forthwith[1] when he heard, he arose and came unto him, and began
(ἄρχειν) to speak with him in words of sadness, as if (ὡς)[2] finding fault with
him. And Theodore's heart was grieved and he wept and went forth from
him. He (*sc.* P.) said unto him,[3] 'Do thou too go and weep unto the
Lord, [even as] I [myself] also have wept.' But (δέ) one of [them that]
heard him answered[4] . . . . .

. . . neither hath[5] Theodore eaten to-day.' He said unto him, 'Leave ye
him ; let him not eat, but (rather) (ἀλλά) let him weep.' And he (*sc.* P.)

[1] Am. *sic.*　　　　　　[2] Am. *sic.*
[3] Am., 'because he had said unto him.'
[4] Am., 'And one of the brethren heard him
while he spake unto him, and he said &c.'

[5] Am., 'Theodore also hath eaten naught
to-day.' And he said, 'And what have ye (to
do) with him (misunderstood for ⲁ ϩ ⲣⲱⲧⲛ̄ ⲛ̄ⲙ-
ⲙⲁϥ)? Let him &c.'

forthwith sat down and did eat with his mind at rest.[1]   And it befell, as
Theodore [2] sat apart alone, sad at heart, two brethren knew that he was
grieved (λυπεῖν) and they betook themselves unto him and said unto him,
' Speak a word unto us.'   But (δέ) he said unto them, ' Now [3] indeed I it
is have need (χρεία) to get comfort from one.'   They said unto him, ' It
may happen . . . . .

Verso (*v.* Am. 414, 415). . . . thy [sadness] of heart and we will comfort
thee.'   But (δέ) he said unto them, ' Not ye it is will together be able to
console me, except (εἰ μήτι) one alone console me.'   But (δέ) the word that
he spake, they knew not what (it meant).   And (δέ) whilst yet (ἔτι) he spake
with them, he looked and lo, the semblance of a man did sit at his feet [4]
and began to speak with him, being like to them that revile our father
Pahômius, tempting (πειράζειν) him and saying, ' Who is Pahômius ? [Is
he (μή)] not

an ignorant (ἰδιώτης) man, knowing nothing ? '   But (δέ) he (*sc.* Theodore)
was indignant (ἀγανακτεῖν) (and) said, ' Our father Pahômius knoweth (then)
nothing ?   Perchance too thou wilt say concerning the apostles (ἀπ.) that
they know nothing, for that it is written [5] concerning them that they were
ignorant men (*ἰδ.*), knowing not how to write.[6]   For (γάρ) he solveth for us
the mysteries (μυστήριον) of the Scriptures (γρ.) and [teacheth] us holy
writings, as it is written.[7]   But not only (οὐ μόνον δέ) . . .,[8] he knoweth
more than thee.'   And after that he had said this, he that spake with him
gave him means that he should know him for an angel (ἄγ.) of the Lord.

Fol. 15.   ↑ *Recto.*

[. . . . . . .]ⲓϣⲓ

[. . . . ⲑ]ⲱⲃ ⲛⲓⲙ’ ⲛ̄-   ⲛⲁ[ⲛ-]

[. . . .]ⲁ[.]ⲉϥ ⲁⲩ-   ⲧⲁϥ[

[ⲣⲱⲙ]ⲉ ⲇⲉ ⲟⲛ ⲉⲓ’ ϣⲁ-   ϥⲥⲟⲩ[ⲧⲱⲛ

[ⲣⲟ]ϥ ⲛ̄ⲟⲩⲟⲩⲟⲉⲓϣ’   ⲁⲩⲱ [

ⲉϥⲟⲩⲱϣ’ ⲉⲣ̄ⲙⲟⲛⲁ-   ⲟⲩⲕⲟ[

---

[1] Am., ' in great grief of heart.'   But read ⲉ͟ⲛ͟ϫ
for ⲛ͟ϫ.   [2] Am. *sic.*

[3] Am. should be, ' I have need that ye two
comfort me.'   And they said unto him, ' It is
indeed possible that the fathers be comforted
even by their children &c.'

[4] Am. (Ac. 51, G ⲣ̄ⲗ̄ⲏ b) ' before him '.
[5] Acts iv. 13.
[6] Am. *sic.*
[7] *Cf.* Luke xxiv. 32.

is &c.'

ϫⲟⲥ · ⲁⲩ[ⲱ] ⲛ̄ⲧⲉⲣⲉϥ⳿- ϩⲃⲏⲩ[ⲉ ⲙⲉ-]
ⲁⲡⲁⲛ[ⲧⲁ] ⲉⲣⲟϥ⳿ ⲁϥ- ⲉⲅⲉ ⲟ̄ⲙ[
ϣⲁϫⲉ ⲛ̄ⲙⲙⲁϥ ⲁϥ- ⲉⲓ ⲉⲃⲟⲗ [·
ϩⲉ ⲉⲣⲟϥ [ⲉ]ϥⲥⲟⲩⲧⲱ̄ ⲟ̄ⲛⲧⲉⲩ[ⲛⲟⲩ ⲉⲧⲙ̄-]
ⲛ̄ⲡⲁϩⲣ[ⲁ]ϥ ⲉⲡϩⲱⲃ ⲙⲁⲩ · ⲛ̄[
[. . .]ᵃ ⲁⲩⲱ ⲁϥϩⲱⲛ [
[ⲉ]ⲧⲟⲟⲧϥ ⲙ̄ⲡⲥⲟⲛ ⲙ̄ⲙⲉⲡⲉⲧ[
ⲉⲧϩⲁⲧⲙ̄ⲙ[ⲣ]ⲟ⳿ ⲛ̄ⲑⲉ- ⲙ̄ⲡⲥⲟⲛ ⲉⲛ[ⲧⲁϥ-]
ⲛⲉⲉⲧⲏ ⲉⲧⲣⲉϥⲉⲓ- ϫⲟⲟⲥ ⲛⲁϥ ⲉ[ϫⲓ-]
ⲛⲉ ⲙ̄ⲙⲟϥ ⲉϩⲟⲩⲛ ⲧϥ ⲉⲉⲓⲛⲉ [ⲙ̄ⲙⲟϥ]
ⲛ̄ⲡⲉⲥⲛⲏⲩ · ⲛ̄ⲧⲉ- ⲉϩⲟⲩⲛ ⲉⲧ[
[ⲣⲉϥ]ⲙⲟⲟϣⲉ ⲇⲉ ⲉⲑⲏ ϫⲉⲙⲁ[
[ⲛⲟⲩⲕ]ⲟⲩ[ⲓ] ϩⲱⲥ ⲉϥ- ⲣⲱⲙ[ⲉ
[ⲛⲁⲃⲱⲕ ⲉϩⲟ]ⲩⲛ ⲉⲧ-ᵇ ⲛ̄[

ᵃ I do not think there is a line missing between this and last; *cf. verso.* ᵇ ⲧⲥⲟⲟⲩϩⲥ
or ⲧⲙⲛ̄ⲧⲉ. So too in col. 2. .

→ *Verso.*

    ]ⲛⲥⲁ ⲗⲉ[ⲡⲉ-]
   ⲉⲃ]ⲟⲗ ⲛ̄- ϫⲁϥ ⲛⲁ[ϥ ϫⲉⲉⲧⲃⲉ-]
[ⲧⲉⲩⲛⲟⲩ] ⲡⲉϫⲁϥ ⲧⲁⲫⲟⲣⲙⲛ [ⲙ̄ⲡⲛⲟ-]
[ⲛⲁϥ ϫⲉⲃⲱⲕ] ⲛ̄ⲡ̄- ⲃⲉ ⲉⲛⲧⲁⲓⲁ[ϥ ϩⲛ̄-]
[ⲙⲟⲩⲧⲉ ⲉⲛ]ⲙ⳿ ⲛ̄- ⲟⲩⲙⲛ̄ⲧⲁⲧⲥⲟ[ⲟⲩⲛ ⲱᵃ]
[ⲥⲟⲛ ϩⲛ̄]ⲙ⳿ ⲁⲩⲱ ⲑⲉⲟⲇⲱⲣⲉ. ⲥⲡⲟⲩⲇⲁ-
[ⲛ̄ⲧⲉⲣⲟⲩⲉⲓ]· ⲡⲉ- ⲍⲉ ⲉⲧⲣⲉⲕϣⲱⲡⲉ
[ϫⲁϥ ⲛⲁⲩ] ϩⲱⲟⲩ ϫⲉ- ⲛ̄ⲧ[ⲟ]ⲕ ϩⲛ̄ⲟⲩⲙⲛ̄ⲧ-
[ⲛ̄ⲧⲁⲓ]ϫⲟⲟⲥ ⲛⲏⲧⲛ̄ ⲁⲧⲛⲟⲃⲉ ⲛ̄ⲟⲩⲟⲉⲓϣ
[ϫⲉⲟⲩ⳿·] ⲡⲉϫⲁⲩ ⲛⲁϥ ⲛⲓⲙ⳿· ⲛ̄ⲑⲉ ⲉⲛⲧⲁⲓ-
        ⲉⲡⲓⲧⲓⲙⲁ ⲛⲁⲕ⳿ ⲉ-

ˣ Scarcely space for ⲱ, though it seems needed.

[ϫⲉⲛ]ⲧⲁⲕϫⲟⲟⲥ ϫⲉ   [ⲡ]ϫⲓⲛϫ[ⲏ] ⲅⲛ̄[ⲟ]ⲩ- ᵇ

[ⲃⲱⲕ] ⲛ̄ⲧⲉⲧⲛ̄ⲡⲁ-   [

[ⲛⲁⲭ]ⲱⲣⲉⲓ ⲛⲏⲧⲛ̄·   ϣⲱ-]

[ⲛ̄ⲧ]ⲟϥ ϫⲉ ⲛ̄ⲧⲉ-   ⲡⲉ ϫⲉ ⲛ̄ⲟⲩⲥ[ⲟⲡ ⲉⲕ-]

[ⲣⲉϥⲥⲱ]ⲧⲙ̄ ⲁϥⲁ[ϣ]   ⲙⲟⲩⲧⲉ ⲉⲩⲣⲱ[ⲙⲉ]

[ⲁϩⲟⲙ]· ⲡⲉϫⲁϥ ϫⲉ   ⲁⲩⲱ ⲛ̄ⲧⲟϥ ⲛ̄ϥ-

...]ⲥⲧᵃ ⲉⲛⲉⲓ-   ⲡⲱⲧ ⲛⲁϥ ⲛ̄ⲧⲉⲩ-

[ϣⲁϫⲉ ⲛⲙ̄]ⲙⲏⲧⲛ̄   ⲛⲟⲩ ⲙ̄ⲡⲣⲛⲟⲩϫⲥ̄

[ⲁⲓⲛⲁⲩ ⲉⲩⲡ]ⲛ̄ⲁ ⲛ̄-   ⲉⲣⲟϥ· ⲁⲗⲗⲁ ⲁϫ[ⲓⲥ]

ⲉ]ϥ-   ⲛ̄ⲧⲟϥ [ϩ]ⲙ̄ⲡ[ⲉⲕϩⲏⲧ]

               ϫⲉⲡⲁⲛ[ⲧⲱⲥ ⲛ̄ⲡϥⲉⲓ-]

               ⲙⲉ ⲉⲩ[ᶜ

ᵃ Am. حين كلامى كنت أكلمكم, Ac. 53 حين كلامى.   ᵇ Whether two or three lines lost is uncertain.
ᶜ Or ϯⲙⲉⲉⲩⲉ ϫ[ⲉ.   But this hardly fills the space.

Fol. 15. *Recto* (*cf.* Am. 416). ... everything that .....[1] But (δέ)
a man also came unto him, once on a time, desiring to become a monk
(μον.). And after that he had met (ἀπαντᾶν) him, he talked with him and
found him fitted (*lit.* upright) before him (*i.e.* in his opinion) for the matter
..... And he bade the brother that was at the gate of the monastery,
that he should bring him in unto the brethren. But (δέ) when he had
gone forward a little, as if (ὡς) he [would go in] unto the [congregation [2]

... in that hour ..... the brother to whom [he] had said to [take] him
and bring [him] in unto the ..., saying,[3] ..... man (?) .....

Verso (*v.* Am. 418). ... went] forth at [once?]. He said [unto him,
'Go (?)] and [call] such a [brother and] such an one.' And [when they
were come,] he [said unto them] likewise, ['What] said [I] unto you?'
They said unto him, 'Thou didst say, ['Go and depart (ἀναχωρεῖν).'[4] But
(δέ) he, when he heard, sighed. He said, '... I [spake with] you, [I beheld
a] spirit (πν.) of .....

... and said unto him, 'Because of the occasion (ἀφορμή) of sin that
I (*sic*)[5] have given (*lit.* done), in ignorance, [O?] Theodore, strive (σπουδά-

---

[1] Apparently not as in Am.'s context. What   [3] An imperative followed here.   [4] Am. *sic*.
follows (§ 46) differs also considerably from Am.,
[2] Or 'midst'.   done.'

ζειν) for thy part to be alway without sin, as I admonished (ἐπιτιμᾶν) thee freely, with[1] . . . . .   But (δέ) if perchance on a time thou call a man and he forthwith hasten away, be not wroth with him, but (ἀλλά) rather say in thy heart, 'Surely (πάντως) he hath not understood . . . . .

Fol. 16.   → *Recto.*

] ⲛⲧⲉⲣⲉϥ-
[ⲛⲁⲩ] ⲛϭⲓ ⲡⲉⲛⲉⲓ-
ⲱⲧ ⲡⲁϩⲱⲙⲉ ⲉⲩ-
ⲡ̄ⲛ̄ⲁ̄ ⲛ̄ⲡⲟⲣⲛⲓⲁ
ⲁⲩⲱ ⲛ̄ⲥⲱⲱϥ' ⲉⲩ-
ⲡⲁⲣⲁⲅⲉ ϩ̄ⲡⲛⲉⲥⲛⲏⲩ,
ⲉⲩⲣϩⲱⲃ' ϩ̄ⲡⲟⲩⲙⲁ·
ⲁϥⲥⲱⲟⲩϩ' ⲛ̄ⲙⲟⲟⲩ
ⲉⲛⲉⲩⲉⲣⲏⲩ ⲉⲣⲟⲩϩⲉ
ⲕⲁⲧⲁ ⲧⲉⲩⲥⲩⲛⲏ-
ⲑⲉⲓⲁ· ⲡⲉⲭⲁϥ ⲛⲁⲩ·
ϫⲉⲁⲣⲓ ⲡⲙⲉⲉⲩⲉ ⲛ̄-
ⲡϣⲁϫⲉ ⲉⲧⲥⲏϩ ϫⲉ-
ⲧⲡⲓⲥⲧⲓⲥ ⲟⲩⲉⲃⲟⲗ

] ?
ⲧⲉⲩⲛⲧⲉ]ⲗⲉⲓⲁ
ᵃⲛ̄ⲡⲁⲓ]ⲱⲛ ⲉⲩ-
]ⲧⲟⲩ ⲁⲛ
[ⲉⲃ]ⲟⲗ ϩ̄ⲡⲛⲉⲩⲥⲱ-
ⲱϥ ⲉⲛⲧⲁⲩ . . ⲁⲥⲉ
[. .] ⲙⲙⲟⲟⲩ ⲛ̄ϩⲏⲧⲟⲩ
[. . . .]ⲛ̄ⲙ̄ⲡ[

ᵃ Perhaps here ⲅⲁⲣ, ⲟⲩⲛ or some such word.

↑ *Verso.*

ⲛ[
ⲉⲛⲧⲁⲩϣ[ⲱⲡⲉᵃ ⲛ-]
ϩⲏⲧⲟⲩ ⲥⲉϣ[ⲱⲡⲉ]
ⲟⲛ ⲧⲉⲛⲟⲩ ⲁⲩⲱ ⲥⲉ-
ⲙⲟⲟϣⲉ ϩ̄ⲙ̄ⲡⲕⲟⲥ-
ⲙⲟⲥ· ϯⲥⲟⲟⲩⲛ' ⲙⲉ̄
ϫⲉⲛϥ   ?

ᵃ Or ϣ[ⲓⲛⲉ], and in next line.

[1] Am. should be, 'As I reprimanded thee freely, with reproof, do thou also, if thou call a man &c.'

ϩⲏⲧ ?

? ?

ⲥⲉⲛⲁϯ ⲙⲁ ⲁⲛ' ⲛ̄-
ϩⲏⲧⲟⲩ ⲛ̄ⲟⲩⲍⲁⲓ-
ⲙⲱⲛ ⲛ̄ⲧⲉⲓⲙⲓⲛⲉ
ϩⲛ̄ⲗⲁⲁⲩ ⲛ̄ϩⲱⲃ·
ⲁⲗⲗⲁ ⲟⲩⲁⲅⲁⲑⲟⲛ
ⲛⲁⲩⲡⲉ ⲉⲧⲣⲉⲩϥⲓ'

ⲟⲩϫⲡⲁⲛ . ⲁϫⲓ
ϩⲛ̄ⲛϣⲁϫⲉ ⲉ[ⲛⲧ]ⲁϥ-ᵃ
ϫⲟⲟⲩ ⲛⲏⲧⲛ̄· ⲁⲗ-
ⲗⲁ ϫⲱⲕ ⲉⲃⲟⲗ' ⲛ̄-

ᵃ Or]ⲁⲓ.

Fol. 16. *Recto* (v. Am. 424). . . . the end (συντέλεια) [. . . of the] age (? αἰών), they not . . .[1] them from out their pollutions wherein they . . . themselves . . . . .

. . . When our father Pahômius saw a spirit (πν.) of fornication (πορνεία) and pollution passing (παράγειν) among the brethren, while they worked in a (certain) place, he gathered them together at evening, according to (κατά) their custom (συνήθεια). He said unto them, 'Remember the word that is written,[2] that Belief (πίσ.) is of [hearing . . . . .

Verso (v. Am. 424). . . . wherein they have been, they are therein[3] now also and do walk in the world (κόσ.). Now (μέν) I know that . . . . . will not give place in themselves unto a demon (δαίμων) such as this, in anything. But (ἀλλά) it (were) good (ἀγαθός) for them that they bear . . . . .

. . . by the words that he (?)[4] spake unto you. But (ἀλλά) fulfil . . . . .

Fol. 17. ↑ *Recto.*

ⲧ[
ⲡⲉᵃ ϣⲁⲉⲛ[ⲉϩ
ⲡϫⲟⲉⲓⲥ . [ⲉⲃⲟⲗ]
ϫⲉⲁⲩⲧⲟ[ϣⲟⲩ ϩⲙ̄-]
ⲡⲉⲩϩⲏⲧ [ⲛ̄ⲙⲙⲓⲛ ⲙ̄-]
ⲙⲟⲟⲩ ⲉⲩϩ[ᵇ

ᵃ Perhaps ϣⲱⲡⲉ.   ᵇ Apparently not ⲉⲩϫ[ⲟⲟⲥ or ϫ[ⲱ ⲙⲙⲟⲥ.

[1] But indic . . .

[2] Rom. x. 17 (probably; *ed.* Wessely, *Stud.* xii. 157).

[3] Or 'have been ashamed, they are ashamed now also'.

[4] Or 'that I'.

ⲭⲉⲡⲉⲩⲟ[ⲉⲓϣ ⲧⲏⲣϥ]

ⲉⲧⲁⲉ . . [ⲛ̄-]

ⲟ̄ⲏⲧ[ϥ] ⲟⲓⲝⲙ̄ⲡⲕⲁϩ   ? [

ⲛ̄ⲧⲛ̄ⲡⲁⲣⲁⲕⲧⲛ̄   ϣⲁ[

ⲁⲛ ⲉⲃⲟⲗ ⲙ̄ⲡⲉⲕⲟⲩ-   ⲡⲣ[

ⲱϣ' ⲕⲁ[ⲛ] ⲉⲕ[ϣ]ⲁⲛ-   ⲝⲓⲛ[

ⲕⲁⲁⲛ ϣⲁⲧⲥ̄ⲩⲡⲧⲉ-   ⲁ . ⲃⲉⲗ[

ⲗⲉⲓⲁ ⲙ̄ⲡⲁⲓⲱⲛ·   ⲅ̄ⲙ̄ⲡⲛ̄[ⲥ ᵃ

ⲛⲁⲓ ⲇⲉ [ⲛ̄]ⲧⲉⲓⲙⲉ-   ⲕⲁ ⲧⲟⲟⲧ[ⲟⲩ

ⲛⲉ ⲕⲁ[ⲛ ⲟ]ⲩⲣⲟⲙⲡⲉ   ⲟ̄ⲙ̄ⲡⲧ[ⲣⲉ

ⲛ̄ⲟⲩⲱⲧ [ⲧ]ⲉⲧⲟⲩ-   ⲟ̄ⲏⲧ' ⲟ̄ⲙ̄ⲡⲟⲩⲉⲕ[ⲟⲩ-]

ⲛⲁⲁⲁⲥ ⲉⲩ[ⲟⲩ]ⲡⲟⲙⲉ-   ⲡⲟⲙⲛ[ⲉ] ⲧⲏⲣⲟ[ⲩ ⲛ̄-]

ⲛⲉ ⲉⲡⲭⲟⲉ[ⲓⲥ] ⲛ̄ ⲙ̄ⲛ̄-   ⲧⲁⲩⲁⲁⲩᵇ [ⲉ]ⲧⲣⲁⲡⲁ[ϥ]

ⲧⲉ ⲛ̄ⲣⲟⲙⲡⲉ· ⲛ̄ ⲟ̄ⲟⲩⲟ   ⲙ̄ⲡⲭⲟⲉ[ⲓⲥ] ⲁⲩⲱ ⲉⲩ[ϯ]

ⲉⲛⲁⲓ ⲉⲩⲡⲟⲗⲓⲧⲉⲩⲉ   ⲟⲩⲃⲉ'ⲡ[ⲁ]ⲓⲁⲃⲟⲗⲟⲥ

ⲕⲁⲧⲁ ⲡⲧⲱϣ ⲛ̄ⲟ̄ⲏⲧ'   ⲟ̄ⲱⲥⲧ[ⲉ .]. ⲓⲛⲉ[

margin

ⲅ̄ ⲙ̄ⲡⲛ̄[

ᵃ Paragraph-mark very doubtful. Can the similar mark and words in smaller script, below the text, have reference to this?   ᵇ One is tempted to read ⲟ̄ⲙ̄ⲡⲟⲩⲉ ⲛ̄ⲁⲓ ⲛ̄ⲧⲉⲓⲙⲛ̄[ⲉ] ⲧⲏⲣⲥ (or -ⲟ[ⲩ]) [ⲉⲡ]ⲧⲁⲩⲁⲁⲥ [ⲉ]ⲩⲣⲁⲡⲁ[ϥ].

→ *Verso.*

                               ]ⲃ̄

                      ⲛ̄]ⲁϣⲱⲡⲉ

                  [ϣⲁⲉⲛⲉ]ⲟ̄' ⲟ̄ⲛ̄ⲧⲙ̄ⲛ̄-

                  [ⲧⲉⲣⲟ ⲉ]ⲛ̄ⲧⲁⲩⲥⲃ̄-

                  [ⲧⲱⲧϥ̄] ⲛⲁⲩ ⲝⲓⲛ-

                  [ⲧⲕⲁⲧⲁ]ⲃⲟⲗⲏ ⲙ̄-

                  [ⲡⲕⲟⲥ]ⲙⲟⲥ ⲉⲃⲟⲗ

                  [ⲭⲉⲁⲩϣ]ⲱⲡⲉ ⲉⲩ-

]ⲱⲡⲉ   ⲛⲅⲟⲧ' ⲙ̄ⲡⲭⲟⲉⲓⲥ

ⲉ]ⲧⲃⲉ-   ⲕⲁⲧⲁ ⲧⲁⲓⲁⲑⲏⲕⲏ

]ⲛ̄ⲛⲣⲱ-   ⲉⲛⲧⲁⲩⲥ̄ⲙ̄ⲛ̄ⲧⲉ

[ⲙⲉ   ]ⲛ̄ⲡⲁⲓⲁⲃⲟ-   ⲛ̄ⲡⲉⲩⲙⲁⳙ · ⲧⲁⲓ ⲟⲛ

[ⲗⲟⲥ   ] ? ⳙⲟ̣   ⲧⲉ ⲑⲉ ⲛ̄ⲡⲣⲉϥⲣ̄ⲛⲟ-

]ⲉⲟⲩⲟ·   ⲃⲉ ⲉⲛⲧⲁⲩⲧⲟⳙⲟⲩ

]ⲃ . . . ⲅⲱ   ⲉⲣⲛⲟ[ⲃⲉ] ⲙ̄ⲙⲛⲉⲧ-

ⲉⲛ]ⲧⲁϥⲣ̄ⲁⲛⲁϥ   ⲙⲏⲛ [ⲉⲃⲟ]ⲗ' ϩⲙ̄-

]ϩ.ⲥ ⲁϥⳙⲱ-   ⲡⲥⲱ[ⲱ]ϥ ⲉⲛⲧⲁⲩ-

ⲡⲉ ⲛⲁⲧⲛⲟⲃⲉ ⲙ̄-   ⲣ̄ⲭⲟ[ⲉⲓⲥ] ⲉⲣⲟⲟⲩ ⲛ̄ϩ[ⲏ-]

[ⲡ]ⲉϥⲙ̄ⲧⲟ ⲉⲃⲟⲗ · ⲧⲏⲣⲟⲩ [ϩⲓ]ⲧⲙ̄ⲡⲁⲓⲁⲃⲟ-

ⲣⲏⲩ ⲉⲓⲉⲣⲓⲭⲱ   ⲃⲟⲗⲟⲥ ⲙ̄ⲡⲉϥⲁ[ⲓ-]

ⲙ̄ⲡⲥⲟ[ⲇ]ⲟⲙⲁ' ⲙ̄-   ⲙⲱⲛ ⲛⲁⲓ ⲉⲛⲧⲁ[ⲩ-]

. ⲁ . ⲉⲣ[.]ⲉⲗⲁⲙⲁ .ᵃ   ⳙⲱⲡⲉ ⲛⲁϥ ⲛ̄-

[ⲙ̄]ⲛ̄ⲥⲉⲃ[ⲟⲓ]ⲙ' ⲉⲁⲩ-   ⳙⲏⲣⲉ · ⲛ̄ⲑⲉ ⲉⲧ-

]ⲩⲕⲱ   ⲥⲛ̄ϩ ϩⲙ̄ⲡⲉⲩⲁⲥ-

margin

ᵃ One is tempted to read ⲉⲗⲁⲙ or ⲁⲇⲁⲙⲁ, preceded by ⲥⲉⲗⲗⲁⲥⲁⲣ or ⲅⲟⲙⲟⲣⲣⲁ. Jericho elsewhere always ϩⲓⲉⲣⲓⲭⲱ.

Fol. 17. *Recto* (*v.* Am. 425). ... unto everlasting ... the Lord,[1] because they have decided in their own heart, being ..., that ['All] the time [where]in we ... upon the earth, we will not decline from Thy will, even (κἄν) shouldest Thou suffer us until the end (συντέλεια) of the age (αἰών).' Those of this sort, whether (κἄν) it be a single year that they shall pass, waiting for (ὑπομένειν) the Lord, or (ἤ) ten years, or (ἤ) more than these, living (πολιτεύειν) according to (κατά) the decision of heart [2] [which . . . .][3] afterwards (?) ... desist ... while . . . .[4] all their perseverance (? ὑπομένειν) that they have done,[4] pleasing the Lord and resisting the devil (δι.), so that (ὥστε) . . . . .

[1] Am. should be, 'And those shall be like unto the Lord; they have decided in themselves saying, in presence of the Lord, with a good conscience and sure. If Thou leave us on the earth, unto the end, we will not decline from Thy will; but all our time for which Thou shalt leave us on the earth, we will continue in Thy will, even shouldest Thou leave us unto the end of the age.'

[2] Am. *sic.*   [3] This passage not in Am.

[4] Slight alterations would give, 'far off, all such-like things that they have done'; but grammatically the changes are hardly admissible.

Verso (v. Am. 425, 426). ...[1] the devil (διάβ.) .... that pleased him ... he was (?) sinless before Him ..... Jericho and Sodom and ... and (?) Elam (?) and Seboim,[2] that did .....

... shall be for ever in the kingdom that hath been prepared for them since the foundation (κατ.) of the world (κόσ.) ; because that they have been faithful unto the Lord, according unto the covenant (κατά, διαθ.) which they did establish with Him. And[3] this likewise is the fashion of the sinners that have decided to sin[4] and those that remain in pollution, whereby the devil (διάβ.) and his demons (δαίμ.) have lordship over them ; unto whom they are become children ; as it is written in the Gospel (εὐ.).....

Fol. 18.   ↑ *Recto.*   → *Verso.*

T̅Ч̅ХПОΥ^a ПЕТЕϢ-	[ПКОС]ΜΟС · ΑΛΛ[Α]
ϢЕ ЕХПОΥЧ ΑΓΩ Μ-	ΑΝΟΝ Μ̅ΠΝ̅СΑΠΕΟ-
ПОΥХООΥЧ · ХЕКАС	ОΥΝ Μ̅ΠΝΟΥΤΕ, Ν̅-
Ν̅ΝΕΠХΑХΕ † ϨΗΥ	ΠΕСϢΩΠΕ ΕΤΡΕΝ-
Ν̅ϨΗΤ, ΤΗΥΤΝ̅ Ε-	ΕΙ' ΕϨΡΑΪ ΕΠΕΪХΩ-
ΠΤΗΡЧ̅ ΚΑΤΑ ΘΕ	Ϩ̅Μ̅ Ν̅ΤΕΪΜΙΝΕ ·
[Ε]ΤСΗϨ' · Ν̅ΤΕΡΟΥ-	ΑΓΩ ΑΥ̅Ρ̅ΤΕΥϢ[Η]
СΩΤΜ ΔΕ ΕΝΑΪ Ν̅ϬΙ	ΤΗΡ̅С̅ ΕΤΜΜΑΥ [ΕΥ-]
[ϨΟΕΙΝΕ Ν̅ϨΗΤΟΥ]	ΜΟΚ̅Ϩ̅ Ν̅ϨΗΤ ΑΓΩ
ΕϨΕΝΑΝΑХΩΡΙΤΗС-	ΕΥΚΡΜΡΜ ΕΤΒΕΝ-
ΝΕ Ν̅ϢΟΡΠ ΕΜΠΑ-	ϢΑХΕ ΕΝΤΑΥСΟΤ-
ΤΟΥΕΙ' ΕΤΚΟΙΝΩΝΙΑ	ΜΟΥ · Ν̅ΤΕΡΟΥΤΩ-
ΑΥΛΥΠΕΙ' ΕΜΑΤΕ Ϩ̅Μ̅-	ΟΥΝ ΔΕ ΕϨΤΟΟΥΕ Ε-

(sic above Ν̅ϨΗΤ line)

^a Or ΤΜХΠΟΥ.

[1] This passage not in Am.

[2] *Cf.* Gen. xiv. 1, 2. It is difficult to complete the names satisfactorily.

[3] Am., 'Even thus also the sinners that have decided to sin and that remain in pollutions which do rule over them by means of the devil and his demons; these (it is) that are become children unto him, and they shall be children also unto him in punishment for ever.'

[4] 'Those (for whom) it hath been decided that they should sin' is grammatically possible.

ⲡⲉⲩϩⲏⲧ' ⲉⲩϫⲱ ⲙ̅-
ⲙⲟⲥ ϫⲉⲣⲉⲟⲩ'ⲡⲉ ⲛⲉⲓ̈-
ϣⲁϫⲉ ⲛ̅ⲧⲉⲓ̈ⲙⲓⲛⲉ·
ⲉϥⲉⲁⲁⲛ ⲛⲁⲅⲣⲓⲟⲥ ⲉ-
ⲛⲉⲛⲉⲣⲏⲩ · ⲙⲏ ⲟⲩⲛ̅-
ⲗⲁⲁⲩ, ⲛⲥϩⲓⲙⲉ ⲛ̅ϩⲏⲧ-
ⲛ̅· ⲙⲏ ⲁⲛⲟⲛ ⲧⲏⲣⲛ̅
ⲛⲉⲛϣⲟⲟⲡ' ⲁⲛ², ⲕⲁⲧⲁ

]ⲉⲣⲏⲥ ·ᵃ
]ϣⲁ
]ϫⲛ̅
]ϣⲱ-
]ⲡⲉ

margin

ⲣⲉⲛⲉⲥⲛⲏⲩ ⲛⲁⲃⲱⲕ
ⲉⲣϩⲱⲃ' ⲉⲙⲡⲟⲩⲃⲱⲕ
ⲛ̅ⲙ̅ⲙⲁⲩ· ⲉⲁⲅⲁⲧⲁ-
ⲛⲁⲕⲧⲉⲓⲡⲉ' ⲉϫⲛ̅-
ⲛⲉⲛⲧⲁⲩⲥⲟⲧⲙⲟⲩ·
ⲙ̅ⲡⲛⲁⲩ ⲇⲉ ⲛ̅ϫⲡ̅-
ϥⲧⲟ' ⲉⲓⲥ ϩⲉⲛⲙⲟⲛⲁ-
ⲭⲟⲥ ⲁⲩⲉⲓ' ⲉⲁⲡⲁⲛⲧⲁ
ⲉⲡⲉⲛⲉⲓⲱⲧ' ⲡⲁ-

ⲛ[
ⲡ[
ϣ[
ⲙ[
ⲓ[
ⲥⲡ[

margin

ᵃ Perhaps ⲥ]ⲉⲣⲏⲥ.

Fol. 18. *Recto* (*v.* Am. 427). . . . while they?] are awake[1] . . . . . not (?)
to ask that which it is meet to ask and he hath not been sent,[2] lest the
enemy have profit of you at all, as it is written.[3] But (δέ) when certain of
them heard these (words), that were aforetime anchorites (ἀναχ.) ere they
had come to the community (κοινωνία), they were much grieved (λυπεῖν) in
their heart, saying,[4] 'What are words such as these? He would make us
ill-disposed (ἄγριος) one to another. Is there (μή) any·woman among us?
Are (μή) not we all according to (κατά) . . . . .

Verso (*v.* Am. 427). . . . the wor]ld (? κόσ.). But (ἀλλά), after the
knowledge of God, let it not be that we descend to pollutions such as these.'
And they passed all that night sad at heart and murmuring because of the
words that they had heard. But (δέ) when they arose in the morning,
when the brethren were about to go forth to work, they went not with them,
being indignant (ἀγανακτεῖν) at that which they had heard. And (δέ) at
the fourth hour,[5] lo, there came monks (μον.) to meet with (ἀπαντᾶν) our
father Pahômius . . . . .

[1] Difficult to accommodate this to Am. Relates
perhaps to the precepts as to sleeping.
[2] *I.e.* unless he hath been sent = Am 'without
a mission.'
[3] Ps. lxxxviii. 22.

[4] Am. should be, saying one to another, ' What
is this word? He hath made us odious and
estranged one from another.'
[5] Am. *om.*

Fol. 19.   → *Recto.*

т]ⲙⲛⲧⲙⲁï·
[ϣⲙⲙⲟ ⲇⲉᵃ] ⲛⲡⲣⲣ-
[ⲡⲉⲥⲱ]ⲃϣ · ϩⲓⲧⲛ-
[ⲧⲁⲓ ⲅⲁ]ⲣ ⲁϩⲟⲉⲓⲙⲉᵇ
[ϣⲡ] ϩⲉⲛⲁⲅⲅⲉⲗⲟⲥ
ⲉⲣⲟⲟⲩ ⲉⲛⲥⲉⲥⲟⲟⲩⲛ
ⲁⲛ · ⲡⲉⲓ̈ⲣⲱⲙⲉ
ⲅⲁⲣ ⲉϥ[ⲛ]ⲁⲩ ⲉⲣⲟϥ
ⲟⲩⲥⲙⲟ[ⲧ] ⲛⲁⲅⲅⲉ-
ⲗⲟⲥ ⲡⲉⲧⲛⲙⲟϥ ·
ⲁϥⲟⲩⲱϣⲃ ⲇⲉ ⲛϭⲓ
ⲑⲉⲟⲇⲱⲣⲟⲥ ⲡⲉϫⲁϥ

ⲥϩ[ⲁⲓ . . . . ᶜ ⲛ̄ⲧⲉⲓ-]
ϩⲉ [ⲉϥϫⲱ ⲙ̄ⲙⲟⲥ]
ϫⲉⲡ[
ⲧ̄ⲡ̄ⲛ[ⲟⲟⲩϥ
ⲉⲧⲉⲡ[
ⲡⲉ ⲛ[
ⲛ̄ϭⲟⲟⲩ[ⲛⲉ ⲡⲉⲓⲱⲧ-]
ⲡⲉ ⲉⲩⲥⲟ[ⲟⲩⲧⲥ ϩⲁϩ-]
ⲧⲏⲛ ⲁⲩⲱ ⲟⲩⲡⲣⲉ-]
[ⲥ]ⲃ̄ⲩⲧⲉⲣ[ⲟⲥ
? [

margin

ᵃ ⲇⲉ inserted in order adequately to fill the gap.
be read, but what remains guarantees the citation.
(' epistle ').

ᵇ Here (and in line 6) scarce a letter can
ᶜ ⲥϩ[ⲁⲓⲥⲟⲩ ('letters') or ⲥϩ[ⲁⲓ ⲙⲙⲟⲥ

→ *Verso.*

]ⲱ
ⲛⲛ]ⲁϯ
]ϩⲏⲧϥ ·
] . ⲡⲉ,
]ϩⲓⲧⲙⲙ-
[ⲡⲛⲟⲩⲧⲉ] · ⲉϣⲱ-
[ⲡⲉ ⲙⲉⲛ ⲉⲕ]ϣⲁⲛϯ
[ⲙⲉⲧⲁⲛⲟⲓ]ⲁ ⲛⲁϥ
[ⲧ̄ⲡⲛⲁϯ ϩⲱ]ⲱⲛ · ⲉⲕ-
[ϣⲁⲛⲛⲟ]ϫϥ ⲇⲉ ⲉⲃⲟⲗ ·
]ⲉ̣ ⲛⲟⲩϫⲉ

ⲧⲉϥⲙⲛ[ⲧ̄ⲡⲣⲉⲥⲃⲩ-]
ⲧⲉⲣⲟⲥ · ⲛ̄ⲥ[ⲉⲛⲟϫϥ]
ⲉⲃⲟⲗ ϩⲛⲧ[ⲥⲟⲟⲩⲧⲥ]
ⲉⲧϥⲛ̄ϩⲏ[ⲧⲥ · ⲙⲁ-]
ⲣⲉϥⲃⲱⲕ' ⲉⲕⲉⲙⲁ
ⲛ̄ϥⲁⲛⲁⲭⲱⲣⲉⲓ' ⲛ̄ϥ-
ⲉⲓⲣⲉ ⲛ̄ⲟⲩⲣ[ⲟ]ⲙⲡⲉ
ϩⲛⲙⲙⲁ̣[ⲁ ⲉ]ⲧ̄ⲙⲙⲁⲩ ·
ⲛ̄ⲧⲉⲧⲙⲗⲁⲁⲩ
ϣⲗⲏⲗ' ⲛ̄ⲙⲙⲁϥ ·
ⲟⲩⲧⲉ ⲟⲩⲱⲙ · ⲁⲩⲱ

margin

Fol. 19. *Recto* (v. Am. 428). ... But (? δέ) love unto strangers neglect not ; for (γάρ) thereby have some received unto themselves angels (ἄγ.) and knew it not.[1] For (γάρ) this man that I see, an angel's form is his.'[2] But (δέ) Theodore answered and said, ...

... had] written [it ?] thus, [saying,] . . . . . [that I] send [thee] . . . . of sackcloth is [the father] of a con[gregation under] us and (?) [a pres]-byter (πρεσβ.) . . . . .

Verso (v. Am. 429). ... the judgement that thou] shalt (?) give . . . . . from [God[3]]. Now (μέν) if thou wilt grant repentance (μετάν.) unto him, [we] also will [grant (it)] ; but (δέ) if thou cast him forth, ... cast [him forth . . . . .

... his presbytership (-πρεσβ.) and (let them) cast him forth from the [congregation] where[in] he is. [Let] him go unto another place and live apart (ἀναχωρεῖν) and pass a year there, and let none pray with him, neither (οὐδέ) eat. And . . . . .

Fol. 20. ↑ *Recto.*

[. . .] γⁱ ⲛ[ⲧⲉϣⲧⲏⲛ ⲛ̄-]
[ⲧ]ⲙ[ⲛ]ⲧⲙⲟ[ⲛⲁⲭⲟⲥ]
ⲉⲧϩⲓⲱⲱϥ [ⲁⲩⲱ]
ⲁϥϯ ϩⲓⲱⲱ[ϥ ⲛⲟⲩ-]
ϣⲧⲏⲛ ⲛ̄ⲕⲟⲥ[ⲙⲓ-]
ⲕⲟⲛ ⲁϥⲕⲁⲁϥ ⲉⲃ[ⲟⲗ]
ⲉⲧⲣⲉϥⲃⲱⲕ' ⲁϥ-
ⲟⲩⲉϩⲥⲁϩⲛⲉ ⲇⲉ ⲟⲛ
ⲉⲛ̄ ϩⲉⲛϭⲉⲣⲟⲟⲃ' ⲁϥ-
ϩⲓⲟⲩⲉ̄ ⲉⲡⲕⲟⲩⲓ̈ ⲉⲧ[ⲛ̄-]
ⲙⲁⲩ · ⲙ̄ⲡⲛ̄ⲥⲱⲥ

]ⲧ
] ?
]. ⲛⲁϥ · ⲁⲛ[ⲉ-]
[ⲥⲛ]ⲏⲩ ⲁⲙⲁϩⲧⲉ ⲛ̄-

margin

ⁱ Perhaps ⲕⲁϩⲏ]ⲩ or ⲙⲙⲁ]ⲩ.

² Steph. Cat. § 228 (?)   ³ Am., 'from Him.'

↑ *Verso.*

[. . . .]ⲇⲉ ⲛ̄[ⲙⲟϥ
[ⲉⲧⲙⲙ]ⲧⲣⲉϥⲙⲟⲟϣ[ⲉ
[ⲙⲛⲡⲣ]ⲱⲙⲉ ⲉⲛϥ-
[ⲛ]ⲁϯ ϩⲏⲩ, ⲁⲛ ⲛ̄ⲙ-
[ⲙ]ⲁϥ · ⲉϣⲱⲡⲉ ⲇⲉ
[ⲉ]ϥϣⲁⲛⲧⲙ̄ⲥⲱ-
[ⲧ]ⲙ̄ ⲛ̄ⲥⲱⲧⲛ̄ ⲁⲗⲗⲁ
ⲛ̄ϥϣⲱⲡⲉ ϩⲛ̄ⲟⲩ-
ⲙⲛ̄ⲧⲁⲧⲥⲃⲱ,
ⲛⲟⲩϫⲉ ⲙ̄ⲙⲟϥ' ⲉ-[a]

[ⲱ] ⲡⲉⲛⲉⲓ[ⲱⲧ ⲛ̄ⲧⲟⲕ]
ⲉⲧϣⲓⲛⲉ ⲛ̄[ⲥⲁⲛⲉⲛ-]
ⲯⲩⲭⲏ ⲉⲧⲟⲩϫ̄[ⲟⲟⲩ]

margin

[a] ⲉ[ⲃⲟⲗ.

Fol. 20. *Recto* (*v.* Am. 429, 430). . . . him.   The brethren laid hold[1] on him . . . . .

. . . [the robe of] monkhood (-μον.) that was upon him [and] he put upon him [a] worldling's (κοσμικός) garment and let him go that he should depart.[2] And (δέ) he bade moreover bring staves and he beat that young(er) one. Thereafter . . . . .

Verso (*v.* Am. 430). . . . but (δέ) [counsel] him that he walk not [with a] man of whom he getteth not profit.   But (δέ) if he shall not hearken unto you, but (ἀλλά) remain unteachable, cast him [forth . . . . .

. . . [O] our fath[er,[3] thou it is] dost seek after [our] souls, to save [them.]

Here an ornament, indicating the end of a section.

---

[1] Am., 'hindered.'　　　[2] Am., *add.* to the world (*sic*).　　　[3] Am. *om.*

Fol. 21. → *Recto.*

[ⲛ]ⲟⲩⲟⲉⲓ[ϣ ⲛⲓⲙ ⲁϥ-]
ⲁⲣⲭⲉⲓ ⲛ[ᵃ
ⲛ̄ⲕⲁⲑⲏⲕⲉⲓ ⲛ̄[ⲛⲉ-]
ⲥⲛⲏⲩ· ⲡⲁⲓ̈ⲡⲉ [ⲡϣⲟ-]
ⲣ̄ⲡ̄ ⲛ̄ⲑ̄ⲣⲏⲧⲟⲛ ⲉ[ⲛ-]

ⲉϣⲁⲣⲉ ⲡⲉ]ⲛ-
[ⲉⲓ]ⲱⲧ ⲡⲁϩⲱ[ⲙⲉ]
[ⲁϩⲉⲣ]ⲁⲧϥ ⲛ̄ϩⲏⲧϥ
[ⲁⲩⲱ] ⲡⲉⲛⲉⲓⲱⲧ· ⲡⲁ-
[ϩⲱ]ⲙⲉ ϩⲱⲱϥ· ⲡⲉϥ-
[ⲁϩ]ⲉⲣⲁⲧϥ ϩⲱⲥ ⲉⲟⲩⲁ·

ⲧⲁϥϫⲟⲟϥ· ⲉⲃⲟⲗ· ϩ̄ⲛ-
ⲡⲉⲅⲣⲁⲫⲏ ϫⲉⲙⲟⲩ-
ⲧⲉ ⲉⲛⲉϩⲓⲟⲙⲉ ⲛ̄ⲣⲉϥ-
ⲧⲟⲉⲓⲧ· ⲙⲁⲣⲟⲩⲉⲓ·
ϫⲟⲟⲩ ⲛ̄ⲥⲁⲛ̄[ⲥ]ⲁⲃⲏ
ⲙⲁⲣⲟⲩⲟⲩⲱⲛ, ⲛ̄ⲣⲱⲟ[ⲩ]

margin

↑ *Verso.*

]ⲛⲧ[
] ⲁⲩⲱ ⲛ̄ⲁϣ
[ⲛ̄ϩⲉ ⲛ̄]ⲧⲱⲧ̄ⲛ̄ ⲁⲧⲉ-
[ⲧ̄ⲛ̄]ϣⲱⲡⲉ ϩⲛⲟⲩ-
[ⲙ̄]ⲛ̄ⲧϫⲁⲥⲓϩⲏⲧ·
ⲉⲁⲧⲉⲧⲛ̄ⲕⲉⲧ·ⲑⲏⲩ-
ⲧ̄ⲛ̄ ⲉⲡⲁϩⲟⲩ ⲉⲧ̄ⲙ̄-
ⲥⲱⲧ̄ⲙ̄ ⲉⲡϣⲁϫⲉ ⲙ̄-
ⲡⲛⲟⲩⲧⲉ· ⲏ̄ ⲙⲉ-
ϣⲁⲕ· ⲙ̄ⲡⲉⲧⲛ̄ⲥⲱⲧ̄ⲙ̄
ⲉⲧⲃⲉⲡϫⲟⲉⲓⲥ ⲛ̄ⲑⲉ

ⲡⲉ ⲧⲉⲛⲟⲩ [ϯϫⲱ]
ⲙ̄ⲙⲟⲥ ⲛⲏⲧ[ⲛ̄ ϫⲉ-]
ⲡⲉⲓ̈ⲛⲟⲃⲉ ⲉⲛⲧ[ⲁⲧⲉ-]
ⲧ̄ⲛ̄ⲁⲁϥ· ⲛ̄ⲥⲉⲕ[ⲁⲁϥ]

margin

Fol. 21. *Recto* (*v.* Am. 431). . . . wherein our father Pahômius was [wont to] stand, while our father Pahômius stood as if (ὡς) (he were) one . . . . .

. . . [at all] times, [he] began (ἄρχειν) [? forthwith] to instruct (κατηχεῖν [1]) the brethren. This is the first word (ῥητόν) that he spake from the scriptures (γρ.),[2] 'Call the mourning women; let them come. Send for the wise women; let them open [their] mouths . . . . .

Verso (*v.* Am. 431, 432). . . . And [how] is it ye have been in pride of heart, having turned you back, not to hear the word of God? Or (ἤ) perchance ye have not heard concerning the Lord, how . . . . .

. . . Now [I say] unto you, this sin that ye [have] done, [it] shall not be forgiven.

Fol. 22. ↑ *Recto.*

[ⲛⲁⲩ] ⲉⲣⲟϥ' ⲙ[ⲙⲓⲛ ⲙ̄-]
ⲙⲟϥ ⲉϥⲃⲏⲕ ⲉⲣⲟ[ⲩⲛ]
[ⲉ]ⲡⲉϥⲥⲱⲙⲁ · ⲟⲁⲟ
[ⲁ]ⲉ ⲟⲛ ⲟ̄ⲡⲛ̄ⲛⲟϭ ⲉⲧ-
ⲡⲟⲗⲓⲧⲉⲩⲉ ⲟ̄ⲛⲛⲉ-
ⲥⲛⲏⲩ. ⲉⲃⲟⲗ' ⲙ̄ⲡⲧⲃ̄-
ⲃⲟ [ⲙ̄]ⲡⲉⲩⲟⲏⲧ' ⲙ̄ⲛ-
[ⲡⲉⲩ]ⲥⲱⲙⲁ · ⲛⲉⲩ-
[ⲛⲁⲩ] ⲉⲟⲁⲟ ⲛ̄ϭⲱⲗⲡ
[ⲉⲃⲟⲗ] ⲟⲓⲟⲟⲣⲁⲙⲁ ·
margin

→ *Verso.*

[. . . .]ⲟ ⲛϭⲉ[. . .]
[. . . .]ⲉⲡⲉⲓⲟⲱⲃ
ⲛ̄ⲁⲡⲓⲥⲧⲟⲛ ⲛ̄ⲛⲁ-
ⲟⲣⲁϥ' ⲉⲧⲣⲉϥϣ[ⲱ-]
ⲡⲉ ⲛⲉϥⲛ̄ⲧⲟⲟ[ⲧϥ̄]
ⲙⲉⲛ, ⲟⲱⲥ ⲣⲱⲙⲉ ⲛ̄-
ⲧⲉ ⲡⲛⲟⲩⲧⲉ. ⲁⲗⲗ[ⲁ]
ⲟⲙ̄ⲡⲉⲓⲟⲱⲃ' [.]ⲉ.[
ⲧⲥ . . . . . [
ⲉⲣⲟϥ · ⲁⲥϣⲱ[ⲡⲉ]
ⲁⲉ ⲛ̄ⲧⲉⲣⲟⲩ[
margin

margin | margin

Fol. 22. *Recto* (*v.* Am. 432). . . . [saw?] it[3] [him]self, entering into his body (σῶμα). And (δέ) many also of the elders (*lit.* great-ones) that lived religiously (πολιτεύειν) among the brethren, by reason of the purity [of] their heart and [their] body (σῶ.), beheld many revelations and visions (ὅραμα) . . . . .

---

[1] That this is the true equivalent of the persistent Coptic form ⲕⲁⲑⲏⲅⲉⲓ is clear from *e.g.* Luke i. 4, Acts xviii. 25, 1 Cor. xiv. 19.

[2] Jer. ix. 17.

[3] The pronoun being masculine, must refer to πνεῦμα, not to ψυχή.

Verso (*v.* Am. 433?). . . . this faithless (ἄπιστος) act (*lit.* thing) before him, that it should befall. He was indeed (μέν) with him (*or* me *or* them) as a man of God; yet (ἀλλά) in this matter . . . . . him. And (δέ) it befell, after they had . . . .

Fol. 23.　→ *Recto* (?).　　　　↑ *Verso* (?).

	ε-]		
	ϣⲱⲡ[ⲉ ⲉϥϣⲁⲛ-]		
	ⲝⲟⲟⲥ ⲛ[ⲁⲓ ⲝⲉ-]		
	ⲱⲛϩ. [	] ⲉϥⲉⲓⲣⲉ	
]ⲱⲡⲉ	ⲝⲉϯⲛⲁ[ⲱⲛϩ ⲉϥ-]	[ⲙ̅ⲡⲙⲉⲉⲩⲉ] ⲙ̅ⲡϣⲁⲝⲉ	ⲡⲉ[
]ⲧⲕⲁ	ϣⲁⲛⲝⲟⲟ[ⲥ ⲝⲉ	[ⲉⲧⲥⲏϩ ϩ̅ⲙ̅]ⲡⲉⲩⲁⲅ-	ⲛⲁⲩ [
	margin	[ⲅⲉⲗⲓⲟⲛ] ⲝⲉⲙⲉⲣⲉⲛⲉ-	ⲉⲃⲟⲗ [
		margin	

Fol. 23. *Recto* (?) (*v.* Am. 433?). . . . 'If so be [he should] say unto me, Live, ...[1] that I shall [live. But (δέ)] if he should say . . . . .

Verso (?). . . . remem[bering] the word [that is written in] the Gos[pel],[2] 'Love . . . . .

Fol. 24.　↑ *Recto.*

	ⲁⲥϩⲉ [ⲉⲝ̅ⲙ̅ⲡⲕⲁϩ]
	ⲁⲩⲱ ⲉⲁ[ⲩⲝⲟⲟⲥ ⲛⲁϥ]
	ϩ̅ⲙ̅ϩⲟⲣ[ⲁⲙⲁ ⲝⲉ-]
]ⲓ	ϯ ϩⲧⲏⲕ' ⲉⲡ[ⲉⲓϣⲁ-]
]ϥ̅.·	ⲝⲉ ⲝⲉϥⲛⲁⲝⲱ[ⲕ']
]ⲱ̣	ⲉⲃⲟⲗ' ⲉⲝⲱⲕ' ⲙ̅ⲡ-
	ⲡ̅ⲥⲁⲟⲩⲟⲩⲟⲉⲓϣ·
	ⲁⲩⲱ ⲛ̅ⲧⲟϥ ⲙ̅ⲡ-
	ⲡ̅[ⲥ]ⲱⲥ ⲁⲩⲧⲁⲙⲟϥ
	[ⲉⲃⲟⲗ ϩⲓⲧⲙ̅ⲡ]ⲉⲡ̅ⲡⲁ̅

---

[1] Perhaps 'I know', 'I believe', though Am.

[2] There is, I think, only one phrase in the

Gospels beginning with ⲙⲉⲣⲉ ⲛⲉ-, *viz.* Matt. v.

[. . ϩορ]ⲁⲙⲁ ⲁϥⲣ-
[ⲡⲙ]ⲉⲉⲩⲉ ⲙ̅ⲡⲉⲛ-
[ⲧⲁ]ϥ̅ⲛⲁⲩ ⲉⲣⲟϥ ϩⲙ̅ⲡ-
ⲡϩⲟⲣⲁⲙⲁ' ϩⲓⲧⲙ̅-
ⲡϫⲟⲉⲓⲥ ⲙ̅ⲡⲉϩⲟⲟⲩ
ⲉⲛⲉⲩⲕⲁⲑⲏⲕⲉⲓ ⲙ̅-
ⲙⲟϥ ⲛ̅ϩⲏⲧϥ̅ ⲉⲣ-
ⲭⲣⲓⲥⲧⲉⲓⲁⲛⲟⲥ ⲛ̅-
ⲑⲉ ⲉⲛⲧⲁϥⲛⲁⲩ
[ϩ]ⲙ̅ⲡϭⲱⲗⲡ̅ ⲉⲃⲟⲗ'
[ⲉ]ⲧⲙ̅ⲙⲁⲩ ⲉϥ̅ⲱ-
[ⲧ]ⲉ ⲛ̅ⲧⲡⲉ' ⲉⲛⲧⲁⲥ-
ⲉⲓ' ⲉϩⲣⲁⲓ̈ ⲉϫⲱϥ·
[ⲙ]ⲛ̅ⲛ̅ⲥⲱⲥ ⲉⲁⲥⲥⲱ-
[ⲟⲩ]ϩ ⲁⲥⲣⲟⲩⲧⲁϭ ⲛ̅-

[ϫⲉⲡ]ⲉⲓⲧ[ⲁϭ ⲛ̅ⲉⲃⲓⲱ
[ⲉ]ⲛⲧⲁ[ϥⲥⲱⲟⲩϩ ⲉ-
ϩⲟⲩⲛ ϩⲛ[ⲧⲉⲕϭⲓϫ
ⲁϥϩⲉ·ᵃ ⲉϫⲛⲡ[ⲕⲁϩ ⲛⲁⲓ-]
ⲛⲉ ⲛⲉⲭⲁⲣ[ⲓⲥⲙⲁ
ⲧⲏⲣⲟⲩ ⲉⲧⲏ[ᵇ
ϣⲱⲡⲉ ⲛⲁⲕ [ϩⲓⲧⲙ̅-]
ⲡϫⲟⲉⲓⲥ· ⲁⲩⲱ [ⲟⲛ]
ⲥⲉⲛⲁϣⲱⲡⲉ ϩⲱ-
ⲟⲩ ⲛ̅ⲛⲉⲕⲥⲏⲩ
ⲉⲧⲉⲡⲁⲓ̈ⲡⲉ ⲡⲏ[ⲁϩ
ⲉⲩϣⲁⲛϣⲱⲡⲉ
ϩⲙ̅ⲡⲉϫⲡⲟ' ⲛ̅ⲕ[ⲉ-]
ⲥⲟⲡ' ⲉϥⲧⲃ̅ⲃⲏⲩ
ⲉⲃⲟⲗ' ϩⲙ̅ⲙⲛ̅ⲧϫ[ⲁ-]

margin

ᵃ ⲁϥ- must refer to ⲧⲁϭ, ⲁⲥ- in line 1 to ⲉⲓⲱⲧⲉ.
ᵇ ⲉⲛⲧ[ⲁⲩ] is inevitable here. Am. (G ⲣⲙ̅ⲏ) لك ماروا التى.

→ *Verso.*

]ⲉⲓ·
ⲛ]ⲁⲙⲉ' ⲛⲉ[ⲧ-]ᵃ
[ⲧⲃ̅ⲃⲟ ⲙ̅]ⲡⲉⲩϩⲏⲧ'
[ⲉⲙⲁ]ⲧⲉᵇ ⲉⲃⲟⲗ' ϩⲙ̅ⲙⲉ-
[ⲉⲩⲉ] ⲛⲓⲙ' ⲙ̅ⲡⲟⲛⲏ-
ⲣⲟⲛ· ⲉⲩⲇⲓⲁⲕⲣⲓⲛⲉ
ⲛ̅ⲧⲙⲏⲧⲉ ⲙ̅ⲡⲉ-
ⲧⲛⲁⲛⲟⲩϥ' ⲙ̅ⲛ̅ⲡ-
ⲡⲉⲑⲟⲟⲩ· [ⲁⲩⲱ ⲁⲥ-]
ϣⲱⲡ[ⲉ ⲛⲉⲣⲉⲟⲩ-]
ϣⲏ[ⲣⲉ ϣⲏⲙ ϣ[ⲱ-]

ᵃ Or ⲛⲉⲧⲛⲁⲧⲃ̅ⲃⲟ or ⲛⲉⲧⲧⲃ̅ⲃⲏⲩ ϩⲙ̅-.   ᵇ Doubtful ; equivalent to من هذه باسرع.

ne[   ]ⲩ · [ⲛ̄ⲧⲁⲙⲛⲧ[ⲉ ⲁ̄ⲛ̄ⲡⲉ-]

          ]ⲛⲉⲥⲱϥ’   ⲧⲛⲁⲛⲟⲩϥ [ⲁ̄ⲛ̄-]

[ⲟⲙⲡⲉϥ]ⲓⲛⲉ ⲛ̄ⲧⲟϥ   ⲡⲡⲉⲑⲟⲟⲩ · [ⲡⲉ-]

         ] ⲛ̄ⲧⲉⲣⲟⲩⲛ̄-   ⲧⲁⲙⲙⲁⲩ ⲇⲉ ⲛ̄ⲧ[ⲉ-]

[ⲧϥ] ⲉⲡⲙⲁ ⲉϣⲁⲩ-   ⲣⲉϥⲛⲁⲩ ⲉⲡⲟⲩ-

[ⲟⲩ]ⲱⲙ’ ⲛ̄ⲟⲏⲧϥ ⲛ̄-   ⲣⲟⲧ’ ⲙ̄ⲡⲉϥϩⲏⲧ
                                          sic
[ϭⲓ] ⲛⲉⲥⲛⲏⲩ ⲉⲧ-   ⲉⲧⲣⲉϥⲇⲓⲁⲕⲣⲓⲛⲉ

ϣⲱⲛⲉ ⲉⲧⲁⲙⲟϥ ·   ⲙ̄ⲡϣⲏⲣⲉ ϣⲏⲙ’

ⲁ̄ⲡⲥⲟⲛ ⲉⲧⲙ̄ⲙⲁⲩ   ⲕⲁⲗⲱⲥ· ⲁⲩⲱ ⲉϥ-

ⲉⲧⲇⲓⲁⲕⲟⲛⲉⲓ̈ ⲉⲛⲉ-   ⲥⲟⲃⲧⲉ ⲛⲁϥ ⲛⲉϥ[ⲁ-]

ⲥⲛⲏⲩ, ⲉⲟⲩⲁⲥⲕⲏⲧⲏⲥ   ϣⲁϩⲟⲙ’ⲡⲉ ϩⲣⲁⲓ̈ [ⲛ̄-]

ⲉⲙⲁⲧⲉⲡⲉ ⲛ̄ⲣⲉϥ-   ϩⲏⲧϥ̄ ⲁⲩⲱ ⲉϥ[ⲇⲓⲁ-]

ⲣϩⲟⲧⲉ ⲉⲡⲉϥⲣⲁⲛ-   ⲕⲣⲓⲛⲉ ⲉϥϫⲱ ⲙ̄-

ⲡⲉ ϯⲧⲟⲩⲉ’ ⲉⲩⲣⲉϥ-   ⲙⲟⲥ ϫⲉⲡϫⲟⲉⲓⲥ

                                          ⲟⲩ’ⲡⲉ ⲡⲉⲓ̈ⲟⲩⲣⲟ[ⲧ]

          margin

Fol. 24. *Recto* (v. Am. 434, 435). ... vision [1] (ὅραμα), and he remembered that which he had beheld in the vision (ὅρ.) from the Lord, on the day whereon he was being instructed (κατηχεῖν) towards becoming a Christian (χρ.); how he had beheld in that revelation the dew of heaven descending upon him, (how) afterwards it had collected and had become a cake of [honey .....

... and it fell [upon the ground] and it had been [said to him] in the vision (ὅρ.), 'Give heed unto this word, for it shall be fulfilled upon thee after a time.' And as for him, he was informed [by the] Spirit (πν.) that 'this [cake of honey] that did [collect] in [thy hand] and fall upon the [ground, these (sic)] are all the gifts (χάρισμα) that came to thee [from] the Lord. And they shall come also unto thy brethren, that is, the earth.[2] When they shall have become born again, being cleansed from [all] pride [of heart] .....

[1] Am. should be 'visions from the Lord, he remembered the revelation of the vision that he (? they) had seen at first, on the day whereon he had been instructed (وعظو) that he should become a Christian (مسیحی); how he had be-

held that the dew of heaven descended upon him and thereafter became in his hand a cake of honey and fell upon the ground ; and (how) it was said unto him in the vision &c.

[2] So G ⲣⲙⲛ̄, omitting Am.'s علی (435, 1).

Verso (*v.* Am. 435). . . . of[1] a truth that [purify] their hearts gre[atly (?)] from every evil (πον.) thought, discerning (διακρίνειν) between good and evil. And it befell [that a] youth [was] sick . . . . . comely [in his] appearance (?). [And] he, when they had brought [him] to the place wherein the sick brethren used to eat, to feed him, that brother[2] that served (διακονεῖν) the brethren and was very ascetic (ἀσκητής) and (God-) fearing, whose name was Titoue, being a . . . . .

. . . discerned] between good [and] evil. But (δέ) that one, when he saw the gladness of his heart that he should serve (διακονεῖν) the youth well (καλῶς) and prepare (food) for him, would sigh[3] within himself and doubt (διακρίνειν), saying, ' Lord, what is this gladness . . . . .

Fol. 25.   → *Recto.*

[ⲁⲅⲱ ⲁϥ]ⲙⲟⲩⲧⲉ ⲉ-
[ⲕⲉⲟⲩ]ⲁ ⲟⲛ︦ⲛⲉⲥⲛⲏⲩ
[ⲁϥ]ϫⲟⲟⲅϥ ⲛ︦ⲙⲙⲁϥ ·
[ⲁⲥ]ϣⲱⲡⲉ ⲛ︦ⲧⲉⲣⲟⲩ-
ⲣ︦ⲡⲁϣⲉ ⲛ︦ⲧⲉ⳿ⲣ︦ⲏ   *sic*
ⲙ︦ⲙⲟⲟϣⲉ ⲁϥ[ϭ]ⲱ-
ϣ︦ⲧ ⲁⲩ[ⲱ] ⲉⲓ[ⲥ ⲟⲩ]ϩ︦ⲣ︦-
ϣⲓⲣⲉ ⲁϥⲉⲓ⳿ ⲉ[ⲃⲟⲗ⳿] ⲟⲛ︦-
ϩⲉⲛϣⲟⲛⲧⲉ ⲕⲁⲧⲁ
ⲑⲉ ⲉⲛⲧⲁϥϣⲁϫⲉ ⲛ︦ⲙ-
ⲙⲁϥ ⲛ︦ϭⲓ ⲡⲉⲛⲉⲓⲱⲧ
ⲡⲁϩⲱⲙⲉ · ⲛ︦ⲧⲉ-
ⲣⲉϥⲛⲁⲩ ⲁⲉ ⲉⲣⲟϥ⳿ ⲁϥ-
ⲧⲁⲙⲉ⳿ ⲡ︦ⲥⲟⲛ ⲉⲧⲙ︦ⲟ-
ⲟϣⲉ ⲛ︦ⲙⲙⲁϥ ⲉⲑⲉ
ⲉⲛⲧⲁϥϫⲱⲕ ⲉⲃⲟⲗ⳿

ⲙ︦ⲛ︦-]
ⲛ︦ⲥⲱⲥ ⲁϥⲕ[ⲧⲟϥ⳿ ⲁϥ-]
ⲃⲱⲕ · ⲁⲥϣ[ⲱⲡⲉ]
ⲁⲉ ⲙ︦ⲛ︦ⲥⲁⲛⲁⲓ [ⲉϥ-]
ϣⲗⲏⲗ⳿ ⲛ︦ϭⲓ ⲡⲉⲛⲉⲓ-
ⲱⲧ ⲡⲁϩⲱⲙⲉ ⲉⲓⲥ
ⲟⲩⲁⲅⲅⲉⲗⲟⲥ ⲛ︦ⲧⲉ
ⲡϫⲟ[ⲉⲓⲥ] ⲁϥⲟⲩⲱⲛ[ϩ︦]
ⲛⲁϥ [ⲉ]ⲃⲟⲗ ⲡⲉϫⲁϥ
ⲛⲁϥ · ϫ[ⲉⲟⲩ⳿ ⲡⲉⲧⲕ︦-]
ⲛⲁⲉⲣⲏ[ⲧ ⲙ︦ⲙⲟϥ ⲉ-]
ⲧⲁⲁϥ⳿ ⲙ︦ⲙ[ⲡ︦ⲧⲛⲁ⳿]
ⲉⲣϣⲁⲛⲡ[ϫⲟⲉⲓⲥ]
ⲕⲱⲗϭⲉ⳿ ⲛ︦[ⲧⲟⲣϭⲏ]
ϩ︦ⲙ︦ⲡⲧⲣⲉϥ[ϣⲱϣ︦ⲧ]
ⲛ︦ⲛ︦ⲃⲁⲣⲃⲁⲣ[ⲟⲥ · ⲛ︦-]

[1] Am. should be, ' And thus they of a truth shall become pure in their hearts from all this and from every evil thought.'

[2] Am. should be, ' And the brother that served the sick brethren, his name was Didûye, and he

was pious and discerned (the nature of) his thoughts aright. And when he saw &c.'

[3] Am. should be, ' He sighed to himself alone and set about doubting within himself, saying, ' O Lord, what is this gladness &c.'

ⲛ̄ϭⲓ ⲡϣⲁϫⲉ ⲉⲛ ⲧ̄   ⲧⲟϥ ⲇⲉ ⲡⲉϫⲁϥ ϫⲉ·
ⲧⲁϥϫⲟⲟϥ· ⲁⲩⲱ ⲟⲛ   ϯⲛⲁϫⲟⲟⲩ ⲉⲧⲉⲕⲕⲗⲏ
ⲁϥⲧⲁⲙⲟⲟⲩ ϫⲉⲁϥ   ⲥⲓⲁ ⲛ̄ⲧⲡⲟⲗⲓⲥ ⲉⲛ
ϩⲱⲛ ⲉⲧⲟⲟⲧϥ̄ ⲉϥϫⲱ   ⲧⲁⲩϣⲟⲗⲥ̄ ⲛ̄ϭⲓ ⲛ̄
ⲙⲙⲟⲥ ϫⲉⲛ̄ⲡⲣ̄ⲣⲟ   ⲃⲁⲣⲃⲁⲣⲟⲥ ⲛ̄ⲟⲩⲁⲡⲥ̄
[ⲧ]ⲉ· ϥⲛⲁϣⲑ̄ⲙ̄ϭⲟⲙ   ⲛ̄ϣⲉ· ⲛ̄ⲥⲟⲩⲟ· ⲙ̄ⲡⲛ̄
[ϭ]ⲁⲣ· ⲁⲛ ⲛ̄ⲣ̄ⲗⲁⲁⲩ ⲙ̄   ϩⲉⲛϫⲱⲙⲉ ⲙ̄ⲡⲛ̄
[ⲡ]ⲉⲑⲟⲟⲩ ⲛⲏⲧⲛ̄·   ϩⲉⲛⲕⲉⲓϩⲟⲥ ⲉⲩⲣ̄ⲭ

margin

↑ *Verso.*

                                                    ⲛ̄]

[ⲡⲟⲩ]ⲱ· ⲉⲛⲉⲥⲛⲏⲩ   ϣⲟⲣⲡ .[. . . ⲧⲥⲟ]
[ⲙ̄]ⲡⲉⲛⲧⲁϥⲛⲁⲩ   ⲛⲁⲛ· ⲛ̄ⲥ[ᵇ   ⲙ̄]
[ⲉⲣ]ⲟϥ ⲉϥⲛⲁϣⲱⲡⲉ   ⲛ̄ϥⲟⲩⲱϣ· ⲛ̄[ⲧⲉ]
ϩⲁⲑⲏ ⲉⲙⲡⲁⲧϥ̄   ⲣⲟⲩⲛⲁⲩ ⲇⲉ ϫⲉ[ⲙ̄]
ϣⲱⲡⲉ· ⲁⲩⲱ ⲛ̄   ⲛ̄ϥⲥⲱⲧⲙ̄ ⲛ̄ⲥ[ⲱ]
ⲧⲉⲓ̈ϩⲉ ⲁⲩ[ϭⲟ]ⲧⲡ̄   ⲟⲩ [ⲁⲩ]ϥⲓ ⲛ̄ⲟⲩⲙⲁ
ⲛ̄ϭⲓ ⲛ̄ⲃ[ⲁⲣⲃ]ⲁⲣⲟⲥ   ⲕⲟⲧ ⲉ]ⲩϫⲱ ⲙ̄ⲙⲟⲥ
ⲙ̄ⲡⲉϥⲣⲁⲥⲧⲉ ⲁⲩⲱ   ⲛⲁ[ϥ ϫ]ⲉⲟⲩⲱⲧⲙ̄
[ⲁ]ⲩⲕ[ⲧⲱⲟ]ⲩ ⲉⲡⲁϩⲟⲩ   ⲉⲃⲟ[ⲗ] ⲉϣⲱⲡⲉ ⲙ̄
[ⲕⲁⲧⲁ ⲑ]ⲉ ⲉⲛⲧⲁⲩ   ⲙⲟⲛ ⲧ̄ⲛ̄ⲛⲁⲕⲟⲛ
[ϫⲟⲟⲥᵃ] ⲛ̄ⲙⲙⲁϥ: ⲥⲕ· ⲁⲩⲱ ⲛ̄ⲧⲉⲣⲉϥ
[ϩⲟⲥⲟⲛ] ⲇⲉ ⲉⲩϫⲣⲁ   ⲣ̄ϩⲟⲧⲉ ϫⲉⲛ̄ⲛⲉⲩ
[ⲉⲓⲧ ⲛ̄]ϭⲓ ⲛ̄ⲃⲁⲣⲃⲁ   ⲕⲱⲡ̄ⲥ̄ ⲙ̄ⲙⲟϥ· ⲁϥ
[ⲣⲟⲥ] ⲁⲩϩⲉ· ⲉⲩⲙⲟⲛⲁ   ⲟⲩⲱⲧⲛ̄ ⲉⲃⲟⲗ·
ⲭⲟⲥ ⲉϥⲁⲛⲁⲭⲱⲣⲉⲓ·   ⲁⲩⲱ ⲙ̄ⲡⲛ̄ⲥⲱⲥ ⲁϥ
ⲛ̄ⲟⲩⲙⲁ· ⲁⲩⲁⲓⲭⲙⲁ   ⲧⲥⲟⲟⲩ ϣⲁⲛⲧⲟⲩ

ⲛ̄ⲧ[ⲟϥ ⲇⲉ ⲙ], or ⲛ̄[ϣⲟⲣⲡ ⲙ̄[ⲡⲁⲧ ̄ⲕ̄ⲧⲥⲟ].

ⲗⲱⲧⲓⲍⲉ ⲛ̄ⲙⲟϥ·
ⲁⲩⲱ ⲁⲥϣⲱⲡⲉ ⲛ̄ⲟⲩ-
ⲥⲟⲡ· ⲛ̄ⲧⲉⲣⲟⲩⲉⲓ· ⲝⲉ-
ⲉⲩⲛⲁⲥⲱ· ⲛ̄ⲟⲩⲏⲣⲡ̄
ⲡⲉⲝⲁⲩ ⲉϧⲟⲩⲛ ⲉϧⲣⲁϥ
ⲝⲉⲙⲟⲣⲕ̄ ⲛ̄ⲧⲟⲩⲱ-
ⲧ̄ϧ ⲉⲣⲟⲛ· ⲁⲩⲱ ⲛ̄ⲧⲉ-

ϯϧⲉ· ⲁⲩⲱⲃⲩϣ ⲁϥ-
ⲡⲱⲧ· ⲛ̄ϭⲓ ⲛ̄ⲙⲟ-
ⲛⲁⲭⲟⲥ· ⲁⲩⲱ ⲙ̄ⲡ-
ⲛ̄ⲥⲁⲛⲁⲓ̈ ⲁⲡⲉⲩϧⲏⲧᵃ
ⲟⲩⲱϣϥ ϧⲱⲥⲧ[ⲉ ⲉ-]
ⲧ̄ⲙ̄ⲧⲣⲉϥⲉϣϭⲙ̄-
ϭⲟⲙ· ⲉⲡⲱⲣϣ̄ ⲉⲃ[ⲟⲗ]

margin

ᵃ So my copy ; but ⲁⲡⲉϥ- is required.

Fol. 25. *Recto* (*v.* Am. 438). . . . [And? he] called another of the brethren and sent him with him. It befell, when they had done half of the journey (*lit.* road of walking), he looked and lo,[1] a youth came forth from some thorn-bushes, even as our father Pahômius had said unto him. But (δέ) when he beheld him, he told the brother that walked with him how the word that he (*sc.* P.) had spoken was fulfilled. And moreover he told him that he had bidden him, saying, Be not afraid, for (γάρ) he shall not be able to do you[2] any ill . . . . .

. . . After]wards he turned about and departed. And (δέ) it befell thereafter, as our father Pahômius prayed, lo, an angel (ἄγ.) of the Lord appeared unto him and said unto him, '[What[3]] wilt [thou] vow [to] give in [charity], if so be the [Lord] hinder (κωλύειν) [the wrath (ὀργή)], in that He [impede] the barbarians (βάρβ.)?' And (δέ) he said, 'I will send unto the church (ἐκκ.) of the city (πόλις) which the barbarians (βάρβ.) have laid waste many (*lit.* an amount of) hundred(weight)[4] of corn, with books and other things (εἶδος) [whereof] they have ne[ed (χρεία) . . . . .

Verso (*v.* Am. 439). . . . related to the brethren what he had seen that should befall ere it had befallen.[5] And thus were the barbarians (βάρβ.) conquered on the morrow and were driven back, even (κατά) as it had been said unto him.[6] And while yet (ὅσον δέ) the barbarians (βάρβ.) were

---

[1] Am. should be, 'they looked and lo (اذا), a youth came forth from the bushes.' (The word, two lines above, translated *cilice*, is not ح but اسلم 'spade'.)

[2] Am. *om.* you.

[3] Am. (Ac. 73 *infra*), 'What wilt thou vow

[ ] (تنذر) to give as charity, if the Lord should calm (هدا) the (*sic*) wrath &c.'

[4] Am., 'an hundred artabae.'

[5] Am. *sic.*

[6] Am., 'as the angel had said unto him.'

victorious, they found a monk living apart ($\mu o \nu$., $\dot{a} \nu a \chi \omega \rho \epsilon \hat{i} \nu$) in a (certain) place and they took him captive ($a \dot{i} \chi \mu a \lambda \omega \tau \dot{i} \zeta \epsilon \iota \nu$).[1] And it befell on a time, when they came and would drink wine, they said unto him, 'Gird thyself[2] and pour (wine) for us.' And when . . . . .

. . . ere [thou give] us [to drink.'][3] But ($\delta \acute{\epsilon}$)] he (?) would not.[4] And ($\delta \acute{\epsilon}$) when they saw that he hearkened not unto them, they took a spear,[5] saying unto him, 'Pour forth[6]; if not, we will slay thee.' And when he was afraid lest they should slay him, he poured forth. And afterwards he gave them to drink until they were drunken and slept; and the monk ($\mu o \nu$.) fled.[7] And thereafter his heart was broken, so that ($\ddot{\omega} \sigma \tau \epsilon$) he was not able to stretch forth . . . . .

Fol. 26.   ↑ *Recto*.

[ⲛⲁϣ] ⲛ̅ⲣ[ⲉ ⲧ̅ⲛⲁⲥⲟⲡⲥ̅]
[ⲙ̅ⲡ]ⲉⲛⲧⲁⲓⲁⲣⲏ[ⲁ′ ⲙ̅-]
ⲙⲟϥ· ϥ[ⲥ]ⲏϩ′ ⲅⲁⲣ ϫⲉ
[ⲡ]ⲉⲧⲙⲁⲁⲣⲛⲁ′ ⲙ̅-
[ⲙ]ⲟⲓ̈ ⲧ̅ⲛⲁⲁⲣⲛⲁ′ ⲙ̅-
ⲙⲟϥ· ⲁϥⲙⲉⲕⲙⲟⲩ-
ⲕ̅ϥ ϫⲉ ⲟⲛ ϩⲣⲁⲓ̈ ⲛ̅ϩⲏ-
ⲧϥ ⲉϥϫⲱ ⲙ̅ⲙⲟⲥ ϫⲉ-
ⲁⲓ̈ⲥⲱⲧⲙ̅ ϫⲉⲟⲩⲛ̅ ⲟ[ⲩ-]
ⲣⲱⲙⲉ ⲛ̅ⲧⲉ ⲡ[ⲛⲟⲩ-]
ⲧⲉ ⲟ′ ⲛ̅ⲉⲓⲱⲧ′ [ⲛ̅ⲧⲕⲟⲓ-]
ⲛⲱⲛⲓⲁ ⲛ̅ⲧ[ⲁ]ⲃⲏ-
ⲛⲏⲥⲉ ϫⲉⲡⲁ[ϩ]ⲱⲙⲉ
ⲧ̅ⲛⲁⲧⲱⲟⲩⲛ ⲛ̅ⲧⲁ-
ⲃⲱⲕ′ ϣⲁⲣⲟϥ ⲛ̅ⲧⲁ-

ⲙ̅ⲙⲁ[ⲩ ϣⲁⲛⲧⲁ-]
ⲡⲁⲛ[ⲧⲁ ⲉⲣⲟⲕ ⲛ̅ϣⲟ-]

[1] Am. 439, 2 (G ⲣ̅ⲡ̅), read ﻉﻣﺤ 'captured him'.
[2] Am., 'thy middle.'
[3] Or 'and afterwards give us to drink'. Am. should be 'Sacrifice unto our gods ere thou give us to drink.'
[4] Am., 'and he did not.'

[5] Lemm, *KKS*. xlv, p. 403, accepts Peyron's ⲙⲁⲕⲱⲧ = $\tau \acute{a} \phi \rho o s$ (Mic. v. 6); but that the usual meaning is there the correct one is shown by Aquila's λόγχη.
[6] Am., 'Raise an offering unto our gods.'
[7] Am., 'arose and fled.'

ⲧⲁⲙⲟⲩ⳿ ⲉⲑⲉ⳿ ⲧⲏⲣⲥ̅
ⲉⲛⲧⲁⲓ̈ⲁⲁⲥ· ⲉϣⲱ-
ⲡⲉ ⲙⲉⲛ, ⲉϥϣⲁⲛ-
ϯ ⲙⲉⲧⲁⲛⲟⲓⲁ ⲛⲁⲓ̈,
ϯⲡⲓⲥⲧⲉⲩⲉ ϫⲉⲡϫⲟ-
ⲉⲓⲥ ⲛⲁϯ ⲛⲁⲓ̈ · ⲉϣⲱ-
ⲡⲉ ⲇⲉ ⲟⲛ ⲉϥϣⲁⲛ-
ϫⲟⲟⲥ ϫⲉⲙ̅ⲛ̅ⲧⲕ̅ⲙⲉ[a]

ⲣ̅ⲡ̅ ⲛ[ϥ̅ⲧⲥⲁⲃⲟⲓ ⲉ-]
ⲡⲱⲣϫ̅ [ⲙ̅ⲡϩⲱⲃ·]
ⲡⲉϫⲁ[ϥ ⲛⲁϥ ϫⲉⲱ⳿]
ⲡⲧⲁⲗ[ⲁⲓⲡⲱⲣⲟⲥ]
ⲙ̅ⲡⲓ[ⲥⲁⲧⲣⲉⲡⲁⲅ-]
ⲅⲉⲗⲟⲥ ⲙ̅ⲡϫ[ⲟⲉⲓⲥ]
ⲁϩ⳿ⲉ ⲣⲁⲧϥ̅ ϩⲓϫ[ⲱⲕ]
ⲉⲣⲉⲡⲉⲕⲗⲟⲙ⳿ [ϩⲓ̅-]

margin

^a ⲙⲉⲧⲁⲛⲟⲓⲁ.

→ *Verso.*

[. . . . ⲁⲩⲱ] ⲁⲛ[ⲟⲕ]
[ϩ]ⲱ ⲛⲉⲙⲙⲁⲩ [ϩⲙ̅-]
ⲡⲙⲁⲩ ⲉ[ⲧ]ⲉⲣⲉⲡ[ϫⲁ-]
ϫⲉ ⲛⲁⲕⲁⲧⲏⲅ[ⲟ-]
ⲣⲉⲓ ⲙ̅ⲙⲟⲕ·
Ⲁⲩⲱ ⲁⲥϣⲱⲡⲉ ⲛ̅-
ⲧⲁⲣⲭⲏ ⲛ̅ⲧⲉⲣⲉϥ-
ⲧⲱϣ ⲛ̅ⲑⲉⲟⲇⲱ-
ⲣⲟⲥ ⲉⲧⲣⲉϥϣⲱⲡⲉ
[ⲛⲉⲓ]ⲱⲧ⳿ ⲉⲧⲥⲟⲟⲩ-
[ϩⲥ̅ ⲛ̅]ⲧⲁ[ⲃ]ⲛⲛⲥⲉ
[ⲁⲩⲱ] ⲛⲧⲟϥ ⲑⲉⲟ-
ⲇⲱⲣⲟⲥ ⲉϥⲥⲟⲟⲩⲛ
ϫⲉϣⲁϥϣⲁϫⲉ
ⲛ̅ϭⲓ ⲡⲉⲛⲉⲓⲱⲧ
ⲡⲁϩⲟⲙⲉ ⲙ̅ⲙⲉⲛ-
ⲛⲉ ⲉⲛⲉⲥⲛⲏⲩ, ϩⲙ̅-
ⲡϣⲁϫⲉ ⲙ̅ⲡⲛⲟⲩ-

[ϩⲱⲛ[a] ⲉⲧⲟⲟ]ⲧϥ̅ ⲉⲧ-
[ⲣⲉϥⲛⲥⲧⲉ]ⲩⲉ ⲙ̅-
[ⲙⲛⲉ ⲁⲩ]ⲱ ⲉⲧⲙ̅-
[ⲟⲩⲉⲙ ⲗⲁⲁ]ⲩ ⲛ̅ⲕⲁ⳿
[ⲉϥⲡⲟⲥⲉ ⲭ]ⲱⲣⲓⲥ ⲁ-

^a Completion of first three lines uncertain, as Am. differs somewhat.

ⲛⲁⲥⲕⲏ ⲛ̄ϣⲱⲡⲉ·　　　　　ⲧⲉ· ⲛⲉϣⲁϥⲥⲡⲟⲩ-

[. . .] . ⲣⲁϲⲓϲᵃ ⲛⲁϥ　　　　ⲁⲁⲍⲉ ⲁⲉⲡⲉ ⲙⲙ-

[ⲭⲉ]ⲕϣⲁⲛⲉⲓⲣⲉ ⲕⲁ-　　　ⲛ̄ⲥⲁⲧⲣⲉϥⲟⲩⲱ· ⲉϥ-

[ⲧⲁ ⲧ]ⲉ̈ⲓϩⲉ· ⲛⲉⲧⲟⲩ-　　　ⲉⲓⲣⲉ ⲙ̄ⲡⲉϥϩⲱⲃ·

[ⲁⲁϥ] ⲛⲁϣⲱⲡⲉ ⲛ̄-　　　ⲛⲉϥⲧⲁⲗⲉ̄ ⲧⲙⲏᵇ

margin

ᵃ Probably [ⲁⲩⲱ] ⲁϥⲭⲟⲟⲥ (Am. ﻭﻗﺎﻝ).　　ᵇ Perhaps followed by ⲅⲁⲣⲡⲉ (Am. ﺍﻻﻥ ﻛﺎﻥ).

Fol. 26. *Recto* (*v.* Am. 439, 440). How [shall I entreat] Him that I have denied ($\dot{a}\rho\nu\hat{a}\sigma\theta a\iota$)? For ($\gamma\acute{a}\rho$) it is written,[1] Whosoever shall deny ($\dot{a}\rho$.) me, him will I deny ($\dot{a}\rho$.).' And ($\delta\acute{\epsilon}$) then he thought within himself, saying, 'I have heard that there is a man of God (that) is father of the community ($\kappa o\iota\nu\omega\nu\acute{\iota}a$) of Tabennêse, namely Pahômius. I will arise and[2] go to him and will tell him of all that I have done. If so be ($+\mu\acute{\epsilon}\nu$) that he give me repentance ($\mu\epsilon\tau$.), I believe ($\pi\iota\sigma\tau\epsilon\acute{\upsilon}\epsilon\iota\nu$) that the Lord shall give (it) me. But ($\delta\acute{\epsilon}$) if so be that he say, There is not for thee repentance ($\mu\epsilon\tau$.) . . . . .

. . . there [is not repentance for me until I] meet with ($\dot{a}\pi a\nu\tau\hat{a}\nu$) [thee[3]] first and thou [show me] the certainty [of the matter.'] He said [unto him, 'O] wretch[ed one ($\tau a\lambda a\acute{\iota}\pi\omega\rho o\varsigma$)], after [that the an]gel ($\ddot{a}\gamma$.)[4] of the Lord had stood by [thee], the crown being [in . . . . .

Verso (*v.* Am. 440). . . . [bade] him to [fast (? $\nu\eta\sigma\tau\epsilon\acute{\upsilon}\epsilon\iota\nu$) daily[5]] and not to [eat aught] of things [cooked], save by ($\chi\omega\rho\acute{\iota}\varsigma$) necessity ($\dot{a}\nu\acute{a}\gamma\kappa\eta$) of sickness. And he said unto him,[6] 'If thou act in this wise, the saints shall be . . . . .

. . . And] I likewise with them, [in] the hour when the enemy shall accuse[7] ($\kappa a\tau\eta\gamma o\rho\epsilon\hat{\iota}\nu$) thee.'

And it befell, at the beginning ($\dot{a}\rho\chi\acute{\eta}$), when he had set Theodore to be father for the congregation of Tabennêse, and Theodore for his part, knowing how our father Pahômius was wont to speak daily unto the brethren the word of God, would be diligent ($\sigma\pi o\upsilon\delta\acute{a}\zeta\epsilon\iota\nu + \delta\acute{\epsilon}$), after that he had ceased to do his work, [for] he wove[8] mats, ...

[1] Matt. x. 33.

[2] Am. *sic*.

[3] Am., 'until I meet with thy paternity.'

[4] Am. *sic*.

[5] Am., 'to fast until evening daily,' for which there seems not space in the Coptic.

[6] Uncertain according to my copy.

[7] So Am., not 'rejoice'.

[8] For this use of ⲧⲁⲗⲟ, *v. Mus. Guim.* 327. 14, with Amélineau's note. Other instances: Dev. xix. 19, Isa. iii. 23, Zoega 375.

Fol. 27.   → *Recto.*

ϣⲗⲏⲗ · ⲁϥϣⲱϣⲧ
ⲁϥⲛⲁⲩ · ⲁⲩⲱ ⲉⲓⲥ ϩⲏ-
ⲛⲧⲉ ⲧϫⲟ' ⲉⲧⲥⲁⲉⲓ̈-
ⲃⲧ ⲁⲥϣⲱⲡⲉ ⲛ̄ⲑⲉ
ⲛ̄ⲟⲩⲛⲟⲩⲃ' ⲧⲏⲣⲥ̄ ·
ⲁⲩⲱ ⲡⲉⲥⲙⲟⲧ' ⲉⲛ-
ⲧⲁⲡϫⲟⲉⲓⲥ ⲟⲩⲱⲛ̄ϩ̄
ⲛⲁϥ ⲉⲃⲟⲗ ⲙ̄ⲡⲛⲁⲩ
ⲉⲧⲙ̄ⲙⲁⲩ ⲡⲁⲓ̈ⲡⲉ
ⲉⲓⲥ ⲡⲉⲥⲙⲟⲧ' ⲛ̄ⲟⲩ-
ⲛⲟϭ ⲛ̄ϧⲟ' ⲛ̄ⲑⲉ ⲛ̄ⲟⲩ-
ⲧⲣⲁⲡⲉⲍⲁ' ⲉϥⲟⲩⲟ-
ⲡ̄ϩ̄ ⲉⲃⲟⲗ' ϩⲓⲧϫⲟ ⲛ̄-
ⲛⲟⲩⲃ' ⲁⲩⲱ ⲉϥϩⲓ-
ϫⲛ̄ⲧⲉϥⲁⲡⲉ ⲛ̄ϭⲓ
ⲟⲩⲕⲗⲟⲙ' ⲉⲙⲙⲛ̄ϣⲓ
ϣⲟⲟⲡ' ⲙⲡⲉϥⲉⲟⲟⲩ ·
ⲁⲩⲱ ⲛⲉⲩϩⲓϫⲙ̄ⲡⲉ-
ⲕⲗⲟⲙ' ⲉϥⲕⲱⲧⲉ ⲛ̄-
ϭⲓ ϩⲉⲛⲉⲓⲛⲉᵈ ⲛ̄ⲙⲉ
ⲉⲛⲁϣⲉ' ⲥⲟⲩⲛ̄ⲧ[ⲟⲩ]
?   ?

]ⲗⲉ ⲉ̣ .
]ⲃ . ⲛ̄ⲑⲉ
[ⲛⲟⲩⲣⲱⲙⲉ] ⲉⲩϩⲟϫ-
[ϩⲉϫ ⲙ̄ⲙⲟϥ] ⲟⲩⲧⲱϥ'
[ⲙ̄ⲛ̄ϫⲟ ⲥ̄ⲛ̄ⲧ]ⲉᵃ ⲁⲩⲱ
[ⲛ̄ⲧⲉⲣϥϭ]ⲗⲓⲃⲉ ⲉ-
[ⲃⲟⲗ ϩ̄ⲛ̄]ⲧⲁⲡⲉⲓ̈ⲗⲏ
[ⲛ̄ⲡⲙⲁ ⲉ]ⲧ̄ⲙⲙⲁⲩ.
[ⲁϥⲉⲓ ⲉ]ϩⲣⲁⲓ̈ ⲁϥ-
[ⲡⲱⲧ ⲛⲁϥ ⲉ]ⲃⲟⲗ'ᵇ
[ϩⲛ̄   ?

ᵃ Does ⲟⲩⲧⲱϥ allow of the construction thus given it by the following words? For the reconstruction here, *cf.* Bo. 105.   ᵇ Or ⲥⲁ]ⲃⲟⲗ [ⲛ.   ᶜ ϥ has been altered, probably to ⲩ.
ᵈ ⲓ erased, leaving ⲉⲛⲉ.

↑ *Verso.*

[ⲕⲁⲓⲟⲥⲩ]ⲛⲏ ·ᵃ ⳁⲣ[ⲛ-]
ⲛⲏ · ⲡⲉⲑⲃⲃⲓⲟ' ⲛ̄-
ϩⲏⲧ · ⲧⲙ̄ⲛ̄ⲧϩⲁ-

ᵃ ⲧⲁⲓ[ⲕⲁⲓⲟⲥⲩ]ⲛⲏ = Am. البرّ.

ⲣϣⲏⲛⲧ· ⲧⲙⲛⲧ-
ⲭⲣⲏⲥⲧⲟⲥ· ⲧⲙⲛⲧ-
ⲣⲙⲣⲁϣ'· ⲧⲉⲥⲕⲣⲁ-
ⲧⲉⲓ'ⲁ· ⲡⲣⲁϣⲉ ⲟⲛ-
ⲑⲉⲗⲡⲓⲥ· ⲧⲁⲅⲁⲡⲏ·
ⲛⲉⲩϣⲟⲟⲡ' ⲇⲉ ⲙⲡⲉϥ-
ⲙⲧⲟ' ⲉⲃⲟⲗ' ⲛϭⲓ ⲛⲟϭ
ⲥⲛⲁⲩ ⲛⲁⲣⲭⲁⲅⲅⲉ-   ⲉϥϩ[
ⲗⲟⲥ ⲉⲩⲧⲁⲉⲓⲏⲩ ⲉ-   ?
ⲙⲁⲧⲉ ⲉⲛⲥⲉⲕⲱ ⲇⲉ   .   ⲍ· ϩ[
ⲁⲛ ⲉⲩϭⲱϣⲧ ⲉⲡⲉⲓ-   ⲙⲁⲣⲉ[ⲧⲉⲕϩⲟⲧⲉ [a]
ⲛⲉ ⲙⲡⲭⲟⲉⲓⲥ ⲉⲛ-   ⲭⲛⲁ[ⲣ̅ϩⲟⲧⲉ]
ⲧⲁϥⲟⲩⲱⲛϩ ⲉⲃⲟⲗ·   ϩⲏⲧ[ⲕ   ⲉϥ-]
ⲡⲉⲛⲉⲓⲱⲧ' ⲛⲁⲣⲱ-   ϣⲗⲏⲗ [ⲁⲩⲱ ⲉϥⲧⲱ-]
ⲙⲉ ⲇⲉ ⲛⲉϥϣⲗⲏⲗ'ⲡⲉ   ⲃ̅ϩ ⲉⲧ[ⲃⲉⲡⲁⲓ ⲉⲓⲥ]
ⲉϥⲧⲱⲃϩ ⲙⲡⲭⲟⲓⲥ   ϩⲏⲛⲧ[ⲉ
ⲉϥϫⲱ ⲙⲙⲟⲥ ϫⲉⲙⲁ-   ⲧ[
[ⲣ]ⲉⲧⲉⲕϩⲟⲧⲉ ⲧⲏⲣⲥ̅   ⲙ[

margin

[a] Perhaps ⲉⲓ ⲉ]ϫⲱⲡ[.

Fol. 27. *Recto* (*v.* Am. 443). ... even as (?) [1] [a man] that is straitened
between [two walls], and [since (*lit.* when) he] was oppressed (θλίβειν) by
reason of the danger (? ἀπειλή) of that place, he [went?] down and [fled?]
forth [from . . .

... whilst he] prayed. He looked and beheld and lo, the wall upon the
eastern side became all as it were of gold. And the form wherein the
Lord did then reveal Himself[2] was this: lo, the form[3] of a great face in
the likeness of a table (τράπ.), appearing upon the golden wall, and upon
its head a crown of immeasurable glory. And there were[4] upon the crown
precious stones round about, of great price . . . . .

to reconstruct a text corresponding with Am.

[2] Am. *sic.*

[4] Am., 'around the crown divers colours, like
to jewels of great price.'

Verso (*v.* Am. 443, 444). . . . righteous]ness (δικαιοσύνη), peace (εἰρήνη), humbleness of heart, longsuffering, kindness (-χρηστός), meekness, temperance (ἐγκράτεια), joy in (*sic*) hope (ἐλπίς), love.[1]   And (δέ) there were in his presence two great archangels (ἀρχάγ.), honourable exceedingly, and (δέ) they ceased not to look upon the likeness of the Lord that had been revealed.   But (δέ) our father Pahômius prayed, beseeching the Lord and saying, 'Let all Thy fear . . . . .

. . . let [Thy fear (?) . . . . . fear] Thee (?) . . . while he] prayed [and] beseeched concerning [this,] lo,[2] . . . . .

Fol. 28.   ↑ *Recto.*

[ρн є]ϥϣ[ⲁ ⲉⲝⲙ̄ⲡⲕⲁϩ]
[ⲡⲉϥ]ⲉⲓⲛⲉ ⲇⲉ ⲉ[ϥ-]
[ⲟⲩⲉ]ⲧⲟⲩⲱⲧ' ⲉⲙ[ⲁ-]
[ⲧⲉ ⲉ]ⲙⲁⲧⲉ · ⲁⲥϣⲱ-
[ⲡⲉ] ⲛ̄ⲧⲉⲣⲉⲥⲧⲁϩⲟϥ'
[ⲛ̄ϭⲓ] ⲑⲟⲧⲉ ⲁϥϩⲉ' ⲉ-
[ⲡⲉ]ⲥⲏⲧ' ⲁⲩⲱ ⲁϥⲥⲱ̄
[ⲉ]ϥϭⲱϣⲉ ϩⲓⲝⲙ̄ⲡⲕⲁϩ
[ⲛ̄ⲑ]ⲉ ⲛⲟⲩⲧⲃ̄ⲧ ⲉϥ-
[ⲟⲛ̄ϩ] ⲉϥϭⲱϣⲉ ϩⲓ-
[ⲝⲙ̄]ⲡⲕⲁϩ· ⲉⲁⲥϫⲱ-
[ⲧⲉ]ᵃ ⲛ̄]ⲛⲉϥⲙⲉⲗⲟⲥ
[ⲙⲛ̄]ⲛⲉϥϩⲁⲣⲙⲟⲥ'
[ⲙⲛ̄]ⲛⲉϥⲁⲗⲧⲕⲁⲥ
[ⲁⲩⲱ ⲡ]ⲉϥⲥⲱⲙⲁ ⲧⲏ-
[ⲣϥ̄ ⲁⲩ]ⲱ ⲧⲉϥ[ψ]ⲩⲭⲏ·
[ⲛ̄ⲧⲉⲣ]ⲉϥⲙ̄ⲕⲁϩ ⲇⲉ

ⲕ[
ϥⲓ ⲁ[ⲛ ϩⲁⲑⲟⲧⲉ ⲧⲏ-]
ⲣ̄ⲥ ⲙ̄ⲡϫ[ⲟⲉⲓⲥ ⲛ̄ⲧⲉ-]
ⲣⲉϥⲑⲗⲓⲃ[ⲉ . . . .]ᵇ
ⲁϥⲁϣⲕⲁⲕ ⲉⲃⲟⲗ ⲛ̄-]
ϩⲁϩ ⲛ̄[ⲥ]ⲟⲡ [ϫⲉⲡⲭⲟ-]
ⲉⲓⲥ. ⲛⲁ ⲛⲁⲓ · [ᶜ
ⲛ̄ⲧⲉⲩⲛⲟⲩ ⲁ[ⲥⲙⲟⲟ-]
ϣⲉ ⲕⲟⲩⲓ̈ ⲕⲟⲩⲓ̈ [ⲛ̄ϭⲓ]
ⲧⲁⲕⲧⲓⲛ' ⲛ̄ⲑ[ⲟⲧⲉ]
ⲁⲥⲕⲟⲧⲉ ⲉⲡⲉⲥ[ⲙⲁ'·]
ⲙ̄ⲛ̄ⲛ̄ⲥⲱⲥ ⲇⲉ ⲟ[ⲛ ⲁϥ-]
ⲙⲟⲟϣⲉ ⲛ̄ϭⲓ ⲡ̄[ⲉⲓⲛⲉ]
ⲙ̄ⲡⲛⲁ' ⲕⲟⲩⲓ̈ ⲕ[ⲟⲩⲓ̈]

ᵃ Bo. p. 107 has ϭⲱ[.   ᵇ ⲧⲟⲧⲉ seems unlikely.   ᶜ Probably nothing here.

[1] *Cf.* Gal. v. 22 (also Budge, *Hom.* 67, Leyden *MSS.* 335). The enumeration corresponds exactly to Am., البر to لياقة, and differs from Bo. 106 (= Av. 46 b).   For 'joy in hope', *cf.*? Rom. xii.

12.   Lemm *KKS.* 432 ff. has discussed similar lists.

[2] Am. should be, 'And while he prayed and beseeched on account of this, lo &c.'

[ⲉⲙⲁ]ⲧⲉ ϩⲱⲥⲧⲉ ⲉⲧ-   ϣⲁⲛⲧϥ̄ⲡⲱ[ϩ̄ ϣⲁⲣⲟϥ]

[ⲣⲉϥ]ⲕⲁ ⲧⲟⲟⲧϥ ⲉ-   ⲁⲩⲱ ⲡⲉϥϭⲓⲛⲉ [ⲛⲉϥ-]

[ⲃⲟ]ⲗ ⲉⲡⲙⲟⲩ · ⲁⲩϭⲱ-   ⲟ' ⲛ̄ⲑⲉ ⲙ̄ⲡⲛⲉϩ' ⲉϥ[ⲕⲓ-]

[ϣ]ⲧ̄ ⲛ̄ⲥⲱϥ ϩ̄ⲛ̄ⲟⲩ-   ⲱⲟⲩ ⲉⲙⲁⲧⲉ · ⲛ̄ⲧ[ⲉ-]

[ⲙⲉ]ⲣⲟⲥ ⲙ̄ⲡⲉϥϩⲟ ⲛ̄ϭⲓ   ⲣⲉϥⲉⲓ' ⲇⲉ ⲉϫⲱϥ' ⲛ̄-ᵃ

margin

ᵃ ? ⲛⲧⲉⲩⲛⲟⲩ.

↑ *Verso.*

                     [. . . . .]ⲛ̄ⲧ[

                     [. .] ϩⲁⲧⲉⲧ[ⲛⲩ-]

[. . . . . .] ⲛ̄ⲧⲉⲓ-   [ⲧ]ⲛ̄ . ⲁⲗⲗⲁ ϯⲡⲁ[ⲙⲉⲛ-]

[ϩⲉ . . . . ⲧⲟ]ⲟⲧϥ   ⲧⲛ̄ ϩ̄ⲙ̄ⲡⲉⲡⲛ̄ⲁ̄ [ϩ̄ⲙ̄-]

[. . . ⲡ]ⲉⲓⲥⲙⲟⲧ'   ⲡⲧⲩⲡⲟⲥ ⲙ̄ⲡ[ⲣⲏ]

[ⲉⲛ]ⲧⲁϥⲧⲥⲁⲃⲟϥ'   ⲉⲧϣⲁ' ⲉϫⲙ̄ⲡ[ⲕⲁϩ']

[ⲉⲣⲟϥ] ⲛ̄ϭⲓ ⲡϫⲟⲉⲓⲥ   ⲧⲏⲣϥ̄ ⲁⲩⲱ ⲉⲣ[ⲉⲛ-]

[ϫⲉⲕ]ⲁⲣⲡ[ⲟⲥ ⲛ]ⲙ' ⲙ̄-   ⲣⲱⲙⲉ ⲉⲧϩⲛ̄ⲭ[ⲱⲣⲁ]

[ⲡⲉ]ⲡⲛ̄ⲁ̄ ⲉⲧϩⲛ̄ⲡⲣⲱ-   ⲛⲓⲙ' ⲙⲟⲟϣⲉ ϩ[ⲙ̄-]

[ⲙⲉ] ⲛⲓⲙ' . ⲉⲩⲛⲏⲩ   ⲡⲉϥⲟⲩⲟⲉⲓⲛ · [ⲧⲁⲓ-]

[ⲉⲃⲟ]ⲗ ϩⲓⲧⲟⲟⲧϥ ⲉ-   ⲧⲉ ⲑⲉ ⲛ̄ⲟⲩⲟⲛ [ⲛⲓⲙ']

[ϫⲱ]ⲟⲩ · ⲕⲁⲧⲁ ⲡϣⲁ-   ⲉⲛⲧⲁⲩⲱⲡ' [ⲉⲡⲉ-]

[ϫⲉ] ⲉⲛⲧⲁⲓ̈ⲁⲕⲱⲃⲟⲥ   ϫⲡⲟ' ⲛ̄ⲕⲉⲥⲟ[ⲡ ϩ̄ⲙ̄-]

[ϫⲟ]ⲟϥ · ϫⲉϯ ⲛⲓⲙ'   ⲡⲉⲩⲁⲅⲅⲉⲗ[ⲓⲟⲛ]

[ⲉⲧ]ⲛⲁⲛⲟⲩϥ' ⲁⲩⲱ   ⲕⲁⲛ ⲉⲛⲥⲉⲥ[ⲟⲟⲩⲛ]

[ⲁ]ⲱⲣⲟⲛ ⲛⲓⲙ' ⲉⲧ-   ⲁⲛ, ⲙ̄ⲡⲉⲩⲉ[ⲣⲏⲩ ⲙ̄-]

[ϫ]ⲏⲕ' ⲉⲃⲟⲗ ⲟⲩⲉⲃⲟⲗ'   ⲡⲣⲟ · ⲁⲗⲗⲁ ⲛ̄[ⲉⲧ-]

ϩ̄ⲛ̄ⲧⲡⲉ'ⲡⲉ ⲉϥⲛⲏⲩ   ϩ̄ⲙ̄ⲙⲁ' ⲛⲓⲙ [ⲥⲉⲥⲟ-]

ⲉⲡⲉⲥⲏⲧ' ϩⲓⲧⲙ̄-   ⲟⲩⲛ, ⲙ̄ⲡⲉⲩⲉⲣ[ⲏⲩ]

ⲡⲉⲓⲱⲧ' ⲛ̄ⲛ̄ⲟⲩⲟ-   ϩ̄ⲓⲟⲩⲥⲟⲡ · ⲁⲩ[ⲱ ⲥⲉ-]

[ⲉ]ⲓⲛ̄' ⲉⲁϥϫⲙ ⲟⲛ   ϣⲟⲟⲡ ϫⲓⲛ

margin

Fol. 28. *Recto* (*v.* Am. 444). . . . the] sun, rising upon the earth.[1] And (δέ) [its] appearance (*lit.* likeness) was bright[2] exceedingly. It befell that when the fear had reached him, he fell down and continued twitching (*lit.* leaping) upon the ground, [even] as a live fish twitcheth upon the ground,[3] after it (*sc.* the fear) had entered into[4] his limbs (μέλος) and his joints (ἁρμός) and his marrow[5] [and] all his body (σῶμα) and his soul (ψυ.). But (δέ) when he had been very sorrowful, even unto (ὥστε) giving himself over unto death, [the angels] looked toward him with a part (μέρος) of their face(s) . . . . .

. . . not bear all [the fear] of the Lord?'[6] After he had been troubled (θλίβειν)[7] . . ., he cried [out] many times, 'Lord, have mercy upon me.' Forthwith the ray[8] (ἀκτίν) of fear went, little by little, and returned to its [place]. And (δέ) thereafter too the [image] of mercy moved, little by little, until[9] it reached [him]. And its appearance [was] like unto oil exceeding thick.[10] And (δέ) when it had come to him, forth[with? . . . . .

Verso (*v.* Am. 444). . . . thus . . . . . this figure that the Lord had shown [him[11]], how that every fruit (καρ.) of the Spirit (πν.) that is in any (*lit.* every) man doth come forth upon them[12] from Him, according to (κατά) the word that James spake,[13] saying, 'Every good gift (δῶρον) and every perfect gift (δ.) is from heaven, coming down from the father of lights.' And he knew also . . . . .

. . . with you. But (ἀλλά) I am with you in the Spirit (πν.), in the type (τύπος) of the [sun], which riseth upon all the [earth], and men that are in all countries (χώρα) do walk in his light. This is the manner of all such as are reckoned [of the] second birth [in?] the Gospel (εὐ.), albeit (κἄν) they know not one another by sight (*lit.* face), yet (ἀλλά) do they that (?) are in every place know one another at once, and are in (?) . . . . .

---

[1] Am. should be, 'like the sun, when he riseth upon the earth. And their appearance was green exceedingly.'

[2] *Cf.* Br. Mus. Or. 7029 Ⳏ, ⲡⲟⲩⲟⲧⲟⲩⲉⲧ ⲙⲡⲛⲟⲩϩ. Am., misunderstanding, اخضر.

[3] Am. *sic.*

[4] Am., 'were broken, injured,' *sc.* his limbs.

[5] Am., 'the place without bones,' translating Bo. ⲁⲧ-ⲕⲁⲥ.

[6] Am. *om.* 'of the Lord'.

[7] Am. should be, 'And when the anxiety had reached him.'

[8] Am. *sic*, sing. [9] G *sic*, Am. 'and'.

[10] Am. should be, 'a very heavy perfume.'

[11] Am. should be, 'And thus passed this similitude that the Lord showed him;' G ⲡⲛϩ b reading 'And thus it passed. And this similitude the Lord showed him, so that '.

[12] Am. should be, 'upon men.'

[13] Jas. i. 17.

Fol. 29. → *Recto* (?).

].·

[. . . . . . εϣ]ϫε
[ⲛ̄ϯϩⲁⲧⲉⲧ]ⲛ̄ⲅⲧ̄
[ⲁⲛ] ⲟ̄ⲛ̄ⲧⲥⲁⲣ︤ⲝ · ⲁ[ⲗ-]
ⲗⲁ ϯⲡ︤ⲗ︤ⲗ︤ⲛ̄ⲧ︤ⲡ
ϩ︤ⲙ︤ⲡⲉⲡ︤ⲛ︤ⲁ · ⲉⲡⲉⲓ-
ϫⲏ' ϫⲉ ⲟⲩ︤ⲛ̄ϩⲟⲉⲓⲛⲉ
ϩⲛ̄ⲡ︤ⲗ︤ⲗ︤ⲛ̄ⲡⲓⲥⲧⲟⲥ' ⲉⲁⲩ-
ϫⲡⲟ' ⲛⲁⲩ ⲛ̄ⲟⲩ︤ⲗ︤ⲗⲉ-
ⲣⲟⲥ ⲛ̄ⲛ̄ⲕⲁⲣⲡⲟⲥ ⲙ̄-
ⲡⲉⲡ︤ⲛ︤ⲁ ⲙ̄ⲡϫⲟⲉⲓⲥ.
ⲛ̄ⲕⲉⲗⲗⲉⲣⲟⲥ ϫⲉ ⲛ̄ⲧⲟϥ
[ⲙ̄ⲡⲁ]ⲧⲟⲩⲉϣ︤ⲙ︤ⲗⲗ-
ϭⲟⲙ' ⲛ̄ϫⲡⲟⲟⲩ ⲛⲁⲩ ·
[ⲉⲧ]ⲃⲉⲡⲁⲓ̈ ⲉϥⲡⲣⲟ-
[ⲧⲣⲉ]ⲡⲉ' ⲛ̄ⲛⲁⲓ̈ ⲛ̄ⲧⲉⲓ̈-
ⲙⲓⲛⲉ ⲛ̄ϭⲓ ⲡ̄ⲣ̄ⲙ̄ϩⲁⲗ' ^{sic}
ⲙ̄ⲡⲛⲟⲩⲧⲉ ⲓ̈ⲁⲕⲱ-
ⲃⲟⲥ ⲉϥϫⲱ ⲙⲙⲟⲥ
ϫⲉⲡⲉⲧϣⲁⲁⲧ' ⲛ̄-
ⲟⲩⲥⲟⲫⲓⲁ ⲛ̄ϩⲏⲧ-
ⲧⲏⲩⲧ︤ⲡ ⲉⲧⲉϩⲟⲉⲓ

ϩⲁⲡⲗ[ⲱⲥ ⲉⲛϥⲛⲟϭ-]
ⲛⲉϭ ⲁⲛ, ⲁ[ⲅⲱ ϥ̄ⲛⲁ-]
ϯ ⲛⲁϥ · ⲡⲉⲓϣ[ⲁϫⲉ]
ϫⲉ ϫⲉϩⲁⲡⲗⲱ[ⲥ ⲉⲛϥ-]
ⲛⲟϭⲛⲉϭ ⲁⲛ ⲁⲩ[ⲱ]
ϥ̄ⲛⲁϯ ⲛⲁϥ. ⲉⲧⲉ-
ⲡⲁⲓ̈ⲡⲉ ⲉϥϯ ⲛ̄ⲟⲩ-
ⲟⲛ ⲛⲓⲙ' ϩ[ⲛ̄]ⲟⲩ︤ⲗ︤ⲗ︤ⲛⲧ-]
ϩⲁⲡⲗⲟⲩⲥ ⲛ̄ϭⲓ ⲡϫ[ⲟ-]
ⲉⲓⲥ, ⲉⲛϥⲛⲟϭⲛⲉϭ [ⲛ̄-]
ⲗⲁⲁⲩ ⲛ̄ⲛⲉⲧⲁⲓⲧ[ⲉⲓ']
ⲙ̄ⲙⲟϥ ϫⲉⲁⲕⲣ̄ⲛⲟ-
ⲃⲉ ⲉⲣⲟⲓ̈ ⲛ̄ ⲁⲕⲣϣⲁϥ-
ⲧⲉ ⲛ̄ϯⲛⲁϯ ⲛⲁⲕ
ⲙ̄ⲡⲉⲕⲁⲓⲧⲏⲙ[ⲁ·]
ⲛ̄ⲧⲟϥ' ϩⲱⲱϥ' ⲡ[ⲉⲧ-]
ⲁⲓⲧⲉⲓ' ϥ̄ϫⲱ' ⲙ̄ⲙⲟ[ⲥ]
ⲉⲧⲃⲏⲛⲧ︤ϥ ϫⲉⲁⲣ-
ⲣⲉϥⲁⲓⲧⲉⲓ ϩ︤ⲛ̄ⲟⲩⲡⲓⲥ-
ⲧⲓⲥ, ⲉⲛϥⲇⲓⲁⲕⲣⲓ-
ⲛⲉ ⲛ̄ⲗⲁⲁⲩ ⲁⲛ · ⲉⲧ[ⲉ-]

margin

↑ *Verso* (?).

[. . . . . . .]ⲡⲙⲁ
[ⲉⲧⲉⲣⲉⲡⲣⲱ]ⲙⲉ ϣⲱ-
[ⲡⲉ ⲛ̄ϩⲏⲧ︤ϥ ⲉⲃⲟⲗ]
[ϩⲓ]ⲧ︤ⲙ̄ⲡⲛⲟⲩⲧⲉ ·

ⲛ̄ϥ[
ⲑⲓⲉ̄ ϩⲏ[ⲧ ? ⲛ̄-]
ⲧⲟϥ ⲙ̄ⲡ︤ⲛ︤ⲥ[ⲁⲧⲣⲉϥ-]
ⲙⲓⲥⲉ ⲛ̄ⲧⲉⲡⲕ[ⲟⲩⲓ̈]

[ⲛ̄]ⲑⲉ ⲛ̄ⲟⲩⲥϭⲓⲙⲉ   ⲙⲟⲩ ⲛ̄ⲧⲉⲩⲛⲟⲩ·
ⲉϣⲁⲥⲱ̄ⲱ̄ ⲕⲟⲩⲓ̈   ⲧⲁⲓ̈ⲧⲉ ⲑⲉ ⲛ̄ⲟⲩⲣⲱ-
ⲕⲟⲩⲓ̈ ⲙ̄ⲡⲛ̄ⲥⲱⲥ   ⲙⲉ ⲙ̄ⲡⲛ̄ⲥⲁⲧⲣⲉϥ-
ⲡ̄ⲥⲙ[ⲓ]ⲥⲉ· ⲛ̄ⲧⲉ-   ⲥⲙⲛ ⲇⲓⲁⲑⲏ[ⲕ]ⲏ
ⲡⲕⲟⲩⲓ̈ ⲍⲁⲧⲉ ϣⲏⲙ'   ⲙ̄ⲡⲛⲟⲩⲧⲉ ⲉⲣ̄-
ϣⲏⲙ' ϣⲁⲛⲧϥ-   ⲡⲉϥⲟⲩⲱϣ' ⲁⲩⲱ
ⲣ̄ⲧⲉⲗⲉⲓⲟⲥ ϩ̄ⲛ̄ⲑⲏ-   ⲉϩⲁⲣⲉϩ' ⲉⲛⲉϥⲉⲛ-
ⲗⲓⲕⲓⲁ· ⲧⲁⲓ̈ⲧⲉ ⲑⲉ'   ⲧⲟⲗⲏ· ⲁⲩⲱ ϥⲡⲣⲟ-
ⲛ̄ⲡ̄ⲕⲁⲣⲡⲟⲥ ⲙ̄ⲡⲉ-   ⲕⲟⲡⲧⲉ ⲕⲁⲧⲁ ⲧⲁⲓ-
ⲡ̄ⲡⲁ ⲉϣⲁⲣⲉⲡⲣⲱ-   ⲁⲑⲏⲕⲏ ⲉⲛⲧⲁϥ-
ⲙⲉ ⲍⲡⲟⲟⲩ ⲛ̄ϩⲏ-   ⲥⲙⲛ̄ⲧⲉ ⲁⲩⲱ ⲙ̄ⲡ-
ⲧϥ ⲕⲟⲩⲓ̈ ⲕⲟⲩⲓ̈ ϩ̄ⲙ̄-   ⲛ̄ⲥⲱⲥ ⲛ̄ϥ̄ⲕⲁ ⲧⲟ-
ⲡⲧⲱϣ' ⲙ̄ⲡⲉϥ-   ⲟⲧϥ ⲉⲃⲟⲗ' ϩ̄ⲛ̄ ⲧ
ϩⲏⲧ' ϣⲁⲛⲧϥ̄ⲣ̄-   ⲕⲁⲣⲡⲟⲥ ⲙ̄ⲡⲉⲡⲛ̄ⲁ̄
ⲧⲉⲗⲉⲓⲟⲥ· ⲛ̄ϩⲏⲧⲟⲩ   ⲉⲛⲧⲁϥⲁⲣⲭⲉⲓ' ⲛ̄-
ⲛ̄ⲑⲉ ⲉⲧⲥϩ̄ϥ'· ⲍⲉ-   ⲣϩⲏⲧⲟⲩ꞉ ⲛ̄ⲧⲟϥ

margin

Fol. 29. (The right position of this fol. is uncertain.)

Recto. . . . ' If I am not among you in the flesh (σάρξ), yet (ἀλλά) am I with you in the spirit (πν.).'[1] And since then (ἐπειδὴ δέ) there are some of the faithful (πιστός) have brought forth for themselves a portion (μέρος) of the fruits (καρ.) of the Spirit (πν.) of the Lord, while (δέ) as for the other portion (μέ.), they have not been able to bring them forth; for this cause doth the servant of God, James, exhort (προτρέπειν) such as these, saying,[2] ' He that lacketh wisdom (σοφία) among you—that is,[3] some . . . . .

. . . liberally (ἁπλῶς), upbraiding not, and he shall give unto him.' And (δέ) this saying : ' liberally (ἁπ.), upbraiding not, and he shall give unto him,' it(s meaning) is this: the Lord giveth unto every one with liberality (-ἁπλοῦς), upbraiding not any one of them that ask (αἰτεῖν) Him, (saying,) ' Thou hast sinned against Me, or (ἤ) Thou hast done iniquity ; I will not

---

[1] Col. ii. 5.
[2] Jas. i. 5.

[3] An explanatory insertion ; so too at end of this page.

grant thee thy request (αἴτημα).'   Rather, of him that asketh (αἱ.) he saith,[1]
'Let him ask (αἱ.) in faith (πίστις), nothing doubting (διακρίνειν)—that
[is . . . . .

Verso. . . . the place [where]in a man is, through God['s will].   Even as
a woman conceiving, little by little, and afterwards bringing forth, and the
little (one) growing by small degrees, until he reach completion (-τέλειος) in
age (ἡλικία) ; such is the fashion of the fruits (κα.) of the Spirit (πν.), a
man bringing them forth within himself, little by little, in the measure of
his heart, until he be complete (τέλειος) therein, as it is written, ...

. . . cause abortion[2] ; [but] then, after that she hath brought forth,
straightway the little (one) dieth.   This is the fashion of a man who, after
that he hath established a covenant (διαθήκη) with God, to do His will and
to keep His commandments (ἐντολή), and hath progressed (προκόπτειν)
according to the covenant (κατά, διαθ.) that he hath established, doth
afterward renounce the fruits (κα.) of the Spirit (πν.), wherein he had made
beginning (ἄρχειν).   He . . . . .

Fol. 30.   ↑ *Recto.*

?	ϩοοⲩ ⲛⲧⲉϥⲙⲛ̄ⲧ-
]ⲧⲉ	ⲕⲟⲩï ⲉϥⲥⲟⲃⲧⲉ ⲛ̄
ⲙⲏ] ⲛ̄ⲧⲁⲧⲉ-	ⲛⲉⲥⲛⲏⲩ · ⲁϥϯ
[ⲧⲛ̄ . . .] . ϥ' ⲛⲁï	ϩⲧⲏϥ' ⲉⲟⲩⲁ' ⲟ̄ⲡⲛ[ⲉ-]
[ⲉⲧⲣⲁϯ ⲡⲉϥ]ϩⲁⲡ'	ⲧⲟⲩⲱⲙ' ⲉϥⲟⲩⲉ[ⲙ']
[ⲟⲩⲡⲉ^a] ⲡⲉⲧⲛ-	ϩⲁϩ' ⲛ̄ⲛ̄ϭⲉ ϩⲓⲧⲉ-
[ϩⲱⲃ ⲁⲛⲁⲭ]ⲱⲣⲉⲓ ⲛⲏ-	ⲧⲣⲁⲡⲉⲍⲁ · ⲡⲉⲧⲙ̄
[ⲧⲛ̄ ⲙ̄ⲡϥ]ⲟⲩⲱϣ ⲇⲉ	ⲙⲁⲩ ⲇⲉ ⲛⲉⲙⲛ̄ⲡⲁⲧϥ[-]
[ⲉⲝⲟⲟⲥ] ⲍⲉⲛ̄ⲧⲟϥ	ⲱⲥⲕ̄ ⲍⲓⲛⲧⲁϥⲉⲓ' [ⲉ-]
[ⲁⲛⲡⲉ ⲍⲉ]ⲕⲁⲥ, ⲉ . ⲛ̄-^b	ⲛⲉⲥⲛⲏⲩ · ⲁϥⲙⲉⲕ-
	ⲙⲟⲩⲕ̄ϥ ⲇⲉ ϩⲣⲁï ⲛ̄-

^a This does not sufficiently fill the space.
perhaps ⲇⲓⲥⲧⲁⲍⲉ ; ⲛⲟⲙⲓⲍⲉ is too rare to be probable.

^b Reading surely mistaken.   The Greek word

[1] Jas. i. 6.

[2] *cf.* Lagarde, *Aeg.* 240 ⲙⲛⲉ̄ⲕⲟⲓⲉ ϩⲏⲧⲥ
ⲛⲟⲩϭϩⲓⲙⲉ ⲉⲡⲉⲥⲏⲧ ; Curzon MS. 108, ⲡ̄ⲁ,

ⲑⲉ ⲟⲛ ⲛ̄ⲧⲁⲕⲟⲓⲉ ϩⲏⲧϥ (*sic*) ⲛ̄ⲛⲉϩⲓⲟⲙⲉ
ⲉⲧⲉⲉⲓ ⲛⲁⲛ.

[ⲍⲉ ⲉⲕⲉⲟⲩⲁ·   ⲟⲏⲧϥ ⲛ̄ⲅ̄ⲓ̈ ⲑⲉⲟⲇ[ⲱ-]
[ⲁⲗⲗⲁ ⲁϥ]ⲕⲁⲣⲱϥ ⲉ-   ⲣⲟⲥ ⲉϥϫⲱ ⲙ̄ⲙⲟⲥ
[ⲛϭⲉ ⲗ]ⲁⲁⲩ ⲛⲁⲩ,   ⲍⲉⲛⲟⲩⲛⲟϥⲣⲉ [ⲁⲛ-]
[ⲁⲛ ⲉ]ⲙⲏⲧⲓ ⲉ-   ⲧⲉ ⲙ̄ⲡⲉⲓ̈ⲥⲟⲛ, ⲉⲧ-
[ⲡⲁⲓ ⲙ̄ⲙⲁ]ⲧⲉ ⲍⲉⲁⲓ̈-   ⲣⲉϥⲟⲩⲉⲙ ⲟⲁⲟ ⲛ̄ⲏ-
[ⲧⲱϣ ⲙ̄ⲡⲣⲱ]ⲃ ⲉⲧⲉ-   ⲥⲉ ⲍⲉⲟ[ⲩ]ⲟ̄ⲣ̄ϣⲓⲣⲉⲡⲉ

margin

→ *Verso.*

ⲙⲙⲟⲛⲁⲭⲟⲥ ⲛϣ-
ϣⲉ ⲁⲛ ⲉⲣⲟϥ ⲉⲟⲩⲉⲙ
ⲛϭⲉ ϣⲁⲛⲧϥⲥⲉⲓ.   ⲡ̄[
ⲉⲃⲟⲗ ⲍⲉⲟⲩⲟⲩⲟⲟⲧⲉ-   ⲑⲉⲟ[ⲇⲱⲣⲟⲥ ⲇⲉ ⲛ̄-]
ⲡⲉ ⲉϥⲧⲣⲉⲡⲣⲱ-   ⲧⲉⲣⲉ[ϥⲉⲓⲙⲉ ⲍⲉ-]
ⲙⲉ ⲟ̄ⲙ̄ϭⲟⲙ· ⲙ̄ⲡ̄ⲛ̄-   ⲡⲉⲓⲥ[ⲟⲛ ⲟⲩ-]
ⲥⲁⲧⲣⲉϥϫⲱ ⲇⲉ ⲙ̄-   ⲱϭ ⲉⲧ[ⲟⲟⲧϥ ⲉⲟⲩ-]
ⲡⲉⲓ̈ϣⲁⲍⲉ ⲁϥⲗⲩ-   ⲉⲙ ⲛ[ϭⲉ
ⲡⲉⲓ ⲉⲙⲁⲧⲉ ⲟ̄ⲙ̄ⲡⲉϥ-   ⲛϭⲉ ⲙ̄[ⲙⲁⲧⲉ ⲛ̄-]
ⲟⲏⲧ ⲛ̄ⲅ̄ⲓ ⲑⲉⲟⲇⲱ-   ⲧⲁϥⲍ[ⲟⲟⲥ ⲁϥⲟⲁ-]
ⲣⲟⲥ ⲉϥϫⲱ ⲙ̄ⲙⲟⲥ ⲍⲉ- ⲣⲉϥ ⲉⲣⲟ[ϥ ⲉⲧⲙⲟⲩ-]
ⲙⲉϣⲁⲕ ⲙ̄ⲡⲟⲩⲱϣ   ⲱⲙ ⲉⲡ[ⲧⲏⲣϥ ϣⲁ-]
ⲙ̄ⲡϫⲟⲉⲓⲥ ⲁⲛⲡⲉ   ⲡⲉⲟⲟⲟ[ⲩ ⲉⲣⲉⲡϫⲟ-]
ⲡϣⲁⲍⲉ ⲉⲛⲧⲁⲓ̈ϫⲟ-   ⲉⲓⲥ ⲟ̄ⲙ̄ [ⲡⲉϥϣⲓⲛⲉ]
ⲟϥ ⲍⲉⲙ̄ⲡⲓⲣⲟⲁⲣϣ   ⲛ̄ⲟⲏ[ⲧϥ
ⲟⲏⲧ ϣⲁⲛⲧϥ̄ⲧⲱ-
ⲃⲥ̄ ⲟ̄ⲛ̄ⲧⲉϥⲡⲣⲟⲁⲓ-
ⲣⲉⲥⲓⲥ ⲙⲁⲩⲁⲁϥ· ⲡϥ-

margin

Fol. 30. *Recto* (*v.* Am. 458). . . . Have ye [(μή) brought] him unto me [that I should give] judgement [upon him ? What then (?) is] your [affair ? [1] De]part (ἀναχωρεῖν).' And (δέ) he wished [not to say,] It [was not] he, lest they should (?) [2] suspect (?) another ; [but [3] (ἀλλά) he] kept silence, [saying] naught unto them, except (εἰμήτι) [this a]lone : ' I have [ordered the] matter that . . . . .

. . . in the] days of his youth, while making ready for the brethren, he observed one of them that did eat, eating many leeks at table (τράπ.). But (δέ) it was not long since he had come to the brethren. And (δέ) Theodore thought within himself, saying, ' It is not a good (thing) for this brother that he eat many leeks, for he is a youth . . . . .

Verso (*v.* Am. 458, 459). . . . monk [4] (μον.) it befitteth him not to eat leeks until he be sated ; for it is a herb that causeth a man to be strong.' But (δέ) when Theodore had said this word, he was much grieved (λυπεῖν) at heart, saying, ' If so be it is not the Lord's will, the word that I have spoken, seeing I had not patience until he should be stirred up by his own purpose (προαίρεσις) and he . . . . .

. . . [But (δέ) Theo]dore when [he] had [known that this] [brother . . . not] contin[ued to] eat leeks [5] . . . . that he had spo[ken, he ke]pt himself [from ea]ting (them) at all, [until] the day where[on] the Lord visited him . . . . .

Fol. 31. → *Recto.*   margin

ογ τωϥ' αγω   μ[ονον ϫεμπεκογ-]
μ̄ν̄ν̄сατρεϥ϶ов-   ωϣ е϶[ов̄κ̄ μ̄πеι-]
с̄ϥ̄ ν̄τετμ̄ν ν̄-   πρнϣ [ν̄сορτ αλλα]
ϭι θеоλωροс · аϥ-   τκеϭι[ϫ' ν̄в̄нне он]
неϫ' τοοτϥ е϶раї   ν̄ϭογω[ϣ ан еϫ̄ιτс]
[е]γν̄κα еϥμе϶ ν̄-   ν̄τοοτ[· аϥογω-]
[в̄]нпе аϥμе϶' τеϥ-   ϣв̄ ϫе πе[ϫаϥ наϥ]
ϭιϫ' аϥсоογτ̄ν̄   ϫееκμе[γе ϫен̄-]
[ν̄]μοογ ероϥ' ϫее-   +ογаϣ[о]γ а[ν τа-]
[ϥ]еϫιτογ ν̄ϭογо-   ογομογ а[λλα +р̄-]

---

[1] Am. ' Have ye brought him &c. ? What is it

[2] Copy inadequate. Am. has ' think '.

[3] Am. *sic.*

[4] Preceded by an adjective, or by ρωμе

[5] The 2nd нϭе ' leeks ' must be wrongly read.

[ⲙ]ⲟⲩ · ⲛ̄ⲧⲟϥ ⲇⲉ ⲉⲙ-
[ⲡ̄]ϥϫⲓⲧⲟⲩ · ⲟⲩⲧⲉ
[ⲙ̄]ⲡϥϫⲟⲟⲥ ⲟⲛ ⲛⲁϥ
[ϫ]ⲉⲥⲉⲕ' ⲧⲟⲟⲧⲕ̄ ⲉⲣⲟⲕ ·
[ⲁⲗ]ⲗⲁ ⲁϥϭⲱϣⲧ̄ ⲛ̄-
[ⲥⲱ]ϥ ⲉⲣⲉⲛⲉϥⲣⲙⲉⲓⲟ-
[ⲟ]ⲩⲉ ϣⲟϭⲟ' ⲉⲡⲉⲥⲏⲧ'
[ⲛ̄]ⲧⲉ[ⲣ]ⲉϥⲛⲁⲩ ⲇⲉ ⲉ-
[ⲣⲟϥ' ⲛ̄]ϭⲓ ⲑⲉⲟⲇⲱⲣⲟⲥ
[ⲉⲣⲉⲛ]ⲉϥⲃⲁⲗ ϯ ⲣ̄ⲙ-
[ⲉⲓⲏ] ⲁϥⲣⲓⲙⲉ ϩⲱⲱϥ
[ⲡⲉϫ]ⲁϥ ⲛⲁϥ ϫⲉⲁ-
[ϩⲣⲟⲕ ⲉⲕ]ⲣⲓⲙⲉ · ⲛ̄ⲧⲟϥ
[ⲇⲉ ⲡⲉϫⲁ]ϥ ⲛⲁϥ ϫⲉ-
[ⲉⲧⲃⲉ]ϫⲉϯⲛⲁⲩ ⲉ-
[ⲣⲟⲕ ⲉⲕϣ]ⲱⲛⲉ · ⲟⲩ'

ϩⲟⲧⲉ ⲉⲧⲃⲉⲡ[ϩⲁⲡ]
ⲙ̄ⲡⲉⲭ̄ⲥ̄ ϫⲉⲛ[ⲛⲉϥ-]ᵃ
ⲕⲣⲓⲛⲉ ⲙ̄ⲙⲟ[ⲓ · ⲡⲉ-]
ϫⲁϥ ⲛⲁϥ ϫⲉ[ⲉⲧⲃⲉ-]
ⲟⲩ' ⲉⲅⲛⲁⲕⲣⲓ[ⲛⲉ ⲙ̄-]
ⲙⲟⲕ · ⲙⲏ ⲡⲉⲧ-
ϣⲱⲛⲉ ⲧⲏⲣⲟⲩ ϩ[ⲛ̄-]
ⲡⲉⲥⲛⲏⲩ ⲙⲉⲛⲁᵇ
ⲛⲁⲩ · ⲏ̄ ⲉⲩϣⲁⲛ[ⲣ̄-]
ⲭⲣⲓⲁ ⲛ̄ⲟⲩⲡⲣⲏϣ [ⲛ̄-]
ⲥⲟⲣⲧ̄ ⲏ̄ ⲟⲛ ⲕⲉⲧ
ⲙⲉⲛⲧⲁⲁϥ ⲛⲁ[ⲩ·]
ⲛ̄ⲧⲟϥ ⲇⲉ ⲡⲉϫ[ⲁϥ]
ⲛⲁϥ · ϫⲉⲁⲕⲙ[ⲉϣⲧ̄]
ⲛ̄ⲕⲁⲗⲩⲃⲏ ⲛ̄[ⲛⲉⲥ-]
ⲛⲏⲩ ⲙ̄ⲡⲉⲓ̈[ⲛⲁⲩ]
ⲁⲕⲉⲓⲙⲉ ϫⲉⲙ̄[ⲙ̄ⲡ-]

margin

ᵃ Or ⲛⲉϥ-.

ᵇ ⲁ is faint; read ⲙⲉⲛⲛⲁ.

↑ *Verso.*

margin

]ⲩⲛⲡⲉⲧ-
[ϣⲱⲛⲉ ⲉϩ]ⲟⲩⲉⲣⲟⲓ̈ ⲙ̄-
[ⲡⲱⲣ ⲛ̄ⲡⲉⲥ]ϣⲱⲡⲉ
[ⲛ̄ⲧⲉⲓⲣⲉ ⲉ]ⲣ[ⲉ]ⲛ̄ⲥⲕⲉⲩ-
[ⲏ ⲛ̄ⲡⲉⲥ]ⲛⲏⲩ ⲛ̄ⲧⲟⲣ-
[ⲡ̄]ⲛᵃ ⲉⲣ̄ⲡⲉⲛⲙ̄-
[ⲧⲟⲛ ⲛ̄ϩ]ⲛ̄ⲧⲟⲩ ⲉϩⲟⲩⲉ-

ⲟⲟⲙ' ⲛ̄ⲧⲁⲓ̈ⲡⲁⲥⲧⲉ
ⲡϥⲛⲁⲣⲱϣⲉ ⲁⲛ
ⲉⲣⲟⲟⲩ · ⲁϥϭⲱϣⲧ̄
ⲇⲉ ⲛ̄ⲥⲱϥ' ⲛ̄ϭⲓ ⲡⲉⲛ-
ⲉⲓⲱⲧ' ⲡⲁϩⲱⲙ[ⲉ]
ⲁϥⲉⲓⲙⲉ ⲉⲡⲙⲟⲕ-
ⲙⲉⲕ' ⲉⲛⲧⲁϥϫⲁⲗ[ⲉ]
ⲉϩⲣⲁⲓ̈ ⲉϫⲙ̄ⲡⲉϥϩ[ⲏⲧ'·]

ᵃ Perhaps ⲁ]ⲛ.

[ⲣⲟⲟⲩ ·] ⲁ[ⲥ]ϣⲱⲡⲉ   ⲡⲉϫⲁϥ' ⲉϩⲟⲩⲛ ⲉ-

[ϩⲙⲡ]ⲉϩⲟⲟⲩ ⲉⲧⲙ̅ⲙⲁⲩ   ϩⲣⲁϥ' ϫⲉⲟⲩ'ⲡⲉ ⲡ[ⲉⲓ-]

[ⲛⲉⲣⲉ]ϩⲉⲛⲥⲛⲏⲩ ⲉⲓ'   ⲙⲟⲕ'ⲙⲉⲕ' ⲉⲛⲧⲁ[ⲕ-]

[ⲉⲡⲃ]ⲟⲟⲩ^a ϩⲓⲟⲩϫⲟⲉⲓ   ᵃⁱᶜ ⲙⲟⲕⲙⲉⲕ' ⲉⲣⲟϥ' ⲑ[ⲉⲟ-]

[ⲙ̅ⲡ]ⲛⲁⲩ ⲛ̅ⲣⲟⲩϩⲉ   ⲇⲱⲣⲉ ·ᶜ ⲟⲩⲡⲉⲧϣ[ⲟⲩ-]

[ϫⲉⲕ]ⲁⲥ ⲉⲩⲉⲧⲁⲗⲉ ⲟⲩ-   ⲉⲓⲧ' ϭⲁⲣⲡⲉ' ⲉⲡ[ⲉⲓ]

[. . .]ⲙ'ᵇ ⲛ̅ⲕⲁⲙ ⲉⲣⲟϥ ·   ⲛ̅ⲧⲟϥ ⲛ̅ϩⲟⲩⲟ' ⲛ[ⲧⲁⲕ-]

[ⲛ̅]ⲧⲟϥ ⲇⲉ ⲑⲉⲟⲇⲱⲣⲟⲥ   ⲛⲁⲩ ⲉⲛⲉⲥⲛⲏⲩ [ⲉⲩ-]

[ⲛ]ⲉⲁϥⲡⲓⲥⲉ' ⲛ̅ⲟⲩϭⲓⲛ-   ⲉⲓ' ϣⲁⲣⲟⲕ ⲉ . ⲛ̅ . [ᵈ

[ⲟⲩ]ⲟⲟⲙ' ⲛ̅ⲛⲉⲥⲛⲏⲩ   ϩⲙⲡⲉⲕϩⲏ[ⲧ ϩⲛ̅-]

[ϩⲙ]ⲡⲉϩⲟⲟⲩ ⲉⲧⲙ̅ⲙⲁⲩ ·   ⲟⲩϣ̅ⲡϩⲙ[ⲟⲧ ϫⲉⲱ]

[ⲁⲩ]ⲱ ⲛ̅ⲧⲉⲣⲉϥϭⲱ-   ⲡϫⲟⲉⲓⲥ ⲛ̅ⲑ[ⲉ ⲛ̅ⲧⲁⲕ-]

[ϣ]ⲧ ⲁϥⲛⲁⲩ ⲉⲛⲉ-   ⲉⲓⲛⲉ ⲛ̅ⲛⲉ[ⲥⲛⲏⲩ]

[ⲥ]ⲛⲏⲩ ϩⲙ̅ⲡϫⲟⲓ ⲙ̅-   ϣⲁⲣⲟⲛ ⲉⲧ[ⲣⲉⲛ-]

[ⲡⲁ]ⲧϥ̅ⲙⲟⲟⲛⲉ ⲁϥ-   ⲛⲁⲩ ⲟⲛ ⲉ[ⲛⲉⲛⲉⲣⲏⲩ]

[ⲙⲉ]ⲕⲙⲟⲩⲕϥ̅ ϩⲣⲁⲓ   ϩⲙⲡⲉⲓⲙ[ⲁ' ⲁⲁⲛ]

[ⲛ̅ϩ]ⲏⲧϥ̅ ⲛ̅ⲧⲉⲩⲛⲟⲩ   ⲟⲛ ⲛ̅ⲙ̅ⲡ[ϣⲁ]

[ⲉϥⲙⲟ]ⲕϩ̅ ⲛ̅ϩⲏⲧ ϫⲉ-   ⲉⲧⲣⲉⲛ[ⲛⲁⲩ ⲉⲛⲉⲛ-]

[ⲙⲉϣ]ⲁⲕ' ⲧϭⲓⲛⲟⲩ-   ⲉⲣⲏⲩ ϩⲙ[ⲡⲕⲉⲙⲁ]

margin

ᵃ Or ϣⲁⲣ]ⲟⲟⲩ.   ᵇ ? ⲉⲧⲛⲱ.   ᶜ Note the vocative form.   ᵈ ⲉ. may be ϣ (? ϣⲁϫⲉ).

Fol. 31. *Recto (v. Am. 552).* . . . his (*sc.* mat).'[1] And after that Theodore had covered him with the mat, he put forth his hand to a vessel full of dates and filled his hand and reached them forth unto him (*sc.* Pachômius), that he might take and eat them. But (δέ) as for him, he took them not, neither (οὐδέ) said, Draw back thy hand. But (ἀλλά) he looked at him, while his tears flowed down. And (δέ) when Theodore beheld him, his eyes shedding tears, he also wept. He (Pach.) said unto him, 'What (lackest) thou, (that) thou weepest?' But (δέ) he said unto him, 'Because that I see thee sick. Not ⌈only (οὐ

[1] ⲟⲩⲧⲱϥ as prep. + suff. seems improbable.

μόνον) that thou] wouldest not [cover thee with this woollen] coverlet, but (ἀλλά)] even the hand[ful of dates also], thou wouldest [not receive it] at my hand.'[1]   But (δέ) [he answer]ed and [said unto him,] 'Thinkest thou I desired them not, to eat them?   Ra[ther (ἀλλά) do I] fear because of the judgement of Christ (Χρ.), lest I be condemned[2] (κρίνειν).'   He said unto him, 'Where[fore] shouldest thou be condemned (κρ.)?   All they that are sick among the brethren, do we not (μή) charity unto them?   Or (ἤ) if they have need (χρεία) of a woollen coverlet or (ἤ) aught besides, do we not give it unto them?   But (δέ) he said unto him, 'Hast thou vis[ited] the cells (καλύβη) of [the] brethren at this [time] and hast found (*lit.* known) that that there is [not

Verso (*v.* Am. 553).   any among them] that is more sick than I?   Nay, [let it not] be [thus, while] the things (σκεύη) [of the] brethren are in our hands[3] (?), ... have our com[fort there]from more than [they.']   It befell on that day that brethren came [to] Pbow (?)[4] in a boat, at eventime, that they might load a ... of reeds thereon.[5]   But (δέ) as for Theodore, he had cooked food for the brethren that day.   And when he had looked, he beheld the brethren in the boat,[6] ere it had come to land; and he thought within himself forthwith, being sad at heart, (saying,) 'Perchance the food that I have cooked shall not suffice for them.'   But (δέ) our father Pachômius looked toward him and knew the thought that had risen into his heart; and he said unto him, 'What is this thought that thou hast thought, Theodore?   Vanity is it indeed (γάρ).   For (ἐπεί) rather the more when thou sawest the brethren coming unto thee,[thou shouldest have said?[7]] in thy heart, in thankfulness, [' O] Lord, even as [Thou hast] brought the [brethren] unto us, that we may see [one another] in this world (*lit.* place[8]), [make us] also wor[thy] that we may [see one] another in [the other world (*lit.* place)].'

[1] Am. *om.* 'at my hand'.
[2] Or ' He condemns me '.
[3] *I.e.* 'in our keeping'.   But if ⲛⲧⲟⲟⲧⲏ ⲁⲛ, '... are not in our hands, that we should have ...'   Am. differs somewhat.   For *couverture*, read *nourriture et vêtement.*   [4] Or 'unto them'.
[5] ? 'a load'.   Am. should be 'that they might load it with *halfâ*'.

[6] Am. should be, 'And when he looked, he beheld the brethren that had come, and he thought within himself, Perchance the cooked food that he had cooked should not suffice for all.'
[7] Or imperat., 'say', if tense of preceding clause would permit.
[8] Am. 'here'.

Fol. 32.　→ *Recto* (?).　　　↑ *Verso* (?).

margin	margin
ⲝⲉ ⲙ̄ⲡ[ⲓϧⲉⲡ ⲗⲁⲁⲩ]	ⲟⲩⲟ]ⲉⲓϣ’ ⲛ̄ⲛ-
ⲉⲣⲱⲧ[ⲛ̄ ⲛⲛⲉⲧⲣ-]	]ⲧⲉ ⲛ̄ⲣⲉϥ-
ⲛⲟϥⲣⲉ [ⲉⲓⲣⲙⲛⲧ-]	]ⲉ · ⲛ̄ⲧⲉⲣⲉϥ-
ⲣⲉ ⲛ̄ⲛ̄[ⲟⲩⲇⲁⲓ ⲙ̄ⲛ̄-]	ⲝⲉ]ⲧⲁⲓ̈ⲧⲉ ⲧϭⲓ̄
ⲛ̄ϩⲉⲑⲛⲟ[ⲥ ⲛ̄ⲧⲙⲉ-]	[ⲱⲛϧ̄ ⲛ̄]ⲛⲉⲧⲟⲩⲁⲁⲃ ·
ⲧⲁⲛⲟⲓⲁ [ⲉϧⲟⲩⲛ ⲉ-]	]ⲅⲉ ⲁⲡⲝⲟⲉⲓⲥ
ⲡⲛⲟⲩⲧ[ⲉ ⲁⲩⲱ]	ⲟ]ⲩⲟⲉⲓⲛ ⲛ̄-
ⲧⲡⲓⲥⲧ[ⲓⲥ ⲉϧⲟⲩⲛ]	]ⲁϥⲝⲓ̈
ⲉⲡⲉⲛⲝ[ⲟⲉⲓⲥ ⲓ̄ⲥ̄ ⲡⲉ-]	ⲟⲩ]ⲟⲉⲓϣ ⲛ̄-
ⲭⲥ̄ · ⲉ[	]ⲧⲉⲛⲉ
ⲛ̄ⲧⲉ[	]ⲛⲁⲓ̈
ⲙⲉ · [	[ⲛ̄ⲧⲁϥⲝⲟⲟⲥ] ⲉⲧⲃⲏ-
ⲝⲉⲁ[	[ⲛ̄ⲧⲟⲩ ⲛ̄ϭⲓ ⲇⲁ]ⲅⲉⲓⲇ’
ⲛ̄[	

Fol. 32.　(The position of this fol. is quite uncertain.)

Recto (?).　. . . 'I[1] have not [hidden aught] from you [of the things that are] profitable, [testify]ing to the Jews and Gentiles (ἔθ.) repentance (μετάν.) [toward] God [and] faith (πίσ.) toward our Lord [Jesus the] Christ (Χρ.) . . . . .

Verso (?).　. . . time of the . . . . . When he had [seen? how] this was the manner-of[-life of] the saints . . . . . the Lord had . . . . . light . . . . . he took (?) . . . . time of . . . . [where]of David [spake] . . . . .

---

[1] Acts xx. 20, 21, but differing considerably from Budge and Woide.

No. 26.

This story of Apollo, ⲫⲓⲗⲟⲥ [ⲛ]ⲛⲁⲅⲅⲉⲗⲟⲥ,[1] and Ammonius of Thône figures in the account of the latter in the *Synaxarium*.[2] A woman had attempted to beguile Ammonius, but had been converted by him. The devil, jealous at this triumph, spreads scandalous reports of the saint among the monasteries, and induces Apollo to visit him and be convinced. Apollo finds there the penitent woman, who, after eighteen years passed in Ammonius' cell, expires in their presence.

→ *Recto.*

[. . .]ⲛϩ·	[ⲉⲓ ⲉϩⲟ]ⲩⲛ ϣⲁ-
[ⲡⲉⲝ]ⲁϥ ⲙ̄ⲡⲁ-	ⲣⲟϥ [ⲁ]ϥⲁⲣⲭⲉⲓ
[ⲧⲡ]ⲅⲗⲏ ⲝⲉ-	ⲛ̄ⲣⲓⲙⲉ ⲛ̄ϭⲓ
[ⲃ]ⲱⲕ ⲧⲁⲙⲉ	ⲡⲁⲓⲁⲃⲟⲗⲟⲥ
ⲡⲉⲛⲉⲓⲱⲧ ⲁ-	Ⲡⲉⲝⲉ·^sic ⲁⲡⲁ ⲁ-

[1] His Life by بوهى ⲡⲁⲡⲟϭⲉ in Paris *arabe*, 4888, f. 139 b, whence in *Synax*. 25 Bâbeh. That this is the Apollo of Bawit has already been pointed out (*PSBA*. xxix. 291. The *Antiphonarium*, at the latter date, calls him ⲡⲓϩⲅⲥⲟⲥ [ⲛ]ⲛⲁⲅⲅⲉⲗⲟⲥ). He appears in the Diptychs, usually confounded with the martyr, son of Justus (*e.g.* Renaudot, *Lit.*, *ed.* 1847, i. 18), rarely distinct (*e.g.* Cairo *Eucholog.* 358). Clédat's *Baouit* ii. 91 gives Hamoi as his father's name; *cf. Synax*., امانى, Life امونة. To what has been elsewhere collected regarding Apollo and his namesakes (Br. Mus. no. 322 n., *Aeg. Z.* xl. 60), I may add : *Miss*. iv. 818 (= Paris 129^13, f. 63) relates probably to this saint. A Life of A. was in the White Monastery Library (*J. Th. St.* v. 566). He is repeatedly invoked at the Jeremias Monastery, alone or with Phib and (or) Anoup ; indeed, two Apollos are there commemorated (Quibell-Thompson, *Saqqâra* nos. 27, 76, 226). The calendaric mention of him with ⲡⲁ ⲛⲉϧⲓⲉⲓⲃ (= ⲁⲡⲁ ⲫⲓⲃ), Leyd. *MSS*. p. 216, remains obscure. The pilgrimage of Herminos and Hôr, related in the Life of the former (Paris *arabe* 148), took them to the church of Apa Apollo. There they beheld the saint's corpse ' adorned and mitred ' مزينا متوجا (f. 322 b). Their preceding visits had been on the W. bank to Apa Jeremias ارميا

(? of Saqqâra), then alive ; thence to the church of Elias the Syrian ; while from Apollo's relics they proceeded to those of Apa Mina in Gebel al-Khaṭṭaf (? Lybian Desert) (f. 323 a). This itinerary is too erratic to make it more than probable that its Apollo is he of Bawit. From the Arabic Life (f. 159 b &c.) it seems that the site of ' The Monastery ' (ⲡⲁⲟⲩⲏⲧ Bawit) was جبل ازكوهى *i. e.* ? ازكوهى = [ⲡ]ϣϭⲉⲛⲟϧⲉ, where a legend placed the cell of Phib (Zoega 367). (Paris 4787, another copy, reads ادكوهى.) A further corruption of this may be ابلوج, *Synax.*, *l. c.* Several other names in this text await elucidation from its Coptic original, announced as in the P. Morgan collection (*Journ. d. Sav.* 1912, 181). J. Maspero points out that the monastery of A. at (?) Aphrodito is named after its historical founder, otherwise identifiable (Pap. Cairo no. 67096). Can this be the same with that near Kom Esfaht (Petrie, *Gizeh and Rifeh* 39), where the patron A. is often called ἅγιος ?

[2] 20 Bashans (Forget ii. 130). Tûnah el-Gebel, W. of Ashmunain, is some 25 miles N. of Bawit. But Apollo was perhaps not, at this time, resident at Bawit ; *v. Aeg. Z.*, *l. c.* Thône often occurs in Ashmunain MSS., *e.g.* Br. Mus. 1042, Rylands 119, Krall *Rechtsurk.* cxxxiv. This Ammonius is invoked, *Deir el-Gebrawi* ii, pl. xxix, Clédat *Baouit* ii. 91.

ⲡⲁ ⲁⲡⲟⲗⲗⲱ
ϫⲉⲉⲓⲥ ⲟⲩⲙⲟ-
ⲛⲁⲭⲟⲥ *(sic)* ⲉⲁⲡⲁ
ⲁⲡⲁ[a] ⲁⲙⲙⲱ-
ⲛⲉⲡⲉ· ⲙⲡⲧⲟⲟ-
ⲟⲩ ⲛⲑⲱⲛⲉ
ⲉϥⲟⲩⲱϣ ⲉ-
ⲁⲡⲁⲛⲧⲁ ⲉ-
ⲧⲉⲕⲙⲛⲧⲉⲓ-
ⲱⲧ·
ⲛ̅ⲧⲉⲣⲟⲩϫⲓ
ⲡⲟⲩⲱ ⲇⲉ
ⲛ̅ⲁⲁⲡⲁ *(sic)* ⲁⲡ[ⲟ-]
[ⲗⲗⲱ

ⲡⲟⲗⲗⲱ ⲛⲁϥ
ϫⲉⲡⲉϣⲃⲏⲣ
ⲁϩⲣⲟⲕ ⲉⲕⲣⲓ-
ⲙⲉ ⲁⲣⲁ ⲛⲧⲁ-
ⲡⲁⲥⲟⲛ ⲁⲙⲙⲱ-
ⲛⲉ ⲙⲟⲩ·
ⲡⲉϫⲉ ⲡⲉⲧⲙ-
ⲙⲁⲩ ⲉⲧⲉⲡ[ϫⲓ-]
ⲁⲃⲟⲗⲟ[ⲥⲡⲉ
?

ª Reading ? ⲉⲡⲁⲁⲡⲁ.

↑ *Verso.*

ϭⲡ[. . . . .]ϥ
ⲁⲡⲇⲓⲁ[ⲃⲟⲗⲟⲥ ⲑ]ⲃ-
ⲃⲓⲟⲥ ⲁϥⲉ ⲉⲃⲟⲗ
ⲙⲡⲟⲩⲥⲟⲓⲙⲉ
ⲁⲩⲱ ⲛⲧⲉⲣⲉϥϭⲉ
ⲉⲃⲟⲗ ⲛϩⲙⲁⲥ
ⲁⲛϩⲓⲥⲉ ⲉⲛⲕⲱ-
ⲣϣ· ⲉⲣⲟϥ ϫⲉⲛⲟ-
ⲭ̅ⲥ̅ ⲉⲃⲟⲗ ⲙⲙⲟⲕ
ϫⲉⲛⲛⲉ ϩⲉⲛⲕⲟ-
ⲟⲩⲉ ⲧⲁⲕⲟ ⲛⲧⲉⲕ-
ⲗⲟⲉⲓϭⲉ· ⲙⲡⲉϥ-
ⲗⲟ ϩⲙⲡⲉϥⲛⲟ-

[
ⲛⲁϥ [ϫⲉⲛⲛⲉ-]
ϩⲉⲛⲕⲟ[ⲟⲩⲉ ⲧⲁ-]
ⲕⲟ ⲛⲧⲉϥ[ⲁϥⲟⲣ-]
ⲙⲏ ⲛ ⲙⲙ[ⲟⲛ]
ⲧⲛ̅ⲛⲟⲟⲩ ⲙⲙ[ⲛⲧ]
ⲛⲥⲟⲛ ⲛⲉⲙⲙ[ⲁⲛ]
ⲛⲧⲛ̅ϭⲟⲡϥ ⲛ̅-
ⲧⲛ̅ⲡⲁⲣⲁⲇⲓ-
ⲇⲟⲩ ⲙⲙⲟϥ ⲛ̅-
ⲧⲉϩⲟⲩⲥⲓⲁ ⲧⲁ-
ⲣⲟⲩⲥⲱⲧⲙ ⲛ̅-
ⲥⲉϣⲗⲁϩ· ϫⲉⲛ-

ⲃⲉ ⲁⲗⲗⲁ ⲁ ϥ-   ⲛⲉⲙⲙⲟⲛⲁ-

[. . .]ⲉ ⲛ̅ⲙⲙⲁⲧⲉ   ⲭⲟⲥ ⲧⲏⲣⲟⲩ ⲧⲁ-

[. . . .]ⲟⲥ ⲛⲙ-   ⲕⲟ ⲛ̅ⲧⲉ ϥ ⲁ ϥ ⲟ[ⲣ-]

                           ⲙⲏ· ⲥⲙⲟⲧ ⲛ [ⲅⲁⲣ]

                           ⲧⲁⲣⲛ̅ⲛⲉ ϫ ⲟⲩ[ⲁ]

                           ⲉⲃⲟⲗ ⲉ ⲛ ϩ ⲟⲥ[ⲟⲛ]

Recto. ... He said unto the door-keeper (-πύλη), ' Go, tell our father Apa Apollo that, lo, (here is) a monk (μον.), namely one from Apa Ammône, of the hill of Thône, who desireth to meet with (ἀπαντᾶν) thy paternity.' But (δέ) when they had brought the news to Apa Apollo . . . . .

... come] in unto him, the devil began (ἄρχειν) to weep. Apa Apollo said unto him, ' Friend, what (aileth) thee, that thou dost weep ? Is then (ἄρα) my brother Ammône dead ? ' That one, who was the devil, said, ...

Verso. ... ' The devil (διάβ.) humbled him and he fell with a woman. And after that he had fallen with her, we were at pains, beseeching him, (saying,) ' Cast her forth from thee, lest others perish by thine example.' He ceased not from his iniquity, rather (ἀλλά) he ... much ' . . . . .

' ... lest] others perish on his account (ἀφορμή). Or (ἤ) if not, send ten brethren with [us] and we will take him and give him over (παραδιδόναι) unto the authority (ἐξουσία), that they may hear and be afraid ; lest all the monks (μον.) perish on his account (ἀφ.). [For ? (γάρ)] it is easi(er ?) that we should cast forth one whilst yet (? -ὅσον) ' . . . . .

No. 27.

This narrative relates (here at least) to a saint named Hôr. Seven of this name can, I believe, be distinguished,[1] and it is impossible so far to decide which of them is here in question. He appears to have visited Alexandria and presumably in peaceful times ; he should therefore not be sought among the martyrs.

[1] A, Anchorites (1) *Hist. Laus.* ix (in Nitria) = Sozomen vi. 28 (in Thebaid) ; (2) companion of Hatre, *Vitae Patr.* v, lib. xv, § 43 = Zoega 299 ; (3) companion of Ambrosius (*cf.* ? the name 'Apa Rasios', Crum, *Ostr.* no. 116, and ? سيوس بدا = ابراسيوس *Synax.* 23 Tûbah) *PSBA.* xxix. 290, Quibell-Thompson, *Saqqâra* nos. 26, 295 ; (4) hermit of 2 Kihak, in Ludolf's Calendar 'the younger', and identical with biographer of Hermi- nos, for in that story his and that saint's deaths are foretold for same date (Paris *arabe* 148, f. 328 b). *Cf.* too his epithets 'Dyer' القصار

↑ *Recto* (?).   → *Verso* (?).

margin   margin

	ϩⲱⲣ ⲉϥϯ ⲉ[ⲟⲟⲩ]	ⲉϩⲟⲩⲛ ⲉⲡⲧⲟ-	
	ⲙ̄ⲡⲛⲟⲩⲧⲉ [ⲙⲛ-]	ⲡⲟⲥ ⲙ̄ⲙⲁⲣⲕⲟⲥ	
]ⲱⲥ	ⲡⲉϥⲁⲅⲅⲉⲗⲟ[ⲥ]	ⲡⲉⲩⲁⲅⲅⲉⲗⲓⲥ-	ⲏ[
]ⲉ	Ⲁⲡⲥⲱⲧⲏⲣ ϯ ⲛⲁ[ϥ]	ⲧⲏⲥ ⲁϥⲣⲥⲁ-	
	ⲛ̄ϯⲣⲏⲛⲏ ⲁϥⲃⲱ[ⲕ]	ϣϥ ⲛ̄ϩⲟⲟⲩ ⲉϥ-	
	ⲉϩⲣⲁⲓ ⲉ[ⲙ̄]ⲡⲏⲩ[ⲉ·]	ⲛⲏⲥⲧⲉⲩⲉ ϩⲛ̄-	
	Ⲡⲁ[ⲓⲕⲁⲓⲟⲥ	[. . . .]ⲡⲉⲕⲟ.	

Recto (?). . . . Apa] Hôr,[1] giving glory unto God and His angels (ἄγγ.). The Saviour (σωτ.) gave (?) him peace (εἰρήνη) and went up to heaven. The ri[ghteous ?. . . . .

Verso (?). . . . in unto the church (τόπος) of Mark the evangelist [2] and passed seven days fasting (νηστεύειν) in . . . . .

No. 28.

From the history of Apa Cyrus, the hermit, narrated by Pambô.[3] Cyrus, reputed a brother of Theodosius I, dwelt in a κατάγαιον,[4] 'at the edge of the world, nigh unto hell.' On Pambô's arrival he falls ill, and, before his death, is aware of that of Shenoute, which, in the Calendar, occurs on the day preceding his own.

(*Synax. ad loc.*) and الٮرجتی (Paris 148, ff. 294 a, 321 b, 330 b), for which I propose ابرختی, *i.e.* ⲡⲣⲁϩⲧ, so explaining the obscure name of his home ابرجت (*alias* اتریب). Yet Amél. *Géogr.* 12 suggests that the latter is a real place-name: B, Martyrs (5) Zoega p. 23 = *CSCO.* vol. 43, 127; (6) *Synax.* 12 Abîb = Amélineau, *Actes* 104: C, Bishop (7) اور (but Abû Sâlih 71 b اوری) Amélineau, *Contes* i. 100. Of these, no. 4 visited Alexandria, as did the subject of our text.

[1] May be subject of a foregoing verb.

[2] *V.* Amélineau, *Géogr.* 37, A. J. Butler, *Arab Conq.* 372.

[3] Br. Mus. Or. 6783 has a complete Life, differing slightly from the other versions (*v.* Rustafjael, *Light of Egypt* 137). Fragments in Saʻidic: Paris 129[13], f. 26, 131[3], f. 37. *V. Synax.* 8 Tûbeh (Hamlê). The Ethiopic text, *ed.* Turaieff, *Zapiski*, Orient. Sect. Imp. Russ. Archaeol. Soc., xv. (1903), is but a slightly longer form of the *Synax.*; but Br. Mus. Or. 701 (Eth.

[4] Paris, *l.c.* So used *Miss.* iv. 763, Rossi I. ii. 11.

→ *Recto.*

ⲧⲁⲟⲩᵃ ϣ[ⲱⲡⲉ ⲱ]
ⲡⲁⲉⲓⲱⲧ [ⲡⲉ-]
ⲝⲁϥ ⲝⲉⲁⲩⲛ[ⲟϭ]
ⲛⲥⲧⲩⲗⲗⲟ[ⲥ]
ϩⲉ ϩⲛ[ⲧⲟ-]
ⲟⲩ ⲛⲁⲧⲣⲓⲡ[ⲉ]   ⲉⲩ[
ⲙⲡⲟⲟⲩ ⲁⲡⲙⲁ-   ϣⲓ[
ⲕⲁⲣⲓⲟⲥ ⲁⲡ[ⲁ]   ⲧⲟⲟ[
[ϣⲉⲛⲟ]ⲩⲧⲉ ⲙ-   ⲥ[
[ⲧⲟⲛ ⲛ̄ⲙ̄]ⲟϥ ⲙ-   ⲝ[
[ⲡⲟⲟ]ⲩ ⲁⲗⲏⲑⲱⲥ
[. . .]ⲟⲥ . . ϣϯ
[. .]ⲛ . . [ⲛⲣ]ϥϯ   ⲡⲉⲝ[ⲁⲓ ⲛⲁϥ
ⲥ[ⲃ]ⲱ ⲁⲩⲱ ⲛⲣϥ-   ⲝⲉϩⲛⲟⲩ[ⲙⲉ ⲡⲁ-]
ⲥⲙ̄ⲛ̄ ⲛ̄ⲟⲙⲟⲥ ⲛ̄ⲡ-   ⲉⲓⲱⲧ [
ⲙⲟⲛⲟⲭⲟⲥ ⲙⲛ-   ⲧⲁⲩ[ⲉⲧ-]
ⁱ ⁱᶜ
ⲛ̄ⲕⲁⲥⲙⲓⲕⲟⲛ[.]   ⲃⲏⲏ[ⲧϥ
        margin

↑ *Verso.*

                      ]ⲟ
        . . .]ⲛⲟⲩ ⲝⲓ ⲙ-
        ⲡⲉⲓⲕⲟⲩ[ⲓ] ⲉⲛⲱ-
        ⲛⲉ ⲛⲥⲧⲁⲁϥ ϩⲁ-
        ⲧⲁⲁⲡⲉ ⲙⲙⲟⲛ
        [ⲁ]ⲓ̈ⲗⲟ ⲉⲓⲉϣⲙ-
ⲡ]ⲕ̄[ⲟ]ⲥⲙⲟⲥ   ϭⲙ ⲉϩⲙⲟⲟⲥ ⲉ-
       ]ⲡⲁϥ-   [ϩⲣ]ⲁⲓ ⲝⲉⲁⲡⲁⲥⲱ-
       ]ⲧⲉⲗⲓ̈ⲟⲥ   [ⲙ]ⲁ ⲣ[ⲧⲥⲟⲙ ⲁ-]
       ?   ⲛⲟ[ⲕ ⲝⲉ ⲁ]ⲓϥⁱ ⲡⲱ-
       ]ⲛϥ   ⲛⲉ [ⲁⲓⲧⲁⲁϥ ϩⲁ-]
       ]ⲁⲟϩ.   ⲝⲱϥ [. . . .]ⲩ
       ]ϩⲁ   . . ⲛⲣⲟ[. . .]ⲡⲉ
]—————   [. .]ⲧ[. . ⲉ'ⲧ-
[ⲙ]ⲛⲥⲁⲛⲁⲓ̈ ⲝⲉ   ⲣⲉϥϣⲟⲡ[ϥ] ⲉ-ᶜ
[ⲡ]ⲉⲝⲁϥ ⲛⲁⲓ̈   ⲣⲟϥ ⲛⲟⲩⲉⲓⲣⲏ-
[ⲝⲉ]ⲙ[. .]ⲧⲛ̄   ⲛⲏ · ⲁⲩⲱ ⲟⲛ ⲛⲉ-
       ]ⲱ   ⲣⲉⲡϥⲥⲧⲟⲙⲁ-
               ⲭⲟⲥ ϣⲟⲅⲱ ϩᵈ[
               . ϥⲛⲛⲟ . [

ᵃ ⲛ̄]ⲧⲁ-.   ᵇ I have noted that ⲝⲓ cannot be read.   ᶜ Or ϩⲙⲛ̄]ⲧⲣⲉϥ-.   ᵈ Or
ϣⲟⲅⲱϩ or as = ϣⲟⲅⲟ.

Recto. . . . What hath happened, O] my father?' He said, 'A great pillar (στῦλος) hath fallen in the mount of Atripe this day; the blessed (μακ.) Apa [Sheno]ute is gone to rest this day. Verily (ἀληθῶς) . . . . teacher and law-maker (-νόμος) for monks (μον.) and worldlings (κοσμικός) . . . . [I?] said [unto him?,] ' In [truth (?), my] father . . . . . concerning [him . . . . .

Verso. . . . the] world (κόσ.) . . . . perfect (τέλειος) . . . . . (*dividing line*). And (δέ) thereafter he said unto me, '. . . . .

... take this small stone and place it beneath my head; verily I am no longer able to sit down, for my body ($\sigma\hat{\omega}$.) is become powerless.' [But ($\delta\acute{\epsilon}$)] I took (?) the stone [and I placed? it] beneath him . . . ., that He would[1] receive him unto Him in peace ($\epsilon\acute{\iota}\rho$.). And also his stomach ($\sigma\tau\acute{o}\mu$.) was[2] . . . . .

No. 29.

This should be part of one of those tales of wandering visits through the desert, paid by a devout inquirer to the cells of various ascetic celebrities, and met with in the collections of *Apophthegmata*, in the Life of Onnophrius,[3] that of Cyrus,[4] of Paul of Tammah,[5] and the like.[6] Here the scene is presumably in the far south, as certain of the characters are connected with Nubia.

Of fol. 3 no translation can be attempted.

Fol. 1. ↑

margin   p. ⲥⲧ

ϣⲱⲛⲉ ⲙ̄ⲛ̄ⲇⲁⲓⲙⲟⲛⲓⲟⲛ ⲉϥ-
ⲛⲟⲩϫⲉ ⲙ̄ⲙⲟⲟⲩ ⲉⲃⲟⲗ · ⲕⲁⲧⲁ ⲑⲉ ⲉⲧⲉ-
ⲣⲉⲡⲉⲛϫⲟⲉⲓⲥ ϫⲱ ⲙ̄ⲙⲟⲥ ϫⲉⲙ̄ⲡ-
ϣⲏⲛ ⲉⲛⲁⲛⲟⲩϥ ⲛⲁⲧⲁⲅⲉ ⲕⲁⲣ-
ⲡⲟⲥ ⲉⲃⲟⲗ ⲉϥϩⲟⲟⲩ · ⲁϥϫⲓ ϩⲁⲣ ⲙ̄-
ⲙⲉⲣⲟⲥ ⲛ̄ⲁⲡⲟⲥⲧⲛⲑⲟⲟⲩⲥ ⲉⲃⲟⲗ ϩ̄ⲛ-
ⲛⲉⲧⲣ[ⲁⲫⲏ] ⲉⲧⲟⲩⲁⲁⲃ · ⲁⲩⲱ ⲛⲉ-
[ϣⲁϥ . . . .]ⲛϥ ⲉⲃⲟⲗ ⲉϥⲙⲉⲗⲉⲧⲁ
ⲡ]ⲉϩⲟⲟⲩ ⲙ̄ⲡⲧⲉⲩϣⲏ ·
     ] . ϫⲉ ⲛ̄ⲧⲉⲩϣⲏ ⲧⲏ-
[ⲣⲥ   ]ⲧⲥ[a] ϫⲉⲛⲁ ⲛⲁⲓ
     ] . . ⲧⲱⲛ[b] ⲉⲣⲟⲟⲩ
     ] . . . ⲱⲧ

[a] Not ⲙⲙ]ⲟⲥ.   [b] ? ⲧⲏⲧⲱⲛ.

---

[1] Or 'when He should'.
[2] This might be read variously: 'was not able to . . .', 'was pouring forth . . .'
[3] *Acta SS.*, June 12, Amélineau in *Rec.* vi. 166.
[4] *Synax.*, 8 Abîb (Forget ii. 215. The Ethiop.,

8 Hamlê, differs much).
[5] *Miss.* iv. 759. The true title of this narrative is not known.
[6] *E.g.* the Life of Athanasius, No. 26.

→ p. ⲥⲁ̄   margin

ⲧⲙ̄ᵃ ⲛ̄ⲥⲱⲃⲉ ⲛ̄ⲟⲩⲟⲉⲓⲯ ⲛⲓⲙ ⲡⲉ-
ⲭⲁⲓ̈ ⲛⲁϥ ⲭⲉⲉⲡⲉⲓⲁⲏ ⲟⲩⲛ̄ⲧⲁⲓ̈ⲉⲓᵇ
ⲉⲯⲁⲭⲉ ⲙ̄ⲡⲉⲕⲙ̄ⲧⲟ ⲉⲃⲟⲗ · ϯⲟⲩ-
ⲱⲯ ⲉⲧⲣⲉⲕⲭⲱ ⲉⲣⲟⲓ̈ ⲙ̄ⲡⲃⲓⲟⲥ ⲛ̄-
ⲛⲉⲥⲛⲏⲩ ⲧⲏⲣⲟⲩ ⲉⲧⲙ̄ⲡⲉⲕⲕⲱ-
ⲧⲉ ⲭⲉⲛⲉⲟⲩⲛ̄ⲕⲉⲟⲩⲟⲛ ⲙ̄ⲡⲥⲁⲣⲏⲥ
ⲙ̄ⲙⲟⲛ · ⲡⲉⲭⲁϥ ⲛⲁⲓ̈ ⲭⲉⲁⲓ̈ϩⲁϩⲉ
ⲥⲟⲛ ⲥⲛⲁⲩ ⲙ̄ⲡⲓⲙⲁⲏ[. . . . .]ⲛ
ϩⲛ̄ⲛ̄ⲁⲛⲟⲩⲃⲁ · ⲉ[ⲣⲉⲡⲣⲁⲛᶜ ⲙ̄ⲡⲟⲩⲁ]
ⲙ̄ⲙⲟⲟⲩⲡⲉ ⲑⲁⲣⲁ[ⲡⲣⲁⲛ ⲙ̄-]
ⲡⲕⲉⲟⲩⲁⲡⲉ ⲓ̈ⲁⲕ[ⲱⲃ   ⲡⲛⲟⲩ-]
ⲧⲉ ⲧⲛ̄ⲛⲟⲟⲩⲥⲟⲩ ⲙ̄[ⲡⲉⲡⲓⲥⲕⲟⲡⲟⲥ]
ⲁⲡⲁ ϩⲉⲣⲙⲓⲁⲥ ⲉⲧ[ⲣⲉϥⲧⲥⲁⲃⲱⲟⲩ]
ⲉⲥϩⲁⲓ̈ ⲛ̄ⲧⲉⲧ[ᵈ

ᵃ ⲥⲱⲧⲙ seems the only possibility.   ᵇ For ⲛ̄ⲧⲁⲓⲉⲓ.   ᶜ Instead of stop, possibly
a letter, ⲛⲉⲣⲉⲡⲣⲁⲛ.   ᵈ ? ⲛ̄ⲧⲉⲣ[ⲉ.

Fol. 1. P. 203. ... maladies and the devils (δαιμόνιον) that he cast out;
according (κατά) as our Lord saith, 'A good tree doth not bring forth
evil fruit (καρ.).'[1] He got many portions (μέρος) by heart (ἀπὸ στηθοῦς)
from the holy scriptures (γρ.). And [he used to . . . . .], repeating (μελετᾶν) . . . . ., day and night . . . . . all the night . . . . . Have mercy upon
me . . . . . resemble (?) them . . . . .

P. 204. ... laughter[2] at all times.' I said unto him, 'Seeing, then
(ἐπειδὴ οὖν), that I have come to speak before thee, I desire that thou
wouldest tell me of the life (βίος) of all the brethren that are in thy
neighbourhood, as to whether there be any other to the south of us.'[3]
He said unto me, 'I came upon two brethren . . . . . among the Nubians,[4]

[1] Luke vi. 43.
[2] Or as an adjective.
[3] Cf. a phrase in Br. Mus. no. 336.
[4] This form, ⲛ̄ⲁⲛⲟⲩⲃⲁ (sing. ⲟⲩⲁⲛⲟⲩⲃⲁ,
pl. ϩⲉⲛⲁⲛⲟⲩⲃⲁ) is used throughout Br. Mus.

Or. 7029, where the barbarians about Philae are so
called; also in *Miss.* iv. 642. (Wessely's Ἀννου-
βάδων, *Ein biling. Majestätsgesuch* 44, is confirmed by Wilcken, *Chrest.* i. II, p. 13.) In
Paris 131¹, f. 62 (homily of Philip, bishop of

[the name of the one] of them being Thara ∴.¹, [the name of] the other Jacob (?) . . . . . God sent them to [the bishop (ἐπ.)?] Apa Hermias,² that [he should teach them] to write. After that (?) . . . . .

Fol. 2. → *Recto.*   ↑ *Verso.*

margin   (*page no. here*)   margin

ΠΕϤΑΪΤΗΜΑ ⲘⲠⲚⲤⲰⲤ ΑΠⲚ[ΟΥ-]
ΤΕ ⲤΩΤⲘ ΕΠΕϤϹΟΠϹ· ⲘⲠⲚⲤΑϩ[ΕⲚ-]
ϩΟΟΥ ϪΕ ΑⲚΕϤΕΙΟΤΕ ⲂⲰΚ ΕΠⲠ[Ο-]
ⲖΕⲙΟϹ ΑΥⲘΟΟΥΤΟΥ· ⲚΤΕΡΕϤϹ[Ⲱ-]
ⲦⲘ ϪΕ ⲚϬⲒ ΠΕΠΙϹΚΟΠΟϹ ΕΠΟΥⲰ
ΑϤϪⲰΚ ΕⲂⲟⲖ ⲘΠΕϤΑΪΤΗⲙ[Α·]
ΑϤϮ ⲚΑΥ ⲘΠⲂΑΠΤΙϹⲙΑ· ⲚΤ[Ε-]
ⲢΕϤⲚΑΥ Ϫ[Ε] ΕϩΟΤΕ ⲘΠⲚΟΥΤΕ .

       ]ᵃ ⲚⲢΗΤΟΥ ΑϤϮ ϩΙⲰΟΥ ⲘⲘ-
[ΠΕϹⲬΗⲙΑ] ⲚⲦⲘⲚⲦⲘΟⲚΑⲬΟϹ ΑΥ-
[Ⲱ   ]ΟΥᵇ ΕϹϨΑΪ· ΑⲨⲰ ⲚΤΕ-
[ⲢΕϤ   ]ΟΥ ⲘΠϹΟΟΥⲚ ΤΗⲢϤ·
[ΑϤϮ ⲚΑΥ ⲚΤΕ]ⲬΕΙⲢΟϪΟΠΕΙΑ· ΠΕ
        ]ⲚⲚⲀⲀϤ ⲘⲘ[

[Ⲙ]ⲘΟϤ ⲘⲠϤⲖΥΠΕΙ ⲘⲘΟΟΥ· Ε̄-
[Ϫ]ⲰΚ ΕⲂⲟⲖ ⲘΠΕϤΑΪΤΗⲙΑ ΚΑΤΑ
[ΘΕ] ⲚΤΑϤϪΟΟϹ· ΑⲨⲰ ΑⲨⲂⲰΚ ΕⲢΗ[Ϲ]
[Ε]ΠΕϤⲙΑ ΕϤΟⲨⲚⲄ ⲘⲘΟⲚ ⲚΑϩΟΟⲨ
[Ϲ]ⲚΑⲨ ⲘⲘΟΟⲰΕ ΕΑⲨΤΑⲘΙΟ ⲚΑⲨ
ⲚΟⲨⲙΑ ⲚϢⲰΠΕ ΑⲨⲰ ΟⲨΚΟⲨΪ
[Ⲛ]ΕΚΚⲖΗϹΙΑ ΑⲨΟⲨⲰϩ ⲚⲢΗⲦϹ·
[Α]ⲨⲰ ΠΕⲨϮ ⲚϬⲦⲏⲨ ΕⲢΟΟⲨ ϩⲚϨⲰⲂ
[Ⲛ]ⲒⲘ· ΑⲨⲰ ΑⲨϢⲰΠΕ ⲚϬⲢΗⲨ Ⲛ-
[Ο]ⲨΟⲚ ⲚⲒⲘ ΕⲦⲚΑⲨ ΕⲢⲞ[Ⲩ ΑⲨ]Ⲱ ΑⲚ-
[Ϲ]ⲰⲦⲘ [Ε]ϩΡΑϩ ⲚΑⲢΕⲦⲎ [ΕⲦΕⲞⲨⲚ-]
ⲦΑⲨ Ⲛ[Θ]Ε ⲚⲚΑⲚΕⲚ[ΕΙΟΤΕ ⲚΑⲢⲬΑⲒ-]
[Ο]Ⲛ· ΑⲚΟΚ ϪΕ Ⲛ[ΤΕⲢΕΙϹⲰⲦⲘ]
[Ε]ⲚΑΪ ΑΪΠΑⲢΑΚΑⲖ[ΕⲒ
[. . . . .]ⲀΪ ϪΕ . . . [

ᵃ ΕⲦ[ⲞⲨⲞⲚϨ ΕⲂⲟⲖ] or ΕⲦ[ⲞⲨⲎϨ ϩⲢΑⲒ].   ᵇ ΑϤⲦϹΑⲂ]ⲞⲞⲨ?

Fol. 2. *Recto.* . . . 'their request (αἴτημα). Afterwards God heard their prayer and (δέ) after some days their parents went to the war (πόλ.) and were slain. But (δέ) when the bishop (ἐπ.) heard the news, he fulfilled their request (αἴτ.) and gave them baptism (βάπ.). But (δέ) when he heard of the fear of God [that dwelt ³?] within them, he put upon them [the habit (σχῆμα)] of monkhood (-μοναχός) and [taught] them to write. And when . . . . . them all knowledge, [he gave them] ordination (χειροτονία)' . . . . .

ⲦΑΠΑⲦΟⲖⲎ, *cf.* Zoega pp. 266, 267) it is
ⲚⲞⲨⲘⲀ. *Cf.* Arab. *Nuba*, Ethiop. *Nuba* (Ludolf,
Comment. p. 68).

¹ My copy would not justify Serapion.

³ Or 'that was manifested'.

Verso. '. . . him and he grieved (λυπεῖν) them not as to fulfilling their request (αἴτ.), according (κατά) as they had said.   And they departed southward to their place, distant from us about two days' walk, when they had made for themselves a dwelling place and a little church (ἐκ.), and therein they dwelt.   And they gave heed unto themselves in everything and became profitable unto every one that beheld them ; and we heard of many "virtues" (ἀρετή) [which were] theirs, like those of our [ancient (? ἀρχαῖος) fathers'].   But (δέ) I [, when I had heard ?] these things, I besought (παρακαλεῖν) . . . . (saying), '. . . . .

Fol. 3.　↑ *Recto* (?).	→ *Verso* (?).
margin	margin
ⲁⲗ]ⲗⲁ ⲉ︤ⲡⲏⲧ︤ⲡ︥	ⲁⲟⲭⲓⲟⲛᵃ ⲁ[. . . . . ⲉⲕ-]
]ⲭⲱ ⳿ⲙ̄ⲙⲟⲥ	ⲕⲗⲏⲥⲓⲁ· ⲧ[
]ⲉϥⲛⲁ†	ⲧⲏ︤ⲣ︤ⲡ︥ ⲡⲉ[
]·ⲟ︦ⲃ̄ⲏⲩⲉ	ⲡⲣⲱⲙ[ⲉ
]ⲭ . . . ⲧⲉ ⲉ	ϩⲓⲧ︤ⲙ︥[ⲡ . . . . ⲭⲓ-]
]ⲙ . . . . ⲟⲩⲛ	ⲧ︥ϥ ⲉⲧⲉⲕⲕⲗ[ⲏⲥⲓⲁ
]ⲏ . . . ⲛ̄ⲑⲉ	ⲛ̄ⲧⲉϥⲯⲩⲭ[ⲏ
]·ⲛ̄ⲛ . . . ⲧⲟⲛ̣	ϩⲓⲟⲩ[ⲥⲟ]ⲡ ⲁ[
]·ⲱⲕ ⲉⲃⲟⲗ	ⲛⲟⲙⲟⲥ ⲙ[. . . . . ⲛ̄ⲧⲉ-]
ⲧ]ⲁϣⲉⲟⲉⲓϣ	ⲣⲉϥⲉⲓ ⲁⲉ ⲉ[
ⲭ]ⲱ ⳿ⲙ̄ⲙⲟⲥ	ⲡⲉϥⲉⲓⲱ[ⲧ
]ⲡ · ⲛ̄ⲑⲉ	ⲙⲉⲛ ⲁ[

ᵃ ? ⲡⲁⲛⲁⲟⲭⲓⲟⲛ, ⲍⲉⲛⲟⲁⲟⲭⲓⲟⲛ.

APPENDIX

ABBREVIATIONS EMPLOYED.

GREEK TEXTS :

AS.	. . . .	*Vita* in *Acta Sanctorum*, Maii iii.
§	. . . .	refers to paragraphs of the above.
Par.	. . . .	*Paralipomena, ibid.*
Nau A	. . . .	*Patrol. Or.* iv. 425-503.
Nau D	. . . .	*ibid.*, 504-511.
Sur.	. . . .	Surius, *De Prob. SS. Vit.*, iii and Nau's copy of the Greek original.

COPTIC TEXTS :

Sa (1 to 6)	. . .	Sa'idic recensions, *v. below*, pp. 183ff.
SaX	. . . .	The new text, No. 25 *above*.
Bo.	. . .	Bohairic recension, *ed.* Amélineau.

ARABIC TEXTS :

Ap.	. . . .	Paris, MS. arabe 261.
Ac.	. . . .	Cairo, printed edition.
Am.	. . . .	Amélineau's printed text.
Av.	. . . .	Vatican, Cod. Arab. 172.

THE main object of this Appendix is to draw attention to two hitherto unnoticed Arabic versions of the Life of Pachomius. Three texts are indeed here described, but two of them (Ap. and Ac.) are, in great part, so closely related that they may be regarded as representing a single version.

M. Amélineau, in publishing his Arabic text, was aware of the existence of the MSS. in Rome and Paris, besides those which he employed[1]; but one must suppose that he did not examine either, since he says nothing of their wide divergence from his own text; and it has thence been hitherto assumed[2] that but one form of the Arabic Life exists.

To the descriptions of these I have added what can provisionally be said as to the six Sa'idic recensions,[3] awaiting for their final valuation the investigations which, it is to be hoped, Professor Lefort will before long publish.

I have no pretext for attempting here a rediscussion of the question of origins; neither our new Sa'idic text nor the new Arabic versions contribute anything

[1] *Mus. Guim.* liv.

[2] Ladeuze 52.

[3] Each of the extant MSS. represents a some-
that the White Monastery alone (whence all these
six came) once possessed twenty (*sic*?) copies of
the Life of P., besides that of P., Horsiese and
Theodore together, such an amount of variation

available as arguments against Ladeuze's contention in favour of a Greek text as the original basis whence the other versions sprang.[1] Yet a reader of AS. and Par., having the requisite familiarity with the popular literary idiom of Egypt in the earlier Byzantine period, and if conversant too with Coptic, would probably be struck by the uncouthness of much of their phraseology, and would incline to admit at least the possibility of certain parts of these texts having been directly translated from Coptic—whether written or oral—and so incorporated in the Greek biography.[2] Not a few examples occur of those ambiguous locutions which, being of identical usage in both languages, it is difficult to assign as original property to either. Such are χεῖρα δοῦναι *help* (Nau D. 511, 15), τόπον εὑρεῖν (AS. § 76 *sup.*, but *cf.* N. Test. τόπον δοῦναι), ὀνόματα λαβεῖν (AS. § 80 *sup.*). Are these to be reckoned evidence for a translation from the Coptic or merely for a Greek composition, written in a Coptic 'atmosphere'; or are they in fact passable Greek and their identical Coptic counterparts simple translations, naturalized and current, like many another Greek phrase and idiom, in the native language?[3]

Paris, MS. arabe No. 261 (= Ap.).

De Slane's catalogue assigns this MS. to the end of the 14th century. A reader's note on the last fol. is dated A. M. 1066 = A. D. 1350. The title runs: 'In the Name of the Father .... the History of our father, the great Pachomius, the saintly, and his favourite disciple, Theodore, the beloved.' *Cf.* the title of Am., where the latter is not mentioned. The limits of this recension are practically conterminous with those of AS. + Par. (*s.* the Table, p. 189). It is indeed a direct translation from the Greek, as we learn from the subscriptions to the MSS. in Cairo[4]; and confirmation of their statements may be had from many of the personal and place-names, where the transcription often reproduces even the Greek case-endings (*e.g.* in § 3 بحومبا. voc.,

---

[1] The main argument against this now generally accepted view (*e.g.* Butler, *Laus. Hist.* ii. 206) is of course its inherent improbability. Despite Prof. Ladeuze's ingenious marshalling of reasons why the Life should have been first composed in Greek, one cannot but feel that such a literary product, in such a time and place, is scarcely credible. (*Cf.* C. H. Turner, in *J. Th. St.* vi. 324.)

[2] Hence there might be instances of mistranslations which have resulted in obscure or improbable readings in the Greek. One case of probable misunderstanding of the Coptic appears to me to be the simile of the devil, bound and placed under foot ὡς στρουθίον (Par. § 4 = Nau A § 15). I suggest that the Coptic here read ϫⲁϫⲉ *enemy*, which the translator mistook for ϫⲁϫ *sparrow*. The corresponding AS. § 67 has θηρίον,

but Am. 531, 9, in paraphrasing that (and translating probably the missing parallel from SaX), has *enemy*. As to στρουθίον, *cf.* Jerome's comment on Eccles. xii. 4, *nunquam passerem in malam partem legisse me novi*, *PL.* 23, 1109. But *v.* Par. § 26, where the word is scarcely open to the explanation here offered.

[3] Ladeuze 43, 44, quotes Tillemont to like effect, but criticizes his remarks. The late E. A. Sophocles (*Lexicon*, List of Authors) appears to have taken the Greek for a 'barbarous translation'. If the much needed revision of the edition of AS. be ever undertaken, we shall learn how far the Bollandists adhered to one MS., how far they compiled their text (*v.* Nau, 409 n.).

[4] *V.* description of Ac.

§ 7 طبانسين acc., § 20 تنتيرون gen. pl., *ib.* سيينس gen., § 38 بلامنس gen., § 68 صورن acc., § 72 فيلونس gen., *ib.* مغفولو gen.), while discarding those forms usual in the parallel texts of Coptic origin (نظريات for شاناسات for شينوفسكيا for بانوس ,برنوج for اخميم, زكشاوس Zακχαῖος sometimes for زكا, زكى). Of features positively significant of a non-Coptic origin, the most noteworthy is the transmutation of the date of Pachomius' death, 14th Pachôns, into its Syrian (or ? Melkite) equivalent, 15th Iyâr, and similarly that of Theodore from 2nd Pachôns to 16th Iyâr; further, the fantastical 'Coptic' etymology of the name Panopolis,[1] and perhaps such omissions as that of the local names in § 52 (fol. 188 b).

The precise relationship between this and the various Greek recensions could only be ascertained by a series of comparisons far more systematic than I have undertaken. This much however may be said: that Ap. is a patchwork of (1) a version following closely AS.+Par.,[2] (2) another, once substantially identical with Am., but since provided with stylistic embellishments—here a further epithet or synonym, there a longer phrase[3]—and (3) independent alterations or additions, sometimes of considerable length. Of these elements (1) is represented, for example, in §§ 1–19, with the exception of §§ 7, 15 (partly), again in §§ 22–25; (2) in §§ 35, 71–96 and in the sections taken from Par. As examples of (3) we may cite (*a*) many additional biblical quotations, throughout the whole text; (*b*) several homiletic developments, *e.g.* in §§ 11, 12, 24, 31, 46, 49, Par. 6, 22, this last of over 7 pages; (*c*) additions or changes in detail, presumably due to the translator, *e.g.* § 2 Abyssinia the scene of P.'s military service; §§ 4, 25 P. and Theodore both tonsured; § 22 P.'s sister writes to him, asking to see him (the whole section is peculiar); § 36 after Υἱοῦ τοῦ Θεοῦ, reference to the Ode of Habakkuk, which, if the wise man meditate, he may dispense with the rest of the Prophets; § 39[2] P. asks water to wash his hands, lest he defile the book he reads; Par. 5 'Permit us to bury him, lest the jackals devour him'; Par. 6 begins with P.'s question, 'Have ye yet more words and blame? They answered, No'[4]; Par. 26 P. exorcises the phantom with a charm[5]; Par. 12 P. in his reply quotes 'a sage'[6]; § 62 (?) referring to P.'s innumerable virtues, 'Who may number the flowers of the desert or the waves of the sea?'; § 65 subsequently P. gave to some the interpretation of his vision, 'and what I long after heard from them I tell to you'; § 72 P. says his monasteries have 7,000 monks.[7] Further, certain additions

---

[1] Fol. 186, 13 (§ 51[2]) الذى هو اسم الزيتون باللغة القبطية.

[2] An instructive specimen of their combination is §§ 66, 67 (ff. 121–129 b). Practically all of AS. and of Par. 2, 3, 4 is included, but the narrative is made up of regularly alternating sections from these two sources.

[3] Often with the object of effecting a rhyme (*cf.* description of Ac.).

[4] So too in Par. 16. *Cf.* Nau A (*Patr. Or.* iv. 443).

[5] Fol. 167, 7. Begins يا لشركم الذى لا ينام وقتالكم الذى ما يكل ويسام.

[6] Fol. 179, 11 بعض الحكماء, 'Whoso setteth fire and water in a vessel without understanding hath done so in madness.'

[7] *Cf.* Am. 380, Ladeuze 204.

would seem to aim at exalting the monastic dignity: § 25 Pekusius first asks P.'s leave to introduce Theodore; § 49 Theodore, before preaching, begs P.'s blessing; Par. 5 the funeral procession reverently salutes P. and takes his blessing; § 50² Petronius, on arrival, performs the humblest menial service during three years (*quot.* Mat. vii. 14); § 51¹ the bishop's deference to P., as if he had been his disciple. Of sheer misunderstandings we may note the name 'Archelaus', given to the anonymous brother in § 42² and originating presumably in the words ἀρχαίῳ ἀδελφῷ.

As is natural in a recension of non-Coptic origin, Ap. shows none of those additional passages which make up so much of Am. (*i. e.* those in Butler's table without Greek, though often with Coptic, equivalents), excepting where taken from the *Laus. Hist.* (*viz.* Am. 366–9, 377, 382–4) and the two anecdotes on Am. 641,¹ which figure in Nau D (*v. Patr. Or.* iv. 509, 43) and are, here as there, followed by the passage *l.c.* 510, 6, ending with Gal. ii. 2.² Indeed a number of the minor peculiarities which differentiate the texts printed or analysed by Nau from those of AS. and Par. reappear in Ap., which likewise has not a few features in common with the pseudo-metaphrastic text of Surius. The following references will suffice to confirm the former statement: Par. 6 ends in Ap. as in Nau D (*l.c.* 440); § 50² Ap. more like Nau D than AS., but much longer; § 52 Ap. = Nau D in certain details, but is longer; § 53 Ap. = Nau D in ref. to πορνεία (*l.c.* 507, 27); § 55² Ap. has συγχωροῦνται κτλ., as in Nau D; § 57 Ap. has τὰ τοῦ πνεύματος; § 58 Ap. = Nau D in omitting 2nd section (AS. καὶ πολλάκις), reading ὑπακούετε—Θεοῦ and in 3rd section οὐ μόνον—ἁμαρτία; § 71 last two lines *om.* Ap. and Nau D. Thenceforth Nau D as well as Ap. generally = Am.

As regards sequence of the paragraphs in Ap., it will be seen from the table, p. 191, that there is an undeniable similarity between their grouping here and in Ac., while in several of the other texts groups appear, identically composed with those in Ap., though at relatively different intervals.

The Cairo Edition (= Ac.).

This print, edited in 1891 by the hegumenus of the monastery of El-Baramûs for the Coptic Orthodox Educational Society in Cairo,³ professes (*s.* Preface) to be reproduced unaltered [from the MS.], so far as the sense remained intelligible. Nothing is said as to sources; but from the colophon in a modern copy in the

---

¹ A Boh. version of the 2nd in Br. Mus. no. 915.

² Instead of being direct translations from AS., the additions in Am. 'from another copy' (Am. 599) must now appear more likely to have come from Ap. (fol. 76 a), which text contains moreover the other passages regarded as directly from AS. (*v.* Ladeuze p. 60).

³ Title . . . كتاب القديس انبا باخوميوس
نقح . . . القمص عبد المسيح المسعودى . طبع
على نفقة جمعية التعليم المسيحى الارثوذكسية
بالقاهرة ١٨٩١

Patriarchal Library, very kindly communicated by Marcus Bey Simaika, we learn that the print was made from it. My informant tells me that the original of this copy (as well as of another in the same library, which expressly states as much) was a MS. in Deir Abû Maḳâr, dated A.M. 975 = A.D. 1251 (*sic*). A third copy of this is, I am further informed, at Deir el-Moḥarraḳ and was made in A.D. 1842. Now this last copy bears the important statement (copied for me by Simaika Bey) that the old MS. at Abû Maḳâr was 'translated from the Greek into the Arabic in the hand-writing of one of the Greek Melkites, named John, son of Metri, son of Ḥamzah, in Cairo.[1] Apparently therefore the date of the MS. is that of the translation itself, which was made only in the 13th century; and if so, we further obtain a *terminus ante quem* for the writing of Ap. The scribe of the Patriarch's copy whence the print was made further observes that from the latter many clauses in rhymed prose (الكلم المسجّع) have been omitted, while, at the same time, such of the more important dates have been inserted as the editor was able to ascertain.[2]

The text as printed is, like Ap., a mixture of the two recensions: the majority of its sections show the same version of AS. + Par. as Ap., and in all but identical wording, while a lesser number agree with Am., though often with modifications in phraseology. But, beyond this, the compiler of Ac. has made a large selection from those independent additions of Am. which Ap. discards (*e.gg.* Ac. p. 8 has Am. 348 *inf.*, p. 29 Am. 390, p. 33 Am. 406, p. 37 Am. do., p. 61 *inf.* Am. 432, p. 65 Am. 562, p. 80 Am. 502, pp. 89–91 Am. 509–18, p. 112 Am. 435, p. 126 Am. 448, p. 136 Am. 591), while in a few cases omitting passages to be found in Ap. (conspicuously that from *Laus. Hist.* = Am. 366 ff., § 27[1] and Par. 32 + § 40[1]). There remain, as elements peculiar to Ac., besides a homiletic development of § 71 (p. 131) and a short apophthegm (p. 163),[3] a long section consisting of excerpts from P.'s sermons (pp. 115, 2–121, 7). Their Sa. original is to be found in Br. Mus. Or. 7024, ff. 18–49 b, while short extracts, partly identical with these, are in Arabic in Or. 4523 (*v.* below), f. 182b ff.[4] For the sequence of paragraphs, *v.* the table, p. 191. How far this is the arrangement of the modern editor it is impossible at present to ascertain.

---

[1] بخط احد الاروام الملكية اسمه جونة بن متري بن حمزة بعحروسة مصر.

[2] These occur on pp. 4, 8, 12, 141, 168 of the edition. The Coptic month-names are of course here employed; *cf.* Ap.

[3] 'By what road can a man expel Satan from within him?' Theodore replies that, as a guest cannot be expelled except his belongings be first ~~put without, so only by first casting forth the~~ vices, can Satan be himself expelled.

[4] Sa. is about to be published by Dr. Budge. It is entitled: '*An Exhortation* (κατήχησις) *pronounced by* ... *Apa Pahomô, concerning a brother that had been wroth, being one of the time of Apa Ebônh, who had brought him to Tabennêse.*' Ebônh is presumably the abbot of Shenesêt (§ 35). *Cf.* perhaps Br. Mus. no. 268. It may be noted here that, among these extracts added after the text in Or. 4523, there is one (f. 185) from the ~~Life of Athanasius~~ No. 27 above).

Amélineau's Text, *Musée Guimet* xvii. 337 (= Am.).

It is not necessary to describe afresh this recension. Of the four MSS. available to me only that at Göttingen (Universitätsbibliothek, Nr. 116, here G) is of any antiquity; it is assigned to the 16th century.[1] The others are all modern copies, the age of whose originals I do not know. M. Amélineau says (*Introd.* liv, lvi) that he had at his disposal copies of three practically identical MSS., in Luxor, El-Moharraḳ, and the Patriarchate, but that his text and translation were made from the last of these. Confronting this statement with Simaika Bey's information (*v.* above), it would appear that the Patriarchate (if not El-Moharraḳ also) possesses copies both of the Ap. and Am. recensions. The MS. which M. Amélineau printed is now Or. 4523 of the British Museum (A.D. 1816), his other two being Nos. 4783 and 4784 (A.D. 1886 and 1839 respectively) of the Bibliothèque Nationale. And yet it is difficult to believe that the translation was indeed made, as one would gather from the author's words (*Introd.* liv), strictly upon his printed text.[2] Wide divergence in detail between them is incessant, and often enough it is possible, by reference to the Am. sections in Ap. and Ac., to account for the discrepancy (*e.gg.* Am. 595 '. . . dont Dieu l'avait sauvé,' *cf.* Ac. 137, 20; Am. 699 'Une certaine nuit . . .', *cf.* Ac. 166, 18; Am. 413 'Quand on eut préparé . . .', *cf.* Ac. 51, 8; Am. 418 '. . . près de moi', *cf.* Ac. 53, 20; Am. *ib.* '. . . Satan qui se montre', *cf.* Ac. *ib.*, 23). The translation in such cases clearly follows the readings of a second MS., more closely related to that whence Ac. (and doubtless Ap.) derived its Am. sections.

As regards the older MS. G, its text is not seldom preferable to that of the printed Am. and agrees occasionally with Ac. Its chief interest however lies in its length as compared with that of Am. For, while containing nothing not found in Am., it omits the incident of Hieracapollo (Am. 365),[3] the passage from the *Laus. Hist.* (Am. 366–9), two other passages (Am. 373, *ult.*–380, 6 and 382, 6–384, 6) and, finally, the long section consisting mainly of Par. (Am. 599, 7–644, 5).[4] The text ends with the death of P., thus, so far as I know, alone of the MSS. of this recension, justifying its title, which in all copies is practically the same as that printed Am. 337 (*cf.* above, title of Ap.).

It may be doubted whether comparative study of the Coptic materials can ever attain to distinguishing among the sources whence Am. was compiled. Help towards such an object might at any rate be had from a tabulation of the Arabic forms under which the commoner personal and place-names appear. It would, I think, then be

---

[1] Flemming in *Vers. d. Hss. im Preuss. Staate* i. (3), 373.

[2] In order to be sure that no other of the three MSS. would account for the peculiarities of the translation, I have collated a number of passages of the latter with each of them. They agree in differing constantly from it.

[3] Otherwise omitted only by Bo. Av.

[4] The connecting link reads as follows (G. ⲥ̄ⲕ̄ⲏ̄ b), after 'Ainsi faisait notre père [P., *sic*], '*And when he had said this to the brethren, and he lying sick*', 'il resta trois jours &c.'

found that *Tabennése* and *Pbow* [1] occur as طبناسين and بافوا in both the earliest and latest portions of the text, while in the intermediate sections [2] they are written دوناسة and ادفوا. So too *Cornelius* is قرناليا in its earlier and later occurrences, قرناليوس between these. The name *Pachomius* offers more confusing evidence; for the form باخوميوس (or بخوميوس), far less common here than the native باخوم—it occurs only 19 times—is found generally in close proximity to the other, sometimes in the selfsame section. [3] The Greek form does not occur between pp. 380 and 600; 14 of the instances are between p. 600 and the end.

It may be noted here that, while Amélineau supposes the 13th–14th century as a probable date for the execution of this translation, Casanova considers that its linguistic character points rather to the tenth. [4]

From some form of Am. is clearly derived the compressed biography of the *Synaxarium* (14 Bashans): *cf.* the forms of place-names, reference to P.'s objection to ordained monks (*cf.* Am. 372), his vision of heaven and hell (Am. 547 ff.), and to his forty years (*sic*) as head of the congregation (Am. 650). Only Athanasius' use of Lu. vi. 48, in praising P.'s institution, does not appear to come from known texts.

Vatican, Cod. arab. 172, foll. 1–98 b (= Av.).

This MS. is dated A.M. 1061 = A.D. 1345. We have here a text of an entirely different type from those already described and one, to all interested in the reconstruction of the Coptic Lives, of far greater importance. Indeed for that purpose Ap.+Ac. are practically negligible, except in so far as their recension affords further testimony to the text of Am. The first 9 leaves of the MS. were unfortunately long ago lost and replaced by a hand probably not much younger than the original scribe's, [5] but from a quite incongruous source, namely the recension Ap. [6] The last words written by this second scribe (fol. 9 b *ult.*) are the first of § 5 and correspond to Ap. f. 15, 5. They are 'And on a certain day', and they are followed in Ap. (and Ac.) immediately by 'there came to them a certain one of the monkish brethren, visiting them; and this brother had been conquered by pride and self-conceit'. But in Av. the two recensions are clumsily pieced together as follows: (f. 9 b) 'And once on a time, (f. 10) in the morning, and they working at their handiwork and repeating by heart (the Scriptures), a brother knocked at the door who dwelt near them.' The preceding context, identical in Ap. and Av., makes it practically certain that the sequel too should have been identical; whereas, with our return to the original scribe, the narrative, forsaking Ap., proceeds as in Bo. (18) and Am. (353).

---

[1] Sa. 1 (*v.* p. 183 *below*) uses the form *Pbau*. Cf. the two Greek forms Πβόου and Παβαῦ (Παβῶ).

[2] Respectively pp. 380–595 and 384–639.

[3] On pp. 380, 632–3, 668, 699. It may be noted that the sections of Ac. coinciding with Am. constantly prefer the Greek to the native form.

[4] *Bull. Instit. Franç.* i. 19, 20.

[5] So Prof. Guidi, who kindly examined these folios for me.

[6] The opening passage in Ac., on the contrary, belongs to the other recension

With the exception, then, of the extraneous title and opening sections (§§ 1–4), we have in Av. a complete, uninterrupted text, closing with P.'s death—a limit which further demonstrates the incongruity of the title transferred here from Ap. Yet the abruptness of the ending (f. 98 b), '. . . lest he should fall into bodily weakness (which would have been) contrary to His will' (*cf.* Am. 650, 3), may point to Av. being but the translation of a first volume, the sequel to which would, like certain of the Coptic Lives, have carried on the story beyond the death of Theodore. Now this abrupt ending happens to coincide exactly with that of an excerpt from the Life in a Sa. anthology of various popular writers,[1] the MS. of which is already known by its extracts from P.'s sermons (= *Miss.* 612–616). The passage here in question is in Paris 129[13], 43 (paged $\overline{qe}$, $\overline{qc}$) and corresponds to Am. 649 *infra*–650, 3. Hence we may assume that one Sa. version did in fact end just as does Av. More-over the subscription[2] to the excerpt is of some interest; for after *A portion* ($\mu\acute{\epsilon}\rho o\varsigma$) *from the Life* ($\beta\acute{\iota}o\varsigma$) *of our father Pahôm*, we read *Apa Theodorus, the archimandrite of Tabennése*, which is proof that in the 11th century at any rate (for that is doubtless the date of the MS.), one Sa. version of the Life was attributed to Theodore himself.[3] Indeed the colophon of Av. (fol. 98 b) refers to the work as a Discourse or Encomium,[4] and P. is, in the course of the narrative, often called *my father*, *Apa P.*, instead of the elsewhere usual *our father*. However, in face of the unvarying reference to Theodore in the 3rd person, these arguments cannot have much weight.

To judge from the identity in sequence between Av. and Bo. up to the point where the latter breaks off (Bo. 214), it may be assumed that what is thereafter lost of P.'s Life followed a course parallel with the remainder of Av. (*i.e.* from f. 88, 5 ظهر له ملاك). Turning now for parallel texts to Am., we find the following correspon-dence: Av. ff. 88, 5–98 b, 2 = Am. 562, 7–564, 8, 542, 1–548, 5, 643 *infra* (only approximate), 596, 5–599, 7, 596, 9–597, 2, 644, 7–650, 3. But though parallel here in matter, details of narrative and phraseology differ widely ; and this is true of Av. and Am. as a whole. I have collated many parallel passages and found nowhere more than a transient identity : a relationship about as close—and this was indeed to be expected—as that between Bo. and Am.

For, at first sight, Av. might be taken for a translation of Bo. : the sequence of paragraphs is identical, and identical too is much of the phraseology, down often to

[1] Besides Pachomius and Athanasius, other foll. (Paris 131[1], 66, 87) have extracts from John of Hermopolis, Severus and Epiphanius ; possibly too from *Acta* (Claudius, Paris 129[16], 43).

[2] *V.* Br. Mus. no. 184, note. That this is the subscription and not the title is clear from the succeeding piece, headed *Likewise* ($\delta\mu o\acute{\iota}\omega\varsigma$) *upon the great Antonius, the anchorite*, the text of which is by *me Athanasius*, and is closed by the

words *Apa Athanasius, the archbishop of Rakote*; then follows an account of Anthony's death, headed *Likewise upon the death of &c.*

[3] Prof. Lefort had arrived at the same conclu-sions from these facts (Letter of 12. ii. 1911).

[4] ميمر القديس انبا بخوم. But ميمر is not an uncommon title where the work is merely narrative and biographical : *e.g.* Bodl. Hunt. 470 (Mart. Pshai and Peter), Paris 148 (Life of Herminos).

the closest details of wording. Yet a comparison with Sa. shows indisputably that it, and not Bo., was the source translated. I have collated them *through all passages where the three texts are extant*, and have found that, in an overwhelming majority of places—some 140 against 30—Av. agrees with Sa. rather than with Bo. The following examples will illustrate their interrelationship [1]:—

I.

	Bohairic (*Mus. Guim.* 91)		Saïdic (*Mus. Guim.* 318)		Av. fol. 41
	avec joie		*om.*		= Sa.
92	= Sa.		et toi vieillard		+ that art above the well
	dans les saints		*om.*		= Sa.
	en présence de tous les frères		*om.*		= Sa.
	les saintes Écritures		*om.*		= Sa.
	terrible		glorieuse		= Bo.
	pleuraient &c.		couverts &c.		= Bo.
	communauté	319	faisceau	41 b	= Sa.
93	sortir		= Bo.		be delivered
	fosse		falaise		= Bo.
	je pense		*om.*		= Bo.
	om.		de sorte . . . la mort		= Sa.
	om.		continuèrent		= Bo.
	arrivés		où il arriva (*sic leg.*)		= Sa.
	à la barque (2°)		= Bo.		*om.*
	près de		*om.*		= Bo.
	tous		*om.*		= Sa.
	envoya (ⲟⲩⲱⲣⲡ)		envoya (ⲭⲉⲩ)		said to (? Sa. misunderstood)
94	dans ta cellule		*om.*		= Sa.
	de l'esprit	320	des esprits	42	= Sa.
	om. (*sic leg.*)		(fit manger) le frère		= Sa.
	ordonnait (*sic leg.*)		t'eût dit		= Sa. (*om.* dative)
	om.		ô mon père		= Sa.
	lui dit aussi (*sic leg.*)		aussi dit		= Sa.
	Je sais que		= Bo.		*om.*
	sagesse, longanimité		patience, sagesse		= Sa.
	à tous &c.		Et nous . . . arrivé		= Sa.
95	démon, démon	321	un, un autre		= Sa.
	en tout ce qu'il fait		en tout ce qui est à lui (*sic leg.*)		= Sa.
	vers le Seigneur		*om.*		= Sa.
	om.		aussitôt		= Sa.
	dit		répondit	42 b	= Sa.
	promptement, beaucoup		*om.*		= Sa.

[1] In these illustrative passages *all* variant places are, of course, recorded.

Bohairic (*Mus. Guim.* 91)	Sa'idic (*Mus. Guim.* 318)	Av. fol. 41
si quelqu'un l'ennemi *om.* inspirant … âmes en dessus de la barque Le lendemain &c.	si un homme (*sic leg.*) = Bo. comme assis sur un trône *om.* l'endroit … abordé et ensuite &c.	= Sa. the lord (? of the house) = Sa. concerning their salva- tion (*cf.* Bo.) beside the boat = Sa.

(with *96* beside the Bohairic column, *322* beside the Sa'idic column)

II.

Bohairic (*Mus. Guim.* 119)	Sa'idic (*Miss. fr.* 547)	Av. fol. 51 b
aussitôt	= Bo.	*om.*
il n'y avait … deux	à cette heure … seulement	alone (*pl.*)
om.	Levons-nous	= Sa.
120 sa main (*sic leg.*)	ses mains	= Bo.
om.	disant	= Sa.
Aussitôt	Sur-le-champ	*om.*
à Dieu	au Seigneur	= Sa.
disant	ils … firent prières	= Sa.
et avec larmes	*om.*	= Sa.
Seigneur [notre] Dieu	*om.*	= Sa.
ta … sur nous	sa … sur eux	= Sa.
fût rendu à lui	548 l'eût [vu]	= Sa.
avant sa mort	*om.*	= Sa.
A l'heure du soir	Mais après l'heure du soir (*sic leg.*)	= Sa. (literally)
à Tmouschons	au couvent	= Sa. + Bo.
le frère	*om.*	= Sa.
121 *om.*	et lorsque …, aussitôt	= Bo.
om.	Nous … prêtre	52 the holy (40 days)
Nous … baptiser		= Sa.
lui révéla	549 leur révéla	= Sa.
de la part du Seigneur	*om.*	= Sa.
conduite (ἀναστροφή)	= Bo.	dignity (قدر)
pour le conduire à Dieu	*om.*	= Sa.
s'il … vertus	si c'est … conduite (2°)	And if his deeds be small
122 Dieu	le Seigneur	= Sa.
envoyait	aillent	= Sa.
om.	avec légèreté	= Sa.
om.	magistrature évidente	= Sa.
puissances	= Bo.	52 b angels
ordre	volonté	= Sa.
om.	sans acception de personnes	= Sa.

Bohairic (*Mus. Guim.* 175)	Sa'idic (Zoega cccix)	Av. fol. 72 *ult.*	
et qu'ils reçussent la vie éternelle	even as he that asked the Saviour, saying, What shall I do &c.		= Sa.
176 vains .	*om.*	73	= Sa.
le besoin du corps	the cares of their maintenance		= Sa.
volonté de Dieu	will of Him that created them		of God that created them
qu'ils fussent . . . éternel	and be saved		*om.*
om. (*sic leg.*)	Likewise too (he prayed)		= Sa.
se trouvaient dans	remain complacently in		= Sa.
parce que . . . égarés	*om.*		= Sa.
qu'ils se connaissent (*sic leg.*) . . . temps	that they should know . . . worthy of life		= Sa.
ainsi, il fait que	and all the other created-things that He hath created for their satisfaction		= Sa.
pendant le jour	daily		= Sa.
afin . . . besoin	*om.*		= Sa.
nous	*om.*		= Sa.
om.	which He hath fixed for them		= Sa.
177 que l'on sème dans les champs	which He hath made on their behalf	73 b	*om.* •

As a further illustration we may take the passage §§ 26–34, where Sa. chances to be available in two decidedly, if slightly, differing forms.[1] A comparison in their variant places of these two and Bo. with Av. shows, as before, a large preponderance of agreements between Av. and Sa. :—

Av. and both Sa.   agree 58 times
Av. and Sa. 1   „   8   „
Av. and Sa. 1 + Bo.   „   13   „
Av. and Sa. 5   „   6   „
Av. and Sa. 5 + Bo.   „   16   „
Av. and Bo.   „   5   „
Av. against all[2]   „   34   „

If it has been sufficiently demonstrated that Av. is translated from Sa., it yet remains to decide which version of that recension was used. The solution of this question involves a comparative examination of all the Sa. material with Av. such as I have not undertaken. In the case of the passage last analysed the claims of the two Sa. versions represented are practically equal; for another, still more fragmentary and

---

mss. 800–810, here called Sa. 1 (= Rhitgardti Cod. …), and … … …
[2] Including of course mere omissions.

only partially parallel Sa. version (Brit. Mus. no. 342) the terms of comparison must be different, for here Bo. is wanting. Pp. п̄–п̄п̄ of this Sa. correspond to Am. 542–544 and Av. ff. 89–91 ; there are some 30 variant places, whereof 20 show agreement between Av. and Sa., 7 between Av. and Am., 3 between Sa. and Am., Av. being independent.[1] As regards the relation of Av. to the other Copto-Arabic text, Am., their paragraph-sequence will, of course, differ, since that of the former coincides with Bo. (*v.* Table, p. 191) ; while the collation of a number of passages—among them those where no Bo. is extant—has shown that they diverge widely, in detail of phrasing, even where not in the construction of the narrative.

Testimony to the Sa'idic origin of Av. could however be had without recourse to comparative methods such as the above. The proper and place-names, to begin with, are, in cases where the Arabic transcript might be ambiguous, generally added (interlined) in Coptic. Of 21 such names, it is true that the majority are not such as to show forms distinctively Sa'idic. пeϭoϣ (*sic*) Av. 17 b, for instance, persists in Bo. 44, 48, beside the true пieϭωϣ, *ib.* 32. But ϣeптace Av. 16 b (Bo. пϣeптaнci), тв̄aкωт Av. 17 b (Bo. өв̄aкaт), ппoγɯ Av. 35 b (Bo. ϕпoγɯ), пϣпaпaрте *ib.* (Bo. пϣeпaпaϩι[2]) and ϯⳓoγe Av. 65 b (Bo. ϯтoγн) speak clearly enough.[3] Then there is a word of frequent occurrence throughout the text which alone goes far to support the claim we make. ' Monastery ' is, in Bo. with rare exceptions, represented ·by ɯoпн (μονή). This corresponds normally to Sa. ϩeпeeтe[4] and in Am. to دير. So too in Av., this last is the usual Arabic equivalent. However, in 11 cases[5] ϩeпeeтe is simply transcribed as هنادة (هنادات, هنادين). But ϩeпeeтe is a word unknown so far in Bohairic literature. In this Arabic form, it is to be met only as a place-name[6] : the dictionaries do not record it.

It is probable moreover that careful examination of the text would reveal unintelligible or questionable readings explicable only when retranslated into Sa'idic. I am only able to point to one undoubted case : Sa. (*Miss.* 526, 2) aϥϣωп eрoϥ ' he approached him '= Bo. 62, 1 eтaϥϭoптϥ eϩoγп ' when he approached ' = Av.

[1] One other independent reading of Av. (90 b) الاودية, where Am. 544, 7 المواضع, Sa. п̄c̄ птoγeiн, might be due to resemblance in sound between the Arabic words, though neither represents the Coptic accurately.

[2] Prof. Mallon confirms this reading, but doubtless Sa. is correct; *v.* Griffith, *ÄZ.* xxxviii. 88.

[3] Conversely in Bo. eв̄ωпϩ, пeϭωϩ, ϕв̄ooγ (*cf.* ϕв̄ωoγ), тcɯiпe confirm the Sa. origin of that version. The remaining Coptic glosses of interest in Av. are : ϣeпecнт, eϥϣпϩ 31 b, пicω 32 b, ϣeптeрϥϣ 35 b, тaɯaγo (= [a]пa ɯaγo) 43 b, also ɯaω, ɯaγω *ib.*, пaтλoλe

57 (*v.* Bo. 133), ϕɯoγп 95 b (*cf.* ппoγɯ), ϩoрcecioc 96, cɯiпe 96 b (*cf.* тcɯiпe).

[4] *E. gg.* Bo. 30, 57, 61, 71, 101, corresponding to Sa. *Miss.* 543, 522, 525, 533, *M. Guim.* 326.

[5] Av. foll. 22 b, 35 b, 36, 37 a, b, 51 b, 52, 54, 66 b, always = Bo. ɯoпн. Once, 32 b = Sa. (*Miss.* 535) cooγϩc.

[6] Abû Ṣâliḥ 89 a gives a monastery so named at Rîfah, S. of Siût, while in *Synax.*, 21 Hatûr (Basset ii. 322, Forget i. 305), it is the name of one at any rate close by Siût, presumably the same. The same too probably is ' the ϩeпнтe of Siût ' in the colophons Zoega 453 and Paris 132[1], 67, though this is hardly a true place-name.

f. 28, 10 اوصاﻩ 'he bade him', the translator mistaking Sa. ϩⲱⲛ 'approach' for ϩⲱⲛ 'bid', a mistake impossible if his original had been Bo., since there the two words are different. That the right meaning here is 'approach' is proved by AS. § 29, πλησιάσας. Perhaps the following also is an error of like origin: Sa. 528, 2 ⲁϥⲭⲟⲟⲩ 'he sent' = Bo. 64, 8 ⲁϥⲟⲩⲱⲣⲡ = Av. f. 29, 6 فقال 'he said', reading apparently ⲁϥⲭⲟⲟⲥ, though elsewhere ⲭⲟⲟⲩ is rightly recognized. Had we a more complete Sa., further conclusions might doubtless be drawn from the numerous corrections in Av., made, with scarcely an exception, by the original scribe, in the actual course of writing. That these are not subsequent alterations is clear; for, in some instances, a word but half written is cancelled and immediately followed by the correction or preferable alternative, *e. g.* f. 95 b, 4 بحنون was begun, but altered to ابمون. This would seem to point to Av. being, not a copy from another Arabic MS., but the original holograph of the translator, written directly from the Coptic before him.[1] The nature of many of the alterations—different readings generally,[2] seldom mere errors corrected—may point to the text being the result of an eclectic process, the translator having perhaps drawn upon more than one of the Coptic versions.

The Saʿidic Recensions.

The prospect of an exhaustive edition of all the Coptic recensions by Professor Théodore Lefort relieves me of the necessity of more than a short description of the MSS. Professor Lefort has expended much labour upon the disentanglement of their mutual relationships; we may therefore leave to him the statement and solution of the various problems involved.

Besides our two new papyri (Nos. 24 and 25 above), fragments are known of six parchment MSS. preserving parts of the Lives.

1 (Lefort No. 4). The Life of P. alone. The script of this MS.[3] is of about the 12th century: facsimile, Mingarelli p. 223, no. 9. Its fragments are:—

Paris 129¹² ff. 45, 46 = *Mus. Guim.* 314   pp. ⲍ-ⲓ̄ = § 2.

„   „   f. 60   = *Miss.* 537   § 4.

Venice (Ming. no. 9) = *Miss.* 800   ⲡⲁ-ⲯ̄ⲅ̄ = §§ 27²–33², *cf. Miss.* 522.

Paris 129¹² f. 47   ⲯ̄ⲍ, ⲯ̄ⲏ (communicated by Prof. Lefort).

[1] The frequent Coptic transcripts of names (*v.* above) may testify to this.

[2] *E. gg.* Av. 14, 9 تعرق altered to تصير = Sa. (Paris 129¹², 11) ⲱⲙⲥ 'were drenched (with blood)'; Bo. wanting; *cf.* Am. 361, 2. Av. 18 b, 8 ليهى altered to ليهتموا, Bo. 35, 4 has both. Av. 21 b, 15 لذات الأطعمة, first word cancelled,

Av. 62, 13 تمتحنﻩ altered to تتميز = Bo. 148, 10

ⲉⲣⲇⲓⲁⲕⲣⲓⲛⲓⲛ. Av. 69 b, 5 و عند ما ارادوا ان altered to يرسوا الى البر ليطلعوا الى الاسكندرية و فى كل ترة يريدوا يصعدوا الى البر فى حال, مضيهم الى الا, which better agrees with Bo. 168, 1, Sa. being here lost.

[3] The same as that of Zoega cxcii, ccxiii**

Vienna, Hofbibl.   = Wessely,*Stud.*xi, no. 1 1 2 a, b pp. p̅ι̅ⲁ̅, p̅ι̅ⲃ̅   = §§ 52, 35².

    „   „   „   „   112 c, d   p̅ⲕ̅ⲍ̅, p̅ⲕ̅ⲏ̅   ⎫

Paris 129¹² ff. 48–54 = *Mus. Guim.* 317   p̅ⲕ̅ⲑ̅–p̅ⲗ̅ⲁ̅ ⎬ = §§ 43–50, 55¹.

   „   78 ff. 27–30 = *Miss.* 547   p̅ⲍ̅ⲉ̅–p̅ⲟ̅ⲃ̅ (*v.* Bo. 119), *cf.* Br. Mus. no. 355 (1).

Vienna, *ut supra*   = Wessely, *l. c.*, 112 e–h   p̅ϥ̅ⲧ̅–p̅ϥ̅ⲧ̅ = § 60, *cf.Miss.*553*inf.*

The text corresponds with another Sa. version in three passages, as here indicated; but, so far as extant, it offers no material not to be already found elsewhere.

2 (Lefort No. 2). This would also appear to consist of the Life of P. alone, although, as in the last case, we have only the argument *e silentio* to support the assumption. The MS. may be of the 6th or 7th century : the script much resembles Br. Mus. *Cat.*, pl. 2, no. 971 (datable about 650). Described with extracts, *l.c.*, no. 342. Its text seems to be generally parallel with Am. (*cf.* sequence of sections), though in detail they differ considerably. One of the passages (p. ⲓ̅ⲧ̅) omitted by Am. (543) reappears in Av. (f. 90, 3–8), and in the same context as here.

3 (Lefort No. 1). Neither is there any evidence here that the MS. included more than the Life of P. The script should be of about the 6th century : facsimile, Hyvernat, *Album*, pl. 2, 2. The two extant fragments are published *Miss.* 538–543 and correspond apparently to §§ 13, 11, 16, though both text and sequence are very different from those of any other recension.

4 (Lefort No. 6). This MS. related solely to Theodore, for on p. ⲣ̅ we see that P. is already dead. The script is of an easily datable type: it must belong to A.D. 1000 or thereabouts: facsimile, Wessely, *Studien* xi, p. 152 (9440). Its fragments are[1] :—

Paris 129¹² ff. 67 + 65 = *Miss.* 560   pp. ⲣ̅, ⲝ̅ = § 75.

Naples (Zoega clxxv) = *Mus. Guim.* 297   = § 77, *cf. Miss.* 567.

Paris 129¹³ f. 54   = *Miss.* 823

Berlin, *Kopt. Urk.*, Nr. 191   ⲕ̅ⲍ̅, ⲕ̅ⲏ̅, *cf. Miss.* 594.

Paris 129¹² f. 63   = *Miss.* 586   ⲗ̅ⲉ̅, ⲗ̅ⲋ̅ = § 81.

Paris 129¹² f. 62   = *Miss.* 584 and *Muséon* xi. 215 (*v.* Bo. 238).

Berlin, Kgl. Bibl., Or. 1607, f. 3   pp. ⲙ̅ⲁ̅, ⲙ̅ⲃ̅ = § 84 (?).

Vienna, Hofbibl.   = Wessely,*l.c.*,no.111a,b ⲙ̅ⲧ̅, ⲙ̅ⲝ̅ = §§ 82, 83, *cf. Miss.* 588.

Paris 129¹³ f. 60 + 129¹² f. 58   ⲙ̅ⲉ̅, ⲙ̅ⲧ̅ = § 93 (?).

   „   129¹² ff. 55–57 = *Mus. Guim.* 328 *ult.*   ⲙ̅ⲧ̅–ⲙ̅ⲏ̅ (*v.* Bo. in Leipzig, Univ. Bibl., vol. xxv, f. 3).

---

[1] On this list *cf.* Lefort in *Muséon* xi. 206, to whom the identification of two of the Paris fragments is due.

The three passages here which have parallels in another MS. (Sa. 5) make it probable that the present is but the second volume of the combined Life, since in the parallel MS. they occur midway in the work, which afterwards proceeds with the history of Theodore.

5 (Lefort No. 5). This is the only MS. which unquestionably combined the history of Theodore with that of P. It was written most probably in the 9th century. Facsimiles: Mingarelli p. 30, nos. 7, 8, Cairo, *Catal. Gén.* no. 8016. Its fragments are :—

Paris 129¹² f. 11		pp. ⲕⲑ, ⲗ̄ = § 9.	
Naples (Zoega clxxiii) = *Mus. Guim.* 295		ⲙⲉ̄, ⲙ̄ⲋ̄ = § 40².	
Paris 129¹² ff. 18–25 = *Miss.* 521		ⲍ̄ – ⲟ̅ⲉ̅ = §§ 26–35, 51, *cf. Miss.* 800, Br. Mus. no. 342, p. ⳅⲉ̄.	
„ f. 26 = *Miss.* 545		ⲡ̄ⲏ, ⲡ̄ⲑ = §§ 41, 42.	
Brit. Mus. no. 355, f. 1		ⲣⲕⲅ̄, ⲣⲕⲁ̄ (*v.* Bo. 122), *cf. Miss.* 549.	
Paris 78 f. 40 = *Miss.* 552		= §§ 61², 56¹, *cf. Mus. Guim.* 328.	
„ 129¹² f. 27 = *Miss.* 553		ⲣⲗⲑ̄, ⲣⲙ̄ = § 60, *cf.* Wessely, *l.c.* 112 e, f, g.	
„ „ f. 39 = *Miss.* 555		[ⲣⲙⲑ̄, ⲣⲡ̄] (*v.* Am. 477).	
Brit. Mus. no. 355, f. 2		ⲣⲡⲁ̄, ⲣⲡⲃ̄ (*v. ib.* 478).	
Paris 129¹² f. 28 = *Miss.* 557		ⲣⲡⲍ̄, ⲣⲡⲏ̄ = § 66.	
Naples (Zoega cccix)		ⲣϥⲅ̄, ⲣϥⲁ̄ (*v.* Bo. 175).	
Leyden no. 88		ⲥⲍ̄, ⲥⲏ̄ (*v.* Am. 507).	
Venice (Ming. no. 7) = *Miss.* 562		ⲥⲡⲍ̄–ⲥⲟ̄ = § 77, *cf. Mus. Guim.* 297.	
„ (Ming. no. 8) = *Miss.* 577		ⲥⲟⲩ̄, ⲥⲡ̄ = § 77.	
Paris 129¹² f. 37 = *Miss.* 588		= § 83, *cf.* Wessely, *l.c.* 111 b.	
„ „ ff. 29–35 = *Miss.* 592		ⲧⲁ̄–ⲧⲓⲁ̄ *cf.* Berlin, *Kopt. Urk.* Nr. 191.	
Brit. Mus. no. 355, f. 3		ⲧⲓⲍ̄, ⲧⲓⲏ̄	
Paris 129¹² f. 36 = *Miss.* 604		ⲧⲗⲁ̄, ⲧⲗⲃ̄ = § 88.	
„ „ f. 38 = *Miss.* 559		= §§ 94, 95, *cf.* Wessely, *l.c.* 111 c, d.	

To the following fragments I do not venture to assign a sequence :—

Cairo Museum no. 8016 (*v.* Am. 515).

Cairo, a fragment in Patriarch's collection (*v.* Bo. 243–5), *cf. Mus. Guim.* 306–8 and p. ⲣⲝⲁ̄ of next MS.

6 (Lefort No. 3). This is the MS. of which the largest number of fragments are

the contents of others, that the character of the recension is hard to define. Its most obvious feature is the homiletic element, more or less prominent in the majority of fragments, and consisting of discourses (or prayers), attributed usually to Theodore, but having little or no visible relation to the narrative or indeed to the incidental discourses of the other recensions or versions. It relates the history of both P. and Theodore. The following list gives the paged fragments, in their order of pagination and irrespective of their contents :—

Naples (Zoega ccxcvi, f. 1)	pp. ⲅ̄, ⲍ̄	= § 1.
Br. Mus. Or. 6954, 40	ⲙ̄ⲁ, ⲙ̄ⲃ	= § 10 (?).
Berlin, Kgl. Bibl., Or. 1350, f. 1	ⲙ̄ⲍ, ⲙ̄ⲏ	= § 12.
Br. Mus. no. 356	ⲛ̄ⲑ, ⲍ̄.	
Paris 129¹² f. 59 = *Miss.* 543	ⲍ̄ⲉ, ⲍ̄ⲋ	= §§ 16, 17.
Naples (Zoega ccxcvi, f. 2)	ⲍ̄ⲑ, ⲟ̄.	
Br. Mus. no. 343, f. 1	ⲟ̄ⲉ, ⲟ̄ⲋ.	
Naples (Zoega ccxcvii, 1 fol.)	ⲣ̄, ⲣ̄ⲁ.	
Br. Mus. Or. 6954, 36	ⲣ̄ⲏ, ⲣ̄ⲑ.	
Paris 131³ ff. 29–33	ⲣ̄ⲓⲁ–ⲣ̄ⲕⲋ.	
Leyden no. 70	ⲣ̄ⲕⲁ, ⲣ̄ⲕⲉ.	
Br. Mus. no. 343, f. 2 (last of qu. ⲓⲋ̄)	[ⲣ̄ⲕⲏ, ⲣ̄ⲕⲑ?].	
Naples (Zoega ccxcvi, f. 3)	ⲣ̄ⲙⲍ, ⲣ̄ⲙⲏ.	
Paris 131⁷ f. 50	ⲣ̄ⲍ, ⲣ̄ⲍⲁ.	
Naples (Zoega clxxvii, ff. 1–4) = *Mus. Guim.* 299	ⲣ̄ⲍⲁ, ⲣ̄ⲟⲁ.	
Oxford, Clar. Pr., no. 35 (*v.* below)	ⲥ̄ⲏ, ⲥ̄ⲑ.	
Vienna, Hofbibl. = Wessely,*Stud.*xi,no,111c,d	ⲥ̄ⲛⲁ, ⲥ̄ⲛⲉ	= §§ 94, 95, *cf.*
		Miss. 559.
Naples (Zoega clxxvii, ff. 5–7) = *Mus. Guim.* 308–314	ⲥ̄ⲅⲁ–ⲥ̄ⲅⲑ	= §§ 80, 96.
Berlin, Kgl. Bibl., Or. 1350, f. 2	ⲥ̄ⲟⲍ, ⲥ̄ⲟⲏ.	
Paris 129¹² f. 42 = *Miss.* 605	ⲧ̄ϥ, ⲧ̄ϥⲁ.	

Here follow those fragments which lack pagination, in a sequence, as far as possible, parallel to Bo. or Am. :—

(*a*) Narrative passages :

Br. Mus. Or. 6954, 35.	
Cairo, a fragment in the Patriarch's collection	*cf.* Bo. 184, Am. 500.
Naples (Zoega ccxcvi, f. 4)	*cf.* Bo. 186, Am. 503.
Br. Mus. no. 343, f. 2	*cf.* Am. 525.
Paris 129¹² f. 61	*cf.* Bo. 260, 276.

(*b*) Homiletic passages :

Br. Mus. no. 343, f. 3.

Naples (Zoega ccxcvii, 2 foll.).

Br. Mus. Or. 6954, 2 fragments (the subject is closely related to that of pp. $\overline{\text{cH}}$, $\overline{\text{c\Theta}}$ above).

Besides these 6 MSS., mention may be made of others relating to the founders of the Pachomian institutions, although they do not contain biographies of them :

α. Paris 129¹³ ff. 43, 44 (*v.* above, p. 178). This is an extract from the Life of P., narrating his death and burial. The MS. was written about A.D. 1000.

β. Paris 129¹² ff. 70–72 = *Miss.* 609–611. From an Encomium (?) on P., attributed, no doubt falsely, to Athanasius. The MS. may be of the 11th century.

γ. Paris 129¹² f. 68 = *Miss.* 590 *ult.*, 591. Hand of about the 11th century: facsimile, Cairo, *Catal. Gén.* no. 8017. This leaf is from an anecdote of Horsiesius. The paging in the edition,[1] $\overline{\text{po\zeta}}$, $\overline{\text{poH}}$, shows that, if indeed it is from the same volume as the other extant leaves by this hand,[2] we may (as M. Amélineau has suggested, *Miss.* 488) have to do with an independent Life of Horsiesius; for the preceding leaves, paged $\overline{\text{o\Theta}}$, $\overline{\text{H}}$, $\overline{\text{p\lambda\Delta}}$, $\overline{\text{p\lambda B}}$, $\overline{\text{p\mu\Gamma}}$–$\overline{\text{p\mu\Gamma}}$, all relate to the patriarchs Peter I and Achillas of Alexandria and the suppression of paganism : they have, that is to say, no apparent relation to the Pachomian communities.

δ. Paris 129¹² f. 74 = *Miss.* 812. The hand may be of the 9th century. This small fragment refers indeed to certain of P.'s companions, but it cannot—if we have regard to the other leaves by this hand and their pagination—belong to any of the Lives. The other extant work of the same hand is: Zoega no. ccxxx, Paris 130³ ff. 59–74, 130⁴ ff. 131–162. There is nothing in the pagination of these long fragments to forbid their being, together with our leaf, all parts of a single volume. On the leaves from 130³ see Leipoldt's observations (*Schenute*, p. 11 n.). The fact that those from 130⁴ are certainly Shenoute's supports his opinion that Zoega's text has at least been edited by that writer.[3]

ε. This fragment is obviously concerned with P. and his disciples, but its relationship to the Lives is obscure, no such incident being discoverable in any other text. I print it from a copy kindly given me (1899) by Professor Guidi, who says the hand is that of the late E. Teza. The copy offers not the slightest information either as to the MS. copied or the number and pagination of its leaves.

---

[1] I have not noted any pagination. Possibly it has (as too often) disappeared in binding.

[2] Cairo no. 8017, Paris 129¹⁶ f. 74, 129¹⁴ ff. 105–108.

[3] The title ⲁⲡⲁ, without following name, rightly claimed by Leipoldt for Pachomius, is however applied to other venerable persons besides, *e.g.* Jeremias of Saqqara (Quibell-Thompson, no. 226, l. 14 n.), Peter of Alexandria (*Texte u. Unt.*, NF. v. 4 b, p. 10), Zoega p. 303, here following.

ⲙⲡⲛⲥⲱⲥ ⲟⲛ ⲁϥϯ ⲕⲉⲕⲟⲧ ⲁϥⲡⲱϩ ⲉⲣⲟϥ ⲟⲛ ⲡⲉϫⲁϥ ⲛⲁϥ ⲙⲡⲙⲉⲣⲥⲉⲡⲥⲛⲁⲩ ϫⲉⲡⲏⲓ
ⲉⲛⲧⲁⲡⲣⲱⲙⲉ ⲕⲟⲧϥ ϥⲉⲓⲣⲉ ⲡⲟⲩⲏⲣ ⲡⲟⲩⲁⲣⲙⲉ · ⲙⲡϥⲉϣϯ ⲁⲡⲟⲗⲟⲅⲓⲁ ⲛⲁϥ ⲡⲁⲗⲓⲛ ⲟⲛ
ⲁϥⲕⲟⲧϥ ⲙⲡⲙⲉⲣϣⲟⲙⲧ ⲛⲥⲟⲡ · ⲁϥⲡⲱϩ ⲉⲣⲟϥ ⲟⲛ ⲡⲉϫⲁϥ ⲛⲁϥ ϫⲉⲡⲏⲓ ⲉⲛⲧⲁⲡⲣⲱⲙⲉ
ⲕⲟⲧϥ ϥⲉⲓⲣⲉ ⲡⲟⲩⲏⲣ ⲡⲟⲩⲁⲣⲙⲉ · ⲡⲉϫⲁϥ ⲛⲁϥ ⲙⲡⲙⲉⲣϣⲟⲙⲧ ⲛⲥⲟⲡ ϫⲉϥⲉⲓⲣⲉ ⲙⲙⲛⲧⲉ
ⲡⲟⲩⲁⲣⲙⲉ · ⲛⲧⲉⲣⲉϥϫⲟⲟⲥ ⲛⲁϥ ϫⲉϥⲉⲓⲣⲉ ⲙⲙⲛⲧⲉ ⲡⲟⲩⲁⲣⲙⲉ ⲁⲡⲁⲅⲅⲉⲗⲟⲥ ⲛⲱⲧϥ ⲣⲱϥ
ⲛⲥⲱⲃⲉ ⲁϥⲙⲟⲟϣⲉ · ⲛⲧⲉⲣⲉⲁⲡⲁ ⲧⲁⲅⲟϥ ⲉⲣⲟⲛ ⲁⲛϫⲛⲟⲩϥ ϫⲉⲧⲁⲙⲟⲛ ⲉⲡⲉϥⲃⲱⲗ · ⲡⲉϫⲁϥ
ⲛⲁⲛ ϫⲉⲡⲣⲱⲙⲉ ⲡⲛⲟⲩⲧⲉ · ⲧⲙⲛⲧⲉ ⲡⲟⲩⲁⲣⲙⲉ ⲙⲡⲛⲏⲓ ⲧⲥⲁϣϥⲉ ⲙⲡⲉ · ⲙⲛⲡⲉ-
ⲥⲧⲉⲣⲛⲱⲙⲁ ⲙⲛⲡⲕⲁϩ ⲙⲡⲁⲙⲛⲧⲉ ⲡⲉϫⲁϥ ⲛⲁⲛ ϫⲉⲛⲑⲉ ⲉⲡⲉ(ⲛ)ⲧⲁⲓⲣⲁⲧⲥⲟⲟⲩⲛ[1] ⲙⲙⲉⲣ-
ϣⲟⲙⲧ ⲛⲥⲟⲡ ⲉⲙⲡⲓϭⲛⲧⲩ ⲉⲧⲁⲟⲩϥ ⲛⲁϥ ⲛⲉⲣⲉⲧⲙⲛⲧⲁⲧⲥⲟⲟⲩⲛ ⲛⲁⲕⲓⲙ ⲁⲛ ⲟⲛⲛⲉⲥⲛⲏⲩ
ϣⲁⲉⲛⲉϩ · ⲡⲉϫⲁⲛ ⲛⲁϥ ϫⲉⲁⲕⲛⲁϩⲙⲛ ⲙⲡⲡⲉⲛⲥⲡⲉⲣⲙⲁ ϣⲁⲉⲛⲉϩ · ⲛⲁⲓⲛⲉ ⲛϣⲁϫⲉ
ⲉⲛⲧⲁⲁⲡⲁ ⲧⲁⲟⲟⲩ ⲉⲣⲟⲓ ⲉⲓⲧⲁⲗⲏ ⲉⲡϫⲟⲉⲓ ⲛⲙⲙⲁϥ ⲁⲛⲟⲕ ⲙⲡⲡⲁⲉⲓⲱⲧ ⲕⲟⲣⲛⲏⲗⲓⲟⲥ ·
ⲡⲉϫⲉ ⲁⲡⲁ ⲕⲟⲣⲛⲏⲗⲓⲟⲥ ⲛⲁϥ ϫⲉⲧⲁⲅⲉⲛϣⲁϫⲉ ⲉⲣⲟⲛ ⲙⲡⲉϩⲟⲟⲩ ⲉⲛⲧⲁⲩϫⲓⲧⲕ ⲉϩⲣⲁⲓ ⲉⲧⲡⲉ ·
ⲡⲉϫⲁϥ ⲛⲁⲛ ϫⲉⲙⲡⲓⲧⲁⲅⲉⲡⲣⲉⲙⲛⲧ ⲙⲡⲁⲥⲁⲗⲁⲡⲛ ⲉⲣⲱⲧⲛ · ⲡⲉϫⲉ ⲁⲡⲁ ⲕⲟⲣⲛⲏⲗⲓⲟⲥ ⲛⲁϥ
ϫⲉⲡⲉⲧⲛⲏϩ ϣⲁⲣⲟⲛ ϩⲱⲱⲛ ⲧⲁⲟϥ ϣⲁⲣⲟⲛ · ⲡⲉϫⲁϥ ⲛⲁⲛ ϫⲉⲛϣⲟⲣⲡ ⲙⲙⲁ ⲉⲛⲧⲁⲩⲛⲧ
ⲉⲣⲱϥ (*sic expl.*).

'And thereafter he turned about[2] again and came up again to him and said unto
him the second time, "The house that the man did build, how many stories hath it?"
He was not able to give him account (ἀπολογία). Again he turned about the third
time and came up to him again and said unto him, "The house that the man did
build, how many stories hath it?" He said unto him the third time, "It hath ten
stories." When he had said unto him, It hath ten stories, the angel smiled and
departed.' When Apa had told it us, we asked him, saying, 'Tell us its meaning.'
He said unto us, 'The man is God. The ten stories of the house are the seven
heavens, with the firmament (στερέωμα) and the earth and hell (*amente*).' He said
unto us, 'Supposing I had been ignorant the third time, not finding what to say unto
him, so would ignorance not have ceased from[3] the brethren evermore.' We said
unto him, 'Thou hast saved us and our seed (σπέρμα) for ever.' These be the
words that Apa spake unto me, I being on board the boat with him, I and my father
Cornelius. Apa Cornelius said unto him, 'Tell us the words (spoken) on the day
when thou wast taken up to heaven.'[4] He said unto us, 'I have not told you the
tenth part of my heart (?)'[5]. Apa Cornelius said unto him, 'That which reacheth
(? = concerneth) us, tell it us.' He said unto them, 'The first place whereunto I was
brought (*sic expl.*).

---

[1] The copy has ⲉⲡⲉ̄ ⲧⲁⲓ &c.

[2] ϯ ⲡⲕⲟⲧ seems equivalent to ⲕⲱⲧⲉ a little
below. Recurs perhaps in Rylands Cat., no. 368.
Whether = ϯ ⲟⲩⲕⲟⲧⲥ (Exod. xxxii. 27 &c.) is
doubtful.

[3] *Cf.* this rare use of ⲕⲓⲙ in Acts v. 42 =
παύεσθαι.

[4] *Cf.* ? Am. 543.

[5] ⲥⲉⲗⲉⲡⲓⲛ = ὑποχόνδρια (or καρδία) in 1 Sam.
xxxi. 3. *Cf.* ? σπλήν. Seems not impossible here.

TABLE I, SHOWING WHERE THE PARAGRAPHS OF AS. AND PAR. OCCUR IN THE UNPUBLISHED ARABIC TEXTS.

AS., §§	Ap., foll.	Ac., pp.	Av., foll.	AS., §§	Ap., foll.	Ac., pp.	Av., foll.
2	7 b		3 b	38¹	98 b	79 (?)	
3	10 a	5	5	38²	99 b		36 b
4	11 a	6	6	39¹	100 a	88	37 a
5	15 a	10	9 b	39²	102 a		
6	17 b	11	11 b	40¹	174 a	41	37 b
7	20 a		12 b	40²	66 b, 103 a	33	
8	21 a	12	12 a	41	67 a	34	38
9	22 b	13	13 b	42¹	70 b	36	38 b
10	24 a		14 b	42²			
11	25 b	14	15 a	43	104 a	56	39 b
12	28 b	16	15 b	44	106 b	50	40 b
13	30 b	,,	16	45	107 b	,,	41
14	32 b	17		46¹	108 b	53	41 b
15	34 a		16 b	46²	109 b		
16	37 b	18	,,	47¹	111 a	54	
17	39 a	,,	,,	47²	112 a		42 b
18	39 b	19	17 b	48	113 a	58, 113	42 b *ull.*
19	42 b	20	18 b	49	115 a	58	44
20¹	73 b	43		50¹	119 a	60	44 b
20²	75 a			50²	183 a	122	35
21	76 a	44		51¹	184 b	123	33 a, 35 b
22	49 a	24	18 b	51²	185 b		33 b
23	54 a	26	21 b	52	188 b	125	35 b
24	56 a	27	20	53	189 b	112	
25	59 b	30	20 b *ull.*, 22 b	54			
26	61 b	31	24 b	55¹	190 b	74	45
27¹	77 a			55²			
27²		87	26	56¹	192 a	,,	45 b
28	78 b	63	26 b	56²			
29	80 b	68	28	57	194 a	76	47 b, 49
30	83 b	64	29	58¹	195 b	126	24 b
31		66	30	58²			48
32	88 b	,,		59¹	198 a	128	55
33¹	65 a	5²		59²			
33²	90 b		30	60	199 a	129	59 b
34¹	92 a	77	30 b	61¹	202 b	71	
34²				61²			45 b
35¹	47 a	23	31 b	62	202 a (?)	130 (?)	
35²	93 a	78		63			
36	94 b	79		64¹	206 a	69	63, 74 b
37	96 b	79 (?)		65¹	207 a	106	75 b

AS., §§	Ap., foll.	Ac., pp.	Av., foll.	AS., §§	Ap., foll.	Ac., pp.	Av., foll.
65²			63 b	81	238 a	149	
66	121 a	91		82	239 a	150	
67	125 a	93		83	240 b	151	
68	208 b	132	63 b	84	242 a	152	
69	211 a	133	65	85	244 b	153	
70	213 a	134	68 b	86	246 b	155	
71	215 a	130		87	247 a	,,	
72	217 b	136		88	249 a	157	
73	221 a	137	70	89¹	251 b		
74	222 b	138	95	90	256 a	160	
75	224 a	140	95 b	91	256 b	161	
76	226 a	142		92	260 b	164	
77	230 a	144		93¹	263 b	165	
78	232 a	146		94	266 b		
79	234 a	147		95	268 a	168	
80	236 a	148		96	270 a	169	

Paralipomena.

Par., §§	Ap., foll.	Ac., pp.	Par., §§	Ap., foll.	Ac., pp.
2	121 a	91	20	147 a	
3	125 b	94 (?)	21	148 b	83
4	127 a	,,	22	150 b (?)	84 (?)
5	129 b	96	23	155 b	82
6	131 a		24	161 b	103
7	140 a	45	25	164 a	104
8	157 a	101	26	167 b	105
9	158 a	,,	27	,,	108
10	159 b	102	28	169 a	81
11	160 b	103	29	170 a	109
12	177 a	121	30	171 b	110
13	135 a	98	31	169 b	82
14	136 a	,,	32	172 b	
15	136 b	99	33	175 a	107
16	138 a	,.	34	180 a	70
17	142 a	46	35	181 a	110
18	144 a	47	36	182 b	111
19	147 a	48			

TABLE II, SHOWING SEQUENCE OF PARAGRAPHS OF AS. AND PAR. IN CERTAIN OF THE RECENSIONS.

Italics here = Paralipomena.

Am.	Bo.	Av.	Ap.	Ac.	Sur.	Nau A.
1	1	As Bohairic.	1	1	1	*1*
2	2		2	2	2	*2*
3	3		3	3	3	*3*
4	4		4	4	4	*4*
5	5		5	5	5	*5*
6	6		6	6	7	*6*
8	8		7	7	8	*13*
7	7		8	8	9	*14*
9	9		9	9	10	*15*
10	10		10	11	11	*16*
11	11		11	12	13	7
12	12		12	13	14	*17–23*
13	13		13	14	15	*8*
15	15		14	16	16	*9*
16+17	16+17		15	17	17	*10*
18	18		16	18	18	*11*
19	19		17	19	19	*24–33*
17	22	(om.)	18	35¹	20	*12*
35¹	20²		19	22	21	*40²*
22	24		35¹	23	22	*38²*
20²	25	As Bohairic.	22	24	23	*39¹*
23	23		*Hist. Laus.* xxxiii.	25	24	*40¹*
24	25		23	26	25	*41*
25	58¹		24	40²	26	43
40²	26		25	41	27	47
26	27²		26	42	28	45
42²	28		33¹	40¹	29	*50¹*
41	29		40²	20	30	44 (*cf.* 62)
42¹	30		41	21	33	51
44	31		42	7	34	57
45	33²		20	*17*	35	*55¹*
46	34		21	*18*	28	*34*
43	35¹		27	*19*	29	*35*
47²	51²		28	44	*32*	*36*
48	50²		29	45	*12*	74
49	51¹		30	33¹	*33*	75
50	52		32	46	38	*31*
53	35²		33²	47	39	
54	38²		34	43	40	
56¹	39¹		35²	48	41	
55¹	40¹		30	50¹	43	
56²	41		37			

Am.	Bo.	Av.	Ap.	Ac.	Sur.
57	4^2	As Bohairic.	3^8	28 (?)	47
5^8	43		39	30	45
59^1	44		40^2	31	50
61^2	45		43	3^2	2
60	46		44	29	3
64^3	47^2		45	64	4
68	48		46	34	51^1
64^1	49		47	61	5
65^1	50^1		48	55	6
66	55^2		49	56	59 }
67	61^2		51^1	57	13 }
55^2	56^1		66	33^2	51^1
33^2	57		67	34	51^2
27^2	58^2		3	35^2	15
29	57		4	36	16
28	59		5	37 (?)	7
30	60		6	38	17
31	64^1		13	28	18
34	65^2		14	31	19
35	68		15	23	21
51	69		16	21	22
50^2	70		7	22 (?)	23
5^2	73		17–23	27^2	8
38^2	64^2		8	39	9
39^1	64^1		9	66	10
68	65^1		10	67	57
69	lacuna	addition	11	2	55^2
70	89^1	74	24–28	3	24
73	88	75	31	4	25
7^2	89^3	addition	29	5	26 (?)
21	90		30	6	64^2
32^1	91		32	13	58
38^1	89^2		40^1	14	27
39^2	93^2		33	15	34
40^2(?)	92		12	16	35
47^1	93^1		34	8	74
48	94		35	9	75
50^1	95		36	10	31
5	96		50^2	11	
6			51	24	
13			52	25	
15			53	26	
16			55	65	
7			56	33	

Am.	Bo.	Av.	Ap.	Ac.
17			57	27
18			58	29
19			59	30
21–27			60	35
29			62 (?)	36
30			61	53
32			64	48
33			65	addition
12			68	12
34			69	50^2
35			70	51
36			71	52
52			v. Nau	58
71			72–96	59
v. Nau*				60
72–96				62 (?)
				71
				v. Nau
				68
				69
				70
				72–87
				90–93
				95
				96

* The two additional sections in Nau D (pp. 509-10); *cf.* Am. 640 *infra*.

ADDITIONS AND CORRECTIONS

Page 1, note a, *read* Should be ⲉⲛⲧ[ⲉⲛⲟⲥ.

,, 9, note 2, *read* vol. 43.

,, 31, note 1. ϣⲁⲙⲓⲥⲉ occurs in 1 Sam. vi. 7.

,, 57, No. 11, *verso*, l. 8, *read* ⲉⲓϣⲁⲛⲕⲧⲟⲓ.

,, 71, note 1. ⲇⲓⲟⲕⲗⲏ in Rossi, *Papiri* i. iii. 24, 26, 31 &c.

,, 73, note 6, *for* 42 *read* 43.

,, 75, note 1. [Ap]a Moui might possibly be a variant of Hamoi. *Cf.* their Arabic
  forms, here and p. 162, note 1.

,, 77, note 1, *read* vol. 43.

,, 83, note 2, ditto.

,, 98, note 1. With ⲉϧⲟⲩⲛ ⲉϧⲣⲁ- *cf.* ⲉϧⲟⲩⲛ ⲉϧⲛ- Num. xiv. 11, Rossi i. i. 19,
  and ⲉϧⲟⲩⲛ ϧⲛ- 2 Sam. iii. 31 ; *v.* also Stern § 572.

INDEX

PERSONS

(In sequence of Coptic alphabet)

ⲁⲃⲓⲙⲉⲗⲉⲭ 51.
ⲁⲃⲣⲁϩⲁⲙ, bibl. 120.
ⲁⲇⲁⲙ 11, 60.
Agripidos (Diocletian) 73.
Athanasius 13 n, 22.
ⲁⲕⲣⲓⲡⲓⲧⲁ (Diocletian) 74.
Amantius, eunuch 22, 23.
Ambrosius (=? Apa Rasios, نداسيوس) 164 n.
ⲁⲙⲙⲱⲛⲉ of Thône 163.
Anatolius 58, 60.
Andrew apostle 64, 65.
Anianus Alex. 67 n.
ⲁⲛⲛⲁ, mother of the Virgin 12.
ⲁⲡⲟⲩϩⲁ (ⲡⲟⲩϩⲁ) 168 n.
Apa Rasios (=? Ambrosius) 164 n.
Apollo, saints so named 162 n.
ⲁⲣⲑⲉⲙⲓⲥ (? ⲑⲉⲙⲓⲥ) 84.
Archelaus 174.

ⲃⲁ[...]ⲥ 59, 60.
Basil of Caesarea 18.
Basilius 58 n.
Bachius 58 n.
Baumstark, Dr. A. 2.
ⲃⲉⲣⲥⲉⲫⲱⲛⲏ (Persephone) 84.

Bilhah, Jacob's wife 52 n.

ⲅⲁⲃⲣⲓⲏⲗ, angel 26.
Gregory Nazianzen 36.
ⲅⲣⲏⲅⲱⲣⲓⲟⲥ 43.

Damianus, patriarch 13 n, 21 n, 23, 33 n.
—, his *Synodikon* 31 n.
ⲇⲁⲛⲓⲏⲗ, bibl. 54.
ⲇⲁⲩⲉⲓⲇ, bibl. 161.
Diocletian 73, 84.
—, his end 73 n.
ⲇⲓⲟⲕⲗⲏ(ⲧⲓⲁⲛⲟⲥ) 72.
ⲇⲩⲣⲁⲡⲟⲥ, (?) goddess 84.

Ebônh 175 n.
ϩⲉⲗⲗⲏⲛ 8, 69, 88.
ϩⲉⲗⲗⲏⲛ, ⲙⲛⲧ- 89.
ⲉⲙⲙⲁⲛⲟⲩⲏⲗ 13, 14 n, 25.
ⲉⲛⲱⲭ 6-10.
Enoch literature 3.
Enoch's mother 4 n.
— sister 4 ff.

ⲍⲏⲛⲱⲛ, emperor 63.

ϩⲏⲗⲓⲁⲥ, bibl. 11.
ⲏⲥⲁⲓⲁⲥ, bibl. 160.
ⲉⲩⲣⲁ, goddess 84.

ⲑⲁⲙⲁⲣ, bibl. 51.
ⲑⲁⲣⲁ[168.
ⲑⲉⲗⲗⲁⲥ, goddess 84.
ⲑⲉⲟⲇⲟⲥⲓⲟⲥ, emperor 64.
ⲑⲉⲟⲇⲱⲣⲟⲥ of Tabennêse, *passim* in No. 25.
— as author of Pachomius' *Life* 178.
Theophilus Alex. 33, 53.

ⲓⲁⲕⲱⲃⲟⲥ, apostle 151, 153.
ⲓⲁⲕ[ⲱⲃ] 168.
ⲓⲁⲣⲉⲇ, bibl. 5, 6.
ⲓⲉⲍⲉⲕⲓⲏⲗ, bibl. 47.
ⲓⲉⲣⲟⲥⲟⲗⲩⲙⲓⲧⲏⲥ 86.
ⲓⲟⲩⲇⲁⲓ 14.
ⲓⲱⲁⲕⲉⲓⲙ, father of Virgin 12.
ⲓⲱⲥⲏⲫ, bibl. 17.
ⲓⲱϩⲁⲛⲛⲏⲥ, Baptist 29.
John *Jejunator* 33.
John of Maiuma 62.

ⲕⲁⲗⲗⲓⲟⲡⲏ 84.
ⲕⲗⲟϫ Coluthus 75 n.
ⲕⲟⲣⲛⲏⲗⲓⲟⲥ 188.
Cyril Alex. 22 n, 59 n.
Cyrus (ⲕⲩⲣⲟⲥ), hermit 165.

Constantine Ladrys 22, 23.

Constantine of Siût 13 n.

ⲗⲁⲣⲧⲏⲥ (Ladrys) 22, 23.
ⲗⲉⲩⲓⲧⲏⲥ 57.

Mathousala (?), bibl. 11.
ⲙⲁⲣⲓⲁ Virgin 26, 27, 30, 60.
— v. also Virgin.
ⲙⲁⲣⲕⲓⲁⲛⲟⲥ, emperor 63.
Mark, evangelist 65, 66, 68 n, 165.
ⲙⲁⲩⲣⲓⲕⲓⲟⲥ Maurice, emperor 21, 23.
ⲙⲓⲗⲓⲧⲓⲏⲓⲁⲛⲟⲥ (Meletian) 11, 13 n.
ⲙⲓⲗⲓⲧⲓⲟⲥ (? Meletius) 58, 61.
ⲙⲓⲭⲁⲏⲗ, angel 77.
ⲙⲟⲩⲓ, martyr 75, 78, 80.
Μωβεῖ, اموى 75 n.
ⲙⲱⲩⲥⲏⲥ, bibl. 16, 38, 50, 59.

Nebuchadnezzar 53.
ⲡⲏⲙⲉⲥⲓⲥ 84.

Pambô, saint 165.
ⲡⲁⲩⲗⲟⲥ, apostle 36, 49, 51, 108.
ⲡⲁⲣⲱⲙ, ⲡⲁⲣⲱⲙⲉ 91, 93, 99, passim in No. 25.
Pachomius, Arabic texts of the Life 172 ff.

Pachomius, forms of the name 100 n, 177.
—, his monasteries pref. n.
—, homily by 175 n.
—, original language of the Life 172.
—, Sa'idic texts of Life 183 ff.
Persephone 84.
ⲡⲉⲧⲣⲟⲥ, apostle 24.
—, σχολάριος 63.
Peter the Iberian 62.
Πλατωνίτης, heretics 33 n.
Psate (Psote), martyr 73, 74.
ⲡⲟⲥⲓⲇⲱⲛ, ⲡϣⲏⲣⲉ ⲙ- 88.
ⲡϭⲱⲗ, saint 75 n, 78.

ⲣⲁⲫⲁⲏⲗ, angel 71.
Rivières, A. des, his copies of MSS. 68.
ⲣⲟⲩⲃⲏⲛ, bibl. 51.
ⲣⲱⲙⲁⲛⲟⲥ, father of Victor 72.

Samaritan, Good 57, 58 n.
ⲥⲩⲗⲏⲏⲏ (Σελήνη) 84.
Severus of Antioch 62 n, 68.
— of Nestarâwah 68 n.
Sibyl, the 4.
ⲥⲙⲁⲣⲁⲅⲇⲟⲛ, name of a calf-god, 68 n.
ⲥⲟⲗⲟⲙⲱⲛ, bibl. 19.

Tabitha, bibl. 4 n, 11.
Timothy Alex. 62 n, 63.

ϯⲧⲟⲩⲉ 141.

ⲫⲓⲃ, saint 162 n.
ⲫⲓⲗⲟⲑⲉⲟⲥ, martyr 68, 70, 71, 72, 81 n.
Philotheus of Dronkah 68 n.

Christ as ship's master 64.

ϣⲉⲛⲟⲩⲧⲉ, archimandrite 166.

Hamoi, father of Apollo 162 n.
ϩⲉⲣⲙⲓⲁⲥ 168.
Herminus, saint 162 n, 175 n.
ϩⲉⲣⲟⲩⲟⲝ, martyr 75 n, 77.
Hôr, saints of this name 164 n, 165.
Horsiesius, a Life of 187.

اموى = Μωβεῖ 75 n.
امويّة Hamoi 162 n.
ﺒﺠﻮﻝ ⲡϫⲟⲗ 75 n.
(ابراسيوس) بداسيوس = ? Ambrosius 164 n.
بوى ⲡⲁⲡⲟⲣⲉ 162 n.
رواخيّاس, Ὠρουώγχιος 75 n.
هروّاج, saint 75 n.

PLACES

Alexandria 21, 22, 75.
Aradus 22.
ⲁⲧⲣⲓⲡⲉ 166.

Auranitis (?) 23.

Berytus 22.

ⲅⲁⲗⲓⲗⲁⲓⲁ 60.

Daphne (Antioch) 23 n.

ⲑⲉⲃⲁⲓⲥ 91.

ⲑⲱⲡⲉ 163.

ⲓⲉⲣⲓⲭⲱ 131.

Cana, Marriage at 60.

ⲕⲁⲡⲡⲁⲇⲟⲕⲓⲁ, ⲧϣⲟⲣⲡ ⲛ- 18.

ⲕⲏⲙⲉ 23, 66, 68 n, 69, 91.

Maiuma, John of 62.

ⲙⲁⲣⲏⲥ 91.

ⲙⲟⲩⲛϭⲟⲩϭ 74.

ⲡⲁⲍⲓⲁⲡⲍⲟⲥ 36.

Nikiou, John of 22.

Nubia 167.

ⲡⲁⲗⲁⲓⲥⲧⲓⲏⲛ 63.

Panopolis, meaning of name 173.

ⲡⲃⲟⲟⲩ 159.

—, forms of name 177.

ⲡⲉⲥⲧⲉⲣⲡⲟⲥⲉⲓⲛ 93 n.

Psoi (Ptolemais) 73.

ⲡⲥⲱ = ⲡⲥⲟⲓ 73 n.

ⲡⲥⲱⲟⲩⲡ (ⲡⲥⲱⲟⲩ) 73 n.

ⲡϣϭⲉⲡⲟϩⲉ 162 n.

ⲣⲁⲕⲟⲧⲉ 23, 66, 75.

ⲥⲉⲃⲟⲓⲙ 131.

ⲥⲉⲣⲁⲡⲉⲓⲟⲛ 93 n.

ⲥⲓⲗⲱϩⲁⲙ 59.

—, meaning of name 59.

Siût 13 n.

ⲥⲟⲇⲟⲙⲁ 131.

Sophene (?) 23.

ⲧⲁⲃⲏⲛⲏⲥⲉ 107, 109, 145, 146.

—, forms of name 177.

ⲧⲙⲟⲩ- (ⲧⲙⲟⲩⲓ-), place-names in 73 n.

Tûnah el-Gebel 162 n.

ⲟⲩϣⲏⲙ, town 24 n.

ⲭⲁⲗⲕⲏⲇⲱⲛ 63

ابسو، ابصاو 73 n.

ابصونة، باصونة 73 n.

(جبل ازكوهى (ادكوهى, site of Apollo's monastery 162 n.

شدسنا, monastery *pref.* n.

منجوج 73 n.

COPTIC

(*A selection only*)

ⲁⲗⲉ 119, 158.

— ⲉϩⲣⲁⲓ 100.

ⲁⲗⲕⲉ 66.

ⲁⲗⲧⲕⲁⲥ 150.

ⲁⲙⲁϩⲧⲉ 93.

ⲁⲙⲛⲧⲉ 42.

ⲁⲡⲁ 23, 59, 74, 75, 77, 78, 80, 93, 162, 163, 166, 168.

— alone as title 187 n.

ⲁⲣⲓⲕⲉ 105.

ⲁⲥⲁⲓ 26.

ⲁⲧⲕⲁⲥ (ⲁⲗⲧⲕⲁⲥ) 152 n.

ⲁϣⲉ 39.

ⲁϩⲉⲣⲁⲧ- ϩⲓϫⲛ- 146.

ⲁϩⲱⲙ 91.

ⲃⲱⲗ, noun 106, 188.

—, vb. 28 n, 61.

ⲃⲟⲗ, ⲛ- 15.

ⲃⲗⲃⲓⲗⲉ 41.

ⲃⲛⲡⲉ 157.

ⲃⲱⲱⲣⲉ (ϭⲱⲱⲣⲉ) ⲉⲃⲟⲗ 28.

ⲃⲟⲩⲃⲟⲩ 19.

ⲉⲃⲟⲧ 23.

ⲉⲕⲓⲃⲉ, ϫⲓ- 8, 88.

ⲉⲡⲱ 101, 102 n.

ⲉⲣⲏⲧ 142.

ⲉⲧⲡⲱ 121.

ⲉϩⲟⲩⲛ ⲉϩⲣⲁ- 98, 98 n.

ⲛϭⲉ 155.

ⲉⲓⲛⲉ, likeness 150.

ⲉⲓⲱⲧ 146.

— ⲛⲧⲕⲟⲓⲛⲱⲛⲓⲁ 145.

ⲉⲓⲱⲧⲉ 92, 140.

ⲉⲓϫⲉⲣⲟⲕ, *v.* ϫⲉⲣⲟ-.

ⲕⲁ ⲧⲟⲟⲧ- ⲉⲃⲟⲗ 154.

ⲕⲱⲕ ⲁϩⲏⲧ 43.

ⲕⲗⲗⲉ 101.

ⲕⲗⲟⲟⲗⲉ 26, 85.

ⲕⲗⲟⲙ 6, 67, 146, 148.

ⲕⲁⲙ 118, 159.

ⲕⲓⲙ, παύεσθαι 188 n.

ⲕⲙⲧⲟ 23.

ⲕⲱⲡⲥ 143.

ⲕⲣⲟ 40.

ⲕⲏⲣⲙⲉⲥ 35.

ⲕⲣⲟⲙⲣⲙ 117, 132.

ⲕⲱⲣϣ 99, 163.

ⲕⲱⲧ, rule 96.

ⲕⲟⲧ, ϯ- 188 n.

ⲕⲟⲩⲓ, ⲙⲛⲧ- 97, 99, 109.

ⲕⲁϣ 9.

ⲕⲱϩⲧ 119.

ⲗⲟ 45, 166.

ⲗⲓⲃⲉ 66.

ⲗⲱⲃϣ 77.

ⲗⲟⲉⲓϭⲉ 163.

ⲙⲟⲩ 23.

ⲙⲟⲕⲙⲕ 92, 145, 155, 159.

ⲙⲁⲕⲟⲧ, ⲙⲁⲕⲱⲧ 143, 145 n.

ⲙⲙⲟⲛ, *minime* 50.

ⲙⲓⲛⲉ, ⲙⲙⲓⲛⲉ 32.

ⲙⲟⲟⲛⲉ, come to port 40, 159.

ⲙⲁⲡⲉⲃⲁⲁⲙⲡⲉ 74.

ⲙⲟⲟⲛⲉ, feed 13.

—, ⲙⲁ ⲙ-, pasture 19.

ⲙⲉⲣⲟⲩⲟⲟϭⲉ 81.

ⲙⲟⲩⲣ 6, 28 n.

ⲙⲟⲩⲥ 77.

ⲙⲁⲥⲉ 69, 70.

ⲙⲛⲥⲉ 48.

ⲙⲓⲥⲉ 154.

—, ⲙⲛⲧⲣⲉϥ- 27.

—, ϣⲁ- 30.

ⲙⲉⲥⲓⲱ 30.

—, vb. 31 n.

ⲙⲉⲥⲟⲏⲧ 45.

ⲙⲥⲁϩ 119.

ⲙⲟⲩⲧⲉ, ⲣⲉϥ- 42.

ⲙⲁⲧⲟⲓ 72.

ⲙⲧⲟⲛ 164.

—, ϯ 99.

ⲙⲁⲁϣⲉ 4.

ⲙⲟⲟϣⲉ ⲉⲃⲟⲗ 15, 19.

ⲙⲉϣϫⲁⲕ 156.

ⲙⲟⲩϣⲧ 43, 158.

ⲙⲟⲩϩ, burn 89.

ⲙⲟⲭϩ 6.

ⲡⲟⲉⲓⲙ 82.

ⲡⲕⲁ 157.

ⲡⲛⲟ 98.

ⲡⲟⲩⲧⲉ ⲛⲥϩⲓⲙⲉ, goddess 84.

ⲡⲧⲁⲓⲣⲉ (? ⲧⲁⲓⲣⲉ), water sprites 88.

ⲡⲟⲩⲧⲩ 19.

ⲡⲱⲧⲩ (ⲡⲟⲩⲧⲩ) 188.

ⲡϣⲟⲧ 55, 82.

ⲡⲉⲉϥ 65.

ⲡⲓϫⲉ 19.

ⲡⲟϥⲣⲉ 156.

ⲡⲉϩ 151.

ⲡⲟⲩϫⲉ 157.

— ⲉⲃⲟⲗ 167.

ⲡⲟϭ, magnate 72.

ⲟⲟϩ 95.

ⲡⲉ, ⲣⲙⲛ- 24.

—, ⲧⲙⲉϩⲥⲁϣϥⲉ ⲙ- 86.

ⲡⲟⲉⲓϣ, step of ladder 39, 40.

ⲡⲱⲗϩ 81.

ⲡⲱⲱⲛⲉ 25.

ⲡⲱⲛⲡ 119, 120.

ⲡⲣⲱ 32.

ⲡⲣⲏϣ 119, 157, 158.

ⲡⲱⲣϫ 112.

— ⲉⲃⲟⲗ 32.

ⲡⲓⲥⲉ 158, 159.

ⲡⲁⲧ 124.

ⲡⲱⲧⲥ 77.

ⲡⲁϩⲟⲩ 45.

ⲡⲁϩⲣⲉ 67.

ⲡⲁϭⲥⲉ 67.

ⲣⲏ 95, 151.

ⲣⲓⲕⲉ ⲉⲃⲟⲗ 112.

ⲣⲱⲕϩ 102.

ⲣⲓⲙⲉ 158.

ⲣⲱⲙⲉ, ⲙⲛⲧⲁⲧ- 75.

ⲣⲙⲙⲁⲟ 49.

ⲣⲟⲙⲡⲉ, ⲧⲣ- 49.

ⲣⲙϩⲉ 84.

ⲣⲁⲛ 6, 7.

ⲣⲡⲉ 88, 93.

ⲣⲣⲟ 64, 72.

—, ⲣ- 90.

ⲣⲏⲥ 84, 88, 91, 169.

—, ⲥⲁ- 168.

ⲣⲟⲟⲩϣ, ⲣ- 77.

ⲣⲁϣ, ⲣⲙ- 69.

ⲥⲟⲓ 77.

ⲥⲱ, ⲙⲁ ⲛ- 27.

ⲥⲁⲃⲉ, ⲙⲛⲧ- 101, 106.

ⲥⲃⲱ 99.

ⲥⲱⲃⲉ 168.

ⲥⲟⲃⲧⲉ 120.

ⲥⲱⲕ 9.

ⲥⲉⲕ ⲧⲟⲟⲧ- 158.

ⲥⲱⲗⲡ 18.

ⲥⲁⲗⲁⲡⲓⲛ (? ὑποχόνδρια) 188 n.

ⲥⲟⲗⲥⲗ 14, 27, 112, 123.

ⲥⲙⲏ 92.

ⲥⲙⲓⲛⲉ 88, 166.

ⲥⲙⲟⲧ 105, 124.

сма2 41.

cıпє 57.

cаапщ 105.

copт 158.

соєıт 6.

cтwт 4.

cıoүp 23.

сооүти 117, 126.

сооүде пхω 77.

сооүес 134, 146.

са2 92.

са2, awl 77.

сооде, put apart 11.

са2тє 76.

сωщє 26.

сωωq 13, 128, 131.

соб̄п 69.

тн̄bo 18.

†b̄с 77.

тωb̄є 102, 156.

тн̄т 150.

тωb̄2 65, 149.

таєıо 12, 17.

таλo 9.

—, weave 147 n.

тмн 147, 157.

тапроүт- 47.

тωрє, щп- 45.

тωрп 23.

тааτє, flap (wings) 47 n.

тооү 6, 163, 166.

таүо 19.

тоүрнс (?) 19.

тоүωт 71.

тоүхо 27.

тωщ, vb. 100, 118, 129, 131, 146.

—, noun 130, 154.

та2о 102, 150.

ѳb̄bıo 163.

тω2м 82.

ѳпо 118.

таб̄ 140.

тωб̄є 20.

— пb̄ppє 110.

оүω, news 163, 169.

оүоєıє 18.

оүоєıм 5.

оүєıпє 19.

оүпоү, рєqка- 42.

оүωпщ 32.

оүωп2 єboλ 99, 101, 113.

оүастп 12.

оүтє 148.

оүоотє 156.

оүωтп єboλ 143.

оүотоүєт 150.

оүωтb̄ 45, 144.

оүωщ 157.

оүωщм 69.

оүωщq 144.

оүω2є 19.

оүа2мє 188.

оүхаı 41, 81.

хоıак2, хоıахк 19, 23.

ωω 154.

ωb̄щ 144.

ωпє 166.

— (єпє) мме 148.

ωрb̄ 31.

ωрк 42.

ωрх 97, 101, 146.

ωск 93, 116, 155.

ωтп, load 121.

ωqє 77.

о2с, п- 18.

ωхп 100.

щє, б̄λ- 52.

щıb̄є 25, 115.

щнı 117.

щоєıх 81.

щıкє 56.

щλнλ 65.

щλ2 18.

щλа2 163.

щнм 23, 24 n.

щωм 31, 32.

щωмє 120.

щммо, р- 42.

щмпоүчє, qаı- 30.

щнп 92.

щпє 19.

щıпє, ма п- 12.

щωпє 57, 90.

щопτє 142.

щап2нτ 57.

щωп 31.

щıпє 98.

щωс 74.

щтєко 82.

щтнп 135.

щаү, аτ- 45.

щооүє 40.

щоүєıτ, пєτ- 159.

щωщ, scatter 35.

щωщ, be equal 60.

щоүщτ 101.

щачтє, мпτ- 4, 9.

щωωсє 67.

чωрє, v. b̄ωрє.

чωб̄є 71, 150.

чоб̄с, хı- 28.

2н (belly), ѳıє- 153.

159.

ϩⲏⲃⲥ 89.

ϩⲱⲃⲥ 157

ϩⲁⲗ, ⲣ- 28.

ϩⲗⲗⲟ 116.

ϩⲁⲗⲗⲟⲩⲥ, meanings of 101 n.

ϩⲁⲗⲏⲧ 56.

ϩⲗⲟϭ 27.

ϩⲙⲙⲉ, ⲣ- 7, 78.

ϩⲟⲙⲛⲧ 45.

ϩⲙⲟⲟⲥ ⲉⲃⲟⲗ 39.

ϩⲙⲟⲧ 104.

—, ϣⲡ- 159.

ϩⲏⲡⲉ 14.

ϩⲡⲟ 43, 45.

ϩⲉⲡⲉⲉⲧⲉ 98, 117, 126, 182.

ϩⲁⲡ 155.

ϩⲣⲉ 31.

ϩⲓⲣⲁⲧ- 82 n.

ϩⲁⲣϣ ϩⲏⲧ 156.

ϩⲣϣⲓⲣⲉ 142, 156.

ϩⲁⲣⲉϩ 97.

ϩⲓⲥⲉ 33.

ϩⲏⲧ, ⲙⲡⲧⲕⲟⲩⲓ ⲛ- 9.

ϩⲧⲟ 93.

ϩⲱⲧⲉ (? ϫⲱⲧⲉ) 77

ϩⲱⲧⲡ 89.

ϩⲏⲩ 99.

—, † 132.

ϩⲟⲩⲙⲡⲉ 19.

ϩⲱϣ 78.

ϩⲟϥ 74.

ϩⲟϫϩⲉϫ 148.

ϫⲏ, ϫⲓⲛ- 127

ϫⲓ 97.

ϫⲓ † 17.

ϫⲟ, wall 148.

ϫⲟⲓ 39, 56, 65, 119, 159.

ϫⲱ, head 98.

ϫⲱⲗⲙ 28 n.

ϫⲟⲗⲙⲉⲥ 27.

ϫⲱⲱⲙⲉ 6, 7, 119.

ϫⲉⲡ-, or 60.

ϫⲉⲡⲉⲡⲱⲣ 107.

ϫⲡⲟ, acquire 153.

— ⲛⲕⲉⲥⲟⲡ 151.

ϫⲱⲣ 18.

ϫⲣⲟ 81.

ϫⲣⲟ, ⲣⲉϥ- 90, 91 n.

ϫⲉⲣⲟ-, ⲉⲓ- 46, 65 n.

ϫⲱⲱⲣⲉ, strong 4, 77.

ϫⲁⲁⲧⲉ, ϫⲁⲧⲉ 18, 154.

ϫⲱⲧⲉ 150.

ϫⲱϫ, ⲁⲛ- 24.

ϭⲱⲗ, gather 52.

ϭⲱⲗⲡ ⲉⲃⲟⲗ 119, 121, 138.

ϭⲗⲟⲟϭⲉ 39, 40.

ϭⲗϭⲓⲗ 77.

ϭⲱⲡⲉ, ϭⲱⲡ 91, 107.

ϭⲉⲣⲱⲃ 135.

ϭⲣⲟⲟⲙⲡⲉ 13.

ϭⲣⲱϩ (ϭⲣⲱϣ) 42.

ϭⲱⲣϭ, people (vb.) 11, 59.

—, lie in wait 15.

ϭⲟⲣϭⲥ 78.

ϭⲱⲧⲛ 91, 143.

ϭⲟⲟⲩⲛⲉ 134.

ϭⲱϣⲧ, ϭⲓⲛ- 27.

ϭⲱϭ 77.

GREEK

ⲁⲅⲁⲑⲟⲥ 9, 17 78, 129.

—, ⲙⲛⲧ- 85, 114.

ⲁⲅⲁⲛⲁⲕⲧⲉⲓ 123, 133.

ⲁⲅⲁⲡⲏ 46, 49, 149.

ἀγαπητός 68 n.

ⲁⲅⲅⲉⲗⲓⲕⲟⲥ 52.

ⲁⲅⲅⲉⲗⲟⲥ 54, 117, 124, 134, 142, 165.

ⲁⲅⲓⲟⲥ 6, 23, 36, 75.

ⲁⲅⲟⲣⲁ 27.

ⲁⲅⲣⲓⲟⲥ 133.

ⲁⲅⲣⲓⲟⲥ, ⲙⲛⲧ- 108 n.

ⲁⲕⲟⲛⲓⲁ (ἀγωνία) 30.

ⲁⲅⲱⲛⲓⲍⲉ 109.

ⲁⲇⲁⲙⲁⲛⲧⲓⲛⲟⲥ 6.

ⲁⲉⲧⲟⲥ 46.

ⲁⲏⲣ 18, 19.

ϩⲁⲓⲣⲉⲥⲓⲥ 13.

ϩⲁⲓⲣⲉⲧⲓⲕⲟⲥ 32.

ⲁⲓⲥⲑⲁⲛⲉ 104, 105.

ⲁⲓⲥⲑⲏⲥⲓⲥ 101, 104, 105.

ⲁⲓⲧⲉⲓ 153.

ⲁⲓⲧⲏⲙⲁ 153, 169.

ⲁⲓⲭⲙⲁⲗⲱⲧⲓⲍⲉ 143.

ⲁⲓⲱⲛ 5, 128, 130.

ⲁⲕⲧⲓⲛ 150.

ⲁⲗⲏⲑⲓⲛⲟⲥ 79, 86.

ⲁⲗⲗⲁ (ἀλλά) 20, 21

ⲁⲛⲁⲅⲕⲁⲍⲉ 23, 98.

ⲁⲛⲁⲅⲕⲏ 57.

—, ⲙⲛⲧ- 15.

ⲁⲛⲁⲅⲛⲱⲥⲧⲏⲥ 84.

ⲁⲛⲁⲗⲁⲙⲃⲁⲛⲉ 5, 10.

ἀναϲταϲιϲ 43.
ἀναϲτροφη 108.
ἀναχωρει 112, 127, 134, 143, 155.
ἀναχωριτηϲ 132.
ἀντικειμενοϲ 78.
ἀξιωμα 63.
ἀξιωματικοϲ 84.
ἀορατοϲ 7, 79.
ἀπο ϲτηθουϲ 97, 119, 167.
ἀπαντα 49, 50, 113, 120, 126, 133, 163.
ἀπαντημα 27
ἀπατη 66.
ἀπειλη 148.
ἀπιϲτοϲ 118, 138.
ἁπλουϲ, μπτ- 153.
ἀπολογια 188.
ἀπορει 59.
ἀποϲτολοϲ 17, 43, 51, 64, 123.
ἀποφαϲιϲ 34, 77.
ἀρα 163.
ἀρτοϲ 43.
ἀρετη 169.
ἁρμοϲ 150.
ἁρπα 145.
ἀρχαγγελοϲ 4, 71, 77, 85, 149.
ἀρχει 123, 124, 137, 154, 162.
ἀρχη 99, 100 n, 146.
ἀρχιεπιϲκοποϲ 23, 63.
ἀρχων 23.
ἀϲεβηϲ 74.
ἀϲκητηϲ 141.
ἀϲτραπη 67.
αὐγουϲτοϲ 90.
ἀγαθηϲ (?) 33.
ἀγαπη 92, 99.

αὐτεξουϲιον 101.
ἀφθαρτοϲ 75.
ἀφορμη 14, 126, 163, 164.

βαπτιζε 30.
βαπτιϲμα 43, 45, 59, 169.
βαρβαροϲ 91, 142, 143.
βαϲανιζε 76.
βαϲανοϲ 76, 77.
βαϲιϲ 69, 71.
βιοϲ 74, 86, 168.
βλαπτει 86.
βοηθει 75, 113, 120.
βοηθεια 33, 34.

γενεα 52.
γενεαλογει 25, 26.
γενηϲιϲ 50.
γενναιοϲ 78, 79.
γιγαϲ 59.
γραφη 97, 100, 124, 137, 167.

δαιμονιοϲ 44, 98, 167.
δαιμων 66, 91, 129, 131.
δημιουργοϲ 31, 32.
δημοϲ 23.
δημευε 84.
διαβολοϲ 87, 130, 131, 162.
διαθηκη 41, 131, 154.
διακοπει 141.
διακονοϲ 84.
διακρινε 49, 104, 119, 140, 141.
διακριϲιϲ 101.
δικαιοϲ 5, 34, 35, 74.
δικαιοϲυνη 4, 148.
διϲταζε 155 n.

δόξον 24 n.

δρακων 74.
δυναμιϲ 31, 79.

εαρ 31.
ἐγκρατεια 149.
ἐγκρατευε 40, 41.
ἐγκωμιαζε 25.
ἐθνικοϲ 93.
ἐθνοϲ 161.
εἴγε 65 n.
εἰδωλομανία 67 n.
εἰδωλον 66, 77.
εἰκων (εἰκών) 4.
εἰρηνη 148, 165, 166.
εἰτα 79.
ἐκκληϲια 24, 37, 59, 86, 169, 170.
ἐλπιϲ 64, 88, 149.
ἐντολη 109, 110, 154.
ἐνωχλει 115.
ἐξητηϲιϲ 18.
ἐξουϲια 163.
ἐξωριϲτεια 63, 75.
ἐπει 110.
ἐπειδη 48.
ἐπιζημια 25.
ἐπιθυμει 51.
ἐπιϲκοποϲ 18, 36, 107, 169.
ἐπιϲτημη 27.
ἐπιτιμα, vb. 126.
ἐπουρανιοϲ 79.
ἐργαϲια 19.
ἑρμηταριον 76.
ἐρωταπόκριϲιϲ 58.
εὐαγγελιον 109, 139.
εὐαγγελιϲτηϲ 24, 32, 165.
εὐϲεβηϲ 74.

ζητημα 61.

ζητεμων 75, 77, 78.

ϩⲏⲗⲓⲕⲓⲁ 25, 88, 95, 154.

ⲑⲁⲗⲁⲥⲥⲁ 64, 65, 72.
ⲑⲉⲁⲧⲣⲟⲛ 71.
ⲑⲉⲟⲗⲟⲅⲟⲥ 36.
ⲑⲉⲱⲣⲉⲓ 17, 21.
ⲑⲏⲣⲓⲟⲛ 71, 119.
ⲑⲗⲓⲃⲉ 148, 150.
ⲑⲗⲓⲯⲓⲥ 120.
ⲑⲩⲙⲟⲥ 76.
ⲑⲩⲣⲟⲩⲣⲟⲥ (θυρωρός) 17.
ⲑⲩⲥⲓⲁⲍⲉ 77, 84.
ⲑⲩⲥⲓⲁⲥⲧⲏⲣⲓⲟⲛ 45.

ϩⲓⲇⲓⲱⲧⲏⲥ 123, 124.
ϩⲓⲥⲧⲟⲣⲓⲍⲉ 25.

ⲕⲁⲑⲁⲣⲓⲍⲉ 30, 117.
ⲕⲁⲑⲁⲣⲱⲛ 54.
ⲕⲁⲑⲏⲧⲉⲓ (κατηχεῖν) 137, 138 n, 140.
ⲕⲁⲕⲓⲁ 54.
ⲕⲁⲗⲁⲙⲁⲣⲓⲟⲛ 9.
ⲕⲁⲗⲩⲃⲏ 158.
ⲕⲁⲗⲱⲥ 40, 43.
ⲕⲁⲛ 98.
ⲕⲁⲛⲟⲛⲓⲍⲉ 44.
ⲕⲁⲣⲡⲟⲥ 11, 100, 151, 153, 154.
ⲕⲁⲥⲓⲥ 77.
ⲕⲁⲧⲁⲃⲟⲗⲏ 130.
κατάγαιον 165.
ⲕⲁⲧⲁⲕⲗⲩⲥⲙⲟⲥ 59.
ⲕⲁⲧⲁⲗⲁⲗⲉⲓ 117.
ⲕⲁⲧⲁⲛⲧⲁ 42.
ⲕⲁⲧⲁⲍⲓⲟⲩ 47.
ⲕⲁⲧⲁⲡⲉⲧⲁⲥⲙⲁ 16.
ⲕⲁⲧⲁⲣⲅⲉⲓ 93.
ⲕⲁⲧⲁⲫⲣⲟⲛⲉⲓ 66.
ⲕⲁⲧⲏⲅⲟⲣⲉⲓ 146.
ⲕⲉⲗⲉⲩⲥⲓⲥ 72.

ⲕⲉⲫⲁⲗⲁⲓⲟⲛ 57.
ⲕⲩⲡⲟⲥ (κῆπος) 19.
ⲕⲏⲣⲩⲍ 103.
ⲕⲓⲛⲇⲩⲛⲉⲩⲉ 56, 102.
ⲕⲗⲏⲣⲓⲕⲟⲥ 47.
ⲕⲟⲓⲛⲱⲛⲓⲁ 132.
—, ⲉⲓⲱⲧ ⲛⲧ- 145.
ⲕⲟⲓⲧⲱⲛ 8.
ⲕⲟⲗⲁⲥⲓⲥ 34, 52, 72.
ⲕⲟⲗⲁⲥⲧⲏⲣⲓⲟⲛ 76.
ⲕⲟⲥⲙⲉⲓ 27.
ⲕⲟⲥⲙⲓⲕⲟⲥ 116, 135, 166.
ⲕⲟⲥⲙⲟⲕⲣⲁⲧⲱⲣ 31.
ⲕⲟⲥⲙⲟⲥ 99, 128, 130, 166.
ⲕⲣⲁⲩⲅⲏ 37.
ⲕⲣⲓⲙⲉ 46, 158.
ⲕⲣⲩⲥⲧⲁⲣⲟⲥ (κρύσταλλος) 31.
ⲕⲱⲗⲩⲉ 142.

ⲗⲁⲓⲕⲟⲥ 46.
ⲗⲁⲙⲡⲁⲥ 67.
ⲗⲉⲍⲓⲥ 37.
ⲗⲏⲥⲧⲏⲥ 89.
ⲗⲟⲩⲓⲕⲟⲥ 31.
ⲗⲟⲩⲟⲥ, sermon 23.
ⲗⲩⲡⲉⲓ 112, 123, 132, 156, 169.

ⲙⲁⲅⲟⲥ 42.
ⲙⲁⲑⲏⲧⲏⲥ 95.
ⲙⲁⲕⲁⲣⲓⲟⲥ 63, 93, 166.
ⲙⲁⲗⲗⲟⲛ 14.
ⲙⲁⲣⲅⲁⲣⲓⲧⲏⲥ 26.
ⲙⲁⲣⲧⲩⲣⲓⲟⲛ 72, 78, 79.
ⲙⲁⲣⲧⲩⲣⲟⲥ 24, 67, 75, 76, 78.
ⲙⲉⲅⲉⲑⲟⲥ 24.
ⲙⲉⲗⲉⲧⲁ 100, 167.
ⲙⲉⲗⲟⲥ 101, 104, 150.
ⲙⲉⲣⲟⲥ 41, 153, 167.
ⲙⲉⲧⲁⲛⲟⲉⲓ 39, 40, 41, 42.

ⲙⲉⲧⲁⲛⲟⲓⲁ 38, 41, 53, 54, 56, 103, 146, 161.
ⲙⲙⲏ (? μῦ) 13.
ⲙⲟⲛⲁⲭⲟⲥ 115, 125, 133, 143, 144, 156, 163, 164, 166.
—, ⲙⲛⲧ- 135, 169.
ⲙⲟⲭⲗⲟⲥ 101.
ⲙⲩⲥⲧⲏⲣⲓⲟⲛ 5, 124.

ⲡⲓⲥⲧⲉⲩⲉ 146, 165.
νικηφόρος 91 n.
ⲛⲛⲏ (? νῦ) 13.
ⲛⲟⲓ 5.
ⲛⲟⲙⲟⲥ (νόμος) 96, 102, 103, 115, 166.
ⲛⲟⲩⲥ 5, 24.
ⲛⲩⲙⲫⲏ 19.

[ⲝⲉⲛⲟ]ⲇⲟⲭⲓⲟⲛ or [ⲡⲁⲛ]-ⲇⲟⲭⲓⲟⲛ 170.
ξυλοκόπος 53 n.

ⲟⲩⲟⲥ 22 n.
ⲟⲓⲕⲟⲛⲟⲙⲓⲁ 29, 90.
ⲟⲓⲕⲟⲩⲙⲉⲛⲏ 55.
ϩⲟⲗⲟⲕⲟⲧⲓⲛⲟⲥ 49.
ϩⲟⲙⲉⲗⲓⲁ 36.
ϩⲟⲙⲟⲓⲱⲥ 51.
ϩⲟⲙⲟⲗⲟⲅⲉⲓ 25, 66, 110.
ϩⲟⲙⲟⲗⲟⲅⲓⲁ 110.
ὁμολογητής 62 n.
ϩⲟⲙⲱⲥ (ὅμως) 50 n, 110.
ⲟⲛⲟⲙⲁⲍⲉ 78.
ⲟⲡⲧⲱⲥ 59.
ϩⲟⲣⲁⲙⲁ 74, 138, 139, 140.
ⲟⲣⲇⲓⲛⲟⲛ 75.
ϩⲟⲣⲓⲍⲉ 54.
ⲟⲣⲓⲛⲏ (ὀρεινή) 27.
ϩⲟⲥⲟⲛ 48, 56, 164.
ⲟⲩⲕ ⲟⲩⲛ 9, 10.

παιδεγcιc 72.

[παι]δοχιοπ(?) or [ξεπο]-
    δοχιοπ 170.

παπογργια 110, 115.

παραβα 51, 109, 115.

παραβατηc 110.

παραγε 128.

παραδιδογ 79, 163.

παρακαλει 75, 79, 169.

παραπομιος 32.

παρθεποc 6, 8, 12, 27.

πατρικιος 23.

πατρις (?) 86.

πειραζε 124.

πειραςιμος 81.

πελαγος 56, 80.

πιθε 66, 110.

πιστεγε 38, 43, 117, 146.

πιστις 43, 44, 60, 109, 128,
    161.

πιστος 105, 153.

πλαςςε 10.

ππεγμα (π̅π̅α̅) 127, 128,
    153.

ποηδης (ποιητής) 88.

πολεμει 66, 91.

πολεμος 78, 85, 169.

πολις 23, 32, 49, 65.

πολιτεγε 38, 130, 138.

πολιτεγομεπος 23.

πολιτια 38.

ποπηρος 140.

πορπεγε 43, 115.

πορπια 128.

ποτηριοπ 46.

πραξις 99.

πρεсβεγε 47.

πρεсβγτερος 84, 134.

—, μπτ- 134.

προκειμεπος 2.

προκοπτε 88, 154.

προσταγμα 91.

προσφορα 46.

προτρεπε 67, 86, 104, 153.

προφητης 38.

πγλη, πατ- 162.

ρραβδος 9.

ρρητοπ 137.

ρρωсατοπ 69.

сαββατοπ 14.

сαρξ 109, 153.

—, ρ- 95.

сεραφιπ 31.

сημαπε (σημαίνειν) 30.

сκαπδαλιζε 60, 109, 110.

сκεπαζε 77.

сκεος (σκεῦος) 91.

сκιρτα 19, 28.

сοφια 79.

сοφος 16.

сπαταλα 95.

сπηλαιοπ 67.

сπογδαζε 95, 126, 147.

сπογδαιος 89.

сτηθος, v. απο.

сτομαχος 166.

сτρατηλατης 23, 29.

сτρατωρ 29.

στρουθίον, use of word 172 n.

сτγλλος (στῦλος) 69, 166.

сγγκελλος 63.

сγμπολιτης 86.

сγπαξις 37.

—, as place of service 119 n.

сγπειδηсιс 101, 102, 103.

сγπετος, μπτ- 114.

сγπηθεια 128.

сγπροδος 63.

сγπταγμα 62 n, 63.

сγπτελεια 128, 130.

σύντεχνος 82 n.

сγπτγχια 27.

сφραγιζε 14, 72.

сφραγις 7, 14.

сχημα 43, 52.

сχολαριος 63.

сωμα 7, 101, 138, 166.

сωτηρ 108, 165.

ταλαιπωρος 89, 146.

ταφος 14.

τάχα 88, 89 n.

ταχγ 9, 119.

τελειος 154.

—, μπτ- 109.

τεχπεαλοκει (? τεχνεαλο-
    γίζειν) 25.

τιμωρια 77.

†ρωπ (τίρων) 29.

τολμηρος 53.

τοπος 165.

τραπεζα 81, 148, 155.

τριας 13.

τγπος 39, 57, 151.

ργπατος 23.

ργπερετης (ὑπηρέτης) 29.

ργπηρετει 63.

ργποθγκη (? ἀποθήκη) 7.

ργπομιπε 77, 81, 130.

ργποτεγε (? ὑποπτεύειν) 13.

ργсος ππαγγελος, epithet
    of Apollo 162 n.

ρηπсιстως (? ὕψιστος) 23.

φιλος ππαγγελος, epithet
    of Apollo 162.

φγλακτηριοπ 42.

ⲫⲱⲧⲓⲥⲙⲁ 79.

ⲭⲁⲓⲣⲉ 26.
χαιρετισμοί 27 n.
ⲭⲁⲗⲓⲛⲟⲥ 93.
ⲭⲁⲣⲓⲍⲉ 9, 72, 75, 79, 93.
ⲭⲁⲣⲓⲥ 105.
ⲭⲁⲣⲓⲥⲙⲁ 140.
ⲭⲉⲓⲣⲟⲧⲟⲛⲉⲓⲁ 169.

ⲭⲓⲙⲱⲛ 19.
ⲭⲓⲱⲛ 31.
ⲭⲟⲣⲏⲅⲉⲓ 60.
χορηγός 60 n.
ⲭⲟⲣⲧⲟⲥ 69.
ⲭⲣⲉⲱⲥ 66.
ⲭⲣⲉⲱⲥⲧⲉⲓ 66.
ⲭⲣⲏⲥⲧⲟⲥ, ⲙⲛⲧ- 149.
ⲭⲣⲓⲁ 49, 50, 158.

ⲭⲣⲓⲥⲧⲓⲁⲛⲟⲥ 42, 43, 51, 72, 84, 140.
ⲭⲗⲟⲛⲟⲅⲣⲁⲫⲟⲩ (χρονογρα-φεῖν) 25.
ⲭⲱⲣⲁ 66.

ⲯⲁⲗⲙⲟⲥ 97.
ⲯⲁⲗⲧⲏⲣⲓⲟⲛ 3.
ⲯⲩⲭⲏ 170.

ARABIC

ابرجتى = ابرختى, epithet of Hôr 165 n.
بنيان 68.

سيرج 69 n.
ظهور 68.
القصار, epithet of Hôr 164 n.

مسحاة, spade 144 n.
ميمر, as 'Encomium' 178 n.
هنادة, ϩⲉⲛⲉⲉⲧⲉ 182.

SUBJECTS

Abbreviations used 171.
Accents on Greek words 63 n, 111 n.
Anthology, a Saʻidic 178.
Antiphonary 62.
Apocryphal Acts 64.
Apophthegmata 167.

Biblical and non-biblical texts in one MS. 1.

Biblical quotations:—
Gen. vi. 4, 59 n.
　,, xiv. 1, 2, 132 n.
　,, xx. 2, 52 n.
　,, xxxv. 22 (21), 52 n.
　,, xxxix. 6, 70 n.
　,, xlvii. 6, 17 n.
Lev. vii. 12, ix. 4, 69 n.
Num. xii. 3, 70 n.
　,, xv. 30 (32), 53 n.
Ruth, Book of, 1.
Ps. iv. 6, 81 n.

Biblical quotations, *contd.*
Ps. xxi. 9, 10, 89 n.
　,, xxviii. 8, 2.
　,, xxxiii. 1, 97 n.
　,, xli. 8, 30 n.
　,, l. 7-9, 2.
　,, lxvi. 2, 2 n.
　,, lxxxiv. 10, 29 n.
　,, lxxxv. 13, 42 n.
　,, lxxxviii. 22, 133 n.
　,, xcvii. 1-5, 2.
　,, cii. 1-5, 106 n.
　,, cviii. 31, 48 n.
　,, cxv. 3, 106 n.
　,, cxviii. 37, 28 n.
　,, cxlii. 10, 93 n.
Psalm verses, 12 n.
Prov. xix. 17 (?), 49 n.
Cant. ii. 11, 19 n.
　,, iv. 16, 20 n.
Isa. xxviii. 15, 18, 41 n.
　,, lvii. 14, 30 n.

Biblical quotations, *contd.*
Isa. lxv. 8, 41 n.
Jer. ix. 17, 138 n.
　,, x. 16, 90 n.
Ezek. iii. 18, 47 n.
Dan. ii. 21, 107 n.
　,, vii. 9, 25 n.
Daniel (doubtful reference), 55 n.
Matt. iii. 16, 62 n.
　,, iv. 2-4, 10, 62 n.
　,, v. 8, 101 n.
　,, v. 22, 59 n.
　,, v. 44, 139 n.
　,, x. 33, 147 n.
　,, xi. 28-30, 39 n.
　,, xix. 19, 58 n.
　,, xxii. 39, 58 n.
　,, xxv. 40, 49 n.
Mark xii. 31, 58 n.
　,, xiii. 19, 35 n.
Luke i. 36, 43, 44, 29 n.

Biblical quotations, *contd.*
Luke i. 39, 28 n.
  ,, ii. 7, 33 n.
  ,, iv. 13, 62 n.
  ,, vi. 43, 168.
  ,, x. 27, 97 n.
  ,, x. 31 ff, 57.
  ,, xiv. 26, 100 n.
  ,, xxii. 30, 81 n.
  ,, xxiv. 32, 125 n.
John ii. 1, 60 n.
  ,, ii. 4, 62 n.
  ,, v. 14, 39 n.
  ,, ix. 3, 7, 59 n.
  ,, x. 18, 21.
  ,, xv. 22, 53 n.
Acts i. 3, 21 n.
  ,, iv. 13, 125 n.
  ,, ix. 15, 92 n.
  ,, xx. 20, 21, 161 n.
Rom. ii. 14, 104 n.
  ,, iv. 15, 36 ff.
  ,, x. 17, 129 n.
  ,, xii. 12, 150 n.
1 Cor. xiii. 5, 47 n, 50 n.
  ,, xv. 50, 92 n.
2 Cor. xii. 2, 87 n.
  ,, xii. 11, 107 n.
Gal. i. 15, 16, 92 n.
  ,, v. 22, 150 n.
Eph. v. 17–20, 2.
Phil. iii. 15, 107 n.
Col. ii. 5, 154 n.
1 Tim. i. 17, 80.
  ,, iv. 2, 103 n.
Titus ii. 11 (?), 2.
Heb. x. 22, 104 n.
  ,, xii. 23, 87 n.
  ,, xiii. 2, 135 n.

Biblical quotations, *contd.*
Jas. i. 5, 154 n.
  ,, i. 6, 155 n.
  ,, i. 17, 152 n.
  ,, ii. 19, 20, 44 n.

Catalogue of books 1 n.
Cathedral church ($\kappa\alpha\theta o\lambda.$ $\dot{\epsilon}\kappa\kappa\lambda.$) 21.
Charity 57.
Christmas 18.
Consonants in name omitted 14 n.
Cow, brazen (torture) 77 n.
Crowns granted to martyrs 68 n.

Dialogue ($\dot{\epsilon}\rho\omega\tau\alpha\pi\acute{o}\kappa\rho\iota\sigma\iota s$) 58.

'Eagles' (*i.e.* clergy) 47 n.
Earthquakes 22.
Edict, Diocletian's 83.
Epiphany 2.
—, sermon on 47 n.

Foot washing 2.

Gnostic names 14 n.
Gods, names of 84.
—, Diocletian's 83.
Greek accents in Coptic MSS. 63 n, 111 n.

Lectionary 2.

Jasper (stone) 27 n.
Judgement, the Last 33.
'Junior' 24 n.

Martyrdom of St. Mark 65.
— of Philotheus 68, 70.

Nativity, homily on the 22 n.

'Power' ($\delta\acute{v}\nu\alpha\mu\iota s$) 11 n.

Quires, how indicated 89.
Quire-marks 15 n, 42, 43.

Red ink 2, 3.
Relics, saints' 13 n.
Repentance, sermon on 53.
Rhymed prose (Arabic), passages in 175.
Rule, the Pachomian 95 n.

Sesame oil 70 n.
'Son of Compassion' (= Christ) 85 n.
'Store-houses' (Book of Enoch) 7 n.
Sunday, Low 2.
Superlineation, peculiar *pref.* n.
Synaxarium 68, 70, 73.
Synodikon of Damianus 31 n.

Temptations of Jesus 62.
'Testimonies' ($\Pi\lambda\eta\rho\circ\phi\circ\rho\acute{\iota}\alpha\iota$) of John of Maiuma 62.
Theotokia, author of 27 n.
Thursday, Holy 2.
Tortures, various 77.
Trinity, the 4, 8 n.

Virgin, the 11.
—, death of the 17.

Water, Blessing of 2.
Wheel (torture) 78 n.

No. 2

ⲕⲛⲁⲃⲉ ⲱ ⲇⲱⲓⲱⲁ
ⲉⲣ ⲟⲗ ...
ⲭⲟ ⲕ ⲙ ⲓ ⲧ

No. 3

ⲑⲟ ⲛ ⲛ
ⲗ ⲟ ⲟ ⲩ ⲉ
ⲉ ϥ ϣ ⲁ ⲛ ⲛ ⲁ ⲩ
ⲉ ⲛ ⲛ ⲟ ⲃ ⲉ ⲩ
ⲥ ⲛ ⲕ ⲧ ⲧ ⲁ ⲣ ⲁ
ⲛ ⲁ ⲅ ⲁ ⲑ ⲟ ⲛ
ϣ ⲁ ϥ ϣ ⲱ

ⲠⲈⲬⲈ

No. 4

ⲡⲉ ⲍⲟ ⲟ ⲩ ⲛ ⲧ ⲁ ⲥ
ⲡ ⲱ ⲩ ⲗ ⲱ ⲧ ⲉ ⲓ
ⲛ ⲟ ⲟ ⲛ ⲧ ⲁ ⲉ ⲓ ⲟ
ⲛ ϩ ⲏ ⲧ ⲩ ⲉ ⲧ ⲣ ⲉ ⲥ
ⲭ ⲧ ⲧ ⲟ ⲩ ⲧ ⲉ ⲭ ⲥ
ⲙ ⲁ ⲣ ⲟ ⲩ ⲭ ⲓ ⲱ ⲓ

No. 4

ⲁⲡⲱⲁⲥ ⲉ ⲡⲉ
ⲛⲩⲛⲁ+ⲕⲁⲣⲡⲟ
ⲁⲛ· ⲛⲩⲧ̄ⲃ̄ⲃⲟ
ⲩⲡⲉⲧⲛⲁ+ⲕⲁⲣ
ⲡⲟⲥⲛ̄ⲟ̄ⲩ̄ⲟ̄ⲩ̄
ⲣⲟ̄ⲧ̄· ⲧ̄ⲥ̄ⲧ̄ⲉ
ⲩⲁⲣ

No. 6

ⲭⲡⲓⲟⲩⲗⲟⲛ
ⲉⲁⲛⲉⲛⲧ̄ⲩⲛ
ⲇⲇⲩ-ⲙⲏⲛ
ⲣⲱⲛⲛⲟⲧⲩⲩ
ⲁⲛⲧⲛ̄ⲧⲩⲩ
ⲁ̄ⲛ̄ⲩⲇ̄ⲥ̄ⲉ
ⲭⲩ·ⲉⲩⲭⲡ̄ⲓ̄ⲟ̄

No. 8

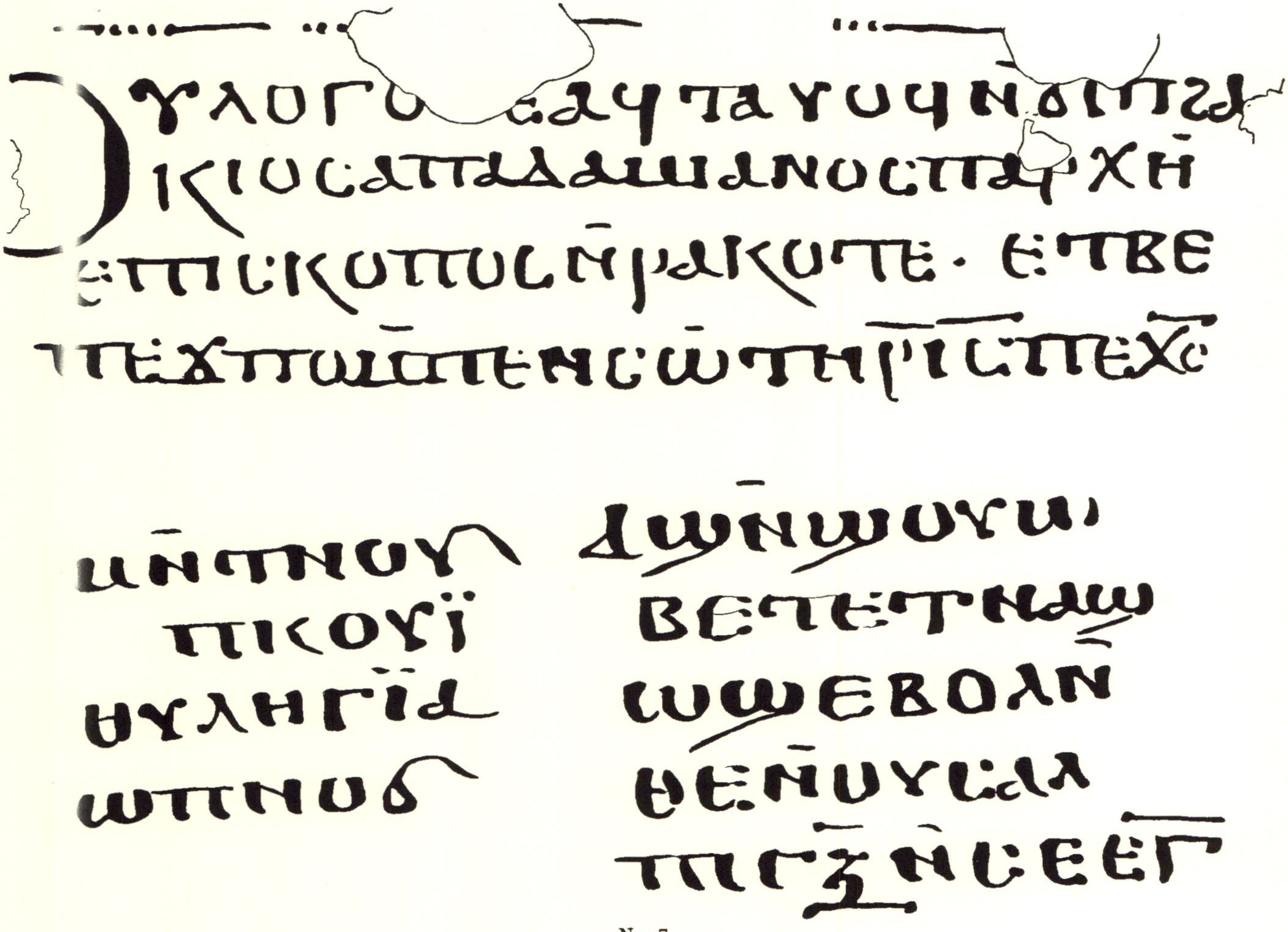

No. 7

ΜΕΝΑΝΤΕΠΓΑΓΙΟϹΓΡΗ¡
ΕΘΕΟΛΟΓΟϹ ΠΕΠΙϹΚΟΠΙϹ
ΕΑΥΠΛΥΟϹ ΕΤΒΕ

ϪΕΠΜΑΙΤΕΜΝ
ΜΝΠΑΡΑΒΑϹΙ¡

ΙΗ
+ ΚΑΛШϹΚΠΙϹ
ΤΕΥΕΕΠΠⲞⲨ
ΝΙϹ ΠΝΤΕ
+ ΑΝΑϹΤΑϹΙϹ:
ΑΚϪⲠΒΑⲠ
ΤΙϹⲘⲁⲁΚ†
ⲠΕΧϹⳌⲓШШΚ

ΕΚШΑΝΚΑ

No. 10

No. 11

No. 12

ⲙⲉⲟⲧⲙⲉ
ⲟⲩⲛⲓⲙⲙⲟⲥ
ⲥⲉⲉⲡⲧⲁⲣⲭⲓⲉⲧⲓ
ⲑⲉⲟⲥ· ⲉⲧⲓⲁⲉⲟⲓ
ⲟⲩⲁⲛⲓⲉⲛⲧⲁⲣ
ⲥⲩⲅⲕⲉⲗⲗⲟⲥ

No. 13

ⲭⲣⲉⲱⲥⲧⲉⲓ
ⲛⲁⲕⲱⲧⲡⲣⲁⲥ
ⲟⲥⲙⲁⲣⲕⲟⲥⲛⲟⲩ
ⲛⲟⲇⲛ̄ⲛ̄ⲭⲣⲉ
ⲱⲥ· ϯⲟⲩⲟⲟⲟⲟ
ⲅⲉⲓ

No. 15

ⲉⲣⲟⲩ ⲓⲥ ⲙⲁⲣⲧⲩ
ⲣⲓⲟⲛ
ⲕⲱⲧ ⲉⲣⲟⲟⲩ
ⲙⲁⲣⲧⲩⲣⲓⲟ
ⲧⲁⲙ·
ⲉ ⲱ ⲫⲓⲗⲟ
ⲁⲛⲉ ⲧⲏⲡ

No. 17

No. 16

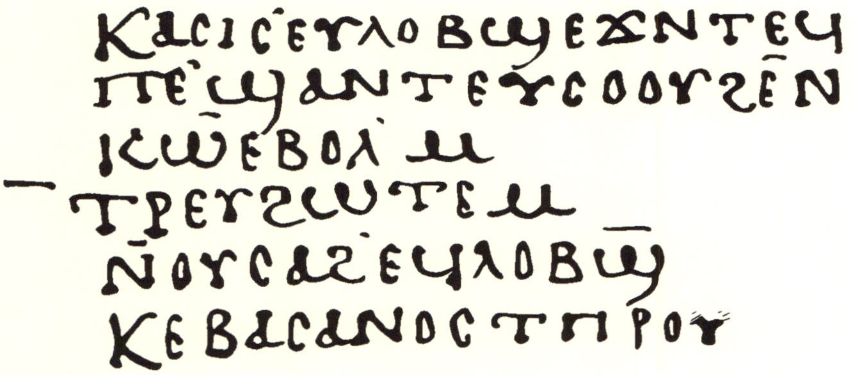

No. 19

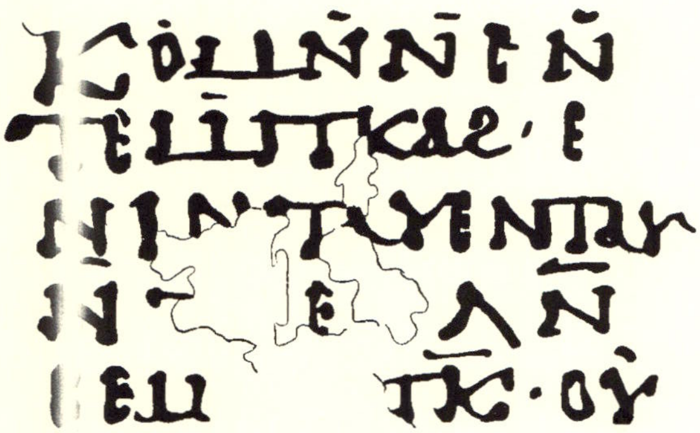

No. 21

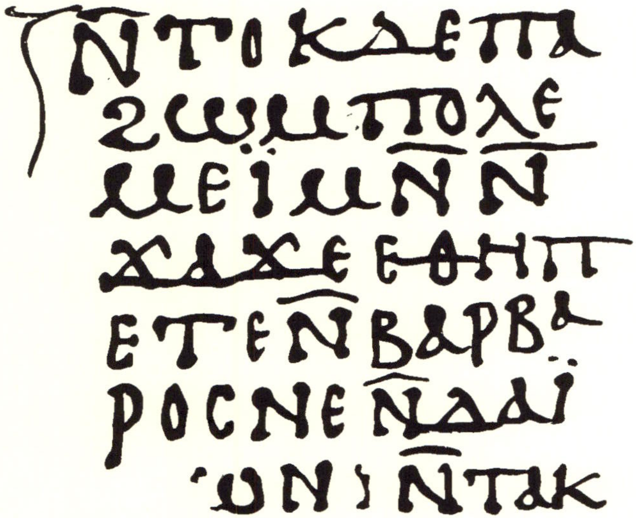

No. 24

ⲥⲕ· ⲁⲩⲱⲛ̄ⲧⲉⲣϥ
ⲣ̄ⲟⲧⲉ ⲭⲉⲛ̄ⲛⲉⲩ
ⲕⲱ ⲛ̄ⲅ̄ⲙ̄ⲙⲟ ⲩ· ⲁϥ
ⲟⲩⲱⲧ ⲛ̄ⲉ ⲃ ⲟ ⲗ ·
ⲁⲩⲱ ⲙ̄ⲛ̄ ⲥ ⲱ ⲃ ⲁⲩ
ⲧ̄ⲥ ⲟ ⲟ ⲩ ϣ ⲁ ⲛ ⲧ ⲟ ⲩ
† ⲍⲉ ⲁⲩⲱ ⲃⲉⲛ̄ ⲁⲩ

No. 25

ⲡ̄ⲡⲁⲡⲟⲗⲗⲱ   ⲭ ⲓ
ⲭⲉ ⲓ̈ⲥⲟⲩⲙⲟ   ⲁ ⲥ
ⲛ ⲁ ⲭ ⲟ ⲥ ⲓ ⲁ ⲡ   ⲙ
ⲁ ⲡ ⲁ ⲇ ⲙ ⲙ ⲱ   ⲡ
ⲛⲓ ⲡⲉ · ⲙ̄ⲡ̄ⲧ̄ⲟ   ⲛⲉ
ⲟⲩ ⲛ ⲑ ⲱ ⲛ ⲉ →   ⲡ

No. 26

ⲧⲁ̅ⲓ̅ⲱ̅ⲧ̅
ⲇⲁⲩⲉⲓⲇⲥ
ⲛ̅ⲧⲁ̅ⲓ̅ⲥ
ϩⲉ̅ⲙ̅ⲙⲉ

ⲥⲱ̅ⲛ̅ⲛⲟ̅ⲩ̅ⲟⲥ̣̅ⲛ̅ⲛ
ⲙⲟ̅ⲛⲁ̅ⲭⲟⲥⲙ̅ⲛ

No. 28

Γ ⲧ̅ⲩⲁ̅ⲓ̅ⲑ̅ⲏ̅ⲙ̅ⲙ̅ ⲙ̅ⲛ̅ⲥ̣̅ⲱ̅ⲑ̅ⲟ̅ⲙ̅ⲛ̅
Π ⲥⲱ̅ⲧⲙ̅ⲡⲉ̅ⲣ̅ⲟⲟ̅ⲧ̅ⲉ̅·ⲙ̅ⲛ̅ⲛ̅ⲧⲁ̅ϩ
ⵐ ⲟ̅ⲩ̅ϫⲁ̅ⲗⲛ̅ⲅⲉ̅ⲓ̅ⲟⲧ̅ⲉ̅ⲃ̅ⲱ̅ϫⲉⲧ̅ⲡ̅ⲡ̅
Λ ⲙ̅ⲙⲟⲥⲁ̅ⲧⲙ̅·ⵯ̅·ⲛ̅ⲧⲟ̅ⲩ̅·ⲛ̅ⲧⲉ̅ⲣ̅ⲉ̅ϥⲥ

No. 29

OXFORD : HORACE HART, M.A.
PRINTER TO THE UNIVERSITY

SAPI FELI
ENTIÆ CITA
ET TIS

Printed in Great Britain
by Amazon